EDUCATING EVERYBODY'S CHILDREN

DIVERSE TEACHING STRATEGIES
FOR DIVERSE LEARNERS

WHAT RESEARCH AND PRACTICE
SAY ABOUT IMPROVING ACHIEVEMENT

ASCD IMPROVING STUDENT ACHIEVEMENT RESEARCH PANEL

ROBERT W. COLE, EDITOR

Association for Supervision and Curriculum Development
Alexandria, Virginia

Association for Supervision and Curriculum Development
1703 N. Beauregard St., Alexandria, VA 22311-1714 USA
Telephone: 1-800-933-2723 or 703-578-9600 • Fax: 703-575-5400
Web site: http://www.ascd.org • E-mail: member@ascd.org

Cover and interior design by Karen Monaco.

Printed in the United States of America.

ASCD Stock No.: 195024
ASCD member price: $21.95   nonmember price: $25.95

Library of Congress Cataloging-in-Publication Data

ASCD Improving Student Achievement Research Panel
    Educating everybody's children : diverse teaching strategies
for diverse learners : what research and practice say about
improving achievement / ASCD Improving Student Achievement
Research Panel ; Robert W. Cole, editor.
        p.   cm.
    Includes bibliographical references.
    ISBN 0-87120-237-9
    1. Education—United States—Experimental methods.
2. Educational equalization—United States. 3. Minorities—
Education—United States. 4. Socially handicapped children—
Education—United States. 5. Academic achievement—United
States. 6. Multicultural education—United States. I. Cole,
Robert W., 1945-   . II. Association for Supervision and
Curriculum Development. III. Title.
LB1027.3A73   1995
371.3—dc20   95-7075
                                    CIP

06 05 04 03 02   15 14 13 12 11 10 9 8

AS OUR STUDENTS BECOME

MORE AND MORE DIVERSE . . .

SO MUST OUR WAYS

OF TEACHING THEM.

This book was generated through a great deal

of spirited dialogue. We hope that it will in turn

generate and support informed dialogue among

others concerned about education that promotes

high achievement for all students. This document

is meant to promote reflection and discussion

among the entire learning community.

EDUCATING EVERYBODY'S CHILDREN

DIVERSE TEACHING STRATEGIES FOR DIVERSE LEARNERS

WHAT RESEARCH AND PRACTICE SAY ABOUT IMPROVING ACHIEVEMENT

FOREWORD

The public schools of today will shape the society of tomorrow. Our fundamental challenge is to foresee change and to shape it to our benefit.

I am firmly committed to a system of quality public education. Education is power. The belief that knowledge empowers people and nations is the foundation on which we must build our commitment to education. Our public schools are fundamental to preparing succeeding generations of young people for participation in American society. We owe it to our children to prepare them for the world they will inherit.

I believe that all children can learn and that public education should enable all children to fulfill their unique potential. Education is the key to developing each child's intellectual, physical, and emotional abilities. Excellence and equity are inseparable. If the movement to improve public education is to be truly meaningful, it must include all students. Educational achievement need not be constrained by race, class, or national origin. Educational equity for some can best be realized when we seek educational advancement and achievement for all. Through the schools, young people gain an appreciation of our cultural diversity and acquire the knowledge and skills to become productive citizens.

I see a bright future for public education—if the schools and the community recognize their mutual needs. All will benefit if we join together for quality public education. As Virgil said, time, indeed, does fly—and the future will be here before we know it. If it is to be the future we choose, we must work to make it so, now.

—Gene R. Carter, *Executive Director*
Association for Supervision
and Curriculum Development

PREFACE

HELENÉ HODGES

The ASCD Strategic Plan for 1990-95 called for the establishment of focus areas to which the organization would devote resources to make a difference in education. The book you hold in your hands is a product of ASCD's work in one of these focus areas, namely, "Improving Student Achievement." A major goal of this focus was to keep ASCD members abreast of research and practice concerned with the improvement of instruction. Meeting the needs of students from diverse cultural, ethnic, linguistic, or socioeconomic backgrounds continues to be a challenge for many practitioners in the field. Too often, students of color and youngsters from low-income areas have been poorly served by U.S. schools.

The reasons for this failure to serve minority youngsters are many. Often teachers' expectations of students are shaped by inaccurate assumptions about innate ability, low expectations for racial minorities or poor children, and a lack of knowledge about students' different cultural backgrounds, including the rules of social interaction between adults and children. In addition, the conditions of schooling in poverty areas often include dilapidated buildings, faulty or nonexistent equipment, low wages for teachers, a preponderance of teachers with minimal teaching skills, fragmented families, and deteriorated and demoralized neighborhoods. Despite these problems, pockets of educational excellence have emerged, and underachievement has been reversed within them.

ASCD's VALUES AND BELIEFS ABOUT TEACHING*

Continuing disparities among the levels of achievement of students of color, low-income students, and the general school population remain a concern. In addition, international comparisons of student achievement, as well as the findings of the National Assessment of Educational Progress (NAEP), suggest a need for significant improvement even among the general school population.

We believe that the effective teaching traditionally provided to the most privileged students must also be provided to students who have, until now, been academically marginal. We also believe that educators must look beyond the stigmas of race and class to meet individual student needs and that students' individual differences require alternative instructional strategies. When we speak of accommodating the needs of diverse learners, it is imperative that we describe how we will alter instruction to improve learning and why we choose the strategies we do. ASCD believes that students are more likely to receive a high-quality education when the learning environment reflects the following values, beliefs, and practices:

• **Balanced Curriculum.** We believe that all students should have a well-planned educational program with opportunities to study the full range of school subjects. A balanced program reflects the nature of knowledge, the needs and interests of individual learners, and the nature of society and the world.

• **Self-Direction.** We believe that students should become responsible for their own learning. Schools should emphasize self-discipline and teach students how to learn, how to think and solve problems, how to teach themselves, and, if necessary, how to bypass their teacher's style when it proves a hindrance rather than an asset.

• **Equity.** We believe that all individuals should be treated equitably. Schools should demonstrate, and foster

---

*For more information, see *Developing Leadership: A Synthesis of ASCD Resolutions Through 1993*, edited by M.B. Howard, D.G. Berreth, and J.S. Seltz (Alexandria, Va.: ASCD) as well as the individual lists of "ASCD Resolutions" approved in a given year.

in their students, respect for the dignity and worth of all persons. Equity of opportunity requires that alternative instructional strategies be available to accommodate the various learning styles of students.

• **Cultural Pluralism**. We believe that cultural diversity in schools and in the curriculum helps prepare students for living in a multicultural society and an interdependent world.

• **Education for Democracy**. We believe that, for the American culture to survive, students must learn democratic values and practices. Educators should model democratic values and practices in their interactions with young people.

• **Responsible Citizenship**. We believe that the future of our world depends on citizens who are well informed and willing to work for civic improvement. Schools should foster social responsibility among their students and provide them with multiple opportunities for helping others within their communities.

THE ORIGINS OF THIS PUBLICATION

This book is the culmination of the work of ASCD's Urban Middle Grades Network, a special Advisory Panel on Improving Student Achievement, and the Improving Student Achievement Research Panel.

The Urban Middle Grades Network was a joint two-year venture of ASCD and the Edna McConnell Clark Foundation. ASCD's charge was to organize a nationwide network of fifteen urban schools serving disadvantaged students in grades 6 through 9 for the purpose of helping school teams provide an education of high content, high expectations, and high support. These three "highs" became the centerpiece of the Three-High Achievement Model, which was a guideline for the schools as they worked to develop high-performing school systems capable of increasing student achievement and retention (see Figure 1). The model emphasized that:

• A **high-content** curriculum should offer: (1) a balanced core congruent with the domains of knowledge, the demands of society, and the developmental needs of learners; (2) high-interest subject matter related to students' daily life experiences; and (3) learning activities based on students' interests.

• Teachers should display **high expectations** for student performance. They should: (1) diagnose how best to teach individual students to improve their academic and behavioral outcomes; (2) use a variety of complementary instructional and management strategies; and (3) display supportive affective teaching behaviors.

• Administrative policies and practices should create a **highly supportive** school environment in which learning is highly regarded and teachers and students are highly respected.

Between 1989 and 1991, school teams consisting of the principal, teachers, parents or guardians, community leaders, and a central office support person worked on developing school improvement plans that incorporated the knowledge base of the best teaching and learning practices in four content areas: reading, writing, oral communication, and mathematics. Participants were guided in setting high standards in each of the content areas and in using new holistic forms of student assessment. Much of the research described in this text has its roots in the work of the Urban Middle Grades Network.

In May 1991, ASCD convened an Advisory Panel on Improving Student Achievement, which was charged with identifying the degree to which young peoples' demographic profiles and social conditions (including gender, socioeconomic status, and cultural, ethnic, and linguistic heritages) influence their performance in school. The panel members agreed that "good teaching"—teaching that is engaging, relevant, multicultural, and that appeals to a variety of learning styles—works well with *all* children, but that children from diverse backgrounds sometimes have educational needs that might not be shared by other students. Panel members were especially cautious about stereotyping, however. They recognized, for example, that not all Asian Americans share the same cultural heritage and that Native American nations and tribes differ by language and culture and heritage. Students bring to the classroom a unique mixture of learning styles and out-of-school experiences; they must be valued for their individuality.

Perhaps the single strongest message of the Advisory Panel was that today's educator needs a repertoire of tools to meet the educational needs of all students. The elements of that repertoire, and the knowledge base behind them, serve as the foundation of this book.

FIGURE 1
ASCD's 3-High Achievement Model

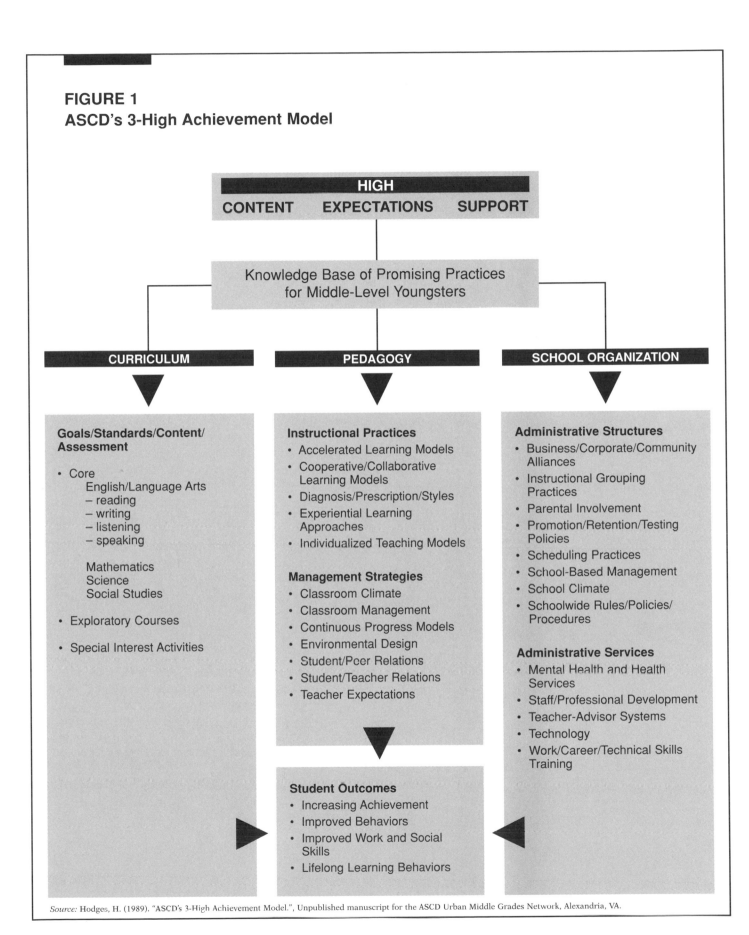

HIGH
CONTENT   EXPECTATIONS   SUPPORT

Knowledge Base of Promising Practices
for Middle-Level Youngsters

CURRICULUM

PEDAGOGY

SCHOOL ORGANIZATION

Goals/Standards/Content/ Assessment

- Core
  English/Language Arts
  – reading
  – writing
  – listening
  – speaking

  Mathematics
  Science
  Social Studies

- Exploratory Courses

- Special Interest Activities

Instructional Practices
- Accelerated Learning Models
- Cooperative/Collaborative Learning Models
- Diagnosis/Prescription/Styles
- Experiential Learning Approaches
- Individualized Teaching Models

Management Strategies
- Classroom Climate
- Classroom Management
- Continuous Progress Models
- Environmental Design
- Student/Peer Relations
- Student/Teacher Relations
- Teacher Expectations

Administrative Structures
- Business/Corporate/Community Alliances
- Instructional Grouping Practices
- Parental Involvement
- Promotion/Retention/Testing Policies
- Scheduling Practices
- School-Based Management
- School Climate
- Schoolwide Rules/Policies/ Procedures

Administrative Services
- Mental Health and Health Services
- Staff/Professional Development
- Teacher-Advisor Systems
- Technology
- Work/Career/Technical Skills Training

Student Outcomes
- Increasing Achievement
- Improved Behaviors
- Improved Work and Social Skills
- Lifelong Learning Behaviors

Source: Hodges, H. (1989). "ASCD's 3-High Achievement Model.", Unpublished manuscript for the ASCD Urban Middle Grades Network, Alexandria, VA.

The Improving Student Achievement Research Panel was convened by ASCD in May 1992. It was composed of eighteen distinguished researchers, representing diverse fields and disciplines. The charge to the panel was to produce a publication that conveys what research and promising practices reveal about the ways in which the achievement of all students might be enhanced. In addition to synthesizing key instructional principles and teaching strategies supported by research as having broad applicability across content areas, the panel explored what research has revealed about successful practice that is specific to the areas of reading, writing, oral communication, and mathematics. The panel also was charged with identifying the principles and strategies that research has shown to be effective in meeting the needs of a broad base of our student population and to explore what research has revealed about successfully addressing the needs of students from economically, ethnically, racially, culturally, and linguistically diverse groups.

Preliminary reviews of the literature suggest that conventional approaches to working with diverse student learners have not been wholly successful. Typically, as evidenced by the school teams in the Urban Middle Grades Network, schools serving low-income, minority populations offer a less challenging, more repetitive curriculum. Teachers often break each learning task into smaller pieces and give students fewer opportunities to engage in higher order thinking skills. While this kind of instruction has positively affected student scores on measures of basic skills, comparable gains have not been seen on measures of more advanced skills. These approaches underestimate what students can do, postpone more challenging and interesting work, and deprive students of a meaningful context for learning and using skills.

In dealing with diverse student populations, it is important to consider language heritage, cultural, and other contextual factors that may influence achievement. Practitioners should focus on the knowledge and abilities that diverse learners bring to the educational setting. Many studies indicate that culture and social circumstances profoundly shape learners' interactions with the environment and influence the ways in which different groups of students respond to classroom activities.

In short, considerable evidence supports the conclusion that the differences in achievement between students of mainstream and nonmainstream backgrounds are not the result of differences in their ability to learn, but rather of differences in the quality of instruction they have received in school. This book offers a wide-ranging assortment of instructional strategies whose effectiveness has been gleaned from an extensive review of both basic and applied research. We believe that if we can improve the quality of instruction, we can improve the performance of all students.

THE FUTURE

During the course of the development of this publication, ASCD adopted a new mission statement for the Association and a set of belief statements and six goals that are intended to guide ASCD into the 21st century (see p. xi). One of these goals lies at the heart of the creation of this book:

By the year 2001, ASCD will mobilize resources to ensure that schools serving children of the poor have access and appropriate opportunity to widely use, and effectively implement, our programs, products, and services.

The ASCD Strategic Planning Commission, composed of affiliate representatives, ASCD members, interested educators, and ASCD staff, has developed a strategic plan that reflects what the Association will become during the last years of the 20th century. The plan is the product of an inclusive process; every segment of the ASCD community was involved in its development, and every segment will be part of its implementation.

ASCD Mission Statement

ASCD, a diverse, international community of educators, forging covenants
in teaching and learning for the success of all learners

ASCD Belief Statements

Fundamental to ASCD is our concern for people, both individually and collectively.

- We believe that the individual has intrinsic worth.
- We believe that all people have the ability and the need to learn.
- We believe that all children have a right to safety, love, and learning.
- We believe that a high-quality, public system of education open to all is imperative for society to flourish.
- We believe that diversity strengthens society and should be honored and protected.
- We believe that broad, informed participation committed to a common good is crucial to democracy.
- We believe that humanity prospers when people work together.

ASCD also recognizes the potential and power of a healthy organization.

- We believe that healthy organizations purposefully provide for self-renewal.
- We believe that the culture of an organization is a major factor shaping individual attitudes and behaviors.
- We believe that shared values and common goals shape and change the culture of healthy organizations.

ASCD Goals

Goal 1

By the year 2001, ASCD will mobilize resources to ensure that schools serving children of the poor have access
and appropriate opportunity to widely use, and effectively implement, our programs, products, and services.

Goal 2

By the year 2001, ASCD will be one of the most influential forces promoting good learning
to educational policymakers worldwide.

Goal 3

By the year 2001, ASCD will have fully integrated its belief in and commitment to diversity
throughout its governance, programs, and affiliations.

Goal 4

By the year 2001, ASCD will actively engage in enhancing the capacity of schools
and school systems for change and self-renewal.

Goal 5

By the year 2001, ASCD will have restructured itself to fully exemplify the principles of learning
and the values and practices of self-renewing organizations.

Goal 6

By the year 2001, ASCD will work together with educators and educational organizations worldwide
to promote quality education through structures that address both national and international issues.

1

EDUCATING EVERYBODY'S CHILDREN

MARIE CARBO

"Children are people. They grow into tomorrow only as they live today."

— JOHN DEWEY IN "SOME FAMOUS AMERICANS ON EDUCATION," *THE EDUCATION ALMANAC 1984* (RESTON, VA.: NATIONAL ASSOCIATION OF ELEMENTARY SCHOOL PRINCIPALS), P. 114.

Author's Note: I thank the following people for their contributions to this chapter: Carol Ascher, Kathryn Au, James Chesebro, Pamela Cooper, Anne Curran, Rita Dunn, Sally Hampton, Kenji Ima, Barbara Kapinus, Marietta Saravia-Shore, Warren Simmons, and Floraline Stevens.

The children of the United States are rapidly becoming more ethnically and culturally diverse. Far too often, unfortunately, diversity is linked closely to poverty. The combination of poverty and diversity plays havoc with performance in school. Disproportionately high numbers of minority, immigrant, and poor children perform consistently in the lower third academically in U.S. schools. The educational course charted in the next few years will play a major role in determining whether we can truly educate everybody's children to be successful, productive citizens in the 21st century.

EDUCATION REFORM 'FLUNKS' THE DEMOGRAPHIC AGENDA

Historically, minority and immigrant students have been poorly served by U.S. schools. Today, the consistently low achievement of young people in these groups is exacerbated by the increasing numbers of Americans who are barely subsisting amid dire economic conditions. By the year 2000, one of every three students in American schools will be from a minority group representing diverse ethnic, cultural, and linguistic backgrounds (though in many parts of the United States today, "minority" students now are the majority).

Our nation's education reform movement has failed to increase the graduation rate of poor, immigrant, or minority children; nor has it contributed to substantial academic gains for them. Unfortunately, the issues and concerns that affect these young people continue to be a low priority not only in education research, but also in local, state, and federal funding allocations.

The demographics of the United States suggest that our most urgent, unmet educational needs are these:

FIGURE 1.1
The National Education Goals in Brief

1. All children ready to learn

2. Ninety percent graduation rate

3. All children competent in core subjects

4. First in the world in math and science

5. Every adult literate and able to compete in the work force

6. Safe, disciplined, drug-free schools

(1) improving the academic performance of the "lower third" of our students, (2) increasing the number of high school and college graduates, and (3) increasing funding that contributes to equity (Hodgkinson 1989).

Two primary factors—the rapidly growing numbers of minority, immigrant, and poor children combined with the higher educational demands posed by current and future jobs in the United States—demand that we collaborate to improve the education and quality of life of the students who are most at risk of academic failure. With that in mind, the contributors to this book have agreed on the following central purpose:

> To give clear focus to what Americans must do to improve substantially the academic performance of the lower third of our students, increase the number of high school and college graduates, and increase the number of high-achieving minority and poverty children.

This book synthesizes some of the most effective instructional strategies for increasing students' confidence, desire to learn, and academic achievement. The strategies selected and described in Chapters 3 through 8 have proven track records, not only with young people at risk of academic failure, but with all students. They are designed to contribute to the building of good programs and good schools and to teach all students successfully.

Strategies were chosen for this document based on direct research or the extension of research-based theory. The knowledge base includes both experimental and descriptive studies. As often as possible, strategies have been included on the basis of several studies rather than a single experimental usage (see Appendix A for a list of the criteria used in selecting research). Underlying the instructional strategies recommended herein are the following general curriculum recommendations:

- an emphasis on concept development, depth of learning, and interpretation of meaning rather than on the learning of isolated facts;
- increased social interaction, collaborative problem solving, and group process skills;
- the inclusion and valuing of the contributions of many ethnic groups;
- an interdisciplinary curriculum in which skills such as reading, writing, mathematics, and oral communication are used as tools for understanding history, the humanities, and science; and
- diversified teaching and learning strategies that reflect students' interests, backgrounds, and learning styles.

Too often, "teaching as usual" in American classrooms consists of children sitting still and listening to the teacher or filling in a series of worksheets; these time-honored practices have proved to be ineffective and actually damaging for students—particularly those at risk of academic failure. This book urges an overhaul of America's educational system. It is intended to bring about a marked improvement in children's learning by focusing on successful classroom practices. The contributors to this book propose a whole new way of educating everybody's children.

WHERE WE ARE NOW: SOME EXCELLENCE BUT LITTLE EQUITY

By the year 2000, American students will leave grades four, eight, and twelve having demonstrated competency in challenging subject matter including English, mathematics, science, history, and geography; and every school in America will ensure that all students learn to use their minds well, so they may be prepared for responsible citizenship, further learning, and productive employment in our modern economy.

— MULLIS ET AL. (1990)

What is the educational status of students in the United States, and how formidable is the task of achieving by the year 2000 the goals set by former President Bush and the nation's governors? Hodgkinson (1992, p. 8) notes that the evidence for the view that all American schools are "terrible" is "very thin." In fact, he found that the "top 15 percent of America's students are world class on any set of indicators." And while we need to do a better job of attending to the "forgotten middle" of the young people in U.S. schools, these students are likely to graduate from high school and go on to contribute to the nation's economic well-being.

In terms of academic attainment, however, the condition of the lowest 35 percent of the young people in our schools is "truly awful," in Hodgkinson's words. Their plight is due to life factors that predated their arrival at school, such as poverty, teen births and out-of-wedlock births, cocaine addiction at birth, too little food, and inadequate housing. Undoubtedly, these factors make it extremely difficult for some children to concentrate and learn, and they put an almost impossible burden on the schools and those who work in them.

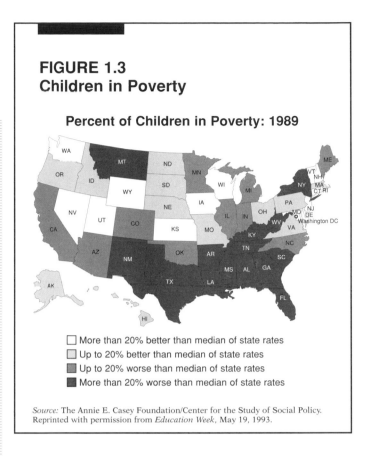

FIGURE 1.3
Children in Poverty

Percent of Children in Poverty: 1989

☐ More than 20% better than median of state rates
☐ Up to 20% better than median of state rates
■ Up to 20% worse than median of state rates
■ More than 20% worse than median of state rates

Source: The Annie E. Casey Foundation/Center for the Study of Social Policy. Reprinted with permission from *Education Week*, May 19, 1993.

LOFTY GOALS BUT INADEQUATE FUNDING

The national goals established at President Bush's 1989 education summit describe only the end product: what young Americans should be able to do by the year 2000. How schools are to fund strategies used to achieve these goals was given little attention at the summit. The matter of funding cannot be dismissed lightly. It lies at the very heart of solving the educational problems of those students who are most at risk of failure. Money alone will certainly not produce better schools, but inadequate funding is a formidable and sometimes insurmountable barrier to improving the desperate conditions in many schools. Funding, for example, is needed for teacher training, teacher time with students in need of extra assistance, materials, building repairs, adequate services, and aides.

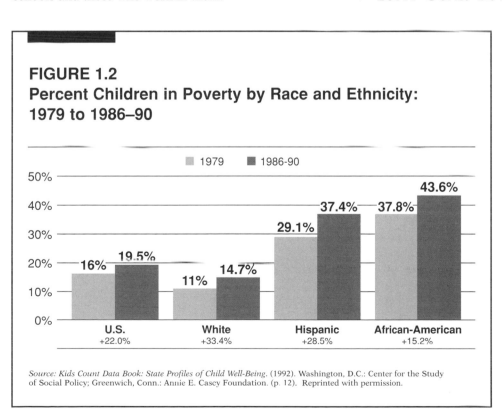

FIGURE 1.2
Percent Children in Poverty by Race and Ethnicity: 1979 to 1986–90

■ 1979 ■ 1986-90

	U.S. +22.0%	White +33.4%	Hispanic +28.5%	African-American +15.2%
1979	16%	11%	29.1%	37.8%
1986-90	19.5%	14.7%	37.4%	43.6%

Source: Kids Count Data Book: State Profiles of Child Well-Being. (1992). Washington, D.C.: Center for the Study of Social Policy; Greenwich, Conn.: Annie E. Casey Foundation. (p. 12). Reprinted with permission.

The stark differences between the extensive resources provided for the education of affluent children and the inadequacies of many schools available to the poor have been illustrated vividly in Jonathan Kozol's (1991) book *Savage Inequalities*. The goal of excellence for all students is just an empty promise unless we attend to the needs and circumstances of poor students and minorities, who comprise one-third of the U.S. school population (Commission on Minority Participation in Education and American Life 1988).

Poor children need the best possible schooling to give them a fighting chance to lift themselves out of poverty. The data indicate, however, that they seldom get such a chance. Not only do poor children live in poor neighborhoods with poor friends and poor classmates, their schools also receive less money to educate each student than do schools educating their more affluent peers.

The difference in spending is enormous. For example, large urban schools, which serve mostly low-income students, spend less money per pupil than the national average—and far less than do suburban school districts. In fact, the financial inequities between the inner cities and their surrounding suburbs have been called "spectacular" even when compared with the disparities between states (Hodgkinson 1992).

Moreover, the spread between rich and poor districts grew even larger during the 1980s (Taylor and Piché 1990). Despite all the special funding for programs such as compensatory education and bilingual education, schools serving predominantly low-income and minority students have become increasingly ill-supported compared with schools serving white, middle-class students (Korbin 1992).

COMPENSATORY AND REMEDIAL PROGRAMS: INAPPROPRIATE INSTRUCTION AND LOW TEACHER EXPECTATIONS

Programs of compensatory and remedial education appear to have done little to improve the academic performance of the lower third of U.S. students. Despite the huge amounts of money spent on these programs, students placed in them "often become lifers" because of the "poor quality of instruction they receive," say the authors of a report on various programs designed to improve the achievement of students who are economically disadvantaged and educationally deficient (Anderson and Pellicer 1990). For example, Chapter 1 programs receive nearly $4 billion dollars per year—20 percent of the budget of the

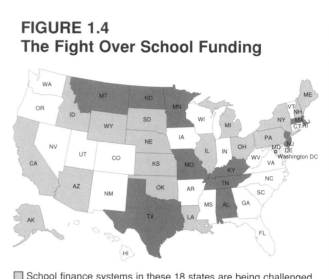

FIGURE 1.4
The Fight Over School Funding

☐ School finance systems in these 18 states are being challenged.

■ Since 1989, court decisions in these 10 states have forced or will likely force changes in their funding systems.

Reprinted with permission from *USA Today*, September 8, 1993, p. 11A.

U.S. Department of Education. Yet according to Anderson and Pellicer (1990), these programs generally "fragment the curriculum" and are so "poorly coordinated with regular programs that student learning is actually impeded."

Anderson and Pellicer also found that the teachers in many compensatory programs have low expectations and use unchallenging, low-level materials. Although students in compensatory and remedial programs badly need the attention of master teachers, they tend to be served by teacher aides and to work alone at their desks—primarily on low-level, pencil-and-paper tasks. The authors also report that remedial and compensatory students would "benefit greatly from increased expectations and demands."

Recognizing the problems faced by Chapter 1 programs, the Commission on Chapter 1 recently outlined the following "most critical deficiencies" of the programs, which must be changed fundamentally (Commission on Chapter One 1992):

• a continued focus on remediation that denies the richness of learning to those who need more, not less, of what makes education engaging and exciting;

• a focus on accounting for dollars that deflects attention from results;

• resources spread too thinly to make a difference in the neediest schools;

• methods for evaluating progress that are antiquated, and even harmful; and

• a perverse incentive structure that discourages schools from improving student performance.

In addition to the need to change Chapter 1 programs themselves, the Commission recognized the urgent need for systemic, whole-school change. Here the message of the Commission is strong and clear:

> If Chapter 1 is to help children in poverty to attain both basic and high-level knowledge and skills, it must become a vehicle for improving whole schools serving concentrations of poor children. There is ample evidence to show that under optimum teaching and learning conditions—those with high expectations and skilled instruction—children *will* learn at high levels. The proof is consistent: those encouraged to work with challenging content, to solve problems, and to seek meaning from what they study will make far greater academic progress than students limited to basic skills instruction.
>
> So, rather than simply building good programs, we must build good schools. We know how to teach *all* students successfully; we can no longer accept any excuses for failing to do so (Commission on Chapter One 1992, p. 7).

HARD REALITIES FOR MANY CHILDREN IN THE UNITED STATES

Children growing up in the United States today face a mind numbing array of hard realities. Consider the potential effects of these glaring facts:

• In 1990, 13 percent of all children in the United States were regularly hungry, 25 percent were born to unmarried parents, over 20 percent of all children under age 18 were poor, and 19 percent had no health insurance (Hodgkinson 1992, p. 4).

• Every year, about 350,000 children are born to mothers addicted to cocaine during pregnancy. Those who survive become children with strikingly short attention spans, poor coordination, and much worse. Getting such children ready for kindergarten costs around $40,000 each (Hodgkinson 1991, p. 10).

• The "Norman Rockwell" family—a working father, a housewife mother, and two children of school age—constitutes only 6 percent of U.S. households (Hodgkinson 1991, p. 10).

• About one-third of preschool children are destined for school failure because of poverty, neglect,

sickness, handicapping conditions, and lack of adult protection and nurturance (Hodgkinson 1991, p. 10).

• Approximately 2.5 million American children were reported to have been abused or neglected last year (Children's Defense Fund 1992).

• The U.S. has the highest rate of poor children and prisoners per capita among industrialized nations (Hodgkinson 1989; Pear 1992).

Too often, we use bleak statistics like the ones above to excuse our inability to teach the children of poverty. We must instead use them to rally support for America's schools. Schools cannot, by themselves, remedy the fearsome problems that our young people face. *The entire society is responsible for creating the problems, and it must be communally responsible for solving them.* And the everyday responsibility for teaching children still rests with individual teachers in individual classrooms. It is that responsibility that gave rise to this book of strategies designed to assist the people who work in classrooms.

The sampling of statistics above suggests some of the problems faced by children of poverty. Now consider some of the outcomes of these problems, as reflected in *The Condition of Education 1993*, published by the National Center on Education Statistics of the U.S. Department of Education:

• Only one in five poor children is enrolled in preschool, compared with more than half of those who are better-off; this disparity has widened since 1973.

• Children from low-income families are more likely to drop out of school than their more affluent peers, and to be older than their classmates.

• Low-income students go to college right after high school at about half the rate of high-income students.

• High school dropouts from poor families are less likely to land jobs than are other dropouts.

• Students whose parents never graduate from high school watch more television and do less homework than students with highly educated parents. Both factors are strongly linked to academic performance.

Ample research tells us that schools provide poor, immigrant, and minority students with instruction inferior to the instruction provided to students of "mainstream" backgrounds. And yet, during the past two decades, little seems to have changed in how our students—regardless of their background—are taught. Despite a huge body of research suggesting alternative teaching strategies better

YOUNG FAMILIES AT RISK

Significant numbers of new families in the United States are "at risk" from the start because the parents are unprepared to take on their new responsibilities, according to a report by the Annie E. Casey Foundation and the Center for the Study of Social Policy.

The fourth annual "Kids Count" report includes an index of the proportion of new families that have at least one of the following risk factors: the mother is under age 20 when she has her first baby; the mother has not completed high school when her first child is born; or the parents of the first baby are not married.

Of the 1.7 million new families begun with the birth of a first child in 1990, 45 percent were at risk for at least one of these reasons, the study says. Each risk increases the likelihood that the families will break up, live in poverty and depend on public assistance, and have children who do poorly in school, the report says.

Each year, the report looks at 10 indicators of child health and well-being and compiles state-by-state comparisons.

FIGURE 1.5
Composite Rankings of States on Measures of Child Well-Being*

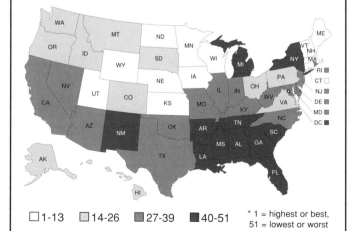

☐ 1-13 ☐ 14-26 ■ 27-39 ■ 40-51

* 1 = highest or best, 51 = lowest or worst

Reprinted with permission from *Education Week*, March 31, 1993.

calculated to bring about increased learning, classrooms in the United States tend to be dominated by textbooks, lectures, and short-answer activity sheets. These outdated instructional practices are, too often, at odds with the learning styles of students, especially students at risk of failure.

Considerable evidence also supports another critical conclusion: that the differences in achievement observed between poor, immigrant, and minority students and students of mainstream backgrounds are *not* the result of differences in their ability to learn. Rather, they are differences *caused by the quality of instruction that young people receive in school*.

Obviously, a multitude of factors—crime, drugs, and poverty, among them—contribute to students' risk of failure today. But the factor that educators have the greatest power to eradicate is *ineffective instructional practices*. Fortunately, research tells us that the risk to young people caused by ineffective instruction is a highly temporary state. Given the means, students at risk of academic failure have the power to make tremendous academic, social, and personal strides.

THE NEED FOR A SHIFT IN PARADIGMS

If America is to educate *all* of its children to higher levels, then Americans must be willing to embrace a major paradigm shift in our beliefs about how students learn. Currently, students are required to *adapt*—to adapt to the prevalent teaching practices and instructional materials and assessment instruments that are used in the school. Those who cannot adapt are rarely accommodated in most classrooms. Instead, they are viewed as being deficient in their ability to learn.

In this outdated paradigm, not knowing English is a deficit; limited life experience is a deficit; being a hands-on learner is a deficit; and requiring demonstration and modeling in order to learn is a deficit. The list of "deficits" is dangerously long. Too often, students who cannot adapt easily are placed in remedial and compensatory programs, or they are placed in low tracks and given inferior, overly simplified objectives and materials and undemanding, repetitive skill work.

The influx into mainstream American of large numbers of students from a variety of cultures calls for *schools* to adapt to their new clientele, not for students to adapt to the schools. Every culture and every student deserves honor and respect. A transformed paradigm of schooling would recognize students for their abilities in their primary language, even though that language may not be English; would identify and accommodate students' learning-style strengths; would encourage students and teachers to learn from each other; would set consistently high expectations for success; and would allow students, teachers, parents, and the entire community to act as mutual resources for learning.

Each youngster brings unique strengths and experiences to school; these strengths and experiences deserve to be recognized and nurtured. Business as usual in U.S. schools—textbook-dominated instruction, lecture-dominated teaching, and short-answer evaluations—simply will not work any longer. Educators need experiences that help them to believe that all children can learn; they need a wide variety of strategies; they need to know when and how to adapt to their students' needs; and they need adequate staff development, modeling, and coaching so that they are confident in using the most effective strategies for particular students. Successful model schools and programs are desperately needed to point the way. And they are needed right away.

Those who believe in the vision of a democratic nation with equal opportunity for all are likely to embrace this challenge and to work toward achieving this new paradigm. Those who find it difficult to accept the need for change should consider the following statement by Hodgkinson (1992, p. 6):

> As pragmatists, we must ensure that the additional 4.4 million nonwhite young people get the best education and access to good jobs as we possibly can, [both] for the nation's health, and also because they will be funding our Social Security payments!

POSTSCRIPT: EDUCATING EVERYBODY'S CHILDREN IS EVERYBODY'S CONCERN

Joe Sweeney teaches mathematics at Middle School 145 in Jackson Heights, New York City. In his school, 58 percent of the students are Hispanic and 12 percent are Asian; about 30 percent of the students are immigrants

representing twenty-five different countries. Some enter Middle School 145 having experienced no compulsory education at all in their native lands.

Sweeney offers neighborhood workshops on "how to help your kids at school"; he calls on volunteer neighborhood interpreters to help him get across his message. He assigns his math students to survey and analyze such problems as graffiti and homelessness; their projects have led to direct social action on very personal levels—finding shelter for a homeless woman through the intervention of a student, for instance.

Of reform, Sweeney says simply, "School cannot be an isolated site that exists only from 9:00 to 3:00. The whole community must get involved with the school. If everyone works together, our schools will succeed."

REFERENCES

Anderson, L.W., and L.O. Pellicer. (September 1990). "Synthesis of Research on Compensatory and Remedial Education." *Educational Leadership* 48, 1: 10–16.

Children's Defense Fund. (1992). *The State of America's Children, 1992.* Washington, D.C.: The Children's Defense Fund.

Commission on Chapter One. (1992). *Making Schools Work for Children in Poverty.* (1992). Washington, D.C.: American Association for Higher Education.

Commission on Minority Participation in Education and American Life. *One-Third of a Nation.* (May 1988). Washington, D.C., and Denver: American Council on Education and the Education Commission of the States.

The Condition of Education 1993. (1993). Washington, D.C.: U.S. Department of Education, National Center for Education Statistics.

Hodgkinson, H. L. (1989). *The Same Client: The Demographics of Education and Service Delivery Systems.* Washington, D.C.: Center for Demographic Policy, Institute for Educational Leadership.

Hodgkinson, H. (1991). "Reform Versus Reality." *Phi Delta Kappan* 73: 9–16.

Hodgkinson, H. (1992). "A Demographic Look at Tomorrow." Washington, D.C.: Center for Demographic Policy, Institute for Educational Leadership.

Korbin, J.E. (January/February 1992). "Child Poverty in the United States." *American Behavioral Scientist* 35, 3: 213–219.

Kozol, J. (1991). *Savage Inequalities: Children in America's Schools.* New York: Crown.

Mullis, I.V.S., et al. (1990). *Accelerating Academic Achievement. America's Challenge. A Summary of Findings from 20 Years of NAEP.* Princeton, N.J.: Educational Testing Service.

Pear, R. (1992). "Ranks of U.S. Poor Reach 35.7 million, the Most Since '64." *New York Times*, pp. A1, A14.

Taylor, W., and D. Piché (1990). *Shortchanging Children: The Impact of Fiscal Inequity on the Education of Students at Risk.* Washington, D.C.: Committee on Education and Labor, U.S. House of Representatives.

2

BARRIERS TO GOOD INSTRUCTION

THE ASCD ADVISORY PANEL ON IMPROVING STUDENT ACHIEVEMENT*

Good instruction is good instruction, regardless of students' racial, ethnic, or socioeconomic backgrounds. To a large extent, good teaching—teaching that is engaging, relevant, multicultural, and that appeals to a variety of modalities and learning styles—works well with all children. Unfortunately, numerous barriers can prevent poor and minority students from receiving good instruction. Some of these barriers are caused by educators' attitudes and beliefs; others are the result of institutional practices. This chapter presents a brief overview of both kinds of barriers. The intent of this chapter is not to provide a thorough cataloguing of every barrier to sound instruction, but rather to place educators on alert.

ATTITUDES AND BELIEFS

RACISM AND PREJUDICE

Despite much progress in U.S. society during the past few decades, racism and prejudice are still ugly realities in all sectors of American life, including education. Today, racism may be less overt and virulent than in the past, but its effects can still greatly harm minority students. In fact, subtle, insidious forms of racism may be even more harmful to young people than are more blatant forms.

Prejudice against the poor, of whatever race or ethnicity, is another force that works against the academic achievement of disadvantaged students. For example, some teachers of poor students don't let them take materials home, out of fear that the materials will never be returned. Yet these same students tend to be very proud of taking materials home and are generally exceedingly careful to return them.

*Members of the panel include Sheryl Denbo, Harriet Doss Willis, Alan Ginsburg, Lois Hirst, Shirley Jackson, Michael O'Malley, Lorraine Valdez Pierce, and Stuart Rankin (Chair).

Obviously, teachers must avoid discriminating, consciously or unconsciously, against students because of their racial, ethnic, or socioeconomic backgrounds. Such discrimination can be as blatant as imposing harsher discipline on minority students or as subtle as lowering expectations for poor children because they have "difficult" home lives. Teachers must be aware that they see students' behavior through the lens of their *own* culture. They must carefully examine their own attitudes and behaviors to be sure that they are not imposing a double standard. Most important, they must believe sincerely and completely that *all children can learn.*

EXPECTATIONS

Educators must hold equally high expectations for affluent white students and poor and minority students—despite the disparity in students' backgrounds. Under the right conditions, low-income and minority students can learn just as well as any other children. One of these necessary conditions, of course, is that the teacher hold expectations of high performance for all students.

High or low expectations can create a self-fulfilling prophecy. Students must believe that they *can* achieve before they will risk trying; and young people are very astute at sensing whether their teachers believe they can be successful. By the same token, teachers must truly believe their students can achieve before they will put forth their best effort to teach them. The teacher's beliefs must be translated into instructional practices if students are to benefit: actions speak louder than attitudes.

Teachers must also be sensitive to the subtle ways in which they can convey low expectations. According to researcher Sandra Graham of the University of California-Los Angeles, when a teacher expresses sympathy over failure, students typically infer that the teacher thinks they are incapable of succeeding, not that they simply may not have tried hard enough. Similarly, when a teacher gives students lavish praise for completing a simple task or offers help before being asked for it, students infer that the teacher thinks they are stupid. In other words, holding high expectations is not simply a matter of cheerleading; it requires insight into how students interpret a teacher's words and behaviors.

Teachers must also resist the temptation to attribute student failure to lack of ability ("I've taught this concept and they didn't understand it; they must not be smart enough"). Failure to learn can stem from many other causes, such as inadequate prior knowledge, insufficient effort or motivation, lack of the right learning strategy, or inappropriate teaching. The bottom line is this: *If students are not learning, the teacher needs to change his or her approach to teaching them.*

Teachers are not the only ones who need to examine their expectations for students, however. Administrators who decide what courses their schools offer should ask themselves whether they are providing too few challenging courses. And counselors must consider whether they are steering students into undemanding courses because they are poor, minority, or female. (Institutional practices that communicate low expectations are discussed below.) The expectation that *all* students can achieve at high levels, under the right circumstances, should be the guiding principle of every school.

LACK OF UNDERSTANDING OF CULTURAL DIFFERENCES

Teachers sometimes misinterpret the behaviors of poor and minority students because they do not understand the cultures they come from. White teachers can easily misread the behaviors of black students, for example. In *Black Students and School Failure*, Jacqueline Jordan Irvine writes:

> Because the culture of black children is different and often misunderstood, ignored, or discounted, black students are likely to experience cultural discontinuity in schools. . . . This lack of cultural sync becomes evident in instructional situations in which teachers misinterpret, denigrate, and dismiss black students' language, nonverbal cues, physical movements, learning styles, cognitive approaches, and worldview. When teachers and students are out of sync, they clash and confront each other, both consciously and unconsciously. . . . (Irvine 1990, p. xix)

Only when teachers understand the cultural backgrounds of their students can they avoid this kind of culture clash. In the meantime, the ways in which teachers comprehend and react to students' culture, language, and behaviors may create problems (Erickson 1987). In too many schools, students are, in effect, required to leave their family and cultural backgrounds at the schoolhouse door and live in a kind of "hybrid culture" composed of the community of fellow learners (Au and Kawakami 1991).

Especially in the early grades, teachers and students may differ in their expectations for the classroom setting; each may act in ways that the other misinterprets. In addition, those teachers (and they are legion) who insist on a

CULTURE'S ROLE IN QUALITY TEACHING
AS REPORTED BY KENJI IMA

In a San Diego elementary school, a teacher of a sheltered English class complained about "cheating" among Hmong students who were submitting homework that appeared to have been worked on by other students and older siblings. In addition to this complaint, the teacher had been upset by what she felt was misbehavior of these same students; she had asked her class aide to telephone the parents.

After a series of phone calls from the aide, some of the Hmong parents removed their children from the school; they felt that the teacher was not doing her job of teaching their children. In effect, they interpreted the telephoned complaints as an indication of the teacher's weakness, since they believed that any competent teacher could surely discipline a misbehaving child without parental intervention. The interactions that shaped this entire incident illustrate the need to bridge the gap between the student's world and the teacher's world.

First, the cheating claim can be understood within the context of the Hmong world with the knowledge that Hmong youngsters feel obligated to help their peers and siblings. (This attitude is also found among many Native American youngsters.) In other words, for these children, helping each other was not seen as inappropriate behavior; they certainly didn't view it as cheating. Second, the teacher/parent misunderstanding highlights the differences in expectations between teachers and parents: The teacher obviously believes that parents are at least partly responsible for the behavior of their children in school, while the parents feel that their obligations for discipline end at the schoolhouse door.

Could the teacher have better addressed both of these issues? Yes, if she would simply have consulted with the Hmong parents. But how does a teacher know when to raise questions about cultural differences, and how could this particular teacher have arrived at appropriate solutions, given her limited understanding of Hmong children and their parents? Only after the parents removed their children from the school did the principal realize that he might have a problem on his hands, but his incompetence led him to allow the situation to continue unresolved. Then other Hmong parents began to complain about treatment of their children, and talk arose about removing still more Hmong youngsters. Given the additional funds received by the school for these children's enrollment, the principal was faced with the definite possibility of declining revenues, which meant he had to discuss the matter with the teacher. He did so, but showed the greatest deference to the teacher. (It should be noted that the teacher was very ethnocentric and unwilling to be flexible, even when the cultural differences were revealed.) Her response was one of "passive aggressiveness"; she refused to agree to contact the Hmong parents on any future occasions that might arise, and she continued to berate those children in her classroom. Some of the Hmong children continue to attend her class, though they have been deliberately misbehaving in response to this "mean" teacher. At this stage, without removal of the teacher there seems to be no easy solution to a festering problem.

Not all teacher are as insensitive as this one, nor are all administrators as incompetent as the principal in this case. Nevertheless, this was clearly a situation in which cultural differences were ignored at the expense of "quality" teaching.

single pedagogical style, and who see other styles as being out of step, may be refusing to allow students to work to their strengths.

As Knapp and Shields (1990, p. 755) suggest, the so-called "deficit" or "disadvantage" model has two serious problems: (1) teachers are likely to set low standards for certain children "because their patterns of behavior, language use, and values do not match those required in the school setting"; and (2) over time a cycle of failure and despair is created that culminates "in students' turning their backs on school and dropping out . . . because teachers and administrators fail to adapt to and take advantage of the strengths that these students do possess."

INSTITUTIONAL PRACTICES

In many schools, institutional practices prevent poor and minority students from receiving good instruction. These practices include tracking, inappropriate instruction, and lack of consequences (for teachers as well as students) for poor performance.

TRACKING

The most notorious of these harmful institutional practices is tracking, which dooms children in the low tracks to a second-rate education by failing to provide them with the support they need to move to a higher track. As a result, they fall further and further behind their peers. Students in the low tracks are stigmatized and lose self-esteem and motivation, while expectations for their performance plummet.

In her book *Keeping Track*, researcher Jeannie Oakes (1985) says "we can be quite certain that the deficiencies of slower students are *not* more easily remediated when they are grouped together." Yet the practice of tracking persists, despite the many negative effects on students documented by Oakes and many other researchers. Tracking is especially harmful to poor and minority students, because these students are more likely to end up in the low tracks.

Effective alternatives to tracking exist. Robert Slavin's Success for All program, for example, uses one-on-one tutoring to immediately help students when they start to fall behind in reading skills. Low achievers in the program have reportedly shown impressive gains. The Accelerated Schools Project, developed by Henry Levin of Stanford

University, creates accelerated programs to bring at-risk students into the mainstream by the end of elementary school; students learn faster because they receive engaging, active, interdisciplinary instruction. The Higher Order Thinking Skills (HOTS) program, developed by Stanley Pogrow of the University of Arizona-Tucson, enhances the general thinking skills of remedial students by showing them how to work with ideas. All of these programs and others, including the Carbo Recorded Book Method, are aimed at helping students get up to speed, rather than permanently segregating them and feeding them a dumbed-down curriculum, as is true of tracking.

LOW EXPECTATIONS

Many institutional practices convey low expectations to poor and minority students. Rhona Weinstein (1994) of the University of California at Berkeley has identified the following through interviews and questionnaires with elementary school children:

> These students often receive barren, remedial materials, which imply the belief that they are unable to grapple with higher-order ideas. In addition, the evaluation system, which typically conveys that intelligence is stable, global, and distributed on a bell curve, implies that some are permanently less intelligent than others and that there is only one kind of intelligence. Further, educators often rely on a system of rewards and punishments to motivate poor and minority students, instead of allowing them some leeway to pursue their own interests. Similarly, these students are typically allowed little input or self-direction; they are not allowed to take responsibility for their own learning. All of these practices reflect the low expectations educators as a group hold for these students.

INAPPROPRIATE INSTRUCTION

Inappropriate instruction harms many poor and minority students. Instead of being presented in a variety of modes, instruction in U.S. schools tends to be abstract, barren of application, overly sequential, and redundant. Bits of knowledge are emphasized, not the big picture, thus handicapping global thinkers. Moreover, the largely Eurocentric curriculum downplays the experiences and contributions of minorities.

Teachers of diverse students find it especially important to use a broad repertoire of strategies. Some children may be global thinkers; others, more analytical. Some children may learn best from lecture and reading; others may learn best through manipulatives and other hands-on experiences. Some children may thrive on competition; others may achieve far more in cooperative groups. Clearly, a diverse array of teaching strategies best meets the needs of diverse students.

Beyond that, there are countless ways, limited only by the teacher's imagination, to tailor instruction to the specific needs of children from varied cultural groups:

• A teacher can make classwork more relevant for children by using illustrations and examples linked to their culture or race. One obvious example is Jaime Escalante's teaching his Hispanic students that the Mayans invented the concept of zero.

• Teachers can highlight role models—figures from history or visiting lecturers, for example—who belong to the same culture or race as students in the class.

• Au and Kawakami (1985, p. 406) describe "the use of a particular event called `talk story,' found in [Hawaiian] children's home culture, that seemed pivotal in improving reading instruction." This form of participatory storytelling begins with a single storyteller but allows listeners to contribute their own extensions to the story, thus revealing their understanding of it. The use of talk story departs from conventional school practice in two ways: the first is "to focus reading instruction on comprehension or understanding of the text, rather than solely on word identification," and the second is "to conduct lessons using a culturally compatible . . . style of interaction."

• Dillon (1989, p. 227) describes the behaviors of a white male teacher who was particularly successful with low-income black students in a rural, secondary, low-track reading class. Dillon ascribes the teacher's success to his ability to do two things: (1) "create a culturally congruent

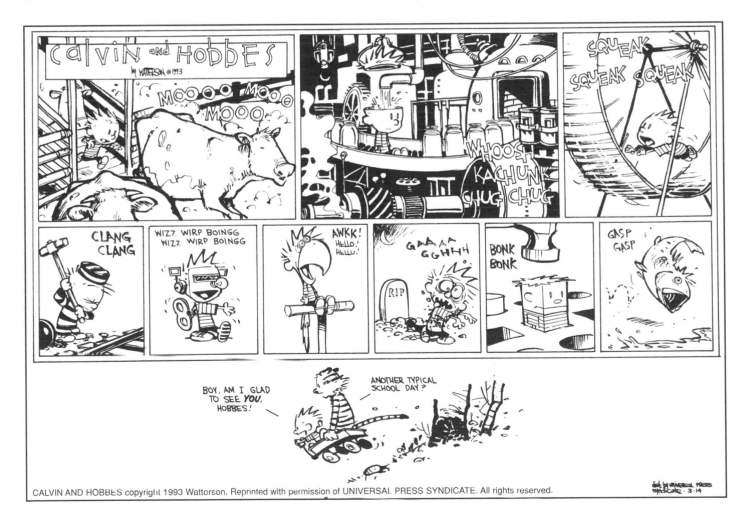

13

social organization in his classroom that accounted for the cultural backgrounds of his students," and (2) to "vary his teaching style to allow him to communicate effectively with his students during lesson interactions, resulting in increased opportunities for student learning and improved student attitudes toward learning and school in general."

Dillon's study, notes Hollins (1993, p. 95) "clearly points to teaching behaviors that have a positive impact on academic performance without changing the social class or ethnic orientation of the learners. These teaching behaviors can be understood and performed by others."

• Citing two other sources (Collins 1988 and Taylor and Dorsey-Gaines 1988) Hollins (1993, p. 95) notes: "Communication is even more effective when cultural meanings are shared. Speaking the same language does not necessarily mean sharing the same cultural understandings. Theoretically, two distinctly different cultural groups may share the same spoken language, but with varying degrees of comprehension due to differences in cultural meanings." Teachers thus need to adjust their "communicative strategies and modes of presentation," identifying those that "best facilitate learning in a particular situation."

In summary, Hollins (1993, p. 96) urges creation of a "social context within the classroom that is comfortable and supportive for every child regardless of background experiences (cultural, ethnic, social, religious, or economic) and social, emotional, psychological, or physical presence. Creating a supportive context for learning means developing friendly and collaborative relationships within the classroom. It has to do with getting children to like themselves and to take pride in their own accomplishments; getting children to be kind, helpful, and respectful toward each other; and building self-confidence and positive interpersonal relationships."

In addition, teachers must use those techniques that will work best with their own students. Competition will probably not motivate a class composed primarily of Native American children, for example, because their culture values cooperation.

DIFFERENTIAL ACCESS

Poor and minority students are often denied access to challenging coursework. Counselors place them in remedial or undemanding courses, and because more challenging courses often require students to have taken specific introductory courses, students can never switch to a more

demanding track. Irvine cites data showing that "black students, particularly black male students, are three times as likely to be in a class for the educable mentally retarded as are white students, but only one-half as likely to be in a class for the gifted and talented" (Irvine 1990, p. xiv). In addition, the pull-out programs intended to help many of these students end up fragmenting their school day. And after pull-out programs end, students are given little support for reentering the regular classroom, so they tend to backslide when they rejoin their peers.

LACK OF CONSEQUENCES

Unfortunately, there are few consequences for students and teachers if poor and minority students do not learn very much. So long as students put in the required seat time, they will receive a diploma; so long as teachers go through the motions, they will have a job. In many cases, nobody—not the education establishment, not the parents or guardians, not the politicians—protests a status quo that is woefully deficient.

Schools that have had success in teaching poor and minority students do not keep ineffective teachers on the faculty; in these schools, teachers are held responsible if their students do not learn. These schools also collaborate with parents or guardians to ensure that students who come to school and strive to achieve are rewarded.

DISCIPLINARY PRACTICES

Teachers sometimes punish poor and minority children more harshly than they do other children for the same offenses. Moreover, suspension is often the punishment of choice, causing students to miss valuable class time. According to Irvine (1990, p. 16),"one factor related to the nonachievement of black students is the disproportionate use of severe disciplinary practices, which leads to black students' exclusion from classes, their perceptions of mistreatment, and feelings of alienation and rejection, which result ultimately in their misbehaving more and/or leaving school."

On the other hand, some teachers are more lenient with poor or minority students, because they believe these children have been socialized differently than mainstream children. For example, teachers might overlook boisterous or aggressive behavior among poor or minority students, while chastising mainstream students for similar behavior. Teachers need to set forth a clear, reasonable discipline policy and require all students to abide by it.

FIGURE 2.1
Factors Affecting Student Achievement

SCHOOL FACTORS

CURRICULUM

Goals/Standards

Content

Teaching

Assessment

LOW EXPECTATIONS

Cultural/Ethnic

Gender

Linguistic

Socioeconomic

SCHOOL ORGANIZATION

Administrative Structures
- Instructional grouping practices
- Retention/promotion policies
- Scheduling practices
- Schoolwide rules/policies/procedures

Administrative services
- Mental health and health services
- Work/career/technical skills training
- Adaptive life skills
- Professional/staff development

NONSCHOOL FACTORS

TEACHER PREPARATION/CERTIFICATION/LICENSING

Content and Teaching/Learning and Knowledge

SOCIAL/ECONOMIC CONDITIONS

Socioeconomic
- Single-parent family
- Nondegreed parent
- Home alone more than three hours a day
- Dropout siblings
- Lack of/inadequate social support services
- Limited English proficiency
- Low socioeconomic status

Economic
- School finance (federal, state, local)

Resource Allocations (programs, services, facilities)

Program Regulations

GOAL: Grade-level performance in basic and advanced academic curricular content areas.

PHILOSOPHY: Prevention vs. Intervention
Proactive vs. Reactive

Hodges 1989

INVOLVEMENT OF PARENTS OR GUARDIANS

Poor and minority parents or guardians too often have no opportunities to create an ongoing relationship with their children's schools; in fact, they often have no communication with the schools at all. In turn, schools tend to make few efforts to develop a relationship with poor and minority parents or guardians, who may be too intimidated or too hard-pressed to initiate contact themselves. For parents who don't speak English, the language barrier can pose another formidable obstacle.

James Comer of the Yale Child Study Center has developed a process to foster good relationships among children, teachers, and parents or guardians. Parents or guardians are encouraged to be an active presence in the school. Social activities bring families and school staff together, helping parents or guardians gain trust in the school. The program has reportedly helped to lower dropout rates, among other benefits.

MASKING THE PROBLEM

Schools sometimes avoid revealing how poorly they serve poor and minority children. They do this by refusing to disaggregate achievement data, for example, and by lowering standards so that students get inflated grades that lull parents or guardians into a false sense of security. It is important to know how well—or badly—poor and minority children are performing, so that necessary changes can be made. But such information should not be used to "blame the victim"—to support arguments that these children are less educable, for example.

UNEQUAL ACCESS TO RESOURCES

Unequal access to resources further reduces poor and minority students' chances of receiving equal opportunities to learn. Poor and minority students typically attend schools that receive less funding than those attended by mainstream students. As a result, they are taught with inferior materials and equipment and have fewer manipulatives, laboratories, and facilities. Teachers in such schools receive less staff development, must cope with larger classes, and have less free time.

THE NEGATIVE IMPACT OF TESTING

Standardized tests can be seen as one way in which a meritocratic society reorders a widely disparate populace into hierarchies of abilities, achievement, and opportunity. Despite the fact that educators have never been fully at ease with the way in which students from different cultures become part of a uniform numerical hierarchy on standardized tests, the main strategy of the excellence movement of the 1980s was to legislate higher educational standards at the state level, most often through increased student testing (ETS Policy Information Center 1990).

Because school districts serving low-income, non-Anglo children were under particular pressure to raise lagging test scores, these districts began to conduct more

testing and to link that testing to promotion and graduation (Bauer 1992). Instead of improving the curriculum and enriching learning in preparation for the test, however, the lack of resources in these districts led teachers to narrow the curriculum and to teach to the test through rote learning and drill work (Dorr-Bremme and Herman 1986). By the end of the 1980s, low-income, non-Anglo students were more at risk than ever of not having the higher order skills now deemed so essential (Ascher 1990).

In fact, the power of tests to translate difference into disadvantage is felt at many points in the world of education, most notably in the decision to place low-income and language-minority students into compensatory or bilingual education classes, where a watered-down, fragmented, and rote curriculum reinforces the disadvantages presumably diagnosed by the tests. Ironically, one of the reasons now given for the lack of success in compensatory and bilingual education is that these movements have been based on a "fundamental misassumption about what was needed" (Fillmore and Meyer 1991, p. 629).

Multiple-choice tests are often used inappropriately as the ultimate measure of students' learning and capabilities. Decisions that significantly affect students' academic destinies are sometimes made on the basis of a single test score. Moreover, norm-referenced tests reinforce the attitude that some students should be expected to do poorly. To be fair to all students, assessment should be primarily criterion-referenced and, as far as possible, based on actual performances. Perhaps most important, a variety of measures should be used to assess student learning.

LACK OF BILINGUAL INSTRUCTION

Not surprisingly, many students who do not speak English fall behind in their studies early, because they are not taught content in their native language. When they eventually learn English, they have lost so much ground in their schoolwork that they find it difficult (and sometimes impossible) to catch up with their peers. In far too many cases, these students become discouraged and drop out of school.

Overall, there is the all-too-common problem of organizational inertia and resistance to change: reluctance to accept bilingual programs, to hire bilingual personnel, to upgrade the status of teachers of English as a second language (ESL), to support the acquisition and development of primary language materials, to monitor and assess the

progress of language-minority students, and to deal with the unique problems facing newcomers, including their needs for counseling.

The number of bilingual teachers in U.S. schools is woefully insufficient, and the use of existing bilingual teachers is far from satisfactory. Bilingual teachers are not used to the best advantage-that is, to take maximum advantage of their dual-language abilities. The training and staffing of ESL and "sheltered English" classes remain inadequate. Beyond staffing, there is a dearth of primary language materials, especially for languages other than Spanish, and bilingual educators regard even those materials as inadequate.

Students who speak a language other than English need to be taught content, for a time, in their native language, while they are also given intensive training in English. Then, when they eventually join their English-speaking peers, they will be up to speed in their studies.

A BEGINNING

Unfortunately, too many educators (and citizens in the larger school community) do not realize that they are guilty of prejudice; they do not realize that their expectations for some young people are lower than their expectations for others. Similarly, many educators fail to take advantage of the rich resources provided by the last two decades of research in education. They have somehow missed the fact that the practice of tracking, for example, has been thoroughly discredited (Oakes 1985).

But naming the barriers to the kind of schooling we want for all of our children is at least a beginning. Naming the problem allows the time-consuming process of treating it to begin. The strategies outlined in this book are intended to provide assistance in treatment.

REFERENCES

Ascher, C. (December 1988). *School-College Collaborations: A Strategy for Helping Low-Income Minorities*. Urban Diversity Series No. 98. New York: ERIC Clearinghouse on Urban Education/ Institute for Urban and Minority Education.

Ascher, C. (March 1990). *Testing Students in Urban Schools: Current Problems and New Directions*. Urban Diversity Series No. 100. New York: ERIC Clearinghouse on Urban Education/Institute for Urban and Minority Education.

Au, K.. and J. Kawakami. (1985). "Research Currents: Talk Story and Learning to Read." *Language Arts* 62, 4: 406-411.

Au, K., and J. Kawakami (1991). "Culture and Ownership: Schooling of Minority Students." *Childhood Education* 67, 5: 280-284.

Bauer, E.A. (1992). "NATD Survey of Testing Practices and Issues." *Educational Measurement: Issues and Practices* 11, 1: 10-11.

Bempechat, J., and H.P. Ginsberg (November 1989). *Underachievement and Educational Disadvantage: The Home and School experience of At-Risk Youth*. Urban Diversity Series No. 99. New York: ERIC Clearinghouse on Urban Education/Institute for Urban and Minority Education.

Benard, B. (April 1991). Moving Toward a "Just and Vital Culture." *Multiculturalism in Our Schools* Portland, Ore.: Western Regional Center for Drug-Free Schools and Communities, Northwest Regional Educational Laboratory.

Cole, M., and P. Griffin, eds. (1987). *Improving Science and Mathematics Education for Minorities and Women: Contextual Factors in Education*. Madison: University of Wisconsin.

Collins, J. (December 1988). "Language and Class in Minority Education." *Anthropology in Education* 19, 4: 299-326.

Connolly, L.H., and S.M. Tucker. (March 1982). *Motivating the Mexican American Student*. Las Cruces, N.M.: ERIC Clearinghouse on Rural Education and Small Schools. (ERIC Document Reproduction Service No. ED 287 657; RC 016 472)

Darling-Hammond, L., and C. Ascher. (March 1991). *Creating Accountability in Big City Schools*. Urban Diversity Series No. 102. New York: ERIC Clearinghouse on Urban Education/ Institute on Urban and Minority Education, and the National Center for Restructuring Education, Schools and Teaching.

Dash, R., ed. (September 1988). *The Challenge—Preparing Teachers for Diverse Student Populations. Roundtable* report. San Francisco, Calif.: Far West Laboratory for Educational Research and Development.

Dillon, D.R. (1989). "Showing Them That I Want Them to Learn and That I Care About Who They Are: A Microethnography of the Social Organization of a Secondary Low-Track English-Reading Classroom." *American Educational Research Journal* 26, 2: 227-259.

Dorr-Bremme, D.W., and J.L. Herman (1986). "Assessing Student Achievement: A Profile of Classroom Practices." Los Angeles: UCLA Graduate School of Education, Center for the Study of Evaluation.

Erickson, F. (1987). "Transformation and School Success: The Politics and Culture of Educational Attainment." *Anthropology and Education Quarterly* 18, 4: 335-356.

ETS Policy Information Center. (1990). *The Education Reform Decade*. Princeton, N.J.: Educational Testing Service.

Farr, M., and H. Daniels. (1986). *Language Diversity and Writing Instruction*. New York: Eric Clearinghouse on Urban Education/Institute for Urban and Minority Education, the ERIC Clearinghouse on Reading and Communication Skills, and the NCTE.

Fillmore, L.W., and L.M. Meyer (1991). "The *Curriculum and Linguistic Minorities." Handbook of Research on Curriculum: A Project of the American Educational Research Association*, edited by P.W. Jackson. New York: Macmillan.

Flaxman, E., C. Ascher, and C. Harrington (December 1988). *Youth Mentoring: Programs and Practices*. Urban Diversity Series No. 97. New York: ERIC Clearinghouse on Urban Education/Institute for Urban and Minority Education.

Haberman, M. (November 1987). *Recruiting and Selecting Teachers for Urban Schools*. New York: ERIC Clearinghouse on Urban Education/Institute for Urban and Minority Education, and the Association of Teacher Educators.

Hodges, H. (1989). "ASCD's 3-High Achievement Model." Unpublished manuscript for the ASCD Urban Middle Grades Network, Alexandria, Va.

Hollins, E.R. (Spring 1993). "Assessing Teacher Competence for Diverse Populations." *Theory into Practice* 32, 1: 93-99.

Irvine, J.J. (1990). *Black Students and School Failure: Policies, Practices, and Prescriptions*. (Contributions in Afro-American and African Studies, Number 131.) New York: Greenwood Press.

Knapp, M.S., and P.M. Shields (June 1990). "Reconceiving Academic Instruction for the Children of Poverty." *Phi Delta Kappan* 71, 10: 753-758.

Knapp, M.S., and B.J. Turnbull. (January 1990). *Better Schooling for the Children of Poverty: Alternatives to Conventional* Wisdom. Washington, D.C.: Prepared under contract by SRI International and Policy Studies Associates for the U.S. Department of Education, Office of Planning, Budget and Evaluation.

Maehr, M.L. (April 1980). "Cultural Differences Do Not Have to Mean Motivational Inequality." Paper presented at symposium entitled "Quality and Equality in Education: Some Motivational Perspectives for Optimizing Development" at the annual meeting of the American Educational Research Association, Boston, Mass. (ED 199 353; UD 021 306).

Mathematical Sciences Education Board. (n.d.) *Making Mathematics Work for Minorities: Framework for a National Action Plan 1009-2000*. (Report of a Convocation).

Miller, S.K., and W.D. Crano. (April 1980). "Raising Low-Income/Minority Achievement by Reducing Student Sense of Academic Futility: The Underlying Theoretical Commonalities of Suggested Strategies." Paper presented at the annual meeting of the American Educational Research Association. (ED 186 575; UD 020 711).

Oakes, J. (1985). *Keeping Track: How Schools Structure Inequality*. New Haven, Conn.: Yale University Press.

Quality Education for Minorities Project. (January 1990). *Education That Works: An Action Plan for the Education of Minorities*. Cambridge: Massachusetts Institute of Technology.

Russell, A. (Summer/Fall 1990). *Carnegie Quarterly* 25, 3-4. New York: Carnegie Corporation of New York. Includes articles on fostering minorities' success in mathematics and science.

Secada, W.G., and D.A. Carey (October 1990). *Teaching Mathematics with Understanding to Limited English Proficient Students*. (Urban Diversity Series, No. 101). New York: ERIC Clearinghouse on Urban Education/Institute on Urban and Minority Education.

Shulman, J.H., and A. Mesa-Bains, eds. (November 1990). *Teaching Diverse Students: Cases and Commentaries*. San Francisco: Far West Laboratory for Educational Research and Development.

Taylor D., and C. Dorsey-Gaines (1988). *Growing Up Literate: Learning from Inner-city Families*. Portsmouth, N.H.: Heinemann.

Weinstein, R. (February 16, 1994). Telephone interview with Kendel Taylor, ASCD.

Willis, S. (June 1991). "Forging New Paths to Success: Promising Programs for Teaching Disadvantaged Students." *ASCD Curriculum Update*. (Available from ASCD, 1250 N. Pitt St., Alexandria, VA 22314.)

PROJECT HOMELESS

"We have to choose Project Homeless. That's the worst problem we talked about. We know more about it, 'cause it's in our neighborhood. What do we know about Los Angeles? What do we care?"

"We care because those people in Los Angeles are black, and we are too. We live in a black neighborhood too. What happened to them could happen here. We could help keep that from happening here. Anyway, I want to know about the Watts riots in the '60s. What happened? Why did it happen again last summer? What could those people have done to keep it from ever happening again?"

"What do you like better, Ms. Shambaugh? What should we do?"

When Kay Shambaugh decided that her 8th grade urban students would choose a long-term project on their own, she had no idea that the democratic process would be quite so noisy. But she was repeatedly reminded of the nature of the democratic process as students argued, discussed, and struggled over choices they had brainstormed earlier.

They had begun with forty ideas and now were down to two. Would they choose to assist the homeless or to research the Watts riots and Los Angeles riots to figure out whether anything had changed in thirty years.

When this pandemonium broke out in her classroom, Kay admonished students for being rude. Later that same day, the vice-presidential debates were broadcast on national television. To the delight of Kay's students, the debating candidates were even more rude than they had been in class. The rapid-fire report on the debates came the next day immediately following the tardy bell.

"Did you see the debates on TV?"

"Yeah, Ms. Shambaugh. Those dudes were rude—a lot louder than us!"

"And that news guy couldn't get him to stop."

"I told my mom that my teacher said democracy was noisy."

"What could you do to come to agreement?" Kay asked tentatively.

"Well, we're not getting anywhere like this. Could each group present their side to the whole class and then we vote?"

The exhibitions took a week to prepare and the whole class period to present. The vote was close, but Project Homeless won. Students from the losing camp were disappointed but agreed to commit themselves to the project.

Within the context of the project, students accomplished these tasks:

• planned, organized, solicited donations, and ran the Halloween party for kids at the Presbyterian Night Shelter;

• published a newsletter containing information from all the shelters and agencies in the community;

• planned, organized, and solicited donations, chaperones, and a disc jockey for a fund-raising dance, with the proceeds going to Bridge Emergency Youth Shelter;

• collected and delivered twenty boxes of canned goods to Loaves and Fishes;

• made a video of visiting speakers, students at work, and fund-raising activities;

• designed and administered surveys of student attitudes toward the homeless;

• interviewed and videotaped homeless children.

Ninety-four percent of the students in the class passed the state writing test that April. Eight of the students were commended for their writing performance. All of the students left for high school with a fat writing portfolio and the understanding that they could make a difference.

3

A BAKER'S DOZEN: EFFECTIVE INSTRUCTIONAL STRATEGIES

LLOYD W. KLINE

Courtesy of Susan Dean, San Francisco, CA

"Children know how to learn in more ways than we know how to teach them."

—Ronald Edmonds (1991)

Author's Note: I thank the following people for their contributions to this chapter: Marie Carbo, Rita Dunn, Helené Hodges, Harriet Doss Willis, Barbara Kapinus, and Floraline Stevens.

The past decade has produced a growing determination among educators, both practitioners and researchers, to crack open some old chestnuts of education reform—the familiar litany of "individual differences," "multiple avenues to learning," and so forth—to see just how meaty some of them might really prove to be. If they do not yield reform, can we at least extract from them some reality-based lessons grounded in the fundamental truths we have known and believed for so many decades?

THE CHAPTER BEFORE YOU

The instructional strategies outlined in this chapter reflect a baker's dozen of the most exciting and determined efforts to change the way America educates its citizens. These "ideas at work" range in complexity and magnitude. They represent concepts that cut across content areas. They overlap so comfortably that they sometimes look like separate facets of a single gem. They are as much about attitude and general approach as about specific pedagogical techniques and classroom application. They have a few characteristics in common:

• They tend to be inclusive, not exclusive.
• They work best in context with other ideas and concepts, not in isolation.

• They often focus on students working within social situations rather than alone.

• The activities, techniques, and goals they suggest or inform are interactive and interdisciplinary, realistic rather than esoteric.

• They empower students to be actively involved in the processes of their own learning, rather than passively receptive.

None of the ideas in this chapter is totally new to education. What *is* new is their rediscovery and renewed emphasis and the effort that has been devoted to exploring and applying them. Although some of these ideas tend to be identified with specific programs, individuals, or locations, they are presented here as generic—that is, as applicable in virtually any classroom in whatever subject area. All are adaptable.

Why ideas *at* work rather than ideas *that* work? Because "ideas *that* work" is part of an older vocabulary in education, a lingo that could be dying out—its connotations of absolute, universal truth increasingly recognized as deceptive and unrealistic. Nothing works every time, everywhere, for everyone. No single strategy, approach, or technique works with all students. The concepts outlined here, however, have been proven to work with many students of diverse backgrounds and widely ranging abilities.

CHALLENGING CONVENTIONAL WISDOM

This chapter encourages newer perspectives on ways of bringing about increased student learning. Knapp and Shields (1990) state that most teachers tend to direct and control the process of instruction and to provide little opportunity for interaction among students, especially between low-achievers and high-achievers. They recommend (p. 756) that teachers provide:

• opportunities for discussion and understanding of meaning;
• project-based or team-learning activities;
• explicit teaching of learning strategies;
• supplemental instruction; and
• reasonable discipline.

THE PURPOSE OF THIS CHAPTER

This chapter draws heavily on the contributions, comments, and advice of the Improving Student Achievement Research Panel, convened by the Association for Supervision and Curriculum Development (ASCD). Given that panel's intent and the fruits of its labor, this chapter seeks to promote:

• instruction that enables students to develop their own ability and disposition to use the fullest dimensions of thinking and learning—that is, not only to solve problems, but also to develop the habits of mind that apply those aspects of thought and development;

• environments that support learning through a wide range of strategies;

• opportunities to deal with topics and texts that are complex and engaging, and tasks that promote the acquisition and application of knowledge that reflects the real world; and

• legitimacy for a wide range of research techniques— experimental, anecdotal, qualitative, and descriptive, as well as empirical—all conducted within coherent theoretical frameworks and involving students of diverse backgrounds.

PRIMARY RESOURCES

Among them, the ASCD panelists reviewed more than 900 research studies. Most of the references cited herein were suggested directly by one or more of those advisors. Pertinent references are cited at the end of each section, then included in the extended bibliography that concludes each chapter.

Because of the corporate genesis of this work, bibliographic citations are neither comprehensive nor within the compass of any single contributor. If pursued, however, both the individual citations and the final bibliography are starting points on a trail of citations that research-oriented professionals can easily use on their own for a more conventional, and complete, review of the literature.

● STRATEGY 3.1: PROVIDE OPPORTUNITIES TO WORK TOGETHER

With the teacher's help, students learn to work in a variety of flexible social configurations and settings—in cooperative learning groups, in pairs, and alone—thus developing proficiencies, skills, and knowledge while at the same time accommodating individual differences in strengths, backgrounds, and interests.

Susie, Ron, Tasha, Jamal, and Juan have a lot in common. They are roughly the same age, sit in the same classroom, have the same teacher, and enjoy many of the same foods, games, and interests. As learners, however, they differ in critical ways. Susie is one of the 13 percent of youngsters in grades K-12 who learn best working alone; Ron, one of the 28 percent strongly oriented to working with a peer; and Tasha and Jamal, two of the 28 percent who learn best with adults (Tasha, by the way, with a collegial adult; Jamal, with an authoritative adult).

Of the five children, only Juan seems to learn reasonably well in any or all of those social configurations. In that respect, he represents fewer than *one-third* of the youngsters in a typical K-12 classroom. Of the five, only Susie and Juan are reasonably well served in the traditional teacher-oriented, teacher-directed classroom. Most of the time, the other three would be much better off in a different kind of learning situation—one far more diverse in its activities, curricular organization, and social configurations.

Few individuals in American business life even think of trying to solve a problem or launch a product or service without massive and persistent teamwork, including open discussion, fact gathering, consideration and argument, trial-and-error experimentation, research, and development. Typically, they not only depend on working with other individuals in their place of business, but also frequently call on outside third-party consultants. Only in U.S. classrooms are individuals expected to find every answer, solve every problem, complete every task, and pass every test by relying solely on their own efforts and abilities.

The concept of cooperative/collaborative learning seeks to tap the potential that group interaction offers for learning and development. In its most formal manifestation, it places students—usually of varying levels of performance—into small groups in which they work together

Courtesy of Sharon Barton, Lee Elementary School, Corsincana, TX

When planning to use cooperative learning approaches or any small-group strategy, remember that some children may need to learn by themselves. Others work well in pairs, some need a small group, and about 28 percent require the direct supervision of a teacher. The use of cross-age tutors, such as secondary students working with elementary school children, has been shown effective for both older and younger students. Some children, however, actually learn better by working alone with material and media than by working often with other people.

toward common goals. At the other end of the continuum, it reinforces the legitimacy of peer tutoring as a learning aid. Those who advocate attending to students' varying learning styles note that some young people work best alone; others work most successfully with authority figures such as parents or teachers. In planning the use of various teaching strategies, teachers must be prepared to make adjustments according to the needs and learning styles of their students (Carbo, Dunn, and Dunn 1986).

"So often teachers tell students to 'get along' or 'cooperate' but spend little time on skill practice and discussion of this basic human need," writes Robert E. Slavin (1986). "Cooperative learning provides the teacher with a model to improve academic performance and socialization skills, and to instill democratic values. A wealth of research supports the idea that the consistent use of this technique improves students' academic performance and helps them become more caring." Slavin cites positive effects in such diverse areas as student achievement at various grade levels and subjects, intergroup relations, relationships between mainstreamed and normal-progress students, and student self-esteem.

David and Roger Johnson (1990), two veteran advocates of cooperation and collaboration in the classroom, note that people in general do not know instinctively how to interact effectively with others. Thus, if cooperative efforts in the classroom are to succeed, students must get to know and trust one another, communicate accurately and unambiguously, accept and support one another, and resolve conflicts constructively.

Cooperative/collaborative learning has been incorporated in a variety of classrooms for a variety of purposes. Those applications have involved student-selected activities, apportioning specific elements of classroom projects or lessons, brainstorming, role playing, problem solving, developing awareness of thinking strategies used by oneself or by one's peers, common interests, group analyses, and team learning.

To implement a technique known as a "circle of knowledge," for instance, a teacher organizes a class into small groups (circles) of four or five students each, appoints a recorder/reporter in each, poses to all a single question to which there are many possible answers, sets a time limit, expects each group member to contribute at least one answer, and then, after facilitating whole-class sharing and challenges, announces a winning group.

Another technique, known as the "Jigsaw," allows a teacher to assign specific components of a major learning project to small task-oriented groups; each group has only a piece of the larger picture under consideration. When all the groups have reported their findings to the entire class, every student has the opportunity to grasp the entire picture.

Some advocates of cooperative/collaborative learning suggest that students be periodically regrouped within heterogeneous classes. They also recognize the value of flexible grouping—that is, regrouping at various times by varying criteria for varying purposes, based on immediate needs. Their reasoning:

• Small-group participation in various contexts for various purposes helps students recognize and learn to function effectively in a variety of social configurations.

• Teaming students who perform at different levels of achievement not only encourages self-esteem and group pride, but also engenders general appreciation and understanding of how individuals differ from each other in attitudes, abilities, points of view, and approaches to problem solving.

"Peer conferencing" and "peer collaboration" offer student writers the critical response of firsthand, face-to-face comments, help them discover what it is to write for an audience, and improve their writing ability as they work on assignments and interact with their peers (Herrmann 1989).

Photo courtesy of Donna L. Clovis, Princeton Junction, NJ

Multicultural students from China, France, Brazil, and Trinidad use computer technology (Internet) to write to their native countries. The students pictured here have lived in the United States for one year. By providing real purposes and real audiences for student communication, their teacher has increased the likelihood that significant student learning will occur (Strategy 3.2).

Tutoring—both cross-age and peer tutoring are other forms of student-to-student interaction—has, like cooperative/collaborative learning, received renewed interest. Several reasons have been cited for its success:

• Many students identify with peers more easily than with adults, especially adult authority figures.

• Many students find it easier to model the behaviors of their peers than of their adult teachers.

• The one-to-one nature of peer tutoring offers immediate response feedback, clarification, extension, and modification—usually in a nonthreatening social relationship (Webb 1987).

REFERENCES

Adams 1990; Carbo, Dunn and Dunn 1986; Dunn and Dunn 1992; Edmonds 1991; Herrman 1989; Johnson and Johnson 1986, 1990; Kilman and Richards 1990; Knapp and Shields 1990a, 1990b; Lehr and Harris 1988; Slavin 1986, 1987, 1989; Stevens et al. 1987; Stover 1993; Webb 1987.

● STRATEGY 3.2: USE REALITY-BASED LEARNING APPROACHES

Teachers provide young people with real purposes and real audiences for reading, writing, speaking, and presenting mathematical and scientific hypotheses or calculations. When students write and speak to intended purposes and audiences, they are more likely to be motivated and to obtain valuable feedback on their efforts.

Jim had trouble writing effectively. To be sure, his sentences were complete and grammatical, the words in them spelled correctly, the syntax straightforward if prosaic. There was one overriding problem with Jim's writing: what he wrote didn't say much of anything. His content and purpose were not specific, precise, or clear. That fact led to a more personal problem for Jim: he had ceased to trust his teacher's judgments of his work. When the teacher observed that his writing wasn't clear, Jim balked. "You're just saying that," he blurted out. "What have you got against me?"

"I'll tell you what, Jim," said the teacher. "Write to me about something you know that I don't know anything about."

After considering two or three possibilities, Jim named a card game his teacher had never heard of.

"Okay," the teacher agreed, "Write step-by-step instructions on how to play the game and bring them to me. I'll follow the instructions, and you can tell me whenever I make a mistake."

"Fair enough!" Jim said.

Jim wrote in his typical style, and his teacher followed the instructions as earnestly as possible. Step by frustrated step, Jim saw the game fall to pieces. He stopped the exercise midway through.

"Give me time for a rewrite," he said, as determined as ever. This time, however, he was convinced that he had a problem with his writing, and he was armed with a clearer perception of it.

Provide students with real purposes and real audiences for their speaking and writing, and you offer them valuable feedback as well as increased motivation. Writing an essay on a topic assigned by the teacher to every member of the entire class lacks the punch and the credibility of writing a personal letter to an editor, a local politician, or a community activist to express a heartfelt compliment, to complain about an injustice, or to inquire about an importance issue. Students derive no satisfaction from succeeding with a mindless, silly activity such as circling the silent *e* in a list of words. Such an activity has no relation to real reading, and no link to real life.

Communicating with real people about real issues, feelings, and beliefs is further enhanced when the content and style of that writing are based in the "outside" reality that the student brings to school. No matter how gilded or gutted its location—in city, suburb, or countryside—the student's community and personal experiences are valuable resources to be explored: they are grounds for inquiry and learning, things that count most in any classroom!

Schema theory firmly undergirds the strategy of reality-based learning. It outlines the belief that individual facts and phenomena are best perceived, learned, and understood within the larger contexts of structure or process. The value of reality-based learning has been firmly documented in the language arts—in reading and writing as well as in the understanding and appreciation of literature. It bridges school and home, classroom and clubhouse, hallway and street.

Extending the recognition and use of authentic purposes, materials, and content into any subject area helps ensure that learning experiences are meaningful and satisfying. Thus, maps, directions, brochures, and directories find a comfortable home in English classes, and community surveys in math classes.

Ideas proliferate in every school—real problems to solve, real issues to resolve: how to manage recycling in the school cafeteria; how to make hallways safer and more hospitable; what to do about truancy or dropouts; whether to lock school doors and when. Problems awaiting study lie just outside the walls of virtually any school in America: traffic patterns; paths for bicyclists, joggers, or rollerbladers; recreational needs and resources for young people; needs of and services for an aging population.

The combined processes of analyzing real problems and then suggesting solutions to them not only motivate learners, but also enable them to range in their thinking processes from recognizing information they need in the resources available to them, to gathering relevant information, to summarizing ideas, to generating potential solutions, and finally to analyzing the consequences and effectiveness of their solutions.

Reality-based learning counters the common notion that many students, particularly those enrolled in Head Start and Chapter 1 programs, suffer from "cultural deprivation" and bring no educationally worthwhile experiences to school. "A more worthwhile approach . . . might be to examine the relationship between what particular groups of children know or how they learn and pedagogical practices," suggests Etta Ruth Hollins (1993, p. 93). "An

improvement in teachers' understanding of how to build on and extend the knowledge and skills these children bring to school, rather than attempting to force the children to fit existing school practices, might get better results."

REFERENCES

Bloom 1976, 1985; Danehower 1993; Hall 1989; Hollins 1993; Knapp and Turnbull 1990; Lozanov and Gateva 1988; Marzano et al. 1992; Marzano, Brandt, Hughes, Jones, Presseisen, Rankin, and Suhor 1988; Palincsar and Klenk 1991; Palincsar et al. 1989; Palincsar and Klenk 1991; Resnick 1987; Richardson 1988; Rowan et al. 1986; U.S. Department of Labor 1992; Walmsley and Walp 1990.

● STRATEGY 3.3: ENCOURAGE INTERDISCIPLINARY TEACHING

Thematic, interdisciplinary teaching helps students connect what they learn from one subject to another, to discover relationships, and, in Thoreau's metaphor of the ideal, to see in every pebble a universe.

Lynn Cherkasky-Davis (1993), lead teacher and project director of the Foundations School (part of the Chicago Public Schools), has described one recent collaborative project at the school: an original version of *Aida*, written, produced, costumed, rehearsed, and staged by students. What did that culminating event represent? It represented what the students had learned about the history, geography, sociology, culture, and drama of ancient Egypt, topics that over preceding weeks both nourished and fed on every subject area in the curriculum.

How useful might it be for a student to know something about the economics and the technology of 19th century New England whaling before reading *Moby-Dick*—and what better opportunity to merge the talents and interests inherent in the respective teachers of social studies, science, and language arts?

How might a thoughtful reading of Aldous Huxley's *Brave New World* illuminate issues, arguments, and ideas as diverse as eugenics, Malthusian economics, and the perceived amorality of certain 20th century mores and technology—again using convergent elements of separate disciplines?

Rarely, if ever, do we live our lives outside of school according to academic pigeonholes. We don't switch to a

When thematic approaches are interesting, students become absorbed and work for long periods of time without stopping. The use of varied methods and materials makes it more possible to respond to students' individual learning preferences.

different frame of reference or way of doing things every twenty or forty or sixty minutes. Even a well-executed shopping trip to the supermarket is an interdisciplinary experience! Scheduling, timing, planning, measuring, counting, reading, identifying, describing, comparing, assessing, affording, budgeting—not to mention spatial orientation, nutrition, and considerations of quality of life— all come into play within a single trip. Consciously or unconsciously, by the time we have negotiated our way from home through traffic to parking lot, then aisle to aisle to the checkout lane and home again, we have routinely called on the skills and content of every basic academic discipline school has to offer.

Most interdisciplinary teaching is not nearly so eclectic nor so involved. Just the same, such teaching does cross traditional subject-area lines and typically involves professional teamwork. It can incorporate into a social studies unit samples of literature and art produced during a given period or by a particular society. Ask students to interpret the samples in light of a specific social context, or to infer specific characteristics of the society from their observations and interpretations. Then let them compare their interpretations with those of their peers, and finally with written records from that period or society.

As another example, how about studying the social impact of a given scientific or technological development at the same time that students are becoming acquainted with the science or technology itself? Mathematics is a natural for interdisciplinary learning. Solving its problems can depend heavily on reading skills. Not only is math an integral component in scientific processes, it plays an appealing role in creating puzzles, music, and architecture.

Interdisciplinary projects promote thinking strategies that cross content areas and transfer solidly into real-life application—analytical observation, for instance, or critical thinking, comparison and contrast, evaluation, perspective, and judgment. The teacher's role includes supporting those processes and helping students, through practice, to become aware of them and comfortable in using them.

Probably no other interdisciplinary approach has won greater acceptance in the past decade, especially in the earlier grades, than that which has integrated five "basic skills"— reading, writing, listening, speaking, and mathematics—into one holistic classroom enterprise. Dorothy Strickland (1985) itemizes how simply and obviously such integration can be attained. *Reading*, for instance, can serve as model and motivation for *writing* that classmates can share by *listening* to such *spoken* activities as story-

---

FIGURE 3.1
Six Options in Curriculum Design

- **Discipline-Based:** The traditional approach, with subjects taught in separate, discrete time blocks.
- **Parallel Disciplines:** Teachers from two or more related subject areas teaching related material simultaneously.
- **Multidisciplinary:** Two or three subject areas are combined in a single course or unit that focuses on a theme, issue, problem, topic, or concept.
- **Interdisciplinary:** Combines all subject areas to focus the full array of disciplines on a theme, issue, problem, topic, or concept.
- **Integrated Day:** Begins with a question, problem, or issue that students want to address, then leads to learning from various disciplines.
- **Field-Based:** Students go outside the school to see how real-world tasks combine skills and knowledge from various subject areas.

Source: These six options are based on the work of Heidi Hayes Jacobs (1991).

---

telling, reporting, oral composition, poetry, and dramatic readings. Reading skills also give a student access to information required in solving *mathematical* problems, and they play a major role in the interpretation of tables, charts, and graphs.

The "whole language" approach to instruction in reading and the language arts is a salutary example of how "disciplines" once viewed and taught as essentially discrete and separate from each other— that is, reading, writing, speaking, and listening—are now recognized and explored as interwoven threads in a single, unified tapestry of individual development.

REFERENCES
Cherkasky-Davis 1993; Jacobs 1991; Marzano, Brandt, Hughes, Jones, Presseisen, Rankin, and Suhor 1988; Paris et al. 1991; U.S. Department of Labor 1992; Strickland 1985.

● STRATEGY 3.4: INVOLVE STUDENTS ACTIVELY

Teachers give every student ample opportunities to experiment actively and directly with oral and printed language, to write, and to apply mathematics to the experiences of daily life.

In collecting lunch money, the 1st grade teacher discovered that eight of her twenty students had apparently brought their lunches to school with them. Rather than simply filing that observation mentally under "classroom administrivia," she posed a question to her class: "Twelve of you brought lunch money today. Knowing that, how many of you apparently brought your own lunches to school with you?"

"Some got out blocks," Mary Lindquist reported, "Some got out toy figures, some used number lines, some used their fingers, and some just thought through it. There were ten or twelve different solutions, and each child wanted to explain his or her own way."

Students passively memorizing a single arithmetic procedure? Not at all. Instead, students actively involved in problem solving, whether or not they agreed on their methods and results.

"Most of us can remember sitting in a math class at one time or another thinking, `When in the world am I ever going to use this?'" Lindquist commented. "Rote memorization is not preparing our children for the future. Kids need to use and understand math."

Mary Lindquist, president of the National Council of Teachers of Mathematics, recounted the anecdote during an interview for an article that appeared in *Better Homes and Gardens* (Atkins 1993). The article notes for its audience of parents that NCTM's current standards for mathematics education "minimize drill-and-practice questions in favor of problems that put kids' thinking skills to the test." The article continues:

> For your child, the goal shifts from getting the right answer to understanding the process behind getting that answer. Math manipulatives—simple, everyday objects that kids can count, combine, subtract, or divide—are being used in many classrooms. Lindquist says anything that turns math into a picture for students helps their understanding.

"By far, the highest percentage of students are tactile/kinesthetic," writes Angela Bruno (1982), "and when these youngsters manipulate hands-on materials they tend to remember more of the required information than through the use of any other sense."

There are several other reasons why students should be allowed to construct their own understandings, generate their own analyses, and create their own solutions to problems:

• It is neither engaging nor authentic to understand a fact or situation exactly as someone else understands it. In real life, we build our own understandings to supplement, change, or confirm for ourselves what we already think we know or what others offer us in knowledge or ideas.

• Teachers promote interest and engagement when they let students address problems for which answers do not exist or are not readily apparent. Students then have real purposes for discovering and applying information and for using all the strategies that might possibly apply and that are available to them.

• Students who are intrinsically motivated and substantially engaged because of interest in meaningful learning activities are more likely to achieve high levels of performance than those for whom the completion of learning activities is simply a means of avoiding punishment.

Integrated throughout the school day and in every area of the curriculum, the range of active learning experiences includes games, simulations, role playing, creative dramatics, pantomime, and contests that demonstrate integration of concepts and allow students to experience the ways in which concepts relate to each other in the world outside school, as well as drawing, storytelling, and other developmentally appropriate activities. Other hands-on, tactile materials and activities include Cuisenaire rods, measuring cups, blocks and cubes, task cards, flip charts, field trips, and laboratory experiences. Many advocates suggest strongly that students be allowed to select for themselves those activities in which they will become involved.

REFERENCES

Atkins 1993; Brown 1990; Bruno 1982; Cohen 1992; Hartshorn and Boren 1990; Hodges 1994; Joyner 1990; NCTM 1989; Roser 1987; Strickland and Morrow 1989.

● STRATEGY 3.5: ANALYZE STUDENTS' LEARNING/READING STYLES

Teachers consider students' individual learning preferences in designing and recommending complementary instructional methods and materials.

Everyone knows that there are all kinds of people: thinkers and doers, audiences and actors, readers and viewers, athletes and couch potatoes. At least one venerated 6th grade music teacher routinely divided her class into "singers" and "listeners."

Probably no other approach attempts to accommodate differences among individual students in greater detail than does that body of thought given the general rubric of "learning styles."

David Kolb (Boyatzis and Kolb 1991) identifies four predominant learning styles. Imaginative learners, he says, excel in watching, sensing, and feeling; analytic learners, in watching and thinking; common-sense learners, in thinking and doing; and dynamic learners, in doing, sensing, and feeling.

Anthony Gregorc (1982, 1985a, 1985b) identifies four basic processes by which individuals differ in their learning patterns: (1) a concrete-sequential process characterized as structured, practical, predictable, and thorough; (2) an abstract-sequential process—logical, analytical, conceptual, and studious; (3) an abstract-random process—sensitive, sociable, imaginative, and expressive; and (4) a concrete-random process—intuitive, original, investigative, and able to solve problems.

Howard Gardner (1983) suggests at least seven different aspects (what he calls "multiple intelligences") by which individuals can come to know the world: linguistic, logical/mathematical, musical, spatial, bodily/kinesthetic, interpersonal, and intrapersonal.

Addressing perennial debates about the "best" approach to teaching reading—e.g., phonics, whole language, sight vocabulary, and so forth—Marie Carbo (1987) writes that "any one of a dozen reading methods is 'best' if it enables a child to learn to read with facility and enjoyment."

No matter how much they echo or differ from each other, all descriptions of "learning styles" are simply attempts to define and accommodate the manner in which a given student learns most readily. The theory holds that learning styles develop through the unique interactions of

biology, experience, personal interests, talents, and energy. A task force commissioned by the National Association of Secondary School Principals considered the many factors that can significantly shape an individual's learning style and selected twenty-four for further study; these range from "perceptual responses," "field dependence/independence," and "successive/simultaneous processing" to "persistence," "environmental elements," and "need for mobility."

Whatever the ultimate taxonomy of learning styles, it seems obvious that while all children can learn, each concentrates, processes, absorbs, and remembers new and difficult information differently. According to Rita and Kenneth Dunn (1988), the factors involved include:

• immediate environment—for example, noise level, temperature, amount of light, furniture type, and room design;

• emotional profile—for example, degree of motivation, persistence, responsibility, and need for structure and feedback;

• sociological needs—for example, learning alone or with peers, learning with adults present, learning in groups;

• physical characteristics—for example, perceptual strengths (auditory, visual, tactile, kinesthetic), best time of day for learning, potential need for periodic nourishment and mobility; and

• psychological inclination—for example, global and analytic strengths.

In the most formal model of matching instruction to learning style, teachers first identify each individual student's style through observation, interview, or questionnaire. They share their observations individually with students and parents, then plan and carry out an appropriate learning program for that child. The program includes compatible instructional practices and management strategies appropriate to what has been observed about the child's learning style. A less formal approach is to emphasize strategies that capitalize on the styles of most students, while accommodating those whose style differs markedly from the group.

Thus, instruction that attends to learning or reading styles capitalizes on an individual student's strengths and preferences while simultaneously removing barriers to learning. Instructional planning extends to such complementary methods, materials, and techniques as floor games, choices among reading materials and ways of receiving or presenting information, and participation in given activities (that is, with the entire class, in a small group, or alone). No one learning style is considered better or worse than any other (Carbo and Hodges 1988; Hodges 1994).

Research in learning styles and reading styles indicates that teaching academic underachievers in ways that complement their style strengths has significantly increased their standardized test scores in reading and across subject areas.

REFERENCES
Andrews 1990, 1991; Bauer 1991; Boyatzis and Kolb 1991; Brunner and Majewski 1990; Butler 1984; Carbo 1987, 1990; Carbo and Hodges 1988; Dunn and Dunn 1988, 1992; Gardner 1983; Gardner and Hatch 1989; Garrett 1991; Gregorc 1982, 1985a, 1985b; Hodges 1994; Lewis and Steinberger 1991; Orsak 1990; Perrin 1990.

● STRATEGY 3.6: ACTIVELY MODEL BEHAVIORS

Teachers model behaviors they would have their students assimilate and practice.

Dorothy had tried for weeks to get her 6th graders to open up in class discussions. After years of traditional teaching, however (that is, the teacher asking the questions and one or two students offering "right" or "wrong" answers), her students were predictably passive. They consistently resisted all her attempts to open up her classroom.

On the rare occasions when an intrepid student asked a question in return or dared to offer a comment, the eyes of every student in the room swung immediately and automatically to Dorothy for her verdict: *right* or *wrong*?

Then, quite by chance, Dorothy happened on a life-sized human figure made of cardboard. She realized at once that it was the very thing she needed to make her point. The following day, she launched a classroom discussion and popped a direct question to see if any of her students would volunteer a response.

Kathy did volunteer, tentatively, of course, and in just a word or two, but her response seemed to the class to merit a judgment from the teacher. All eyes fell in silence on Dorothy.

Without uttering a word, Dorothy walked to her closet, pulled out the cardboard figure, and set it in the chair behind her desk. Then, with every eye following her in

amazement, she sat down beside Kathy and stared silently at the cardboard figure, waiting like her students for its response.

Dorothy was modeling the behavior she saw in her students—behavior she was hoping they would overcome. And they got the point. The humor in the situation engaged their trust, demonstrated Dorothy's sincerity as a teacher, and dramatized their own responsibility as participants in their own learning. Real class discussions began to pick up, and Dorothy found fewer and fewer occasions to pull her cardboard counterpart out of the closet.

Most modeling, of course, is intended to work the other way around—that is, teachers usually behave as they would have their students behave. Learners gain when teachers practice what they preach, try out ideas in front of the class, even participate actively in projects or tasks *with* the class.

For years, sustained silent reading (SSR) periods have been standard procedure in many schools. The basic technique is simple: At a given time—say, for thirty minutes just before lunch every Monday, Wednesday, and Friday—*everyone* in the school chooses something to read and does just that for the entire thirty minutes: students, teachers, principals, secretaries, custodians—everyone! Proponents ascribe grand accomplishments to the practice, including motivation, reinforcement, shared learning, increased

Photo courtesy of Sherry Willerton, Washington Education Center, Joplin, MO

As Brian, a high school student, reads to the preschoolers and observes their enthusiasm, he comes to realize the importance of reading aloud to young children. This teenager provides a positive role model for his young charges.

library use, even improved scores in reading achievement. SSR is modeling at its purest and simplest. Do as I'm doing, not just what I tell you to do.

When modeling, teachers in whatever subject area follow the same assignments or suggestions that they give their students: write on the same topics, figure out the same problems, play the same games, and ask themselves the same questions. And they do so in full view and hearing of their students, often as co-participants in small-group activities, or one-to-one with a student.

The practice is neither demeaning nor condescending. Instead, it dramatizes desired behavior, one of the surest means available to demonstrate process, motivate and guide students, and help develop perspective on a given task or concept. As a teacher, let your students hear you think aloud. Teachers who share thoughts on how they have completed a certain task or arrived at a particular conclusion help students become aware of their own thinking strategies.

Modeling enables teachers to furnish appropriate cues and reminders that help students apply particular problem-solving processes or complete specific tasks—in storytelling, for instance, or inquiry, or evaluation. Among such techniques, *scaffolding* is one of the most generic and useful approaches. Scaffolding is a device by which the teacher builds on the point of reference at which a student hesitates or leaves off—in telling a story, in explaining a process, in seeking an answer, in any moment of discourse, analysis, or explanation. In scaffolding, the teacher simply suggests the next step, both reinforcing what the student has already achieved and guiding the student to greater understanding or accomplishment.

More generally, Costa and Marzano (1987) identify seven starting points by which teachers can create a classroom "language of cognition":

- using precise vocabulary;
- posing critical and interpretive questions, rather than simple recall;
- providing data, not solutions;
- giving directions;
- probing for specificity;
- modeling metacognitive processes; and
- analyzing the logic of language.

"Most teachers put too much emphasis on facts and right answers and too little attention on how to interpret those facts," writes school administrator Robert Burroughs

(1993), commenting specifically on the teaching of literature. "The result has been growth in basic literacy at the expense of thoughtfulness—the kind of critical thinking the nation's governors and President Clinton are emphasizing."

Burroughs outlines specific preferred techniques among those he has seen teachers use to guide learning processes and thus structure growth in understanding and appreciation. The techniques are adaptable to discourse, inquiry, or discussion in any subject area:

- Focusing—refocusing students' efforts at refining their own responses if, for instance, they begin wandering from the specific content at hand.
- Modifying or shaping—rephrasing a student's idea in slightly different language; for instance, if a student suggests that a character in a novel is resisting change, the teacher might add a word or two to encourage consideration of other explanations for the character's behavior.
- Hinting—calling attention to a passage in the text that challenges a student's view.
- Summarizing—restating ideas to bring them to everyone's attention and to spur discussion, or summarizing various positions students have taken along the way (Burroughs 1993, pp. 27-29).

REFERENCES
Burroughs 1993; Costa and Marzano 1987; Langer 1991; Marzano, Brandt, Hughes, Jones, Presseisen, Rankin, and Suhor 1988; Paris et al. 1991; Rosenshine and Meister 1992; Vygotsky 1962, 1978.

● STRATEGY 3.7: EXPLORE THE FULLEST DIMENSIONS OF THOUGHT

Teachers provide *all* students with meaningful opportunities to develop and apply the fullest dimensions of thinking, helping them become critical thinkers and creative problem solvers while engaging them in their own learning.

"What a beautiful horse," said the city-bred dude. "How much is it worth?"

"Depends if you're buyin' or sellin'," answered the well-practiced cowhand.

"Thinking cannot be divorced from content," writes Carr (1988) "In fact, thinking is a way of learning content. In every course, and especially in content subjects, students should be taught to think logically, analyze and compare, question and evaluate. Skills taught in isolation do

Working in small groups, students are given an opportunity to process information, interact with peers, and offer solutions to a variety of problems. The teacher pictured here incorporates strategies that help students become critical thinkers and creative problem solvers.

little more than prepare students for tests of isolated skills."

If any of the "ideas at work" described in this chapter challenges the conventional wisdom of classroom practice, it is the notion that students, regardless of their performance level, are capable of using higher order thinking skills. This concept contrasts sharply with the attitude and practice of the high school English teacher who on the first day of school gave all 125 of her seniors a writing assignment. She collected and corrected their papers, pointed out the various lapses in spelling, grammar, and punctuation (lapses, by the way, both predictable and inevitable in a student sample of that size), and then used those errors to justify an unproductive, unchallenging year spent reviewing the same sterile exercises in spelling, grammar, and punctuation that her students had seen countless times before.

No one condones faulty grammar and inaccurate spelling, of course. At the same time, however (and far more important), teachers need not wait until students have mastered "basic skills" before they introduce the more complex skills of analysis, synthesis, criticism, and

metacognition into their classroom routines. The process of gathering information, evaluating it critically, drawing inferences, and arriving at logical conclusions is based on evidence, and evidence can be expressed and recognized by many different means and in many different formats. While we believe that every student should learn to spell accurately, the fact remains that one typically need not know that *i* comes before *e* except after *c* in order to test the fairness or bias in an editorial statement or to detect straightforwardness or ambiguity in a politician's promise.

Wiggins (1992) notes that tests typically overassess students' knowledge and underassess their know-how. Onosko (1992) reports measurable "climates of thoughtfulness" in the classrooms of social studies teachers who reflect on their own practices, who value thinking, and who emphasize depth over breadth in content coverage.

Carr (1988) and others suggest various ways by which to introduce and pursue higher order thinking skills in the classroom. Here are four examples:

Use of all major news media—newspapers, magazines, television, and radio—motivates students, and comparing different accounts of the same story helps them develop questioning attitudes. "In the process," writes Carr (1988), "they become more discriminating consumers of news media, advertising, and entertainment."

"All classification tasks," she notes, "require identification of attributes and sorting into categories according to some rule. While sorting concrete objects is an appropriate activity for the young child, verbal analogies (for example, `How are a diamond and an egg alike?') are appropriate for learners of any age. . . . Applications to mathematics and science, especially the inquiry approach to science, are readily apparent."

"Schema theory," she continues, "holds that information, if it is to be retained, must be categorized with something already stored in memory. Brainstorming techniques that aid comprehension . . . help students to access their prior knowledge about a topic to be introduced, and thus to classify and retain the new information."

Children's literature becomes its own "powerful tool," Carr concludes, citing Somers and Worthington (1979): "Literature offers children more opportunities than any other area of the curriculum to consider ideas, values, and ethical questions."

Just how seriously should Chicken Little's neighbors have taken her complaint that the sky was falling? Why?

Why not? Was it fair for the Little Red Hen to keep all the bread she had baked for herself?

How true is it that sticks and stones can break your bones, but names will never hurt you? Why does a rolling stone gather no moss? If water is heavier than air, how do raindrops get up in the sky? How does science differ from art, music from noise, wisdom from fact?

What is truth?

REFERENCES

Adams 1986; Bransford et al. 1986; Carr 1988; Chi et al. 1989; Lambert 1990; Onosko 1992; Paul 1984; Rosenshine and Meister 1992; Somers and Worthington 1979; Wiggins 1992.

● STRATEGY 3.8: USE A MULTICULTURAL TEACHING APPROACH

Teachers recognize and explore multicultural perspectives in all areas of the curriculum, emphasizing through example and instruction the strength and value of a unified society forged from cultural diversity.

Multiculturalism doesn't mean what it used to mean in American education—and not even what it meant less than a decade ago. Adding a speech by Martin Luther King, Jr., to the literature anthology and offering parental instructions in Spanish—both good ideas in their own right—simply doesn't go far enough toward filling the bill anymore. Teaching multiculturally throughout the curriculum is more than simply an attempt to combat racism. The more important aim of studying human cultures in all their diversity is to understand what it is to be human.

Unfortunately, such study has too often been skewed to a single perspective while more inclusive perspectives have been labelled as somehow disloyal to the American tradition. The fact that racism is so prevalent in American society has until recently led many theorists to concentrate primarily on the study of specific ethnic groups, on their characteristics and unique contributions to the more "general culture"—usually that described from a Euro-American or Anglo-American point of view.

By contrast, the history of the United States is actually the history of all the cultures that comprise it. Until recently, multicultural education has focused mostly on minority groups, even though Euro-Americans and Anglo-Americans also spring from a culture that was not originally and purely "American." Such skewing sets up the fallacy that Euro- and Anglo-American descendants are the 'real' Americans, while all others, particularly people of color, are culturally different.

The controversy and sensitivities that surrounded the question of how most appropriately to mark the Columbus Quincentenary in 1992—if indeed to celebrate it at all—were perhaps evidence of a New World in education, or at least of newer awarenesses blowing in the wind.

Classroom instruction in a multicultural context is enhanced when it involves students in learning about themselves first—through oral history projects, for example, in which children involve their parents, grandparents, and other older, living adults who can relate information about family backgrounds and histories. Shared in the classroom, such information becomes a powerful tool both for identifying similarities among students and for highlighting how they differ from one another in positive rather than negative ways.

The Association for Supervision and Curriculum Development supports a mosaic approach to multiculturalism in the classroom, focusing on the whole of society, but recognizing society's various components as important to the whole. Among its goals (see Howard, Berreth, and Seltz 1993, as well as the individual lists of "ASCD Resolutions" passed for any given year):

• Developing comprehensive policies on multiculturalism that guide and inform curriculum, instructional methods, teacher preparation and inservice training, staffing, instructional materials, and school and classroom climate.

• Identifying unifying concepts such as "education for a democracy" that will accommodate the recognition, valuing, exploration, and use of cultural differences in the classroom.

• Emphasizing multicultural perspectives in all schools, regardless of their community demographics.

• Assuring the accuracy of scholarship that underlies new curriculum materials and perspectives.

• Guaranteeing curricular and program review processes that include representatives whose backgrounds reflect cultural diversity.

In short, teaching multiculturally cultivates a school culture that celebrates diversity; supports mutual acceptance of, respect for, and understanding of all human differences; and provides a balanced viewpoint on key issues involved in such teaching. It provides students with a

FIGURE 3.2
Eight Characteristics of the Multicultural School

1. The teacher and school administrators have high expectation for all students and positive attitudes toward them. They respond to them in positive and caring ways.

2. The formalized curriculum reflects the experiences, cultures, and perspectives of a range of cultural and ethnic groups as well as both genders.

3. The teaching styles used by the teachers match the learning and motivational styles of the students.

4. The teachers and administrators show respect for the students' first languages and dialects.

5. The instructional materials used in the school show events, situations, and concepts from the perspectives of a range of cultural, ethnic, and racial groups.

6. The assessment and testing procedures used in the school are culturally sensitive and result in students of color being represented proportionately in classes for the gifted and talented.

7. The school culture and the hidden curriculum reflect cultural and ethnic diversity.

8. The school counselors have high expectations for students of color and help these students to set and realize positive career goals.

Source: Banks 1990.

global, international perspective on the world in which they live. It seeks to eliminate racial, ethnic, cultural, and gender stereotypes and to resolve or ameliorate problems associated with racism and prejudice. And it underscores the importance of teaching ethics, values, and citizenship in promoting our nation's democratic heritage.

REFERENCES

Au and Kawakami 1985; Banks 1990; Bennett 1986; Bloom 1985; Collins 1988; Dillon 1989; Fullinwider 1993; Hall 1989; Hollins 1993; Kendall 1983; Quellmalz and Hoskyn 1988; Taylor and Dorsey-Gaines 1988; Tiedt and Tiedt 1986.

● STRATEGY 3.9: USE ALTERNATIVE ASSESSMENTS

Because they recognize and understand its multiple roles, teachers demonstrate positive attitudes toward assessment and use various modes to evaluate student achievement and behavior, as well as all other aspects of learning and teaching.

The student report card is no longer the primary measure of success in schooling. The general American vocabulary now includes a whole range of assessment terms: SATs, standardized tests, norms, criterion references, outcomes, portfolios, and on and on. Little wonder that teachers and administrators feel pressured by "assessment" and more than a little harried by the public clamor and misunderstanding that often surround the term.

Various modes of assessment yield critical and useful information to inform and shape tools and methods that promise to improve academic achievement. "Why do we evaluate students?" ask Rasbow and Hernandez (1988). Among the answers are to determine:

- if objectives have been achieved;
- the knowledge and skills that students have acquired;
- areas in which the curriculum needs improvement;
- the effectiveness of a teaching process or methodology;
- student responses to specific aspects of the curriculum; and
- students' ability to use knowledge and skills.

Evaluations are also used to:

- design instruction for individuals, groups, or entire classes;
- diagnose a student's level of understanding before recommending further instruction on a given topic;
- gather information on the quality of the learning environment;
- guide the direction of future study;
- summarize an activity, topic, or unit of work;
- provide a basis for extra help where needed; and
- identify the most useful information to communicate to students and parents.

Traditional assessment techniques and instruments for filling one or another of those roles are as familiar to most teachers as they are widespread in use: the National Assessment of Educational Progress, the Scholastic Aptitude Test, norm- and criterion-referenced tests (many of them mandated by state legislatures), standardized tests in specific subject areas (the Stanford, the California, and the Metropolitan, among others), performance scales, and checklists. And, of course, among teacher-made instruments, the essay exam and the ubiquitous multiple-choice test.

In recent years, however, researchers and curriculum specialists have given increased attention to alternatives in assessment: to exhibitions or demonstrations, for instance, that serve as culminating activities in a student's learning experience; to observation and analysis of hands-on or open-ended experiences; to portfolios (collections of records, letters of reference, samples of work, sometimes even including videotapes of student performance or task accomplishment—in fact, any evidence that appropriately documents a student's skills, capabilities, and past experiences).

If two of the primary purposes of assessment are to determine whether the goals of education are being met and to inform various stakeholders of the progress of education, assessment techniques must be sufficiently varied to perform these functions as appropriately and accurately as possible. Those goals vary, after all, from very broad national goals (for example, those embraced by the National Governors' Association) to the individual teacher's lesson plan. They encompass diagnoses of ability or style in teaching and learning, measurements of proficiency and achievement of individual students or entire classes, and the effectiveness of entire schools, districts, state systems, or national programs. The audiences for assessments may include students, teachers, parents, policy makers, colleges, and businesses, among other interests. Some assessments serve gatekeeping roles—college admission tests, for instance.

Increasingly, large-scale assessments are tied more closely to tasks that reflect activities in the world beyond the classroom. These assessments are characterized as being "authentic" or "performance" assessments. They encourage us to consider educational success in terms of the skills and knowledge that young people will need as adults.

Some of the newer assessments reflect some of what we have come to realize are preferred teaching practices; consequently, they contain activities that are congruent with and that support good instruction. They tend to invite diverse responses and promote a range of thinking—hands-on science and mathematics problem-solving activities, for example. In some cases, assessment tasks may extend over several days, allowing students to reflect on their work, to polish and revise it. Some assessments give students the opportunity to respond in any of several ways, including writing, drawing, and making charts or graphic organizers.

In general, trends in alternative assessment tend to:

• use a variety of progress indicators, such as projects, writing samples, interviews, and observations;
• focus on an individual's progress over time rather than on one-time performance within a group; and
• bring teachers into conference with students about their work and progress, helping students to evaluate themselves by perceiving the results of their own work.

Finally, more and more teachers are recognizing the value of multiple assessments in analyzing and reshaping their own instructional delivery skills, and in serving as a catalyst for change.

REFERENCES
Buechler 1992; Grace 1992; Hewitt 1993; Johnson 1993; Lockwood 1991; Rasbow and Hernandez 1988; Marzano et al. 1992; Marzano, Pickering, and McTighe 1993; Perrone 1991; *Redesigning Assessment 1992*; Schnitzer 1993; Sweet and Zimmerman 1992; Worthen 1993..

● STRATEGY 3.10: PROMOTE HOME/SCHOOL PARTNERSHIPS

Through well planned, comprehensive, long-lasting programs, parents are involved in a variety of meaningful school roles, including decision making and participation in activities as well as in the educational development of their children.

The professionals at Harlem Park Middle School in Baltimore, Maryland, take parental involvement seriously. They have added three parent coordinators to their staff and located them full-time in the neighborhoods the school serves rather than in the school building itself. Living and working in those neighborhoods, the coordinators help fight a steady rise in the school's dropout rate by teaching parents how to keep their children in school, help with homework, keep track of progress, and work with school representatives before a crisis develops.

Photo courtesy of Ann E. Snyder, Bledsoe County Schools, Pikeville, TN

Successful programs usually have home/school or parent education components. Here, parents participate in learning how to make classroom manipulatives for tactile, hands-on learners at a workshop conducted at the teachers' center. Considerable research supports that each of us learns and remembers information differently. Parents who are aware of their own child's learning preferences are better able to support their child's learning.

School officials in Mesa, Arizona, have recognized that parenthood is "eighteen years of on-the-job training." So they organized a "Parent University," filled a Saturday with forty workshops ranging from creative art activities for preschoolers, to helping young people survive junior high, to financing a college education. More than 800 people attended (Education Leaders Consortium 1989).

In South Carolina, parents participate in making important decisions about schools as members of local School Improvement Councils.

Since the state legislature in Illinois passed a School Reform Act in the late 1980s, each of Chicago's more than 500 schools has been governed by a local school council consisting of two teachers, two community representatives, one school principal, and six parents elected by and from the community.

Epstein (1989) outlines five broad avenues by which parents and schools can share in a child's development:

Parents have the basic obligation to provide food, clothing, and shelter; to assure a child's general health and safety; and to provide child rearing and home training. But parents can also provide school supplies, a place for schoolwork at home, and positive home conditions for learning.

The school, in turn, is obliged to communicate to the home such important information as school calendars; schedules; notices of special events, school goals, programs, and services; school rules, codes, and policies; report cards, grades, test scores, and informal evaluations; and the availability of parent/teacher conferences.

Parents can be directly involved in the work of the school: assisting teachers and students with lessons; chaperoning class trips; participating in classroom activities; aiding administrators, teachers, and school staff in the school cafeteria, library, laboratories, and workshops; organizing parent groups in fund raising, community relations, political awareness, and program development; attending student assemblies, sports events, and special presentations; and participating in workshops, discussion groups, and training sessions.

Parents can involve themselves in learning activities at home by developing a child's social and personal skills and by contributing to basic skills education, development of advanced skills, and enrichment.

In governance and advocacy, parents can assume decision-making roles in the PTA/PTO, on advisory councils, or through other committees and groups at the school, district, or state levels. They can become activists in monitoring schools and by working for school improvement.

Among private philanthropic organizations, the Rockefeller Foundation has funded a $3 million effort to launch a five-year project incorporating the pioneering practices of James Comer, a child psychiatrist at Yale University. The Comer Model is based on the belief that parental involvement is the cornerstone of effective and responsible school change. Comer maintains that one cannot separate academic development from the child's social and cultural background. Thus, one of several programs within the project emphasizes a school's obligation to work cooperatively with parents and mental health professionals in meeting the needs of children.

In another initiative for developing home/school relationships, the National Urban League offers its affiliates competitive grants to help them mobilize local communities in school reform efforts.

Williams and Chavkin (1989) report that successful home/school programs tend to share seven characteristics: (1) they are guided by written policies; (2) they enjoy administrative support; (3) they include training of staff, parents, or both; (4) they take a partnership approach; (5) they maintain two-way communications; (6) they encourage networking; and (7) they are constantly informed and reshaped by project evaluation.

Having abstracted and reviewed almost fifty studies of home/school cooperation, Henderson (1987) concludes:

The family provides the primary educational environment.

Involving parents in their children's formal education improves student achievement.

Parent involvement is most effective when it is comprehensive, long-lasting, and well-planned.

The benefits of family involvement are not confined to early childhood or the elementary levels of schooling; there are strong effects from involving parents continuously throughout high school.

Involving parents in their own children's education at home is not enough. To ensure the quality of schools as institutions serving the community, parents must be involved at all levels of schooling.

Children from low-income and minority families have the most to gain when schools involve parents. Parents can help, regardless of their level of formal education.

We cannot look at the school and the home in isolation from one another; we must see how they interconnect with each other and with the world at large.

REFERENCES

Becher 1984; Comer 1980; Education Leaders Consortium 1989; Epstein 1987, 1989; Epstein and Dauber 1991; Goodson and Hess 1975; *The Harvard Education Letter* 1988; Henderson 1987; Leler 1983; U.S. Department of Education 1990; Williams and Chavkin 1989.

● STRATEGY 3.11: USE ACCELERATED LEARNING TECHNIQUES

Teachers recognize and base instruction on the fact that accelerated learning techniques can be effective with students at every level of ability and performance.

Colin Rose (1985) declares in *Empowering the Spectrum of Your Mind* that most of us are probably using only four percent of the enormous potential of our brains. "The more you use your brain," he maintains, "and the more facts and experience you store, the more associations and connections you make. Therefore, the easier it is to remember and learn yet more new material."

Once considered appropriate for use almost exclusively with students identified as gifted and talented, accelerated learning is now believed to be effective with students of any level of performance or ability. In 1991, with support from the Rockefeller Institute of Government, fifty schools nationwide embarked on a six-year Accelerated School Program designed to serve students who had been identified as "disadvantaged."

How does one "accelerate learning"? What is the theory behind the phrase? Rose (1985) begins with a seemingly obvious fact: no learning can take place without memory. How does one best encode things into memory? By creating concrete images of sights, sounds, and feelings, and by strong association of one image with another. The stronger the original encoding, the better the ultimate recall. "To achieve good memory," Rose (1985) writes, "you need to link a series of facts or ideas together, so that when one is remembered, it triggers recall for a whole series of others."

Thus, an ideal learning pattern becomes:

• Immediate rehearsal of new facts in the short term.
• Repetition or testing of the facts a few minutes later.
• Review of the facts an hour later.
• A short recap of them after a night's rest. (Sleep appears to help memorization; new information is reviewed during REM—Rapid Eye Movement—sleep.)
• Short review a week later.
• Short review a month later.

Rose claims that such a schedule of learning can enable the recall of up to 88 percent of the new information an individual receives—four times better than the usual rate of recall.

Among other techniques recommended by advocates of accelerated learning:

• Chunking, that is, reducing new information to manageable bits—a "chunk" no longer than seven words or seven digits, for instance.
• Use of music and rhyme as aids to memory.
• Peripheral learning and the use of memory "maps" to encourage association and thus recall.
• Encoding as specifically as possible by principles rather than through isolated examples by rote.

Psychiatrist Georgi Lozanov (Lozanov and Gateva 1988) urges maintaining an upbeat classroom presentation at all times, with constant attention to physical surroundings, self-esteem, goals and outcomes, competition, right and wrong answers, and individual learning styles, expectations, and outcomes.

REFERENCES
Galyean 1983; Levin 1988a, 1988b, 1991a, 1991b; Lozanov and Gateva 1988; Means and Knapp 1991; Pritchard and Taylor 1980; Richardson 1988; Rose 1985; Russell 1975; Suggestive Accelerated Learning and Teaching 1985.

● STRATEGY 3.12: FOSTER STRATEGIES IN QUESTIONING

To engage students in more active learning and response, teachers encourage them to generate their own questions and lead their own discussions.

The "discussion" dragged on. Invariably, the teacher asked one factual-recall question at a time about the short story at hand. Each question invariably elicited a right-or-wrong answer from one, sometimes two, student volunteers. Then the teacher reached that point in the story where the main character faced what seemed like a life-or-death, personal dilemma. "I wonder how many of you have ever faced such a situation," the teacher remarked offhandedly. Every hand in the room shot up, some flapping in anticipation. "Oh, my! I'm afraid I've touched some raw nerves," the teacher exclaimed. "Let me withdraw the question." All the raised hands dropped. So did students' attention to the topic.

Our teacher couldn't have read Lehr and Harris (1988). They suggest (and their suggestions are well supported by research) how even that age-old classroom practice of questions from the teacher can be adapted to elicit individual involvement rather than passive response. They also show how to follow through for even greater student participation and response. Their advice, in part (Lehr and Harris 1988, pp. 43-44):

• Structure questions so that students can succeed.
• Encourage students to respond. (Most teachers answer two-thirds of their own questions.)
• Ask questions in all modes. (Most questions are asked at the level of basic recall or recognition. More complex questioning increases student achievement.)
• Pause. The number and quality of student answers increase when teachers provide "wait time" of three to five seconds after asking a question. Appropriate wait time is particularly important in teaching low achievers. Some higher-level questions might require as much as 15 to 20 seconds of wait time.
• Call on students randomly, but be sure not to forget the low achiever.
• If a student's response is vague, call for clarification or elaboration—for example, "Tell me more." Probe students to higher levels of thinking.
• Encourage students to develop and ask their own questions, thus increasing their opportunities for thinking.
• Use techniques that require students to pose their own questions and to make discoveries on their own. For example, ask students in a science class to make predictions, based on their own experiences, before a demonstration or experiment. The processes of observing, comparing, and describing are as important as the product.

Other students of questioning technique suggest that teachers break the total content of their questioning into bits small enough so that students are assured of being able to answer at least three-quarters of the questions correctly. They urge a high proportion of questions that are well beyond mere factual recall—questions that encourage interpretation or that challenge critical thinking.

Questioning need not simply follow a lesson or assignment as a means of checking to see if students have completed or understood it. Reading specialists, for instance, have long advocated the use of prereading questioning techniques, using teacher- or student-generated questions to develop background knowledge, preview key concepts, and set purposes for the reading. Questioning after reading should provide students with opportunities to practice or rehearse what they have learned from the text, as well as increase associations between textual information and their own background knowledge ("Questioning Promotes" 1987).

To stimulate student discussions, Dillon (1984) suggests a three-step process:

• Carefully formulate one or two questions to get the discussion going.
• From then on, ask questions only when perplexed and genuinely in need of more information.
• Then make more statements that present facts or opinions, that reflect students' opinions to them, that register confusion, or that invite elaboration and student-to-student exchanges.

Student-generated questions and student-led discussions give students a higher stake and interest in their classroom activities and learning. Framing their own questions requires young people to interact with the meaning of content or text from a variety of perspectives. Generating their own questions, they support and challenge each other and recognize the social aspects of exploring the meaning of what they encounter in reading or in other learning activities.

Teachers need to model effective questioning and discussion strategies, including how to interact with others as well as how to think about and discuss text or content.

Touch a raw nerve now and then—not to aggravate, but to stimulate!

References
Adams 1986; Carlsen 1991; Dillon 1984; Goatley and Raphael 1992; Lehr and Harris 1988; "Questioning Promotes" 1987; Roberts and Zody 1989; "Teachers' Questions" 1987.

● Strategy 3.13: Emphasize Brain-Compatible Instruction

Teachers develop programs and techniques that build on the full and complex functional capabilities of the human brain.

Think of your most recent drink of water. Exactly what did you do in taking it? What facts, what prior experiences, what understandings did you call on? What steps did you take? It's been estimated that you performed fifty or so actions while taking that drink of water. Did you think of all fifty—that is, did you bring any of them, in isolation, to the forefront of your consciousness while drinking?

Probably not. Your brain handled all the necessary steps for you. At the same time, your brain was probably helping you consider your plans for the weekend, reminding you of the slight soreness in your left thumb, telling you it was a warm afternoon, and juggling countless other "programs"—chains of thought needed to accomplish some foreseen goal, whether soaking your thumb or quenching your thirst (Neve et al. 1986).

Brain-compatible instruction builds on the notion that the human brain operates as an incredibly powerful parallel processor, always doing many different things simultaneously (Caine and Caine 1991). The brain is capa-

ble of such a vast number and array of functions that its functioning can be visualized most easily only in terms of programs and patterns— one program, perhaps, for getting a glass of water at the kitchen sink, a different program for sipping from the water fountain outside your classroom door.

How does the brain differentiate among the vast array of programs it stores? By recognizing an apparently endless number and variety of patterns among them. Thus "brain-compatible instruction defines learning as *the acquisition of useful programs*," write Neve and her colleagues (1986). "The human brain is exceedingly intricate. For educational purposes, however, what counts is a broad, holistic understanding of what the brain is *for* (it did not evolve to pass tests or fill in worksheets), its principal architecture, its main drives, and its way of *relating to the real world*."

The program in which Neve works (at Drew Elementary School in East Windsor, New Jersey) "stands in marked contrast to the conventional 'brain-antagonistic' approaches that reflect tradition rather than new knowledge available from the neurosciences and other disciplines."

Carnine (1990) describes some of the misunderstandings that can result in teachers, students, or both after "brain-antagonistic" instruction:

> Very young children know that the name of an object stays the same even after the orientation of the object has changed. For example, when a chair is turned to face the opposite direction, it remains a chair.
>
> Consequently, in preschool, when a *b* is flipped to face the opposite direction, children often assume that it still goes by the name of *b*. Making this error doesn't necessarily imply that a student's visual brain function is weak or that the student would benefit from a kinesthetic approach to learning lower-case letters. Extensive research has shown that students are more likely to confuse objects and symbols that share visual and/or auditory samenesses, such a *b* and . . .
>
> In solving simple computation problems, such as 24 + 13, first-graders learn that they can start with the bottom number in the units column or with the top number: 4 + 3 equals 7, and so does 3 + 4. The sameness they note is that these problems can be worked in either direction, from top to bottom or the reverse.
>
> Soon thereafter come subtraction problems, such as 24 − 13. Students can still apply the sameness learned in addition, thinking of the difference between 4 and 3 or between 3 and 4 and always sub-

tracting the smaller number from the larger. However, when students encounter a problem such as 74 – 15, applying the sameness noted earlier leads them to subtract the smaller from the larger number and come up with the answer 61. Such a mistake is a sensible application of a mislearned sameness. . . .

"The brain's search for samenesses," Carnine concludes, "has little regard for the intentions of educators." At the same time, he notes that while the brain's relentless search for patterns helps explain certain common student misconceptions, it can also help educators develop more effective classroom activities.

The team at Drew Elementary developed their own "seven principles"; the principles serve as focal points to guide teachers in designing and implementing brain-compatible instruction:

1. Create a nonthreatening climate.

2. Input lots of raw material from which students can extract patterns—a vast array of activities, aided by an ample supply of materials, equipment, and print and audiovisual resources.

3. Emphasize genuine communication in talking, listening, writing, and reading as ways to interact with other people.

4. Encourage lots of manipulation of materials. Students need to be in command and able to push things around, encouraging them to work toward goals and explore a range of means.

5. Emphasize reality. By using problems, examples, and contacts drawn from the "real world" rather than contrived exercises, texts, worksheets, and basal readers, students can see the real value of their own learning.

6. Address learning activities to actual, productive uses.

7. Respect natural thinking, including intuitive leaps, a grasp of patterns (as in number tables or good writing), and aesthetic and nonverbal interests and activities.

"Brain-based instruction," Caine and Caine (1991) warn, "stems from recognizing that the brain does not take logical steps down one path like a digital computer, but can go down a hundred different paths simultaneously like an enormously powerful analog computer."

Finally, Caine and Caine (1991) add, "Each brain is unique. Teaching should be multifaceted to allow all students to express visual, tactile, emotional, and auditory preferences. Providing choices that are variable enough to attract individual interests may require the reshaping of schools so that they exhibit the complexity found in life."

REFERENCES
Bateson 1980; Caine and Caine 1991; Campbell 1989; Carnine 1990; Cousins 1989; Della Neve et al. 1986; Hart 1983, 1986; Vygotsky 1962, 1978.

BIBLIOGRAPHY

Adams, M.J. (1986). "Teaching Thinking to Chapter 1 Students." In *Compensatory Education: Conference Proceedings and Papers (Washington, D.C.: June 17 18, 1986)*, edited by B.I. Williams et al. Chapel Hill, N.C.: Research and Evaluation Associates, Inc.

Adams, M.J. (1990). *Beginning to Read: Thinking and Learning About Print* Cambridge, Mass.: Bradford Books/MIT Press.

Andrews, R.H. (July September 1990). "The Development of a Learning Styles Program in a Low Socioeconomic, Underachieveing, North Carolina Elementary School." *Journal of Reading, Writing and Learning Disability International* 6: 307-314.

Andrews, R.H. (1991). "Insights into Education: An Elementary Principal's Perspective." *Hands-on Approaches to Learning Styles: Practical Approaches to Successful Schooling.* New Wilmington, Pa.: Association for the Advancement of International Education.

Atkins, A. (February 1993). "New Ways to Learn." *Better Homes and Gardens* 71, 2: 35-36.

Au, K., and J. Kawakami. (1985). "Research Currents: Talk Story and Learning to Read." *Language Arts* 62: 406-411.

Banks, J.A. (Fall 1990). *Preparing Teachers and Administrators in a Multicultural Society.* Austin, Texas: Southwest Development Laboratory.

Bateson, G. (1980). *Mind and Nature: A Necessary Unity.* New York: Bantam.

Bauer, E. (1991). "The Relationships Between and Among Learning Styles Perceptual Preferences, Instructional Strategies, Mathematics Achievement and Attitude Toward Mathematics of Learning Disabled and Emotionally Handicapped Students in a Suburban Junior High School." Doctoral diss., St. John's University.

Becher, R.M. (1984). *Parent Involvement: A Review of Research and Principles of Successful Practice.* Washington, D.C.: National Institute of Education.

Bennett, C.I. (1986). *Comprehensive Multicultural Education: Theory and Practice.* Newton, Mass.: Allyn and Bacon.

Bloom, B.S. (1976). *Human Characteristics and School Learning.* New York: McGraw-Hill.

Bloom, D. (1985). "Reading as a Social Process." *Language Arts* 62: 134-141.

Boyatzis, R.E., and D.A. Kolb. (1991). "Assessing Individuality in Learning: The Learning Skills Profile." *Educational Psychology: An International Journal of Experimental Educational Psychology* 11, 3 4: 279-295.

Bransford, J.D., et al. (October 1986). "Teaching Thinking and Problem Solving: Research Foundations." *American Psychologist* 41, 10: 1078-1089.

Brown, S. (October 1990). "Integrating Manipulatives and Computers in Problem-Solving Experiences." *Arithmetic Teacher* 38, 2: 8-10.

Brunner, C.E., and W.S. Majewski. (October 1990). "Mildly Handicapped Students Can Succeed with Learning Styles." *Educational Leadership* 48, 2: 21-23.

Bruno, A. (October 1982). "Hands-on Wins Hands Down." *Early Years* 13, 2: 60-67.

Buechler, M. (April 1992). "Performance Assessment." Policy Bulletin. Bloomington: Indiana Education Policy Center.

Burroughs, R. (July 1993). "The Uses of Literature." *The Executive Educator* 15, 7: 27-29.

Butler, K.A. (1984). *Learning and Teaching Styles: In Theory and Practice.* Maynard, Mass.: Gabriel Systems.

Caine, R.N., and G. Caine. (1991). *Teaching and the Human Brain.* Alexandria, Va.: ASCD.

Campbell, J. (1989). *The Improbable Machine.* New York: Simon and Schuster.

Carbo, M. (October 1987). "Matching Reading Styles: Correcting Ineffective Instruction" *Educational Leadership* 45, 2: 40-47.

Carbo, M., and H. Hodges. (Summer 1988). "Learning Styles Strategies Can Help Students at Risk. *Teaching Exceptional Children* 20, 4: 55-58.

Carbo, M., R. Dunn, and K. Dunn. (1986). *Teaching Students to Read Through Their Individual Learning Styles.* Englewood Cliffs, N.J.: Prentice-Hall.

Carlsen, W.S. (Summer 1991). "Questioning in Classrooms: A Sociolinguistic Perspective." *Review of Educational Research* 61, 2: 157-178.

Carnine, D. (January 1990). "New Research on the Brain: Implications for Instruction." *Phi Delta Kappan* 71, 5: 372-377.

Carr, K.S. (Winter 1988). "How Can We Teach Critical Thinking?" *Childhood Education* 65, 2: 69-73.

Cherkasky-Davis, L. (June 11, 1993). Presentation at the Annual Conference of the Educational Press Association of America in Philadelphia, Pa..

Chi, M.T.H., et al. (1989). "Self-Explanations: How Students Study and Use Examples in Learning to Solve Problems." *Cognitive Science* 13: 145-182.

Cohen, H.G. (March 1992). "Two Teaching Strategies: Their Effectiveness with Students of Varying Cognitive Abilities." *School, Science and Mathematics* 92, 3: 126-132.

Collins, J. (1988). "Language and Class in Minority Education." *Anthropology in Education* 19: 299-326.

Comer, J.P. (1980). *School Power.* New York: Macmillan, The Free Press.

Costa, A.L., and R. Marzano. (October 1987). "Teaching the Language of Thinking." *Educational Leadership* 45, 2: 29-33.

Cousins, N. (1989). *Head First: The Biology of Hope.* New York: E. P. Dutton.

Danehower, V.F. (Summer 1993). "Implementing Whole Language: Understanding the Change Process." *Schools in the Middle* 2, 4: 45-46.

Della Neve, C., et al. (October 1986). "Huge Learning Jumps Show Potency of Brain-Based Instruction." *Phi Delta Kappan* 68, 2: 143-148.

Dillon, D.R. (1989). "Showing Them That I Want Them to Learn and That I Care About Who They Are: A Miroethnography of the Social Organization of a Secondary Low-Track English-Reading Classroom." *American Educational Research Journal* 26: 227-259.

Dillon, J.T. (November 1984). "Research on Questioning and Discussion." *Educational Leadership* 42, 3: 50-56.

Dunn, R., and K. Dunn. (1992). *Teaching Secondary Students Through Their Individual Learning Styles: Practical Approaches for Grades 7 12.* Needham Heights, Mass.: Allyn and Bacon.

Edmonds, R. (program consultant). (1991). *Effective Schools for Children at Risk* (videotape). Alexandria, Va.: ASCD.

Education Leaders Consortium. (1989). "Schools, Parents Work Best When They Work Together." Washington, D.C.: Education Leaders Consortium.

Epstein, J.L. (1987). "Toward a Theory of Family-School Connections: Teacher Practices and Parental Involvement. In *Social Intervention: Potential and Constraints*, edited by K. Hurrelmann, F.X. Kaufmann, and F. Lasel. New York: Walter de Gruyter.

Epstein, J.L. (1989). "Effects on Student Achievement of Teachers' Practices of Parental Involvement." In *Literacy Through Family, Community, and School*, edited by S. Silvern. Greenwich, Conn.: JAI Press.

Epstein, J.L., and S.L. Dauber. (January 1991). "School Programs and Teacher Practices of Parent Involvement in Inner-City Elementary and Middle Schools." *The Elementary School Journal* 91, 3: 289-305.

Fullinwider, R.K. (Spring 1993). "Multiculturalism: Themes and Variations." *Perspective—Council for Basic Education* 5: 2.

Galyean, B.C. (1983). *Mind Sight-Learning through Imaging.* Long Beach, Calif.: Center for Integrated Learning.

Gardner, H. (1983). *Frames of Mind: The Theory of Multiple Intelligences.* New York: Basic Books.

Gardner, H., and T. Hatch. (November 1989). "Multiple Intelligences Go to School." *Educational Researcher* 18, 8: 4-9.

Garrett, S.L. (1991). "The Effects of Perceptual Preference and Motivation on Vocabulary and Test Scores Among High School Students." Doctoral diss., University of La Verne, California.

Goatley, V.J., and T.E. Raphael. (1992). "Non-traditional Learners' Written and Dialogic Response to Literature." In *Literacy Research, Theory, and Practice: Views From Many Perspectives. 41st Yearbook of the National Reading Conference*, edited by C.K. Kinzer, and D.K. Leu. Chicago: National Reading Conference.

Goodson, B.D., and R.D. Hess. (1975). *Parents as Teachers of Young Children: An Evaluative Review of Some Contemporary Concepts and Programs.* Washington, D.C.: Bureau of Educational Personnel Development, DHEW, Office of Education.

Grace, C. (1992). "The Portfolio and Its Use: Developmentally Appropriate Assessment of Young Children." *ERIC Digest.* Urbana, Ill.: ERIC Clearinghouse on Elementary and Early Childhood Education.

Gregorc, A.E. (1982). *An Adult's Guide to Style*, Columbia, Conn.: Gregorc Associates, Inc.

Gregorc, A.E. (1985a). *Inside Styles: Beyond the Basics.* Columbia, Conn.: Gregorc Associates, Inc.

Gregorc, A.E. (1985b). *Gregorc Style Delineator.* Columbia, Conn.: Gregorc Associates, Inc.

Hall, E.T. (Fall 1989). "Unstated Features of the Cultural Context of Learning." *Educational Forum* 54, 1: 21-34.

Hart, L. (January 1983). "A Quick Tour of the Brain." *School Administrator* 40, 1: 13-15.

Hart, L. (May 1986). "All `Thinking' Paths Lead to the Brain." *Educational Leadership* 43, 8: 45-48.

Hartshorn, R., and S. Boren. (June 1990). "Experiential Learning of Mathematics: Using Manipulatives." *ERIC Digest* Charleston, W.V.: ERIC Clearinghouse on Rural Education and Small Schools.

The Harvard Education Letter. (November/December 1988). 4, 6: 1-8.

Henderson, A.T. (1987). *The Evidence Continues to Grow: Parent Involvement Improves Students Achievement.* Columbia, Md.:

National Committee for Citizens in Education.

Herrmann, A.W. (May 1989). "Teaching Writing with Peer Response Groups." *ERIC Digest* Bloomington, Ind.: ERIC Clearinghouse on Reading and Communication Skills.

Hewitt, G. (May June 1993). "Vermont's Portfolio-Based Writing Assessment Program: A Brief History." *Teachers & Writers* 24, 5: 1-6

Hodges, H. (January 1994). "A Consumer's Guide to Learning Styles Programs: An Expert's Advice on Selecting and Implementing Various Models in the Classroom." *The School Administrator* 51, 1: 14-18.

Hollins, E.R. (Spring 1993). "Assessing Teacher Competence for Diverse Populations." *Theory into Practice* 32, 1: 93-99.

Howard, M.B., D.G. Berreth, and J.S. Seltz, eds. *Developing Leadership: A Synthesis of ASCD Resolutions Through 1993.* Alexandria, Va.: ASCD.

Jacobs, H.H. (October 1991). "Planning for Curriculum Integration." *Educational Leadership* 49, 2: 27-28.

Johnson, D.W., and R.T. Johnson. (1986). *Learning Together and Alone,* 2nd ed. Englewood Cliffs, N.J.: Prentice-Hall.

Johnson, D.W., and R.T. Johnson. (December/January 1990). "Social Skills for Successful Group Work." *Educational Leadership* 47, 4: 29-33.

Johnson, N.J. (1993). "Celebrating Growth Over Time: Classroom-Based Assessment in Language Arts." Literacy Improvement Series for Elementary Educators. Washington, D.C.: Office of Educational Research and Improvement.

Joyner, J.M. (October 1990). "Using Manipulatives Successfully." *Arithmetic Teacher* 38, 2: 6-7.

Kendall, F.E. (1983). *Diversity in the Classroom: A Multicultural Approach to the Education of Young Children.* New York: Teachers College Press.

Kilman, M., and J. Richards. (1990). *Now That We've Done the Calculation, How Do We Solve the Problem? Writing, Sharing, and Discussing Arithmetic Stories.* Newton, Mass.: The Literacies Institute, Education Development Center, Inc.

Knapp, M.S., and B.J. Turnbull. (January 1990a). *Better Schooling for the Children of Poverty: Alternatives to Conventional Wisdom. Study of Academic Instruction for Disadvantaged Students. Volume I: Summary.* Washington, D.C.: Policy Studies Associates; Menlo Park, Calif.: SRI International.

Knapp, M.S., and P.M. Shields, eds. (January 1990b). *Better Schooling for the Children of Poverty: Alternatives to Conventional Wisdom. Study of Academic Instruction for Disadvantaged Students. Volume II: Commissioned Papers and Literature Review.* Washington, D.C.: Policy Studies Associates; Menlo Park, Calif.: SRI International.

Knapp, M.S., and P.M. Shields. (June 1990b). "Reconceiving Academic Instruction for the Children of Poverty." *Phi Delta Kappan* 7, 10: 753-738.

Lambert, M. (1990). "When the Problem Is Not the Question and the Solution Is Not the Answer: Mathematical Knowing and Teaching." *American Educational Research Journal* 27, 1: 29-63.

Langer, J.A. (1991). *Literary Understanding and Literature Instruction.* Report Series 2.11. Albany, N.Y.: National Research Center on Literature Teaching and Learning.

Lehr, J.B., and H.W. Harris. (1988). *At-Risk, Low-Achieving Students in the Classroom.* Washington, D.C.: National Education Association.

Leler, H. (1983). "Parent Education and Involvement in Relation to the Schools and to Parents of School-Aged Children." In *Parent Education and Public Policy*, edited by R. Haskins and D.

Addams. Norwood, N.J.: Ablex Publishing Co.

Levin, H.M. (April 5 9, 1988a). "Structuring Schools for Greater Effectiveness with Educationally Disadvantaged or At-Risk Students." Paper presented at the annual meeting of the American Educational Research Association, New Orleans, La.

Levin, H.M. (September 1988b). *Accelerated Schools for At-Risk Students.* CPRE Research Report Series RR-010. New Brunswick, N.J.: Center for Policy Research in Education, Eagleton Institute of Politics, Rutgers, The State University of New Jersey.

Levin, H.M. (January 1991a). "Don't Remediate: Accelerate." *Principal* 70, 3: 11-13.

Levin, H.M. (1991b). *Accelerating the Progress of ALL Students.* Rockefeller Institute Special Report, Number 31. Albany: State University of New York, Nelson A. Rockefeller Institute of Government.

Lewis, A., and E. Steinberger. (1991). *Learning Styles: Putting Research and Common Sense into Practice.* Arlington, Va.: American Association of School Administrators.

Lockwood, A.T. (March 1991). "Authentic Assessment." *Focus in Change* 3, 1. (Available from the National Center for Effective Schools, Madison, Wisc.)

Lozanov, G., and E. Gateva. (1988). *The Foreign Language Teacher's Suggestopedic Manual.* New York: Gordon and Breach Science Publishers.

Marzano, R.J., D. Pickering, and J. McTighe. (1993). *Assessing Student Outcomes: Performance Assessment Using the Dimensions of Learning Model.* Alexandria, Va.: ASCD.

Marzano, R.J., et al. (1992). *Toward a Comprehensive Model of Assessment.* Aurora, Colo.: Mid-continent Regional Educational Laboratory.

Marzano, R.J., R.S. Brandt, C.S. Hughes, B.F. Jones, B.Z. Presseisen, S.C. Rankin, and C. Suhor. (1988). *Dimensions of Thinking.* Alexandria, Va.: ASCD.

Means, B., and M.S. Knapp. (1991). *Teaching Advanced Skills to Educational Disadvantaged Students. Final Report.* Washington, D.C.: Prepared under contract by SRI International and Policy Studies Associates for the U.S. Department of Education, Office of Planning, Budget, and Evaluation.

National Council of Teachers of Mathematics. (1989). *Curriculum and Evaluation Standards for School Mathematics.* Reston, Va: NCTM.

Onosko, J.J. (April 1992). "Exploring the Thinking of Thoughtful Teachers." *Educational Leadership* 49, 7: 40-43.

Orsak, L. (October 1990). "Learning Styles Versus the Rip Van Winkle Syndrome." *Educational Leadership* 48, 2: 19-20.

Palincsar, A.S., and L.J. Klenk. (1991). "Learning Dialogues to Promote Text Comprehension." In *Teaching Advanced Skills to Educationally Disadvantaged Students.* Washington, D.C.: U.S. Department of Education.

Palincsar, A.S., et al. (December/January 1989). "Collaborative Research and Development of Reciprocal Teaching." *Educational Leadership* 46, 4: 37-40.

Palincsar, A.S., C.S. Englert, T.E. Raphael, and J.R. Gavalek. (May June 1991). "Examining the Context of Strategy Instruction." *Remedial and Special Education (RASE)* 12, 3: 43-53.

Paris, S.G., et al. (1991). "The Development of Strategic Readers." In *Handbook of Reading Research, Volume II*, edited by R. Barr, M.L. Kamil, P.B. Mosenthal, and P.D. Pearson. New York: Longman.

Paul, R.W. (September 1984). "Critical Thinking: Fundamental to Education for a Free Society." *Educational Leadership* 42, 1: 4-14.

Perrin, J. (October 1990). "The Learning Styles Project for Potential Dropouts." *Educational Leadership* 48, 2: 23-24.

Perrone, V. (1991). *Expanding Student Assessment*, Alexandria, Va.: ASCD.

Pritchard, A., and J. Taylor. (1980). *Accelerated Learning: The Use of Suggestion in the Classroom*. Novato, Calif.: Academic Therapy.

Quellmalz, E.S., and J. Hoskyn. (April 1988). "Making a Difference in Arkansas: The Multicultural Reading and Thinking Project." *Educational Leadership* 46, 7: 52-55.

"Questioning Promotes Active Reader/Text Interaction." (Spring 1987). *IRT Communication Quarterly*.

Rasbow, J., and A.C.R. Hernandez. (June 1988). "The Price of the `GPA Perspective': An Empirical Study of `Making the Grade.'" *Youth and Society* 19, 4: 363-377.

Redesigning Assessment (videotape). (1992). Alexandria, Va.: ASCD.

Resnick, L.B. (1987). "Learning in School and Out." *Educational Researcher* 16, 9: 13-20.

Richardson, R.B. (March 1988). *Active Affective Learning for Accelerated Schools*. Stanford, Calif.: Center for Educational Research at Stanford University.

Roberts, J., and M. Zody. (March 1989). "Using the Research for Effective Supervision: Measuring a Teacher's Questioning Techniques." *NASSP Bulletin* 73, 515: 8-14.

Rose, C. (1985). *Empowering the Spectrum of Your Mind*. Flushing, N.Y.: Spectrum Educational Services, Inc.

Rosenshine, B., and C. Meister. (April 1992). "The Use of Scaffolds for Teaching Higher-Level Cognitive Strategies." *Educational Leadership* 49, 7: 26-33.

Roser, N.L. (1987). "Research Currents: Returning Literature and Literacy." *Language Arts* 64: 90-97.

Rowan, B., et al. (1986). "The Design and Implementation of Chapter 1 Instructional Services: A Study of 24 Schools." San Francisco: Far West Laboratory for Educational Research and Development.

Russell, P. (1975). *The Brain Book*. New York: E.P. Dutton.

Schnitzer, S. (April 1993). "Designing and Authentic Assessment." *Educational Leadership* 50, 7: 32-35.

Sinatra, R. (May 1983). "Brain Research Sheds Light on Language Learning." *Educational Leadership* 40, 8: 9-12.

Slavin, R.E. (1986). *Using Student Team Learning*, 3rd ed. Baltimore, Md.: Johns Hopkins University Press.

Slavin, R.E. (October 1987). "Making Chapter 1 Make a Difference." *Phi Delta Kappan* 69, 2: 110-119.

Slavin, R.E., N.L. Karweit, and N.A. Madden. (1989). *Effective Programs for Students at Risk*, Boston: Allyn and Bacon.

Somers, A. B., and J.E. Worthington. (1979). *Response Guides for Teaching Children's Books*. Urbana, Ill.: National Council of Teachers of English.

Stevens, R.J., et al. (1987). "Cooperative Integrated Reading and Composition: Two Field Experiments." *Reading Research Quarterly* 22: 433-454.

Stover, D. (May 25, 1993). "School Boards Caught Up in Debate Over Tracking," *School Board News* 13, 9: 1, 8.

Strickland, D.S. (1985). "Integrating the Basic Skills Through the Content Areas." Workshop Materials. New York: Teachers College, Columbia University.

Strickland, D.S., and L.M. Morrow. (1989). *Emerging Literacy: Young Children Learn to Read and Write*. Newark, Del.: International Reading Association.

"Suggestive Accelerative Learning and Teaching: A Manual of Classroom Procedures Based on the Lozanov Method." (1985). Ames, Iowa: Society for Accelerated Learning and Teaching (SALT).

Sweet, D., and J. Zimmerman, eds. (November 1992). "Performance Assessment." *Education Research Consumer Guide* (Report no. ED/OERI-92-38; OR-92-3056). Washington, D.C.: Office of Educational Research and Improvement.

Taylor, D., and C. Dorsey-Gaines. (1988). *Growing Up Literate: Learning from Inner-city Families*. Portsmouth, N.H.: Heinemann.

"Teachers' Questions: Why Do You Ask?" (May 1987). *The Harvard Education Letter* 3, 3: 1.

Tiedt, P.L, and I.M. Tiedt. (1986). *Multicultural Teaching*. Newton, Mass.: Allyn and Bacon.

U.S. Department of Education, Office of Educational Research and Improvement. (August 1990). "Parental Involvement In Education." *Issues in Education* (0-861-983). Washington, D.C.: U.S. Government Printing Office. (2-page newsletter)

U.S. Department of Labor. (1992). *Learning a Living: A Blueprint for High Performance. A SCANS Report for America 2000*. Washington, D.C.: Secretary's Commission on Achieving Necessary Skills, U.S. Department of Labor.

Vygotsky, L.S. (1962). *Thought and Language*, edited and translated by E. Hanfmann and G. Vakar. Cambridge, Mass.: M.I.T. Press.

Vygotsky, L.S. (1978). *Mind in Society: The Development of Higher Psychological Processes*. Cambridge, Mass.: Harvard University Press.

Walmsley, S.A., and T.P. Walp. (1990). "Integrating Literature and Composing into the Language Arts Curriculum: Philosophy and Practice." *Elementary School Journal* 90, 3: 251-274.

Webb, M. (Spring 1988). "Peer Helping Relationships in Urban Schools." *Equity and Choice* 4, 3: 35-48.

Wiggins, G. (May 1992). "Creating Tests Worth Taking," *Educational Leadership* 49, 8: 26-33.

Williams Jr., D.I., and N.F. Chavkin. (October 1989). "Essential Elements of Strong Parent Involvement Programs." *Educational Leadership* 47, 2: 19-20.

Worthen, B.R. (February 1993). "Critical Issues That Will Determine the Future of Alternative Assessment." *Phi Delta Kappan* 74, 6: 444-454.

TEAMWORK

Students in grades K-5 at the Alice Carlson Applied Learning Center are having a unique and different experience in their Applied Learning classrooms. They are being encouraged and challenged to make choices and decisions and to take responsibility for their learning and their education.

The students in these classrooms represent the diverse population of the Fort Worth Independent School District. All of these students chose to attend the Applied Learning Center; many of them were not successful at their previous schools.

At the beginning of the 1992-93 school year, these diverse young people began their learning by forming assigned groups in which they would work together, make decisions, and solve problems. When teachers discovered that group work and decision making were new strategies for many students, they devoted time to practicing these strategies. Early in the year, some students could make only peripheral decisions, but as the school year progressed and as students began to routinely work together, they learned strategies to help them make more meaningful decisions as a team.

One group of 4th grade students served on the Playground Representative Committee and worked together on the design and choice of the equipment for the school's new playground. They worked within a $10,000 budget and presented reports explaining their progress and the direction they were taking. The group reported routinely to a

larger committee made up of parents, teachers, and other students. They made decisions based on student surveys and input from the staff and the larger committee.

All of these young people have learned to make decisions about what they learn and how they go about learning such concepts as managing their time, materials, and resources as they become involved in their projects.

"We use projects to help us learn, and we've learned to allocate our time and use it wisely. Teachers let us make decisions about our work and let us put our minds to work," says one student. "When I do a project on Texas history, I'll know enough to tell other people."

Another student says, "We have access to lots of resources, our teachers, and other people on staff. Not only have I learned to work in groups, but now I can tutor other kids."

At Alice Carlson, students can be found routinely working in small groups and large groups, and working

independently with peers, teachers, and community members.

Through classwork and individual work, students will be able to develop interpersonal skills, communication skills, negotiation skills, and teamwork strategies—tools that will enable them to put academic knowledge to work.

"We're all treated equal, teachers pay attention to you, not just your work," says one student. "I'm so proud of myself. I feel I can do almost anything, and in the future I know I'll do more good things."

4

DIVERSE TEACHING STRATEGIES FOR DIVERSE LEARNERS

MARIETTA SARAVIA-SHORE AND EUGENE GARCIA

Photo courtesy of Goodman/Van Riper Photography, Washington, DC

That minority and low income children often perform poorly on tests is well known. But the fact that they do so because we systematically and willfully expect less from them is not. Most Americans assume that the low achievement of poor and minority children is bound up in the children themselves or their families. "The children don't try." "They have no place to study." "Their parents don't care." "Their culture does not value education." These and other excuses are regularly offered up to explain the achievement gap that separates poor and minority students from other young Americans.

But these are red herrings. The fact is that we know how to educate poor and minority children of all kinds—racial, ethnic, and language—to high levels. Some teachers and some entire schools do it every day, year in and year out, with outstanding results. But the nation as a whole has not yet acted on that knowledge . . .

—Commission on Chapter 1 (1992, pp. 3-4).

This chapter treats a multitude of teaching strategies shown by research to be effective in educating diverse student learners. Diverse student learners include students from racially, ethnically, culturally, and linguistically diverse families and communities of lower socio-economic status. Subsequent chapters offer a sampling of strategies that hold promise for increased student learning in reading, writing, mathematics, and oral communication. If we can act on this knowledge, we can realize the educational excellence we desire for *all* our children.

SCHOOLING ISSUES

Historically, "Americanization" has been a prime institutional educational objective for culturally diverse children (Gonzalez 1990). The desired effect of Americanizing students has been to socialize and acculturate an increasingly diverse community. In essence, people believed that if schools could teach students "American" values, then students could be "saved" from educational failure.

In a variety of ways, Americanization is still the goal of many programs aimed at culturally diverse students (Rodriguez 1989). For these students, unfortunately, Americanization still means the elimination not only of linguistic and cultural differences but of a culture deemed somehow undesirable by the mainstream culture.

Programs of Americanization seem to assume a single, homogeneous, modern culture; the relationship between the dominant culture and the myriad subcultures that exist is not that of equals. The dominant community, enjoying greater wealth and privilege, claims its position by virtue of cultural superiority (Ogbu 1987). In one way or another, nearly every child not born into the dominant culture—whether born in the United States or elsewhere—

47

FOCUSING ON EDUCATION

Members of the three largest racial or ethnic minority groups in the United states agree that education is the most important issue facing their communities, according to a survey by a Florida-based marketing firm reported in the May 26, 1993, *Education Week*.

Market Segment Research Inc., of Coral Gables, conducted more than 3,500 face-to-face and telephone interviews with African-Americans, Hispanics, and Asian-Americans.

FIGURE 4.1
Most Important Issues Facing Minority Groups

	Percent Citing Issue
AFRICAN-AMERICANS	
Education	45%
Drugs	17%
AIDS	12%
Crime	7%
Gang Violence	3%
HISPANICS	
Education	36%
AIDS	15%
Drugs	15%
Child Abuse	11%
Gang Violence	7%
ASIAN-AMERICANS	
Education	29%
Crime	19%
Drugs	9%
AIDS	9%
Health Care	8%

Source: Market Segment Research Inc. This figure is reprinted with permission from *Education Week* (May 26, 1993), p. 3.

is subject to being treated as a foreigner, an alien, an intruder.

In 1923, Susan M. Dorsey, the superintendent of the Los Angeles public schools, speaking to principals in the district, reportedly voiced a common complaint: "We have the [Mexican] immigrants to live with, and if we Americanize them, we can live with them. . . ." Even today, the objective of many figures in the dominant culture is to transform the diversity in our communities into a monolithic English-speaking and American- thinking and -acting community.

This context of "us versus them" is exemplified at many levels in education. In a nationwide survey of families, Wong-Fillmore (1991) found evidence that serious disruptions of family relations occur when young children learn English in school and lose the use of their home language. Many of the parents interviewed in this study expressed concern that their children will lose their language and become estranged from their families and their cultural heritage; others reported that their children had already lost or were losing their home language.

An interviewer told the story of a Korean immigrant family in which the children had nearly lost the ability to speak their native language after just a few years in American schools. The parents could speak English only with difficulty, and the grandmother who lived with the family could neither speak nor understand it; she felt isolated and unappreciated by her grandchildren. The adults spoke to the children exclusively in Korean. They refused to believe that the children could not understand them and interpreted the children's unresponsiveness as disrespect and rejection. Only when the interviewer, a bilingual Korean-English speaker, tried to question the children in both languages did the parents come to realize that the children could no longer speak or understand Korean. The father wept as he spoke of being unable to talk to his children. One of the children commented that she did not understand why her parents always seemed to be angry.

Today, as in the past, teachers are being challenged to broaden their repertoire of teaching strategies to meet the needs and strengths of students from a staggering diversity of backgrounds and cultures. These learners—African Americans, Native Americans, Asian Americans, Hispanic Americans, and many, many others—face societal discrimination or live in conditions of poverty. The ways in which we teach these young people exert a powerful influence on their linguistic, social, cognitive, and general educational development.

Research suggests, for instance, that effective instruction acknowledges students' gender differences and reaffirms their cultural, ethnic, and linguistic heritages. Many effective instructional approaches build on students' varying backgrounds to further the development of their abilities in reading, writing, mathematics, and oral communication. Of critical importance is the recognition that the use of effective instructional practices as demonstrated by research will improve achievement for *all* children, including those who are not minorities or children of poverty. The implementation of sound, research-based strategies that recognize the benefits of diversity can build a better future for all of us (see, for example, Tharp 1989a, 1989b, 1991; Tharp, Jordan, Speidel, Au, Klein, Calkins, Sloat, and Gillmore 1984; and O'Donnell and Tharp 1990).

THE VALUE OF DIVERSITY

The broad range of experiences and perspectives brought to school by culturally, linguistically, and ethnically diverse students is a powerful opportunity for *everyone* to learn more—in different ways, in new environments, and with different types of people. Every single person in this enormously diverse and ever-changing system has the power to serve as an invaluable resource for all others—students, teachers, and the community as a whole. Rather than constituting a problem for students and educators, the growing diversity in U.S. classrooms necessitates and encourages the development and use of diverse and varied teaching strategies designed to respond to each student as an individual.

The United States is a privileged nation, for it includes not only immigrants, but also political refugees, indigenous Americans, and descendants of peoples (sometimes brought against their will) from every continent on the globe. This boundless diversity has resulted in the inventions, discoveries, ideas, literature, art, music, films, labor, languages, political systems, and foods that enrich American culture. These same resources also have the potential for enriching the American classroom. They are opportunities to be explored and treasures to be appreciated, as well as challenges to the status quo.

Adopting a truly global perspective allows us to view culturally and linguistically diverse students and their parents or guardians as resources who provide unparalleled opportunities for enrichment. Naturally, we need a greater repertoire of approaches to teaching and learning to cope with varied styles of learning. Teachers and students alike must cultivate interpersonal skills and respect for other cultures. The new world economy demands this global view. After all, our markets and economic competition are now global, and the skills of intercultural communication are necessary in politics, diplomacy, economics, environmental management, the arts, and other fields of human endeavor.

Surely a diverse classroom is the ideal laboratory in which to learn the multiple perspectives required by a global society and to put to use information concerning diverse cultural patterns. Students who learn to work and play collaboratively with classmates from various cultures are better prepared for the world they face now—and the world they will face in the 21st century. Teaching and learning strategies that draw on the social history and the everyday lives of students and their cultures can only assist this learning process.

Teachers promote critical thinking when they make the rules of the classroom culture explicit and enable students to compare and contrast them with other cultures. Cross-cultural skills develop naturally in culturally and linguistically diverse classrooms. For such learning to take place, however, teachers must have the attitudes, knowledge, and skills to make their classrooms effective learning environments for all students. Given the opportunity, students can participate in learning communities within their schools and neighborhoods and be ready to assume constructive roles as workers, family members, and citizens in a global society.

Zeichner (1992) has summarized the extensive literature that describes successful teaching approaches for diverse populations. From his review, he distilled 12 key elements for effective teaching for ethnic and language minority students:

1. Teachers have a clear sense of their own ethnic and cultural identities.

2. Teachers communicate high expectations for the success of all students, and a belief that all students can succeed.

3. Teachers are personally committed to achieving equity for all students and believe that they are capable of making a difference in their students' learning.

4. Teachers have developed a bond with their students and cease seeing their students as "the other."

5. Students are provided with an academically challenging curriculum that includes attention to the development of higher- level cognitive skills.

6. Instruction focuses on students' creation of meaning about content in an interactive and collaborative learning environment.

7. Students see learning tasks as meaningful.

8. The curriculum includes the contributions and perspectives of the different ethnocultural groups that compose the society.

9. Teachers provide a "scaffolding" that links the academically challenging curriculum to the cultural resources that students bring to school.

10. Teachers explicitly teach students the culture of the school *and* seek to maintain students' sense of ethnocultural pride and identity.

11. Community members and parents or guardians are encouraged to become involved in students' education and are given a significant voice in making important school decisions related to program, i.e., resources and staffing.

12. Teachers are involved in political struggles outside the classroom that are aimed at achieving a more just and humane society.

Photo courtesy of William Mills, Rockville, MD

The student diversity in this classroom offers valuable learning experiences for each youngster. By working together in multicultural groups, students learn to appreciate the capabilities of their classmates as well as identify their own strong points. When instruction is offered in a student's primary language, content can more easily be learned. In addition, students who are not bilingual can develop skills in another language when the teacher is able to capitalize on student resources in the classroom.

THE STRATEGIES IN THIS CHAPTER

For the sake of clarity, this chapter breaks the teaching strategies into two main sections. A brief introduction precedes each section. The first section, "Strategies for Culturally and Ethnically Diverse Students," contains strategies appropriate for culturally and ethnically diverse students whose primary language may or may not be English. The second section, "Strategies for Linguistically Diverse Students," contains strategies that specifically address the unique needs of linguistically diverse students. Each strategy entry includes a brief discussion of the strategy as well as examples of the strategy at work in the classroom. References at the end of each entry allow the reader to explore additional information and resources.

STRATEGIES FOR CULTURALLY AND ETHNICALLY DIVERSE STUDENTS

Generally, U.S. schools provide students of diverse backgrounds with instruction quite different from that provided to students of mainstream backgrounds. For example, poor children and culturally and linguistically diverse students tend to receive inferior instruction because they are usually placed in the bottom reading groups or sent out of the classroom for remedial instruction.

Research also shows that schools tend to discriminate against students of diverse backgrounds through assessments that do not value their home language and through the use of teaching procedures that fail to build on the strengths of their culture or home languages (see Garcia and Pearson 1991, Goldman and Hewitt 1975, and Oakland and Matuszek 1977). Still other studies demonstrate that many teachers fail to communicate effectively with students; typical and hard-to-change instructional procedures often violate the behavior norms of students' home cultures (see Au 1980, Cazden 1988, Delpit 1988, Heath 1983, and Ogbu 1982). Also, teachers may have low expectations for students of diverse backgrounds and thus fail to present them with challenging and interesting lessons.

Kenji Ima (1988, 1991) has aggregated a large body of research which, though it relates primarily to Asian and Pacific Islanders newly arrived in the United States, has implications that reach far beyond that particular immigrant population. Ima and other researchers (First 1988, National Coalition of Advocates for Students 1988, Quality Education for Minorities Project 1990) found many identifiable factors associated with the level of these young people's performance in school; schools have control over some factors but not others. If teachers understand these factors and their effects on young people who are newly arrived in the United States, they will be better able to assess their needs and find innovative ways of helping them adjust to new schools and to life in a new culture. Some of these critical factors and their effects mind include the following:

• The level of the family's socioeconomic resources is associated with success in school but is conditioned by other factors, such as immigrant status.

• Prior education in the country of origin is associated with success in school.

• Student performance is associated with country of origin and ethnicity; however, these factors are associated with other factors, such as whether schooling was disrupted in the home country.

• The age of entrance into the United States affects success in the English language, as well as other academic areas, but the degree of success is also conditioned by literacy in the home language. Those children who enter the United States before puberty will have an advantage in school.

• The longer the length of the stay in the United States, the greater the success in school. Unfortunately, this effect is offset by a reduction of motivation that comes through acculturation into the American culture.

• Intact family and home support systems are associated with success in school. Not surprisingly, unaccompanied minors and students from single-parent families, for example, are at greater risk of failure in school.

In this context, it is important to understand that Asian Americans, for instance, are often viewed incorrectly as a single ethnic group. There are, however, many distinct subgroups of Asians Americans, each having its own culture, religion, and perspective. Generalization across such subgroups can lead to misperceptions and a failure to recognize and address specific concerns and needs. It is also

---

FIGURE 4.2
Major Ethnic Groups

Minority refers primarily to five ethnic groups: Alaskan Natives, American Indians, Black Americans, Mexican Americans, and Puerto Ricans.
   Other minority groups can include Cuban Americans, Asian immigrants, Central American immigrants, and others.

Alaskan Natives refers to those residing in Alaska who are Eskimo, American Indian, or Aleut.

American Indians refers to members of one of the 300 to 400 tribes (both federally and nonfederally recognized) that exist in the United States with ancestors who lived here before the arrival of Europeans. American Indians are also often referred to as Native Americans or Indians, and individuals are frequently identified by tribal affiliation.

Black Americans or Blacks refers to individuals of African heritage, most of whom were born in the United States, making up the largest ethnic group in America. The label, as used by the Bureau of the Census and other data sources, includes U.S.-born and non-U.S.-born blacks, such as those from the West Indies. Hispanic blacks are included under the specific national affiliation, for example, Cuban or Cuban Americans, or the border label of Hispanics. Other labels include African Americans and Afro Americans.

Puerto Ricans refers to persons born in Puerto Rico, as well as those born on the mainland, but of Puerto Rican descent.

White refers to those of European, Near Eastern, and north African heritage. As counted by the Bureau of the Census, this category includes those who identify themselves as white. Low-income whites share many of the educational barriers as other minority groups, including high dropout rates, limited educational opportunities, and poverty.

Source: Quality Education for Minorities Project 1990.

---

important to understand that the overall descriptor "Southeast Asian" generally refers to those who report their own ethnic identity as Vietnamese, Laotian, Cambodian, or Hmong. The recent tendency to stereotype

Asians as "high achievers" may mask significant and unique educational problems and needs.

Along this same line, Hispanic Americans or Latinos are also composed of many distinct subgroups. Although the U.S. Census Bureau classifies all Spanish-speaking peoples under the general heading "Hispanic origin," this term includes all persons who identify themselves as Mexican, Puerto Rican, Cuban, Central or South American, or of other origins. Furthermore, people of Hispanic origin may be of any race.

Finally, it is important to be aware that agencies dealing with population data refer to Alaska natives or Native Americans as one group, even though the customs, languages, and cultures of the many tribes and nations of these two groups are vastly different.

Considerable evidence supports this crucial conclusion: The differences in achievement observed between and among students of culturally and ethnically diverse backgrounds and students of mainstream backgrounds are *not* the result of differences in ability to learn. Rather, they are the result of *differences in the quality of the instruction* these young people receive in school. Moreover, many students who are at risk of failure in U.S. schools have styles of learning that are at odds with traditional instructional practices. Naturally, a multitude of complex factors contribute to students' at-risk status; many of these factors—crime, drugs, and poverty, among others—are beyond the control of educators. But educators *do* have the power to eradicate ineffective instructional practices. The strategies that follow have been demonstrated to be effective in increasing student achievement.

Among the teaching strategies strongly recommended are the following:

- Maintain high standards and expectations for all students.
- Offer challenging, advanced coursework.
- Learn about students' home cultures.
- Encourage active participation of parents or guardians.
- Capitalize on students' backgrounds.
- Use culturally relevant curriculum materials.
- Identify and dispel stereotypes.
- Recognize students' learning styles, cultures, and native languages.
- Structure cooperative learning environments.

REFERENCES
Commission on Chapter 1 1992; Ogbu 1987; Rodriguez 1989; Wong-Fillmore 1991.

● STRATEGY 4.1: MAINTAIN HIGH STANDARDS AND EXPECTATIONS

Teachers maintain high standards and demonstrate high achievement expectations for all ethnically, culturally, and linguistically diverse students; this includes offering challenging and advanced coursework.

DISCUSSION

Students learn more when they are challenged by teachers who have high expectations for them, encourage them to identify problems, involve them in collaborative activities, and accelerate their learning. Teachers who express high expectations for students convey a belief that students have the ability to succeed in more demanding activities. Rather than focusing exclusively on repetitive, rote learning, teachers involve young people in problem-solving activities that require them to use their judgment, form opinions, do research, do homework, use analytic skills, evaluate, make connections, and manage time effectively.

CLASSROOM EXAMPLES

Jaime Escalante captured media attention with his success in teaching calculus to Hispanic students. His high expectations for his students and their subsequent accomplishments were the subject of the film *Stand and Deliver*. Many teachers who will never be the subject of a Hollywood film have inspired and guided pupil achievement. Research emphasizes the overwhelming importance of the teacher's believing that *all students can learn* (see Gibson and Ogbu 1991; Knapp et al. 1993; Winfield and Manning 1992).

When teachers believe that students can learn, they not only communicate these expectations explicitly, thus encouraging young people, but they also spend more time on more challenging activities—for instance, asking higher order questions that require not only identification and categorization but also comprehension and analysis, application to other situations, synthesis, and value judgments.

Heath and McLaughlin (1994) have found that one of the reasons for the effectiveness of after-school youth programs organized by community-based organizations is that the staff, often operating on a shoestring budget, must depend on the students to assist in taking responsibility for the activities. Young people plan, teach others, and perform. When students are brought into the planning of a performance or dramatic production and become coaches for others, they are being given "adult" responsibilities and challenges; everyone must be able to depend on everyone else to show up on time and do his part. In addition, involving students in the financial aspects of such operations—raising funds by organizing activities or making requests of foundations—fosters involvement, responsibility, and the learning of math skills. Students learn social skills, too, as well as communication skills and performance skills.

In such collaborative work, diversity of skills is seen as a resource for the entire group; everyone brings something different to the table. Finally, by making journal writing a required part of students' group responsibilities, teachers provide students the opportunity to reflect on what they are learning, practice writing skills, and keep the staff informed of their individual progress and well-being.

REFERENCES
Carter and Chatfield 1986; Chall, Jacobs, and Baldwin 1990; Gibson and Bhachu 1991; Gibson and Ogbu 1991; Heath and McLaughlin 1994; *The Harvard Education Letter* 1988; Knapp et al. 1993; Levin and Hopfenberg 1991; Quality Education for Minorities Project 1990; Tharp and Gallimore 1988; Winfield and Manning 1992.

● STRATEGY 4.2: INCORPORATE THE HOME CULTURE

Teachers learn about their students' home-community culture in order to better comprehend students' behavior in and out of the classroom.

DISCUSSION

Teachers can enlist parents or guardians as resources to help clarify their cultural expectations concerning the roles of teachers and students, discipline patterns, reward systems, and the values held by young people from linguistically and ethnically diverse cultures.

Educators must understand and respect the many different ways of being a parent and expressing concern about the education of one's children. For example, Gibson (1983, 1988) reports that Punjabi immigrant parents in California believe it is the teacher's task to educate and that parents should not be involved in what goes on at school. Punjabi parents support their children's education by requiring that homework be done and ensuring that their youngsters do not "hang out" with other American students but instead apply themselves to schoolwork. Even though the parents themselves may be forced to take more than one job, they prevent their children from working so that they have time for homework. As a result, Punjabi students as a group have higher rates of graduation and college acceptance than other immigrant groups.

CLASSROOM EXAMPLES

Teachers can ask students to interview their parents about their lives as children, the stories they remember, favorite poems, and family recipes. The results of these interviews can be made into booklets and, subsequently, reading materials for the entire class. Parent-teacher organizations can hold meetings at times convenient for parents to attend, and they can provide translators for those who do not speak English. A room in the school can be set aside for parents to meet and discuss issues concerning their children's education or related to the school community. Teachers can visit parents in their homes. Teachers can use parent-teacher meetings as a time to discuss homework and discipline.

Parents who are welcomed into the school in ways that are culturally appropriate for them become more accessible both as resources and as learners. Immigrant parents can learn both English as a second language and survival skills for their new culture. Parents who are bilingual may be asked to translate for those who have not yet achieved fluency in a new language. Parents who attend workshops can learn family literacy and family math activities that enhance their own abilities to support their children's learning of these skills. When students see that their parents are respected by the school, there may be less of the conflict between home and school cultures that can cause a breakdown of discipline within the family.

REFERENCES
Arvizu 1992; Coballes-Vega 1992; Gibson 1983, 1987, 1988; Gibson and Bhachu 1991; Hamilton, Blumenfeld, Akoh, and Miura 1989; Heath 1986; Jordan, Au, Joseting 1983; Laosa 1982; Phillips 1972; Saravia-Shore and Martinez 1992; Strickland and Ascher 1992; Wong-Fillmore and Valadez 1986.

● STRATEGY 4.3: ENCOURAGE ACTIVE PARTICIPATION OF PARENTS OR GUARDIANS

Teachers inform parents of the importance of talking with their children, taking the time to read to them (in their home language), sharing oral histories and traditional folktales, and labeling objects and events around the home.

DISCUSSION

Parents or guardians are a child's *first teachers*, but they are not always aware of the ways in which they mold children's language development and communication skills. By sharing information about the parent or guardian's important role in a child's learning and by offering specific suggestions, teachers support this crucial role. *Children learn their language at home*; the more interaction and communication, the more children learn.

Teachers can act as "culture brokers" by interacting and talking with parents to emphasize the key role parents play in their children's education. Teachers can assist parents in understanding the expectations of the school and their classroom as well as eliciting from parents their expectations of teachers and students. Teachers can suggest ways in which parents might converse more often with their children to prepare them for communication in the classroom.

CLASSROOM EXAMPLES

Children can learn the importance of language in expressing ideas, feelings, and requests if parents or guardians respond to them and acknowledge their thoughts. Children also need guidance in learning patterns of communication that will be necessary in the classroom, including how to make a request, ask a question, and respond to a question.

If parents or guardians are literate in *any* language, they can read to their children in that language to encourage reading for pleasure and to help children begin to make the connection between oral language and reading. Even if parents or guardians are not literate, they can use wordless books or create prose as they hold their children and "read" with them.

Even the simplest evidence of contact and caring about the importance of literacy pays huge dividends in a young person's schooling. Parents or guardians can take time to talk with their children about any activity they are doing together, such as eating a meal, thereby encouraging language development. Parents or guardians can ask their children questions about whatever activity they are engaged in and how it relates to another activity, as well as asking how they feel about the activity, or what they predict may happen next. They are thus modeling the kinds of communication patterns that young people will use in school. At the same time, simply giving children the gift of attention pays huge dividends.

Programs in family literacy can help parents acquire or strengthen their own literacy skills, making them better able to assist their children's development of literacy. The National Center for Family Literacy, which has its headquarters in Louisville, Kentucky, is a leader in this effort. Other techniques, such as the use of recorded books, allow adults and children to learn reading skills together. Children are encouraged to read when they see their parents reading and have their parents read to them. Reading for fun also encourages more reading.

REFERENCES
Arvizu 1992; Carbo 1978, 1989; Carbo, Dunn, and Dunn 1986; Dornbusch, Ritter, Leiderman, Roberts, and Fraleigh 1987; Lee 1986; McIntosh 1983; Snow 1986; Tharp, Jordan, Speidel, Au, Klein, Calkins, Sloat, and Gallimore 1984; Valverde, Feinberg, and Marquez 1980.

● STRATEGY 4.4: CAPITALIZE ON STUDENTS' BACKGROUNDS

Teachers recognize that learning is strongly influenced by students' cultural backgrounds. Although students differ in their knowledge of oral and written language, research demonstrates that all children come to school with a background of experience that teachers can capitalize on during the learning process.

DISCUSSION

Students' self-esteem and motivation are enhanced when teachers elicit their experiences in classroom discussions and validate what they have to say. Young people become more engaged in lessons when they are brought into the initial dialogue by being asked what they know about the topic and what they want to know. If their ques-

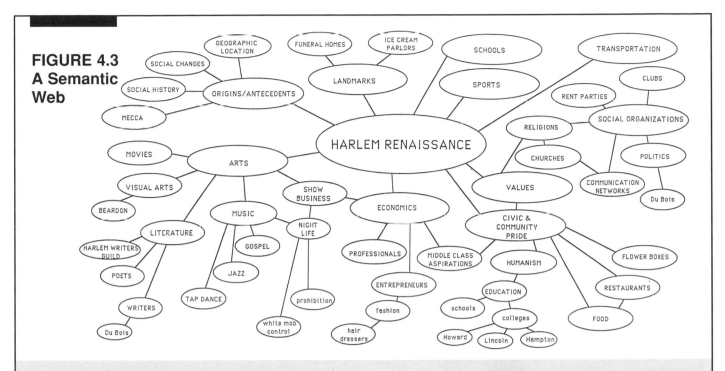

**FIGURE 4.3
A Semantic
Web**

Using a semantic web is an excellent way of eliciting what students know about a theme or topics they will be studying. Since some teachers are unfamiliar with webbing, the CICL Collaborative Professional Development at Teachers College, Columbia University, models the use of semantic webbing so that teachers have an opportunity to become familiar with it and see the benefits of its use.

The theme of the Harlem Renaissance elicited many kinds of responses during the brainstorming stage. These topics were later categorized—another activity that enables learners (teachers and students) to organize their learning. In this case, each teacher then chose a topic (such as architecture or writers during the Harlem Renaissance), researched it, and wrote a lesson plan addressing the topic (such as taking a tour of the major landmarks of Harlem). The CICL then staff pulled together all the lesson plans to produce a curriculum unit developed collaboratively by all the teachers. The process modeled how teacher/learner interests can shape a curriculum.

Marietta Saravia-Shore, 1993.

tions are written down and form a guide for some of the research on the topic, students are far more likely to be interested in doing the research than if the questions simply come out of a text. The teacher also obtains a better understanding of the students' previous knowledge about a subject—a pre-assessment, as it were—that can guide the planning of the lesson that follows.

CLASSROOM EXAMPLES

One way in which teachers can ensure recognition of students' contributions is to use "semantic webbing." At the beginning of learning a new topic, teachers can ask students what they know about that topic; the simplest way to do this is to brainstorm with the students a multi-tude of associations with the topic. The teacher (or one of the students) puts the topic— "culture," for example—in a center circle on the chalkboard and then records the students' associations in circles around the center circle.

As a next step, the class can discuss (and connect with lines) all the related aspects of "culture," making a spider's web of relationships on the board. This work can be expanded by categorizing the subtopics.

The teacher can also ask students what they want to know about the topic at hand. Students' questions, recorded for later use, can serve as guides for research. Students are more likely to be interested in researching a topic when they begin with their own real questions. Their real questions lead them on an ever-widening path of investigation.

Implementing this strategy can be as simple as asking children to voice their questions about a given topic at the beginning of a lesson. After gathering student questions, the teacher can ask whether any student already has information about the topic. Before drawing on books and other resources, the students themselves can be resources by using their own knowledge and prior experiences.

REFERENCES
Au and Jordan 1981; Boggs 1985; Coballes-Vega 1992; Gallimore, Boggs, and Jordan 1974; Heath 1983; Jordan 1981; Lee and Lee 1980; Protheroe and Barsdate 1992; Tharp 1989a, 1989b, 1991; Taylor 1983; Tharp 1992; Torres-Guzman 1992; Trueba, Jacobs, and Kirton 1990.

● STRATEGY 4.5: USE CULTURALLY RELEVANT CURRICULUM MATERIALS

Teachers use culturally relevant curriculum and instructional materials that recognize, incorporate, and accurately reflect students' racial heritage and the contributions of various ethnic groups.

DISCUSSION

Students' self-esteem is strengthened when they see and read about the contributions made by their own racial or ethnic group to the history and culture of the United States. Whenever possible, teachers adapt the curriculum to focus lessons on topics that are meaningful to students. This kind of focus allows students to practice language, thinking, reading, and writing skills in real, meaningful, and interactive situations. Students also come to realize that teachers value and appreciate each child's culture and language.

CLASSROOM EXAMPLES

Teachers can select texts or, if necessary, supplementary materials (such as children's literature written by a variety of authors) that incorporate the perspectives, voice, historical events, poetry, artwork, journals, and illustrations of the range of racial and ethnic groups that make up U.S. society (and that may well be represented in the classroom). Teachers can ask students to interview their parents about their history, including their culture, poetry, music, recipes, novels, and heroes. The student can videotape, audiotape, or write the interview and share it with the rest of the class.

In interviews conducted by the Latino Commission (Rodriguez 1992), high school students observed that they feel left out when the curriculum of the school contains nothing that relates to their own culture. Conversely, they feel that both they and their culture are valued when their culture is included in the curriculum. For younger students, children's books about young people in their own cultural context can provide avenues for discussion and comparison of the similarities and differences between the culture of their parents and that of the school or community in which they now live.

REFERENCES
Banks 1993; California State Department of Education 1986; Cummins 1986; Heath 1983; Knapp and Turnbull 1990; Rodriguez 1992; Saravia-Shore and Arvizu 1992; Staton-Spicer and Wulff 1984; Taylor 1983; Valverde, Feinberg, and Marquez 1980; Wong- Fillmore and Valadez 1986.

● STRATEGY 4.6: IDENTIFY AND DISPEL STEREOTYPES

Teachers use language and instructional resources that are nonsexist, nonracist, and nonethnocentric; if stereotypes are present in lectures or texts, teachers point them out to students.

DISCUSSION

If the teacher allows sexist or racist language and stereotypes to pass unchallenged, students will be harmed in two ways: (1) by the demeaning depiction of their group, which may become part of their self-concept, and (2) by the limitations they will feel on their ability to live and work harmoniously with others in their classroom and in their society.

Teachers can select texts or, if texts are unavailable, supplementary materials to address this issue. The supplementary materials should be written by a variety of authors who incorporate a wide range of perspectives on historical events, poetry, artwork, journals, music, and illustrations of women and men, as well as varied ethnic and racial groups. Teachers can also point out sexist language and ethnic, racial, or gender stereotypes in instructional materials.

CLASSROOM EXAMPLES

The teacher points out examples of sexist language, such as the use of "man" for "human" or the use of the pronoun "he" in referring to both men and women, and then asks how this makes the young people in the class feel.

To encourage the exploration of how it feels to be in another's shoes, the teacher can also ask students if they would like to be labeled "non-Eastern" because they live in the Western Hemisphere—just as many North Americans refer to those who live in the Eastern Hemisphere as "non-Western." The teacher might also ask white and Asian students whether they would prefer to be called "nonblack," in the same manner that blacks and Asians are often referred to as "nonwhite."

The teacher can also compare the dichotomy used in categorizations of racial groups in the United States (i.e., black and white) with the continuum of racial/ethnic groups in South America, where there are more than twenty such categories or distinctions. These striking differences lend themselves to a discussion of the social construction or definition of racial groups; students will enjoy the opportunity to research the history and derivation of these definitions.

REFERENCES
Boutte et al. 1993; Demetrulias 1991; Haw 1991; McIntosh 1983; Martinez and Dukes 1991; Rakow 1991; Sadker et al. 1989; Sadker, Sadker, and Long 1993; Valverde, Feinberg, and Marquez 1980.

● STRATEGY 4.7: CREATE CULTURALLY COMPATIBLE LEARNING ENVIRONMENTS

Teachers recognize the influence of students' learning styles, culture, and native language on the ways in which they learn and use language.

DISCUSSION

Research has shown that students learn more when their classrooms are compatible with their own cultural and linguistic experience (see Au 1980; National Coalition 1988; Jordan 1984, 1984; Saville-Troike 1978; Trueba and Delgado-Gaitan 1985). When the norms of interaction and communication in a classroom are very different from those to which the student has been accustomed, students experience confusion and anxiety, cannot attend to learning, and may not know how to appropriately seek the teacher's attention, get the floor, or participate in discussions. By acknowledging students' cultural norms and expectations concerning communication and social interaction, teachers can appropriately guide student participation in instructional activities.

Research on the effectiveness of culturally compatible classrooms has been conducted with Hawaiian children as well as with Navajo and African American children (see Au 1980; Pepper and Steven 1989; Little Soldier 1989; Gilbert and Gay 1985; Henry and Pepper 1990; Irvin 1990). The aspects of culture that influence classroom life most powerfully are those that affect the social organization of learning and the social expectations concerning communication.

The organization of the typical U.S. classroom is one of whole-class teaching in which the teacher as leader instructs, assigns text, and demonstrates to the whole class; this whole-class instruction is often followed by individual practice and assessment. By contrast, the Kamehameha Early Education Program (KEEP) found small-group classroom organization to be more culturally compatible for Hawaiian children (Au 1980). While a teacher works with one small group of students, the others are able to work independently in other small groups with a variety of peer teaching and learning interactions. A group of Navajo children was also found to benefit from small-group classroom organization but differed somewhat in demonstrating fewer offers of, and requests for, peer assistance (Little Soldier 1989).

A group of African American students worked most effectively when the social organization of the classroom involved group interactions and competitions in which one student performed in front of the class while the rest were an attentive and critical audience eager to discover errors and to replace the "performer" in front of their peers. Research showed that students performed most competently when speaking and interacting in complex ways— in their community church, for example, where expectations were compatible among adults and children (Heath 1982, 1983, 1986).

According to Tharp (1992), teaching and learning are more effective when they are contextualized in the experiences, skills, and values of the community and when learning is a joint productive activity involving both peers and teachers. Learning is furthered by "instructional conversations"—dialogues between teachers and learners about their common, shared, jointly experienced learning activities.

CLASSROOM EXAMPLES

A teacher notices that a Chinese American girl tends not to raise her hand to participate in discussions. The teacher discovers that the child is afraid to respond in front of the whole class because she is still learning English and is worried that other students will laugh at her. The teacher divides the class into groups of four to do collaborative research so that the girl can practice speaking in English with a smaller group of students.

Too often, when young people speak a language other than English and are learning English as a second language, teachers of ESL or reading in English may restrict their activities to the lowest level of decoding and phonics, levels that do not challenge the students intellectually. *Only when students have the opportunity to continue learning in their native language can they operate at their cognitive level and grow intellectually.* After reading a book or article in their native language, they can be challenged with questions of comprehension and application and analysis—the higher order thinking skills. Moll, Diaz, Estrada, and Lopes (1992) found that the level of questioning is much more restricted in ESL reading groups than in native-language reading groups.

Jordan, Tharp, and Baird-Vogt (1992) found that Hawaiian children's academic achievement increased when certain aspects of their home culture were integrated into the elementary classroom. The use of a culturally appropriate form of communication called "talk story" engaged the students more fully. Hawaiian students were also more comfortable in school when they were recognized as being able to take responsibility for maintaining the order and cleanliness of their classroom. In their homes, Hawaiian children have many responsibilities for the care of younger siblings and cooperate in doing household chores. They felt more "at home" when they could come in early, straighten up the room, and set out the work of the other students for the day. Teachers made the classroom more *culturally compatible* by learning about the culture of the home.

REFERENCES
Au 1980; Au and Jordan 1981; Au and Mason 1981; Bloome 1985; Calfee, Cazden, Duran, Griffin, Martus, and Willis 1981; Dunn, Beaudy, and Klavas 1989; Dunn and Griggs 1990; Hirst and Slavik 1989; Jordan, Tharp, and Baird-Vogt 1992; Michaels 1981; Moll, Diaz, Estrada, and Lopes 1992; Philips 1983; Saravia-Shore and Arvizu 1992; Teale 1986; Tharp 1992; Wong-Fillmore 1983.

● STRATEGY 4.8: USE COOPERATIVE LEARNING

Teachers use cooperative learning approaches that increase the likelihood of interethnic friendships and improved attitudes and behaviors toward classmates of different backgrounds. Methods that include group goals and individual accountability are the most effective.

DISCUSSION

One of the most difficult issues faced by teachers in multiethnic classrooms is that students, particularly those from ethnic groups suffering social discrimination, tend to cluster in groups based on ethnicity. Students may observe that one peer group draws itself apart and, in reaction, may come to feel that they have to do so as well.

To break down this defensive withdrawal into ethnic groups, students need to have time to get to know each other and to find that they share common ground, common problems, and common feelings. Participating in a small group over an extended period of time in a shared activity with a shared goal that can only be achieved by working together is one way to break down artificial barriers between students.

Students who have an opportunity to learn in cooperative learning groups with students of other racial and ethnic groups get to know their fellow students as real people rather than stereotypes. When students learn together and get to know one another, mutual respect and friendships can develop.

CLASSROOM EXAMPLES

The teacher assigns students to groups of five or six and gives each student a specific task in the scientific experiment they are to do collaboratively. One reads and sets up the materials for the experiment, one performs the experiment, another records it, another illustrates it, another reads the recorded experience to the rest of the class, and so forth.

Cooperative learning needs to be taught. Students need to learn appropriate social skills: to communicate, to listen and give feedback, to manage conflict, to take leadership, to contribute, and to take responsibility for a part of the task. Teachers need to allow groups ample time to "process" their own performance in a task by talking about their interaction and how it could be improved. Tasks that include positive interdependence as part of the activity—that is, tasks requiring each person in the group to be dependent on the whole group's doing well in order to achieve the goal—are more likely to be successful. "Jigsaw" tasks, for instance, which cannot be completed unless everyone helps or unless each participant learns one piece of the job and teaches the others, are especially effective. Cooperative learning is *not* simply having students sit next to each other; it involves structuring young people's need to communicate, to get to know one another, and to work together.

REFERENCES
Au 1980; Carbo, Dunn, and Dunn 1986; Coballes-Vega 1992; Dunn 1989; Garcia 1992; Hirst and Slavik 1989; Johnson and Johnson 1982; Johnson, Johnson, and Holubec 1994; Philips 1972; Saravia-Shore 1993; Slavin 1980, 1986, 1991.

● STRATEGY 4.9: CAPITALIZE ON STUDENTS' CULTURE, LANGUAGE, AND EXPERIENCES

Teachers construct lessons in ways consistent with students' home-community culture and language to take advantage of students' cognitive experiences and to allow students opportunities to engage in behaviors conducive to achievement.

DISCUSSION

Learning is more likely to occur when young people's expectations about how to interact with adults and other children match the teachers' and administrators' expectations for such interaction.

Saravia-Shore and Martinez (1992) found that Puerto Rican high school dropouts who had succeeded in an alternative high school credited their increased achievement to the difference in the way they were treated by the adults in each school. They reported that they felt they were treated as children in the regular high school but as adults in the alternative school. Their new teachers expected that they would do their homework, since they had enrolled in order to pass the GED examination. Moreover, teachers in the alternative high school showed an understanding of the students' cultural norm of having families at an early age and being responsible for other members of their family. Since they knew the students had other (and very pressing) responsibilities—caring for their families and working to support them—they did not criticize students for being late to class, so long as their work was completed. Simply put, the students felt that the teachers cared about their success.

CLASSROOM EXAMPLES

Jordan, Tharp, and Baird-Vogt (1992) have shown that when teachers incorporate the home culture's expected patterns of interaction and discourse, students feel more comfortable in school and participate more actively in learning situations. When students are used to caring for other children at home, they have a foundation for cooperative learning and peer teaching, given the opportu-

nity and the support of the teacher. If they are accustomed to having responsibilities in caring for their physical environment at home, they feel comfortable in caring and managing the school environment.

References
Au 1980; Au and Mason 1981; Calfee, Cazden, Duran, Griffin, Martus, and Willis 1981; Heath 1986; Jacob and Jordan 1987; Jordan, Tharp, and Baird-Vogt 1992; Knapp and Turnbull 1990; Philips 1983; Saravia-Shore and Martinez 1992; Torres-Guzman 1992.

STRATEGIES FOR LINGUISTICALLY DIVERSE STUDENTS

The term "linguistically and culturally diverse" is a relatively new one—and one that conveys little sense of the vast differences among the various populations identified in this manner. Such populations (Native Americans, Mexican Americans, Chicanos, Puerto Ricans, Cubans and other Latinos, Russians, Chinese, and Southeast Asians, among others) have long been perceived by the majority society as linguistically, cognitively, socially, and educationally vulnerable because of their minority culture and lack of ability to speak English; the period of greatest vulnerability for young people in these groups coincides with the critical age for schooling (Cavazos 1989).

Very simply, this population is best defined as the set of students who enter the formal process of education from homes and communities in which English is not the primary language of communication. Since 1980, according to the Center for Demographic Policy (CDP) of the Institute for Educational Leadership (Center for Demographic Policy 1993), the number of U.S. residents for whom English is a foreign language has increased by more than one-third—to 31.8 million in 1990, or 14 percent of the population of the United States. In 1990, six of ten immigrants were from either Mexico, or Central or South America, the CDP reports. After English, Spanish is the language most commonly spoken in the United States.

Over time, a variety of social and educational programs have aimed to rid this population of the characteristics that are perceived to place them "at risk" (Barona and Garcia 1990). Recent research has redefined the nature of our linguistically and culturally diverse students' educational vulnerability. It has destroyed stereotypes and myths

LEADING LANGUAGES

One in seven U.S. residents speaks a language other than English at home, according to data released by the Census Bureau.

The bureau says 31.8 million Americans speak a foreign language at home, up from 23.1 million a decade ago, according to an article in the May 12, 1993, *Education Week.*

FIGURE 4.4
Fifty Most Common Languages: 1990

Language	Total Speakers Over 5 Years Old 1990	Percentage Change From 1980
Spanish	17,339,172	50.1%
French	1,702,176	8.3%
German	1,547,049	–3.7%
Italian	1,308,648	–19.9%
Chinese	1,249,213	97.7%
Tagalog	843,251	86.6%
Polish	723,483	–12.4%
Korean	626,478	127.2%
Vietnamese	507,069	149.5%
Portuguese	429,860	19.0%
Japanese	427,657	25.0%
Greek	388,260	–5.4%
Arabic	355,150	57.4%
Hindi, Urdu and related	331,484	155.1%
Russian	241,798	38.5%
Yiddish	213,064	–33.5%
Thai	206,266	131.6%
Persian	201,865	84.7%
French Creole	187,658	654.1%
Armenian	149,694	46.3%
Navajo	148,530	20.6%
Hungarian	147,902	–17.9%
Hebrew	144,292	45.5%
Dutch	142,684	–2.6%
Mon-Khmer	127,441	676.3%

Source: Census Bureau. This figure is reprinted with permission from *Education Week* (May 12, 1993), p. 3.

and laid a foundation on which to reconceptualize existing educational practices and launch new initiatives. This new foundation recognizes the homogeneity/heterogeneity within and between such populations.

Current thinking emphasizes the value of speaking more than one language. Prior to this recognition of the advantages of bilingualism, children were often considered "disadvantaged" when they spoke a language other than English. Now a child's first language is considered a resource on which to build "additive" bilingualism (learning a second language while becoming literate in their first language).

Public school systems have been among the first institutions to tackle this increasing societal and cultural diversity, reports the Center for Demographic Policy (1993); consider these examples:

In Prince George's County, Maryland (outside Washington, D.C.), for example, students in the school system speak more than 100 languages. Programs geared at helping students learn both English as a second language as well as understanding cultural differences are offered throughout the school system.

In Arlington, Virginia (also outside D.C.), one in three students is an immigrant who speaks one of 50 languages. Arlington also offers programs for non-English-speaking students. Arlington has taken an approach that is somewhat different from others. Students receive several hours a day of intensive English instruction and spend the rest of the day with native English-speaking peers for lessons in other subjects.

Texas, with the third largest non-English-speaking population, launched a program [in November 1992] which is aimed at helping immigrant parents. The program, Even Start, teaches everything from English to coping with American culture. The immigrant mothers go to school for four hours and eat breakfast and lunch with their children in the cafeteria.

No one set of descriptions or prescriptions will suffice. It is worthwhile, however, to consider a set of intertwined commonalties that deserve particular attention; these commonalties include the bilingual/bicultural and the instructional circumstances of these populations. The brief discussion that follows provides a simple overview of recent research that has addressed the effective instruction of linguistically diverse students.

One trend in the field of foreign and second language learning that is affecting the education of linguistically diverse students is the popularity of dual-language programs. In these dual-language programs, monolingual English-speaking students spend part of the day immersed in a second-language learning situation—learning children's literature, songs, and sometimes math and science in a second language. In some of these programs, students who are native speakers of the foreign language are in the same classroom. Thus, English speakers can use their new language with both the teacher and with native language speakers with whom they share the classroom.

Some bilingual programs are also dual-language or two-way programs that follow the same pattern, with two sets of students learning a second language from each other as well as from their teacher. Monolingual English-speaking students learn Spanish, for example, while native Spanish speakers learn English as a second language. This new perspective—viewing language minority students as resources for monolingual English-speaking students—follows the trend of building on the strengths that students bring rather than concentrating solely on that which they still need to learn. Another advantage to this approach is that it facilitates the education of children in integrated classrooms rather than the segregation of children on the basis of their ability to speak and write English.

Today educators prefer that students develop linguistic facility in both English and their home language, rather than develop English only and lose the home language, only to have to relearn a second language later in their school years. Research shows that students' *cognitive* development proceeds more readily in their native language and that students learn content more easily in the native language while they are learning English as a second language.

Life in today's multicultural society makes it easy to see the benefits of proficiency in more than one language. Consequently, teachers are encouraging young people to learn in two languages rather than learning only in English. This approach is linked to a new emphasis on the integration of content and the learning of English as a second language (ESL), as opposed to the traditional focus on ESL as a discrete area.

An interdisciplinary approach to curriculum—breaking from many decades of separation among the various disciplines—is a powerful ally in teaching culturally and linguistically diverse children. Instead of teaching reading as a discrete subject, for instance, teachers now view reading as a process for learning concepts and exploring subjects and their connections. Cooperative learning groups

and peer tutoring work splendidly in conjunction with computer-mediated language learning. And parents are partners in their children's schooling, as well as resources for teachers in understanding young people's cultural patterns of communication and interaction.

The following strategies offer a synthesis of those which research emphasizes as most promising in raising the achievement levels of linguistically diverse students. Among the teaching strategies strongly recommended are the following:

- Affirm and build on students' culture, language, and experiences.
- Incorporate dual-language strategies; integrate English speakers with English language learners.
- Use integrated, whole language approaches.
- Teach the second language through content.
- Use "sheltered English" strategies.
- Practice English in cooperative problem-solving groups.
- Use cross-age and peer tutoring; integrate native English speakers with English language learners.
- Allow community language norms in informal learning situations.
- Use interdisciplinary, thematic teaching.
- Use computers and peer tutors to enhance language learning.

REFERENCES

Barona and Garcia 1990; Bredo, Henry, and McDermott 1990; Cavazos 1989; Center for Demographic Policy 1993; Chan 1983; Cummins 1981; Cummins and Swain 1986; DeAvila and Duncan 1980; Dolly, Blaine, and Power 1988; First and Willshire-Carrera 1988; Hakuta 1986; Hakuta and Garcia 1989; Hakuta and Gould 1987; Ima and Rumbaut 1989; Matute-Bianchi 1986; Ogbu 1987; Pang 1990; Wong-Fillmore 1983; Wong-Fillmore and Valadez 1986.

● STRATEGY 4.10: CREATE TRULY BILINGUAL CLASSROOMS

Teachers provide literacy and content instruction for students in their native language while they are learning English.

DISCUSSION

Students who come to school with a home language other than English learn more from programs in which their native language is *one* of the languages of instruction.

Photo courtesy of Monica Lee Photography, San Francisco, CA

In a 3rd grade classroom we see rural Mexican-American children engaged in purposeful activities. Students are brainstorming solutions, reading from big books, and working in small or large groups. Notice that the experience chart on the left is written in both English and Spanish, thus demonstrating respect for the primary language of many of the students and helping them to translate more easily to English.

By continuing to learn subject content in their native language, such students do not fall behind in their academic subjects while acquiring English. Potentially bilingual students who are in developmental or late-exit bilingual programs for five years seem to progress at a faster rate in subjects in presented in English than do their counterparts in early-exit bilingual programs.

Potentially bilingual students are able to continue to learn in their home language while learning English; they continue to develop cognitively and acquire skills (such as reading) that can later be transferred to English. Once they have learned the vocabulary in English, they can comprehend what they decode. The context of learning is more difficult if it is entirely in the student's second language. These students also risk losing the opportunity to become bilingual and biliterate.

A school that respects the language and culture of its ethnically and linguistically diverse students and parents or guardians can develop educational situations that maximize the resources these students bring to school. Instead of being confused and distressed by trying to cope in a language they cannot understand, students can continue to learn content and skills and develop a feeling of efficacy as well as belonging to their new school. If the school context does not allow for this linguistic and cultural diversity, students are more likely to feel confused, adrift, and alienated.

CLASSROOM EXAMPLES

When the number of students in a school who speak the same language merits the establishment of a bilingual program, the practice of encouraging young people to learn content in their native language while learning English as a second language is likely to increase their learning overall. Students learn content (mathematics, science, social studies) in their native language until they have learned sufficient English as a second language to learn academic content in English.

With the help of such programs as LogoWriter O™, students can learn to use computers to do programming and word processing in their native language. In one 6th grade classroom, for example, new immigrant students compared dwellings around the world. They saw photographs of different types of dwellings and learned that cultural responses to different ecological systems were one of the reasons for differences among earlier cultures. Igloos were adaptations to their environment, just as the adobe "apartments" of Native Americans were adaptations to theirs; the builders of both types of dwellings used available resources. Using Spanish, students learned to program geometrical shapes to represent igloos and Anasazi dwellings and to write about them, also in Spanish.

REFERENCES
California State Department of Education 1986; Carter and Chatfield 1986; Cummins 1981, 1986; Cziko 1992; Hakuta and Garcia 1989; Hakuta and Alvarez 1992; Hakuta and Gould 1987; Chamot and O'Malley 1994; Ramirez, Yeun, Ramey, and Pasta 1990; Saravia-Shore and Arvizu 1992; Wong-Fillmore and Valadez 1986.

● STRATEGY 4.11: INCORPORATE DUAL-LANGUAGE STRATEGIES

Teachers incorporate dual-language strategies in the classroom.

DISCUSSION

In dual-language learning situations, students proficient in languages other than English learn more effectively. They continue to learn content in their native language while learning English as a second language by interacting with monolingual English-speaking students who are also learning a second language.

First, young people's native language is affirmed and respected when it becomes a subject being taught to their English-speaking peers. Second, potentially bilingual students can share their native-language expertise as peer tutors to English-speaking students who are learning a second language for enrichment. Third, the long-term gains are greater since, in this additive bilingual strategy, students proficient in languages other than English become bilingual and biliterate. Fourth, students are not segregated into classes for potentially bilingual students or monolingual English-speaking students; all are integrated and become bilingual over a period of five or six years.

In some schools, students spend half the day in an immersion situation, learning content in English, and the other half immersed in learning content in the other language. In other schools, students initially learn specific subjects such as math, art, music, or physical education in their second language. Monolingual English-speaking students are immersed in a second language, such as Spanish, with native Spanish speakers.

CLASSROOM EXAMPLES

Teachers enhance the learning of a second language by structuring informal situations in which students who are proficient in languages other than English can be peer tutors for monolingual English-speaking students learning a second language, and vice versa. Second-language learning for both groups is enhanced when they can communicate informally at certain times during the school day in their second language. This alternative social organization of learning a second language does not rely solely on the teacher as the locus of teaching. Students become teachers and resources for one another; *second language learning is reciprocal.*

Students learning Spanish as a second language, for example, can be encouraged to use the language in functional situations. Younger students can learn aspects of Latino cultures by using recipes in Spanish to cook Mexican, Dominican, and Puerto Rican dishes. Or they can learn about the music of each culture by learning to sing songs in Spanish. Older students may learn about the rain forests in Central and South America and graph the number of medicines derived from plants in this ecosystem.

REFERENCES
Deem and Marshall 1980; Garcia 1987/88, 1988, 1991, 1992; Gee 1982; Herbert 1987; Krashen and Biber 1988; Lindholm 1988; Saravia-Shore and Arvizu 1992; Short, Crandall, and Christian 1989.

● STRATEGY 4.12: USE INTEGRATED, HOLISTIC APPROACHES

Teachers use integrated, holistic approaches to language experiences for second-language learners instead of rote drill and practice. Students practice English in oral and written forms in ways that are nonthreatening, have a real purpose, and are enjoyable.

DISCUSSION

Rote drill and practice are boring and lack meaning for young people. Holistic experiences are much more engaging. For instance, students can use language-experience approaches to learn science in English. In doing so, they connect speaking, writing, and reading; since their oral language is written down for later reading, they can understand what they read, and their reading has meaning.

Research on the learning of second languages shows the value of an increased emphasis on "communicative competence" (Carpenter 1983; Valdez-Pierce 1991; Garcia 1987, 1988). To be competent in communicating, students need to go beyond mastering the rules of grammar. They must learn how to apply social and cultural rules as well. Students learning a second language must learn, for

Photo courtesy of Monica Lee Photography, San Francisco, CA

In schools that respect the language and culture of a diverse student population, youngsters are less likely to be confused, adrift, and lacking in self-esteem. In this picture, the young girls are learning content but are still able to use their home language, Spanish, to acquire understandings. Notice the numbers spelled out in both Spanish and English.

example, that the informal language used with peers and friends may not be appropriate in more formal situations—for example, making a request of a teacher or being interviewed for a job. Students must learn how to take turns in a conversation, when to talk and keep still, how to "demonstrate" listening, and when to be direct or indirect. These culturally appropriate ways of speaking can be learned when students hear stories, see dramas, read books with dialogue, and write and act out plays.

Classroom Examples

The teacher begins reading a children's story by first showing the illustrations and asking the students to describe them. After reading the story, the teacher asks a student to retell it. Subsequently, the teacher may ask the students to write the story as a play with a different ending or to write a continuation of the story. This technique helps young people see the connection between writing and reading.

The teacher asks students to break into groups of five. Each group is responsible for writing and illustrating a story. Group members must first negotiate who will do which tasks in English, then which events to illustrate. They must agree on the sequence of events and number them sequentially. One way of structuring this activity is to provide pages labeled "main characters," "problem to be solved," "first event," "second event," "third event," and "resolution of problem."

In another example, students are given a painting and asked to describe what they see and how it makes them feel. The teacher or another student writes down their words. The teacher places the written words of the student under a postcard of the painting. The student is later asked to read what has been written.

High school students can be assigned to watch one scene of a play that takes place in the culture they are learning about. They then form groups and write the scene as they recall it. After the groups respond to each others' efforts and refine the dialogue (perhaps by referring to the video of the play), they can act out the scene. A subsequent assignment might call on them to change the role and status of one of the characters and decide how that character would speak: What might he or she say differently? How would the other characters respond? The students can then act out the scene, using the same basic content but saying things in a different way to someone with a different social role.

Students can also imagine real-life situations in which they might find themselves and act out the parts of

different speakers, alternating in social roles. They can get feedback from peers who are members of the linguistic group they are studying.

References
Heath 1986; Garcia 1987/88; Krashen 1982; Ovando 1993.

● Strategy 4.13: Use Subject Matter to Teach Language

Teachers use subject matter, rather than specific linguistic skill exercises, to teach English to students with limited proficiency in English.

Discussion

The learning of language cannot be separated from what is being learned. Too often, students with limited proficiency in English are required to learn the abstract or grammatical aspects of language as opposed to the functional and communicative aspects of language. These more important functional skills are best developed in conjunction with the learning of content material.

When students learn a second language in a *functional* way (similar to the way they learned their first language), the process has real meaning, and learning makes sense and is more interesting. Students also benefit by learning cross-cultural skills. Learning greetings in a second language, as well as the "polite" behavior associated with that language, will enable young people to communicate more easily in their new culture. Learning how to request food at a dinner table requires basic grammar and "polite" behavior. Students can go on to discuss how polite behavior differs in different cultures, and what it means in the classroom and in the school cafeteria.

Classroom Examples

Instead of removing students from a content lesson in mathematics because they are not yet proficient in English, the teacher can pair bilingual and monolingual students in small groups and provide math-related tasks within those groups. Bilingual students will assist the monolingual students in completing these tasks while providing natural models of language development within the content domain.

Pairs of students may perform a simple experiment in their classroom: They are to find out "what will happen if. . . ?" They are guided by labels on the objects they use. Students write the steps of their experiment in the form of an experience chart and tell what happened when they followed the steps. If they are stuck, they can ask another pair of students for help. The sequence of steps is then written and may be illustrated with pictures. Another day, they can use the experience chart to practice reading aloud in English.

For older students who have learned the processes of math (addition, subtraction, multiplication, division) in their native language, and particularly for those who already know the Arabic number system, a review of the math process in English is an effective way of learning functional English. When young people understand the process in numerical form, they can learn the vocabulary and the rules for asking questions and stating solutions.

References
Carter and Chatfield 1986; Cuevas 1984; Garcia 1987/88; Lucas, Henze, and Donato 1990; Wong-Fillmore and Valadez 1986.

● Strategy 4.14: Use Sheltered English Strategies

In multilingual schools that are too linguistically diverse to form bilingual classrooms, teachers further the learning of English for students who are proficient in languages other than English by teaching content-embedded English as a second language and by using "sheltered English" strategies.

Discussion

For multilingual schools that are too linguistically diverse to form bilingual classrooms, sheltered English and content-embedded English-as-a-second-language programs are beneficial to students who are proficient in languages other than English. Pull-out programs should be avoided; they stigmatize children. Care must be taken, however, to allow students ample time to use English themselves and not simply to be a passive "audience" for the teacher.

Classroom Examples

The "sheltered English" strategy makes the learning of subject matter simple and comprehensible. Visuals are used as referents for vocabulary; language is simplified.

Grammatical structures are presented sequentially, and vocabulary is presented in reasonable quantities. Teachers provide many examples and hands-on activities, so students can comprehend abstract as well as concrete instructional materials.

The teacher can demonstrate an activity and describe simply what she is doing. As she draws a face, she tells the children, "I am drawing eyes," and "I am drawing a mouth," and "These are teeth." The visual references make comprehension quicker and easier, and the modeling of language enables children to learn new grammatical structures. Even the use of drawing as a teaching device may model for students the effectiveness of nonverbal means of mastering their new language and new culture; this activity may lead to the use of drawing as a tool for peer tutoring as well.

References
Cummins 1984; Edward, Wesche, Krashen, Clement, and Krudenier 1984; Garcia 1987/88, 1988, 1991, 1992; Krashen 1982, 1985.

● Strategy 4.15: Practice English by Solving Problems in Cooperative Groups

Teachers organize classrooms into flexible, heterogeneous, cooperative learning groups composed of native and non-native speakers of English in order to give language-minority and limited-English-proficient students opportunities to practice English in problem-solving situations.

Discussion

Students proficient in languages other than English learn more by being *actively engaged in cooperative learning* than by being passive listeners. Students whose native language is something other than English benefit from being in cooperative learning groups with native English speakers, since they can hear a native model of English and practice their English in authentic communicative situations.

Teachers who structure cooperative learning situations for students proficient in languages other than English enable their students to become more actively engaged in learning. Potentially bilingual students need to practice generating and rehearsing their second language. Small groups in which each child has a specific role and specific tasks enable youngsters to learn more than if they are merely passive listeners. For this reason, *cooperative learning groups* are more productive than whole-class instruction, because small groups (three or four students) challenge children to use language more frequently. Young people need to be grouped around meaningful tasks so that they use language for *work-related* communication. Cooperative strategies have been demonstrated to work well with Chicano (Garcia 1991), Laotian, Cambodian, Hmong (Ima, Galang, Lee, Dinh Te 1991), and Japanese students.

CLASSROOM EXAMPLES

In a junior high science class, students first identify some of the problems in their neighborhood. They then collaboratively develop a questionnaire to use in interviewing people in the community to find out what they identify as neighborhood problems. If their community has many residents who speak a language other then English, they may need to have a second version of the questionnaire in that language. After forming teams to interview community members about the neighborhood problems, they return to the school and then record the responses and graph them by frequency. They can then discuss whether there is a problem that they can work together to solve, what resources they need to solve it, and the pros and cons of various suggestions for achieving a solution.

In another example, younger students may be assigned to research one of two groups: the Algonquian speakers and the Iroquoian speakers. Their goal is to discover the adaptive strategies each group used to take advantage of the environment for their dwellings, clothing, food, and transportation. The students are assigned to different roles, such as researcher, recorder, reporter, illustrator, or graph maker (to graph the results of the research).

The teacher gives each group a coloring book containing line drawings of people from the Algonquian and Iroquoian nations pursuing many activities of daily life. The students can interpret the drawings to identify means of transportation, materials from which dwellings were made, and so forth. They display their findings on a chart provided by the teacher, and they can also write a brief narrative describing the drawing.

REFERENCES
Cummins 1986; DeAvila and Duncan 1979; Garcia 1991, 1992; Ima, Galang, Lee, and Dinh Te 1991; Saravia-Shore 1993; Slavin 1980, 1986, 1991; Tharp and Gallimore 1991.

● STRATEGY 4.16: USE CROSS-AGE AND PEER TUTORING

In bilingual programs, teachers use peer tutoring, including cross-age tutoring, to engage English-speaking and limited-English-proficient students in conversations that lead to enhanced literacy and language acquisition.

DISCUSSION

For many students whose culture emphasizes the care of younger children by their older siblings (Puerto Rican, Hawaiian, and Chicano cultures, for instance), teachers have a foundation on which to build cross-age peer tutoring in school. Research shows that learning is enhanced both for those who are tutored and for the tutors themselves. Heterogeneous cross-ability grouping promotes student tutoring through the sharing of different skills in different contexts; for instance, a student who is still learning English may be a strong math student who can assist an English-speaking classmate with a mathematics project.

Teachers can provide learning opportunities for students who are proficient in languages other than English by organizing their classroom to include cross-age tutoring and peer tutoring. Students who are proficient in another language, such as Spanish, can provide language models and practice for monolingual English speakers learning Spanish. In some learning situations, Spanish can be used to converse about a shared activity. In another situation in which English is the primary language, the roles of the tutor and tutee can be reversed.

CLASSROOM EXAMPLES

Students are studying number systems. Using the chalkboard, a student who speaks only English demonstrates the use of zero in the Arabic number system to a native Spanish speaker by showing math problems and then working with the other student to solve them. After learning the Mayan number system, the native Spanish speaker can then demonstrate, in Spanish, the Mayan number system and its use of zero and place to show its meaning to the English-speaking student.

REFERENCES
Moll, Diaz, Estrada, and Lopes 1992

● STRATEGY 4.17: RESPECT COMMUNITY LANGUAGE NORMS

Teachers demonstrate respect for each student's language and do not prevent bilingual students from alternating between English and their native language (code switching) while they work together.

DISCUSSION

The most important consideration in teaching is that *communication be accomplished*. In many bilingual populations, language alternation (code switching) is frequently used for more effective communication. In conversations, either teacher or student may change the language in midstream to catch the listener's attention, to give emphasis, to clarify, to elaborate, or to address those in a group who may understand the second language more readily. Therefore, students and teachers should be able to readily use these naturally occurring alternations to achieve communication in the classroom.

In discussing the whole language approach, in which language is taught naturally as it occurs within any social environment, Goodman (1986) has noted, "Whole language programs respect the learners—who they are, where they come from, how they talk, what they read, and what experiences they [have] already had." Both Edelsky (1986) and Huerta-Macias and Quintero (1992) include code switching as part of this whole language approach.

CLASSROOM EXAMPLES

In a reading exercise conducted in English, a student hesitates in answering a comprehension question posed by the teacher. The teacher rephrases the question in the child's native language, and the child proudly responds to the question in her native language. In this scenario, the teacher focuses on the goal of story comprehension and alternates language use to achieve this goal.

In a family literacy program, five families come together for an hour and a half once a week after school. Their teacher conducts the classes in both Spanish and English, alternating according to the linguistic abilities and preferences of both parents and children. This strategy enables parents and children to feel comfortable in expressing themselves in either language. Their activities include conversing, reading, writing, and art projects. The parents tend to use Spanish to express themselves; the

teacher alternates between speaking Spanish with the parents and English with the children. The children also use both languages freely as they speak to their parents, their brothers and sisters, and the teacher.

In developing literacy, the specific language used is not as important as encouraging communication between parents and children. The intent here is to use the language skills of the parents as a resource, so that they can continue assisting their children with reading and writing

Photo courtesy of Robert Kerly

Teachers who demonstrate sincere respect for their pupils and are willing to learn about their students' home-community culture are more apt to be effective instructors because they promote students' self-confidence and relate instruction to students' backgrounds. While recognizing the role of the home culture, the effective teacher does not lose sight of each student's distinctiveness as a learner with unique needs and capabilities.

skills at home. This communication—and the development of an enjoyment of reading and writing together—are the primary goals of this approach. Other outcomes include developing respect for the parents' native language, helping the student to develop biliteracy, and developing the native language as a resource while acquiring literacy in English.

REFERENCES
Bowman 1989; Carter and Chatfield 1986; Duran 1981; Edelsky 1986; Garcia 1988, 1991, 1992; Garcia, Maez, and Gonzalez 1983; Genishi 1981; Goodman 1986; Huerta 1980; Huerta-Macias and Quintero 1992; Poplack 1981; Valdez-Fallis 1977; Zentella 1992.

● STRATEGY 4.18: USE THEMATIC, INTERDISCIPLINARY TEACHING

Teachers integrate the learning of subject matter and the learning of a second language by providing learning opportunities related to a theme.

DISCUSSION

Students proficient in languages other than English can learn content with greater comprehension if their learning is *interdisciplinary*. Linguistically diverse students have been shown to benefit from interdisciplinary approaches. For students learning English as a second language, thematic approaches enhance learning and comprehension, because the new learning is incremental and added to a theme that the students already understand. Having a base vocabulary related to the theme enables students to have a context in which to fit new learning from the various disciplines. And vocabulary is reinforced by its use in different subject contexts.

Focusing on a theme and relating various disciplines to that theme enables students to better understand each new area, since it is connected to a known core. When there is a theme, the vocabulary and skills can be developed in connection with the content. This approach provides coherence to students who are proficient in languages other than English; instead of trying to learn about several separate and distinct areas with diverse vocabularies simultaneously, they can work within a broad, but unifying, theme.

CLASSROOM EXAMPLES

The bilingual science program *Descubrimiento* (DeAvila and Duncan 1980) is an example of an interdisciplinary program that integrates science content and processes, foreign language learning, and English as a second language. Because students set up, conduct, analyze, report, and write up the experiments as group members, they can learn a second language, either English or Spanish, while they are learning science skills and content. They also learn to work cooperatively. All the skills of communication in each language (on different days) are used to learn, question, record, and share what has been learned from the science experiment.

REFERENCES
Carter and Chatfield 1986; Garcia 1992; Gardner 1983; Krashen 1982, 1985; Lucas, Henze, and Donato 1990; Pease-Alvarez, Garcia, and Espinosa 1991.

● STRATEGY 4.19: USE COMPUTERS AND PEER TUTORS TO ENHANCE LANGUAGE LEARNING

Teachers provide students with the use of a computer in learning English as a second language.

DISCUSSION

Teachers who create situations in which two students can use a common computer enable students to more readily learn English as a second language. Computers can assist potentially bilingual students in learning English as a second language. With a word processing program and a partner who is also a second-language learner, students have the opportunity to generate language, create dialogues, interview each other, assist each other by being an audience for the other's writing, and assist with corrections of vocabulary and grammar.

The ways in which computers are integrated into the social organization of the classroom make a difference in their effectiveness for second language learning. One computer shared by a whole class of students does not allow for as much language practice as does pairing students on a computer and giving them interactive tasks. Scheduling students in this way allows for more sessions at the computer per week and also allows the computer to be used for communication tasks. If ESL students have access to a

CLASSROOM EXAMPLES

A teacher can show a photograph of two people interacting to a pair of students at the computer. Their task is to imagine the identity of each person and to develop a dialogue in which each of them assumes the voice of one of the people in the photograph. Each responds to the other and can give the other feedback if he or she is "out of character" or needs assistance with the activity.

The teacher can structure situations in which students use computers to strengthen writing skills in their second language by providing assignments that have an immediate communicative purpose. Teachers assign two students to a computer and ask each to provide peer tutoring to the other. Students can interview each other via the computer, one asking questions via the computer and the other writing the answers.

Another activity that students find enjoyable and rewarding is writing a play or a news story together. If the task is to write a news story, one student can act as the correspondent and interview the "newsmaker" or "informant." Students can also interview one another about their various countries of origin and write a book for the whole class by combining their individual accounts.

At the high school level, as an ongoing classroom project, bilingual students can learn to use desktop publishing software to collaboratively produce a bilingual monthly newsletter that they can exchange with a bilingual class in a "sister school" in another district. The newsletter may include poems, jokes, community surveys, methods of dealing with problems at school, or interviews with conflict mediators, faculty members, or parents who tell about their jobs. By exchanging newsletters with a "sister school" (and possibly including a questions column in which students from the other school can tell how they deal with concerns and problems), students are using language to learn about their real-life concerns.

In using computers, teachers challenge students to provide more of their own interpretation and to generate their own text, rather than simply perform rote drill-and-practice activities.

REFERENCES
Mehan 1989; Mehan et al. 1985; Moll, Diaz, Estrada, and Lopes 1992; Philips 1972; Roberts et al. 1987; Sayers 1989; Sayers and Brown 1987.

Photo courtesy of Lynn Ward, El Centro, CA

When youngsters are able to work with many different materials and resources, including newer technologies such as computers and electronic networks, they are likely to learn more. These students clustered about one computer are also able to share ideas about the assigned activity.

computer laboratory, however, they will have even more possibilities to generate language together with a partner who can give them feedback.

The kinds of software used for language learning also make a difference. Some language-learning programs simply translate drill and practice into computer formats. Other software—word processing programs or programs such as LogoWriter, which combines language, programming, and geometry—challenge students to generate sentences and to use the second language for communication purposes, thus promoting greater language learning. Desktop publishing software is another way to motivate students to write in their second language, since they know that their writing will be edited collaboratively and then published, to be read by classmates and parents or guardians.

Computers can also be used to hook into electronic networks and correspond with "sister schools" in the same city, in another state, or even in another country. Individual correspondence or bilingual newsletters written by students can develop their writing and literacy skills in both their native and second languages.

BIBLIOGRAPHY

Arvizu, S.F. (1992). "Home-School Linkages: A Cross-Cultural Approach to Parent Participation." In *Cross-Cultural Literacy: Ethnographies of Communication in Multiethnic Classrooms,* edited by M. Saravia-Shore and S.F. Arvizu. New York: Garland.

Au, K.H. (1979). "Using the Experience-Text-Relationship Method with Minority Children." *Reading Teacher* 32, 6: 677-679.

Au, K.H. (Summer 1980). "Participation Structures in a Reading Lesson with Hawaiian Children: Analysis of a Culturally Appropriate Instructional Event." *Anthropology and Education Quarterly* 11, 2: 91-115.

Au, K.H., and C. Jordan. (1981). "Teaching Reading to Hawaiian Children: Finding a Culturally Appropriate Solution." In *Culture in the Bilingual Classroom,* edited by Henry Trueda, et al. Rowley, Mass.: Newbury House.

Au, K.H., and J.M. Mason. (1981). "Social Organizational Factors in Learning to Read: The Balance of Rights Hypothesis." *Reading Research Quarterly* 17, 1: 115-152.

Banks, J.A. (1993). "Approaches to Multicultural Curriculum Reform." In *Multicultural Education,* edited by J.A. Banks and C.A.M. Banks. Boston: Allyn and Bacon.

Barona, A., and E. Garcia. (1990). *Children at Risk: Poverty, Minority Status, and Other Issues in Educational Equity.* Washington, D.C.: National Association of School Psychologists.

Bloome, D. (1985). "Reading as a Social Process." *Language Arts* 62: 134-142.

Boggs, S.T. (1985). *Speaking, Relating and Learning: A Study of Hawaiian Children at Home and at School.* Norwood, N.J.: Ablex.

Boutte, G.S., et al. (November 1993). "Racial Issues in Education: Real or Imagined?" *Young Children* 49, 1: 19-23.

Bowman, B.T. (October 1989). "Educating Language-Minority Children: Challenges and Opportunities." *Phi Delta Kappan* 71, 2: 118-120.Bredo, E., M. Henry, and R.P. McDermott. (1990). "The Cultural Organization of Teaching and Learning." *Harvard Educational Review* 60, 2: 247-258.

Calfee, R., C. Cazden, R. Duran, M. Griffin, M. Martus, and H. Willis. (1981). *Designing Reading Instruction for Cultural Minorities: The Case of Kamehameha Early Education Program.* Cambridge, Mass.: Harvard University, Graduate School of Education. (ERIC Document Reproduction Service No. ED 215039).

California State Department of Education. (1981). *School and Language Minority Students: A Theoretical Framework.* Los Angeles: Evaluation, Dissemination, and Assessment Center, California State University.

California State Department of Education. (1986). *Beyond Language: Social and Cultural Factors in Schooling Language Minority Students.* Los Angeles: Evaluation, Dissemination, and Assessment Center, California State University.

Carbo, M. (December 1978). "Teaching Reading with Talking Books." *The Reading Teacher* 32, 3: 267-273.

Carbo, M. (1989). *How to Record Books for Maximum Reading Gains.* Roslyn Heights N.Y.: National Reading Styles Institute.

Carbo, M., R. Dunn, and K. Dunn. (1986). *Teaching Students to Read Through Their Individual Learning Styles.* Englewood, N.J.: Prentice-Hall.

Carpenter, L.J. (August 1993). *Bilingual Special Education: An Overview of Issues.* Los Alamitos, Calif.: National Center for Bilingual Research.

Carter, T.P., and M.L. Chatfield. (1986). "Effective Bilingual Schools: Implication for Policy and Practice. *American Journal of Education* 95, 1: 200-234.

Cavazos L. (1989)."Building Bridges for At-Risk Children." *The Education Digest* 55, 3: 16-19.

Cazden, C.B. (1988). *Classroom Discourse: The Language of Teaching and Learning.* Portsmouth, N.H.: Heinemann.

Center for Demographic Policy. (Summer 1993). *CDP Newsletter* 1, 4. [entire issue]

Chall, J.S., V.A. Jacobs, and L.E. Baldwin. (1990). *The Reading Crisis: Why Poor Children Fall Behind.* Cambridge, Mass.: Harvard University Press.

Chamot, A.U., and J.M. O'Malley. (1994). "Instructional Approaches and Teaching Procedures." In *Kids Come in All Languages: Reading Instruction for ESL Students,* edited by K. Spangenberg-Urbschat and R. Pritchard. Newark, Del.: International Reading Association.

Chan, K.S. (1983). Limited English Speaking, Handicapped, and Poor: Triple Threat in Childhood. In *Asian- and Pacific-American Perspectives in Bilingual Education: Comparative Research,* edited by Mae Chu-Chang. New York: Teachers College Press.

Coballes-Vega, C. (January 1992). "Consideration in Teaching Culturally Diverse Children." *ERIC Digest* EDO-SP 90/2. Washington, D.C.: ERIC Clearinghouse on Teacher Education.

Commission on Chapter One. (1992). *Making Schools Work for Children in Poverty,* pp. 3-4. Washington, D.C. American Association for Higher Education.

Cuevas, G.J. (1984). "Mathematics Learning in English as a Second Language." *Journal for Research in Mathematics Education* 13, 7: 134-144.

"Cultural Differences in the Classroom." (March 1988). *The Harvard Education Letter* 4, 2: 1-4.

Cummins, J. (1981). "The Role of Primary Language Development in Promoting Educational Success for Language Minority Students." In *Schooling and Language Minority Students: A Theoretical Framework.* Los Angeles: California State University.

Cummins, J. (1984). *Bilingualism and Special Education: Issues in Assessment and Pedagogy.* Clevedon, England: Multilingual Matters.

Cummins, J. (1986). "Empowering Minority Students: A Framework for Intervention." *Harvard Education review* 56, 1: 18-36.

Cummins, J., and M. Swain. (1986). *Bilingualism in Education: Aspects of Theory, Research and Practice.* London: Longman.

Cziko, G.A. (March 1992). "The Evaluation of Bilingual Education." *Educational Researcher* 21, 2: 10-15.

DeAvila, E.A., and S.E. Duncan. (1979). "Bilingualism and Cognition: Some Recent Findings." *NABE Journal* 4, 1: 15-50.

DeAvila, E.A., and S.E. Duncan. (1980). "Definition and Measurement of Bilingual Students." In *Bilingual Program, Policy and Assessment Issues.* Sacramento: California State Department of Education.

Deem, J.M., and W.J. Marshall. (1980). "Teaching a Second Language to Indochinese Refugees When No Program Exists." *Journal of Reading* 23: 601-605.

Delpit, L.D. (1988). "The Silenced Dialogue: Power and Pedagogy in Educating Other People's Children." *Harvard Education Review* 48: 280-298.

Demetrulias, D.M. (Spring 1991). "Teacher Expectations and Ethnic Surnames." *Teacher Education Quarterly* 18, 2: 37-43.

Dolly, J.M., D.D. Blaine, and K.M. Power. (1988). "Performance of Educationally At-Risk Pacific and Asian Students in a Traditional Academic Program." Paper presented at the annual meeting of the American Educational Research Association, New Orleans, La.

Dornbusch, S.M., P.L. Ritter, P.H. Leiderman, D.F. Roberts, and M.J. Fraleigh. (1987). "The Relation of Parenting Style to Adolescent School Performance." *Child Development* 55: 1233-1257.

Dunn, R. (Summer 1989). "Do Students from Different Cultures Have Different Learning Styles?" *International Education* 16, 50: 40-42. (Available from the Association for the Advancement of International Education, New Wilmington, Pa.

Dunn, R., and S. Griggs. (1990). "Research on the Learning Styles Characteristics of Selected Racial and Ethnic Groups." *Reading, Writing and Learning Disabilities* 6: 261-280.

Dunn, R., J.A. Beaudy, and A. Klavas. (1989). "Survey of Research on Learning Styles." *Educational Leadership* 46, 6: 50-58.

Duran, R., ed. (1981). *Latino Language and Communicative Behavior*, pp. 133-152. Norwood, N.J.: Ablex.

Edelsky, C. (1986). *Writing in a Bilingual Program*. Norwood, N.J.: Ablex.Edward, H., M. Wesche, S. Krashen, R. Clement, and B. Krudenier. (1984). "Second Language Acquisition Through Subject-Matter Learning: A Study of Sheltered Psychology Classes at the University of Ottawa." *Canadian Modern Language Review* 41, : 268-282.

First, J.M. (November 1988). "Immigrant Students in U.S. Public Schools: Challenges and Solutions." *Phi Delta Kappan* 70, 3: 205-210.

First, J.M., and J.W. Willshire-Carrera. (1988). *New Voices: Immigrant Students in U.S. Public Schools*. Boston: National Coalition of Advocates for Students.

Gallimore, R., J. Boggs, and C. Jordan. (1974). *Culture, Behavior and Environment*. Beverly Hills, Calif.: Sage.

Garcia, E. (Winter 1987/1988). *Effective Schooling for Language Minority Students*. (New Focus, NCBE Occasional Papers in Bilingual Education, No. 1). Wheaton, Md.: National Clearinghouse for Bilingual Education.

Garcia, E. (1988). "Attributes of Effective Schools for Language Minority Students." *Education and Urban Society* 20, 4: 387-398.

Garcia, E. (1991). *The Education of Linguistically and Culturally Diverse Students: Effective Instructional Practices*. Santa Cruz: National Center for Research on Cultural Diversity, University of California.

Garcia, E. (1992). "Linguistically and Culturally Diverse Children: Effective Instructional Practices and Related Policy Issues." In *Students At Risk in At Risk Schools: Improving Environments for Learning*, edited by H. Waxman, J. Walker de Felix, J.E. Anderson, and H.P. Prentice Jr. Newbury Park, Calif.: Corwin Press.

Garcia, E., L. Maez, and G. Gonzalez. (1983). *The Incidence of Language Switching in Spanish/English Bilingual Children of the United State*. (ERIC Document Reproduction Service No. BE015018)

Garcia, G.E., and P.D. Pearson. (April 1991). *Literacy Assessment in a Diverse Society*. (Technical report no. 525). Champaign, Ill.: Center for the Study of Reading, University of Illinois.

Gardner, H. (1983). *Frames of Mind: The Theory of Multiple Intelligences*. New York: Basic Books.

Gee, P.L. (1982). "Reading and Mathematics Achievement of Eighth-Grade Chinese-American Students Enrolled in Bilingual or Monolingual Program." Doctoral diss., University of San Francisco.

Genishi, C. (1981). "Code-switching in Chicano Six-Year-Olds. In *Latino Language and Communicative Behavior*, edited by R. Duran. Norwood, N.J.: Ablex.

Gibson, M.A. (1983). *Home-School-Community Linkages: A Study of Educational Opportunity for Punjabi Youth. Final Report*. Stockton, Calif.: South Asian American Education Association.

Gibson, M.A. (December 1987). "The School Performance of Immigrant Minorities: A Comparative View." *Anthropology and Education Quarterly* 18, 4: 262-275.

Gibson, M.A. (Spring 1988). "Punjabi Orchard Farmers: An Immigrant Enclave in Rural California." *International Migration Review* 22, 1: 28-50.

Gibson, M.A., and P.K. Bhachu. (1991). "Ethnicity and School Performance: A Comparative Study of South Asian Pupils in Britain and American." *Ethnic and Racial Studies* 11, 3: 239-262.

Gibson, M.A., and J.U. Ogbu, eds. (1991). *Minority Status and Schooling: A Comparative Study of Immigrant and Involuntary Minorities*, New York: Garland Publishing.

Gilbert, S.E., and G. Gay. (October 1985). Improving the Success in School of Poor Black Children." *Phi Delta Kappan* 67, 2: 133-137.

Goldman, R.E., and B. Hewitt. (1975). "An Investigation of Test Bias for Mexican American College Students." *Journal of Educational Measurement* 12: 187-196.

Gonzalez, R.D. (January 1990). "When Minority Becomes Majority: The Changing Face of English Classrooms." *English Journal* 79, 1: 16-23.

Goodman, K. (1986). *What's Whole in Whole Language?* Exeter, N.H.: Heinemann.

Hakuta, K. (1986). *The Mirror of Language: The Debate on Bilingualism*. New York: Basic Books.

Hakuta, K., and E. Garcia. (1989). "Bilingualism and Education." *American Psychologist* 44, 2: 286-299.

Hakuta, K., and L. Gould. (March 1987). "Synthesis of Research on Bilingual Education." *Educational Leadership* 44, 6: 38-45.

Hamilton, V.L., P.C. Blumenfeld, H. Akoh, and K. Miura. (Winter 1989). "Japanese and American Children's Reasons for Things They Do in School." *American Educational Research Journal* 26, 4: 545-571.

Haw, K.F. (Spring 1991). Interactions of Gender and Race—A Problem for Teachers? A Review of the Emerging Literature." *Educational Research* 33, 1: 12-21.

Heath, S.B. (1983). *Ways With Words: Language, Life and Work in Communities and Classrooms*. New York: Cambridge University Press.

Heath, S.B. (1986). "Sociocultural Contexts of Language Development." In *Beyond Language: Social and Cultural Factors in Schooling Language Minority Students*, developed by the Bilingual Education Office, California State Department of Education. Los Angeles: National Evaluation, Dissemination, and Assessment Center, California State University.

Heath, S.B., and M.W. McLaughlin. (September-October 1994). "Learning for Anything Everyday." *Journal of Curriculum Studies* 26, 5: 471-489.

Henry, S.L., and F.C. Pepper. (1990). "Cognitive, Social, and Cultural Effects on Indian Learning Style: Classroom Implications." *The Journal of Educational Issues of Language Minority Students* 7: [entire issue].

Herbert, C. (1987). San Diego Title VII Two-Way Bilingual Program, San Diego Unified School District, Calif.

Hirst, L., and C. Slavik. (1989). "Cooperative Approaches to Learning." In *Effective Language Education Practices and Native American Language Survival*, edited by J. Reyhner. Billings, Mont.: Eastern Montana College Press.

Huerta, A.G. (1980). "The Acquisition of Bilingualism: A Code-Switching Approach." In *Language and Speech in American Society: A Compilation of Research Papers in Sociolinguistics*, edited by R. Bauman and J. Sherzer. Austin, Texas: Southwest Education Development Lab.

Huerta-Macias, A., and E. Quintero. (Summer-Fall 1992). "Code-Switching, Bilingualism and Diliteracy. A Case Study." *Bilingual Research Journal* 16: 69-90.

Ima, K., R. Galang, E. Lee, and H. Dinh Te. (Summer 1991). "What Do We Know About Asian and Pacific Islander Language Minority Students?" A Report to the California Department of Education's Bilingual Education Office. San Diego: San Diego State University.

Ima, K. and E.M. Labovitz. (1991). *Language Proficiency, Ethnicity and Standardized Test Performance of Elementary School Students*. (ERIC Document Reproduction Service No. ED 341700)

Ima, K., and R.G. Rumbaut. (June 1989). "Southeast Asian Refugees in American Schools: A Comparison Between Fluent-English-Proficient and Limited-English-Proficient Students." *Topics in Language Disorders* 9, 3: 54-75.

Irvine, J.J. (1990). *Black Students and School Failure: Policies, Practices, and Prescriptions.* Westport, Conn.: Greenwood Press.

Johnson, D.W., and R.T. Johnson. (1982). *Joining Together: Group Theory and Group Skills.* 2nd ed. Englewood Cliffs, N.J.: Prentice-Hall.

Johnson, D.W., R.T. Johnson, and E.J. Holubec. (1994). *The New Circles of Learning.* Alexandria, Va.: ASCD.

Jacob, E., and C. Jordan. (1987). "Explaining the School Performance of Minority Students." Theme Issue of *Anthropology and Education Quarterly* 18, 4.

Jordan, C. (1981). "Educationally Effective Ethnology: A Study of the Contributions of Cultural knowledge to Effective Education of Minority Children." Doctoral diss., University of California at Los Angeles.

Jordan, C. (1984). "Cultural Compatibility and the Education of Hawaiian Children: Implications for Mainland Educators." *Educational Research Quarterly* 8, 4: 59-71.

Jordan, C. (Summer 1985). Translating Culture: From Ethnographic Information to Educational Program." *Anthropology and Education Quarterly* 16, 2: 104-123.

Jordan, C., K.H. Au, and A.K. Joseting. (1983). "Patterns of Classroom Interaction with Pacific Islands Children: The Importance of Cultural Differences." In *Asian- and Pacific- American Perspectives in Bilingual Education: Comparative Research,* edited by Mao Chu-Chang. New York: Teachers College Press.

Jordan, C., R. Tharp, and L. Baird-Vogt. (1992). "Just Open the Door: Cultural Compatibility and Classroom Rapport." In *Cross-Cultural Literacy: Ethnographies of Communication in Multiethnic Classrooms,* edited by M. Saravia-Shore and S.F. Arvizu. New York: Garland.

Knapp., M.S., and B. Turnbull. (1990). *Better Schooling for the Children of Poverty: Alternatives to Conventional Wisdom. Study of Academic Instruction for Disadvantaged Students. Vol. 1: Summary.* Washington, D.C.: Policy Studies Associates; Menlo Park, Calif.: SRI International.

Knapp, M.S., N.E. Adelman, C. Marder, H. McCollum, M.C. Needels, P.M. Shields, B.J. Turnbull, A.A. Zucker. (1993). *Study of Academic Instruction for Disadvantaged Students: Academic Challenge for the Children of Poverty: Findings and Conclusions.* Washington, D.C.: U.S. Department of Education, Office of Policy and Planning.

Krashen, S. (1982). *Principles and Practices in Second Language Acquisition.* Hayward, Calif.: Alemany Press.

Krashen, S. (1985). *The Input Hypothesis: Issues and Implications.* New York: Longman.

Krashen, S., and D. Biber. (1988). *On Course: Bilingual Education's Success in California.* Sacramento: California Association for Bilingual Education.

Laosa, L. (1982). "School, Occupation, Culture, and Family: The Impact of Parental Schooling on the Parent-Child Relationship." *Journal of Educational Psychology* 74: 791-827.

Lee, E. (1986). "Chinese Parents' Support for the Bilingual Education Program." Doctoral diss., University of the Pacific.

Lee, E.S., and M.R. Lee. (1980). "A Study of Classroom Behaviors of Chinese American Children and Immigrant Chinese Children in Contrast to Those of Black American Children and White American Children in an Urban Head Start Program." Doctoral diss., University of San Francisco.

Lee, E. (June 1988). "Cultural Factors in Working with Southeast Asian Refugee Adolescents." *Journal of Adolescence* 11, 2: 167-179.

Lee, E.W. (Winter 1989). "Chinese American Fluent English Proficient Students and School Achievement." *NABE: The Journal for the National Association of Bilingual Education* 13, 2: 95-111.

Levin, H., and W. Hopfenberg. (January 1991). "Don't Remediate: Accelerate!" *Principal* 70, 3: 11-13.

Lindholm, K.J. (1988). "Edison Elementary School Bilingual Immersion Program: Student Programs After One Year of Implementation." Los Angeles: Center for Language Education and Research.

Little Soldier, L. (October 1989). "Cooperative Learning and the Native American Student." *Phi Delta Kappan* 71, 2: 161-163.

Lucas, T., R. Henze, and R. Donato. (1990). "Promoting the Success of Latino Language Minority Students: An Exploratory Study of Six High Schools." *Harvard Educational Review* 60: 315-334.

Martinez, R., and R.L. Dukes. (March 1991). "Ethnic and Gender Difference in Self-Esteem." *Youth and Society* 22, 3: 218- 338.

Matute-Bianchi, M.E. (1986). "Ethnic Identities and Patterns of School Success and Failure Among Mexican-Descent and Japanese- American Students in a California High School: An Ethnographic Analysis." *American Journal of Education* 95, 1: 233-255.

McIntosh, P. (1983). "Interactive Phases of Curricular Re-Vision: a Feminist Perspective." Wellesley, Mass.: Wellesley College Center for Research on Women.

Mehan, H. (1989). "Microcomputers in Classrooms: Educational Technology or Social Practice?" *Anthropology and Education Quarterly* 20: 4-22.

Mehan, H., et al. (1985). *Computers in Classrooms: A Quasi-Experiment in Guided Change. Final Report to National Institute of Education (NIE).* La Jolla, Calif.: Interactive Technology Laboratory.

Michaels, S. (1981). "Sharing Time: Children's Narrative Styles and Differential Access to Literacy." *Language in Society* 10, 3: 423-442.

Moll, L.C., S. Diaz, E. Estrada, and L.M. Lopes. (1992). "Making Contexts: The Social Construction of Lessons in Two Languages." In *Cross-Cultural Literacy: Ethnographies of Communication in Multiethnic Classrooms,* edited by M. Saravia-Shore and S.F. Arvizu. New York: Garland.

National Coalition of Advocates for Students. (1988). *New Voices: Immigrant Students in U.S. Public Schools.* Boston: The Coalition.

Oakland, T., and P. Matuszek. (1977). "Using Tests in Nondiscriminatory Assessment." In *Psychological and Educational Assessment of Minority Children,* edited by T. Oakland. New York: Brunner/Mazel.

O'Donnell, C.R., and R.G. Tharp. (1990). "Community Intervention Guided by Theoretical Development." In *International Handbook of Behavior Modification and Therapy* (2nd ed.). New York: Plenum Press.

Ogbu, J. (1982). "Cultural Discontinuities and Schooling." *Anthropology and Education Quarterly* 13: 291-307.

Ogbu, J.U. (1987). "Variability in Minority School Performance: A Problem in Search of an Explanation." *Anthropology and Education Quarterly* 18, 4: 312-334.

Ovando, C.J. (1993). "Language Diversity and Education." In *Multicultural Education,* edited by J. Banks and C.M. Banks. Needham Heights, Mass.: Allyn and Bacon.

Pang, V.O. (Fall 1990). "Asian-American Children: A Diverse Population. *Educational Forum* 55, 1: 49-66.

Pease-Alvarez, C., E. Garcia, and P. Espinosa. (1991). "Effective Instruction for Language Minority Students: An Early Childhood Case Study." *Early Childhood Research Quarterly* 6: 347-362.

Pepper, F., and S. Henry. (1989). "Social and Cultural Effects on Indian Learning Style: Classroom Implications." In *Culture, Style and the Educative Process,* edited by B.J. Shade. Springfield, Ill.: Charles C. Thomas.

Philips, S. (1972). "Participant Structures and Communicative Competence." In *Functions of Language in the Classroom*, edited by C. Cazden, et al. New York: Teachers College Press.

Philips, S. (1983). *The Invisible Culture: Communication in Classroom and Community on the Warm Springs Indian Reservation*. New York: Longman.

Poplack, S. (1981). Syntactic Structure and Social Function of Code-Switching. In *Latino Language and Communication Behavior*, edited by R. Duran. Norwood, N.J.: Ablex.

Protheroe, N.J., and K. Barsdate. (March 1992). "Culturally Sensitive Instruction." *Streamlined Seminar* 10, 4. (Available from National Association of Elementary School Principals, Alexandria, Va.)

Quality Education for Minorities Project. (January 1990). *Education That Works: An Action Plan for the Education of Minorities: Report Summary*. Cambridge: Massachusetts Institute of Technology.

Rakow, L.F. (Summer 1991). "Gender and Race in the Classroom: Teaching Way Out of Line." *Feminist Teacher* 5, 1: 10-13.

Ramirez, J.D., S. Yuen , D.R. Ramey, and D.J. Pasta. (1990). (February 1991). *Final Report: Longitudinal Study of Structured English Immersion Strategy Early-Exit and Late-Exit Transitional Bilingual Education Programs for Language Minority Children*, Vols. 1 and 2. Washington, D.C.: U.S. Department of Education.

Roberts, L., J. Andelin, N.C. Naismaith, L. Roberts, M. Fever, K. Fulton, J. St. Lawrence, M. Zuckerkandel, M. Fenn, C. Clary, M. Haahr. (1987). "Trends and Status of Computers in Schools: Use in Chapter 1 Programs and Use with Limited English Proficient Students." Washington, D.C.: U.S. Congress Office of Technology Assessment.

Rodriguez, C.E. (1989). *Puerto Ricans Born in the U.S.A.* Winchester, Mass.: Unwin Hyman, Inc.

Rodriguez, C.E. (1992). *Student Voices: High School Students' Perspectives on the Latino Dropout Problem*. Report of the Fordham University, College at Lincoln Center Student Research Project. New York: Latino Commission on Educational Reform.

Rumbaut, R.G. (August 1990). *Immigrant Students in California Public Schools: A Summary of Current Knowledge*. (Report No. 11). Baltimore, Md.: Center for Research on Effective Schooling for Disadvantaged Students.

Rumbaut, R.B., and K. Ima. (January 1988). *The Adaptation of the Southeast Asian Refugee Youth: A Comparative Study. Final Report to the Office of Resettlement*. San Diego, Calif.: San Diego State University, Department of Sociology.

Rumbaut, R.G., and J.R. Weeks. (Summer 1986). "Fertility and Adaptation: Indochinese Refugees in the United States." *International Migration Review* 20, 2: 428-465. [special theme issue titled "Refugees: Issues and Directions"]

Sadker, M., D. Sadker, and S. Steindam. (1989). "Gender Equity and Educational Reform." *Educational Leadership* 46, 6: 44-47.

Sadker, M., D. Sadker, and L. Long. (1993). "Gender and Educational Equity." In *Multicultural Education*, edited by J. Banks and C. Banks. Needham Heights, Mass.: Allyn and Bacon.

Saravia-Shore, M. (1993). "Professional Development for an Education That Is Multicultural: The Cross-Cultural Interdisciplinary Cooperative (CICL) Model." In *Reinventing Urban Education: Multiculturalism and the Social Context of Schooling*, edited by F. Rivera-Batiz New York: IUME Press, Teachers College, Columbia University.

Saravia-Shore, M., and S.F. Arvizu, eds. (1992) *Cross-Cultural Literacy: Ethnographies of Communication in Multiethnic Classrooms*. New York: Garland.

Saravia-Shore, M., and H. Martinez. (1992). "An Ethnographic Study of Home/School Role Conflicts of Second Generation Puerto Rican Adolescents." In *Cross-Cultural Literacy: Ethnographies of Communication in Multiethnic Classrooms*, edited by M. Saravia-Shore and S.F. Arvizu. New York: Garland.

Saville-Troike, M. (1978). *A Guide to Culture in the Classroom*. Arlington, Va.: National Clearinghouse for Bilingual Education.

Sayers, D. (1989). "Bilingual Sister Classes in Computer Writing Networks." In *Richness in Writing: Empowering ESL Students*, edited by D. Johnson and D. Roen. New York: Longman.

Sayers, D., and K. Brown. (April 1987). "Bilingual Education and Telecommunications: A Perfect Fit." *The Computing Teacher* 14, 7: 23-24.

Short, D.J., J. Crandall, and D. Christian. (1989). "How to Integrate Language and Content Instruction: A Training Manual." Los Angeles: Center for Language Education and Research. (ERIC Document Reproduction Service No. ED 292-304)

Slavin, R. (1987). "Cooperative Learning: Can Students Help Students Learn?" *Instructor* 96, 7: 74-78.

Slavin, R. (1986). *Using Student Team Learning*. 3rd ed. Baltimore, Md.: Johns Hopkins University Press.

Slavin, R. (February 1991). "Synthesis of Research on Cooperative Learning." *Educational Leadership* 48, 5: 71-82.

Snow, M. (1986). Innovative Second Language Education: Bilingual Immersion Programs. Los Angeles: University of California, Center for Language Education and Research

Staton-Spicer, A.O., and D.H. Wulff. (October 1984). "Research in Communication and Instruction: Categorization and Synthesis." *Communication Education* 33, 4: 377-391.

Strickland, D., and C. Ascher. (1992). "Low Income African- American Children and Public Schooling." In *Handbook of Research on Curriculum*, edited by P. Jackson. New York: Macmillan.

Taylor, D. (1983). *Family Literacy: Young Children Learning to Read and Write*. Portsmouth, N.H.: Heinemann.

Teale, W.H. (1986). "Home Background and Young Children's Literacy Development." In *Emergent Literacy: Writing and Reading*, edited by W.H. Teale and E. Sulzby. Norwood, N.J. Ablex.

Tharp, R.G. (1989a). "Psycho-Cultural Variables and Constants. Effects on Teaching and Learning in Schools." *American Psychologist* 44: 349-359.

Tharp, R.G. (1989b). "Culturally Compatible Education: A Formula for Designing Effective Classrooms. In *What Do Anthropologists Have to Say About Dropouts?*, edited by H.T. Trueba, G. Spindler, and L. Spindler. New York: Falmer Press.

Tharp, R.G. (1991). "Cultural Diversity and Treatment of Children." *Journal of Cultural and Clinical Psychology* 49: 799-812.

Tharp, R.G. (1992). "Cultural Compatibility and Diversity: Implications for the Urban Classroom." In *Teaching Thinking and Problem Solving* 14, 6: 1-4. (Available from Research for Better Schools, Philadelphia, Pa.

Tharp, R.G., C. Jordan, G.E. Speidel, K.H. Au, T.W. Klein, R.P. Calkins, K.C.M. Sloat, and R. Gallimore. (1984). "Product and Process in Applied Developmental Research: Education and the Children of a Minority." In *Advances in Developmental Psychology, Vol. III*, edited by M.E. Lamb, A.L. Brown, and B. Rogoff. Hillsdale, N.J.: Lawrence Erlbaum.

Tharp, R., and R. Gallimore. *Teaching Mind and Society: A Theory and Practice of Teaching Literacy and Schooling*. New York: Cambridge University Press.

Tharp, R., and R. Gallimore. (1991). *The Instructional Conversation: Teaching and Learning in Social Activity*. Santa Cruz: National Center for Research on Cultural Diversity, University of California.

Torres-Guzman, M.E. (1992). "Stories of Hope in the Midst of Despair: Culturally Responsive Education for Latino Students in an Alternative High School in New York City." In *Cross-Cultural Literacy: Ethnographies of Communication in Multiethnic Classrooms*, edited by M. Saravia-Shore and S.F. Arvizu. New York: Garland.

Trueba, H., and C. Delgado-Gaitan. (1985). "Socialization of Mexican Children for Cooperation and Competition: Sharing and Copying." *Journal of Educational Equity and Leadership* 5: 3.

Trueba, H.T., L. Jacobs, and E. Kirton. (1990). *Cultural Conflict and Adaptation: The Case of Hmong Children in American Society.* New York: Falmer.

Valdez-Pierce, L. (1991). *Effective Schools for Language Minority Students.* Chevy Chase, Md.: The Mid-Atlantic Equity Center. (Available from the publisher at 5454 Wisconsin Ave., Suite 1500, Chevy Chase, MD 20815)

Valverde, L., R.C. Feinberg, and E.M. Marquez. (1980). *Educating English-Speaking Hispanics.* Alexandria, Va.: ASCD.

Valdez-Fallis, G. (1977). *Code-Switching and the Classroom Teacher.* Arlington, Va.: Center for Applied Linguistics.

Williams, M.D. (1981). "Observations in Pittsburgh Ghetto Schools." *Anthropology and Education Quarterly* 12: 211-220.

Winfield, L.F., and J. Manning. (1992). "Changing School Culture to Accommodate Student Diversity." In *Diversity in Teacher Education: New Expectations,* edited by M.E. Dilworth. San Francisco: Jossey-Bass.

Wittrock, M. (1986). *Handbook of Research on Teaching.* New York: Macmillan.

Wong-Fillmore, L. (1983). "The Language Learner as an Individual: Implications of Research on Individual Differences for the ESL Teacher." In *On TESOL '82: Pacific Perspectives on Language Learning and Teaching,* edited by M.A. Clarke and J. Handscombe. Washington, D.C.: Teachers of English to Speakers of Other Languages (TESOL).

Wong-Fillmore, L. (1991). "When Learning a Second Language Means Losing a First." *Early Childhood Research Quarterly* 6: 323 346.

Wong-Fillmore, L., and C. Valadez. (1986). "Teaching Bilingual Learners." In *Handbook of Research on Teaching,* edited by M.C. Wittrock. New York: Macmillan.

Zeichner, K. (1992). Educating Teachers for Cultural Diversity." East Lansing, Mich.: National Center for Research on Teacher Learning.

Zentella, A.C. (1992). "Individual Differences in Growing Up Bilingual. In *Cross-Cultural Literacy: Ethnographies of Communication in Multiethnic Classrooms,* edited by M. Saravia- Shore and S.F. Arvizu. New York: Garland.

5

STRATEGIES FOR INCREASING ACHIEVEMENT IN READING

Marie Carbo and Barbara Kapinus

Reading is the most important, fundamental ability taught in the nation's schools. It is vital to society and to the people within it. It is the door to knowledge and a capability that can liberate people both intellectually and personally.

— National Assessment of Educational Progress (1991, p. 1).

Authors' Note. We thank Denise Verley-Matthews for her contributions to this chapter.

Our schools shoulder the responsibility for bringing about world-class levels of literacy in the United States. Despite evidence showing that the reading ability of U.S. students has declined only slightly in recent decades (Mullis et al. 1990), the current levels of reading achievement for too many young Americans still fall short of what is needed in the workplace, in colleges, and in the international arena. A high level of literacy is essential to the vitality of our democratic society, but low reading ability holds back many American students, making it virtually impossible for them to understand their subjects and causing them to fall ever further behind in their school work.

The inability to read has a direct relationship to the tendency of more and more young people to drop out of school. In fact, a study conducted by the Chicago Public Schools found lack of ability to read to be "the single most important factor in predicting which students would drop out of school" (Griffin 1987). The number of poor readers in the United States remains dangerously high: only 19 percent of our "disadvantaged" youngsters reach the "adept" level of reading by age 17. Illiteracy among our minority youth has been estimated at about 40 percent (Carroll 1987).

As the problems that young people experience outside of school continue to mount—poverty, abuse, neglect, handicapping conditions, lack of adult protection and nurturance, to name a few—so do the number of students who are so far behind their peers in reading and language development that they have little hope of ever catching up. As Kameenui (1993, p. 379) observes:

> What is profoundly and unequivocally the same about them is that they are behind in reading and language development. Moreover, they constantly face the tyranny of time in trying to catch up with

their peers, who continue to advance in their literacy development. Simply keeping pace with their peers amounts to losing more and more ground for students who are behind.

Kameenui's analysis is perfectly accurate, according to Anderson and Pellicer (1990), whose work was described in Chapter 1. In examining the achievement of economically disadvantaged and educationally deficient students, they found that, despite the billions of dollars spent annually on compensatory education, most of the youngsters targeted for assistance made very little progress in reading, becoming "lifers" in the programs. Anderson and Pellicer strongly recommended both the use of challenging materials in these programs and master teachers who have high expectations for their students.

If every young person is to have equal educational opportunity, sweeping changes are necessary in the way young people are taught to read and then tested on what they are able to read. Now, more than at any other time in American history, we need clear guidelines for accelerating the development of the most important, fundamental, and vital ability addressed in the schools: the ability to read.

ENHANCING STUDENTS' READING ACHIEVEMENT

Data gathered as part of the National Assessment of Educational Progress (NAEP) describe the learning conditions in American schools that relate positively to reading achievement. Unfortunately, the data do not appear to have greatly affected classroom practice. According to the 1990 NAEP study of students in grades four, eight, and twelve, the following conditions correlate positively with reading achievement (Foertsch 1992):

- large amounts of reading done in and outside of school;
- major deemphasis of workbook activities;
- discussions of reading that emphasize higher-level thinking;
- opportunities for connecting reading and writing;
- reading a great variety of texts (novels, poems, stories); and
- support for literacy in the home.

THE STATE OF THE ART OF READING INSTRUCTION

In sharp contrast to the above listing of desirable conditions, the same 1990 NAEP study (Foertsch 1992) described the following characteristics that actually exist in the United States today:

- U.S. students read very little, either in or outside of school.
- Schools continue to place overwhelming emphasis on activities involving the use of reading workbooks.
- U.S. students have "difficulty in constructing thoughtful responses" when asked to "elaborate upon or defend their interpretations of what they read."
- The majority of students still do not write each week about what they read.
- Library use decreases throughout the grades; most 12th graders report only *yearly* use of the library.
- Access to reading materials in the home has declined somewhat; only 25 percent of the students reported discussing reading with family and friends.
- Approximately 20 percent of the students reported reading for fun only *yearly or never*.

A particularly disturbing trend in the NAEP data came to light in the period between 1988 and 1990 (Foertsch 1992). While there was a slight increase in the amount of student reading both in and outside of school, the study also showed a sharp increase in the number of students who "never read for fun." These data suggest that between 1988 and 1990, students were being assigned more reading in and outside of school, but that more students were growing to dislike reading.

Making the process of learning to read enjoyable for the learner is critical. Learning to read must be a pleasurable activity for young people rather than simply a skills-based source of stress; if they are to continue to read on their own, students must associate reading with enjoyment and good books. Our aim must be for young people to *spend more time reading*—a crucial step toward becoming lifelong readers.

The implications of a 1983 study of the reading styles (that is, the learning styles for reading) of students in grades two, four, six and eight were consistent with the NAEP findings (Carbo 1983). The responses of youngsters in the primary grades indicated a low preference for work-

FIGURE 5.1
A Summary of New Standards for Curriculum and Instruction in Reading

CURRICULUM

TRADITIONAL EMPHASIS	NEW EMPHASIS
teaching reading as a discrete subject area	integration of process and content
functional literacy	ability to communicate with and understand written language
reading for "right answer"	inquiry-based approach
basal readers	wide variety of genre, including high-quality literature
mainstream culture and language	students' home/community culture and experiences

INSTRUCTION

TRADITIONAL EMPHASIS	NEW EMPHASIS
uniform instruction	identifying individual student's learning/reading styles
remediating weaknesses	building on reading and literacy strengths
workbooks and worksheets	dialogue and discussion
skills teaching: decoding	modeling and interactive guided practice
	strategy teaching: cognitive (comprehension) and metacognitive
ability grouping	scaffolding to guide students in completing complex tasks
	extended silent reading
	heterogeneous grouping: flexible
	cooperative/team learning activities
	peer tutoring

Source: Hodges 1989.

book exercises along with a high preference for writing activities, choice of high-interest reading materials, and time to read both alone and in pairs. Older students preferred far fewer workbook exercises, a wide choice of high-interest reading materials, and more time to read alone and to work with peers.

The NAEP data strongly suggest that during the past decade of reading instruction, the education community has failed to accommodate the natural reading strengths and preferences of U.S. students. In fact, many reading programs hamper the reading progress of students; in doing do, these programs actually create poor readers. When reading instruction has matched, rather than mismatched, students' preferred styles of reading, reading achievement and enjoyment of reading have tended to increase significantly (Carbo 1987, LaShell 1986, *Reading Styles Progress Report* 1990, Sudzina 1987).

THE CHARACTERISTICS OF GOOD READERS

According to the NAEP (1991), "an obvious goal of reading literacy education" is to develop good readers. An understanding of the characteristics of good readers is a critical element in providing direction for reading instruction. In a comparison of good readers and less proficient readers, the NAEP (1991, p. 9) noted that good readers:

- have positive habits and attitudes about reading;
- read with enough fluency so that they can focus on the meaning of what they read;
- use what they already know to understand what they read;
- form an understanding of what they read, and extend, elaborate, and critically judge its meaning;
- use a variety of effective strategies to aid their understanding and to plan, manage, and check the progress of their reading; and
- can read a wide variety of texts and can read for different purposes.

ASSESSING ACHIEVEMENT IN READING

Although the reading scores of U.S. students have declined only slightly over the past few decades (Farr, Fay, Myers, and Ginsberg 1987; Mullis et al. 1990), the public's belief that there has been a serious deterioration in reading scores has contributed to a "new focus on standards and assessment" (Farr 1993, p. 27). Often, the new focus has not reflected important research findings.

For example, the Commission on Reading defined reading as "the process of constructing meaning for written texts" and as "a complex skill requiring the coordination of a number of interrelated sources of information" (Anderson, Heibert, Scott, and Wilkinson 1985); the Commission recommended "broad-gauged" measures of reading achievement that reflect these new definitions. Yet most standardized tests of reading achievement used in the United States still tend to overemphasize a student's knowledge of discrete, low-level skills; the result is an overemphasis on the mechanics of reading and on skill sheets and workbooks. (For a summary of what reading achievement tests should measure, see Carbo 1988b.)

For poor readers in particular, this strong emphasis on test scores can have disastrous consequences. Even more than their peers, poor readers need to learn with interesting and challenging reading materials, but they are often required to do even more skill work and paper-and-pencil activities than are good readers (Anderson and Pellicer 1990).

In 1988, the International Reading Association (IRA) expressed the concern "that inappropriate assessment measures are proliferating for the purpose of school by school, district by district, state by state, and province by province comparisons." The IRA passed two resolutions: the first affirmed that reading assessments should "reflect recent advances in the understanding of the reading process," and the second, "that assessment measures defining reading as a sequence of discrete skills be discouraged" (International Reading Association 1988).

A related problem (and a thorny one to attempt to solve, given teachers' general tendency to rely on standardized testing) has been the number of U.S. teachers who teach to the test, thus contaminating our understanding of students' actual reading ability. As Farr (1993, p. 31) noted: "A good score on a standardized reading test no longer indicates that the student can read in general. It means only that the student can do those limited things the test covers."

Though the task ahead is daunting, reading assessment has broken new ground in recent years. Notably, the NAEP and the states of Illinois, Maryland, Michigan, and Wisconsin have developed more global measures of reading achievement which, compared to previous standardized achievement tests, include longer passages and attempt to assess both strategic reading behaviors and deeper levels of thinking. Some of these assessments have moved away from relying solely on multiple-choice items; they include such open-ended items as written responses and student-designed charts and illustrations.

The relatively wide acceptance of a constructivist, context-specific definition of reading has led to an emphasis on more authentic assessment. This trend has caused educators to analyze the authenticity of the testing situation. Of particular interest has been the validity of a test's content in considering the reader's purpose, interests, and background, and the accuracy of a test's measurement of a student's reading performance.

The use of portfolios is a relatively new approach to the assessment of reading performance that has gained wide acceptance. Portfolios may be collections from students and teachers of samples of the student's writing in draft form or final form, responses to reading, records of interviews and observations of students, and students' own reflections on their progress. The collection is used to demonstrate the student's development and progress, over time, in reading, writing, and thinking.

Last, and perhaps most important, is the notion that students must become the primary assessors of the development of their own literacy, and that youngsters need to learn how to authentically assess their own progress. Within this new paradigm, students are encouraged to become good self-assessors, learning how to select, review, think, and revise. In effect, they learn how to take responsibility for their own learning (Farr 1993).

READING STRATEGIES THAT PROMOTE ACHIEVEMENT

The remainder of this chapter presents a number of strategies, drawn from both research and experience in the field, that are especially recommended as means of accelerating reading ability and creating good readers, particularly among those students characterized as being at risk of failure. The strategies include the following techniques:

- provision of good reading models;
- literacy-rich environments;
- ample time to practice and enjoy reading;
- home/school partnerships;
- integration of language activities;
- accommodation of young people's interests,

abilities, and reading styles;
- systematic and varied instruction;
- use of a variety of reading methods;
- activation of prior knowledge;
- authentic purposes for learning and assessment;
- emphasis on constructing, examining, and extending meaning;
- meaning-driven activities;
- explicit instruction of "what," "when," and "why"; and
- use of a variety of heterogeneous and homogeneous groups.

Douglas Monk knows that his efforts have paid off. In 9th grade, he gained 27 points on the Normal Curve Equivalent in reading in only four months. His teacher, Linda Queiruga, used the recorded book method described in Strategy 5.1. Doug was one of Queiruga's students with learning disabilities. At the beginning of the taped books program, Douglas could read on his own only 3rd grade level books. He was unable to read even the titles of the short stories recorded by Queiruga. After four months of working with the book tapes, Douglas was reading 6th grade material with no assistance. His parents reported that his self-esteem had shot up. In a year, he advanced to 7th grade books, and after two years, at the end of 10th grade, Doug could read and comprehend on a 9th grade level. He had nearly closed a six-year gap and had improved his spelling and written language. In the 11th grade, and mainstreamed for most of his classes, Doug commented: "I really believed I was stupid. This class proved to me that I'm not."

● STRATEGY 5.1: READ ALOUD

Teachers read aloud to young people, providing good reading models that serve to improve their students' reading accuracy, fluency, and comprehension.

DISCUSSION

Students need to hear good reading models in order to become familiar with the patterns and rhythms of well-written language. This modeling is especially important for young people with a limited knowledge of English and for those who have had little or no experience listening to written English.

Each day, teachers, volunteers, or peer tutors can read to students a selection of different types of literature, including expository texts. To help young people better understand the content, teachers relate the reading materials to the students' background and experiences; they can encourage them to read a text selection silently to themselves before they are asked to read it aloud.

Hoffman, Roser, and Battle (1993) suggest that a "model" read-aloud program include seven features: (1) designating a daily legitimate time and place for reading aloud; (2) carefully selecting quality texts that include stories with "enduring themes and meaty plots, [and] poems that touch and enlighten"; (3) allowing readers and listeners to explore interrelationships among books; (4) encouraging personal responses to the readings; (5) establishing small conversation groups; (6) offering a variety of opportunities to respond to the readings and to extend them; and (7) rereading selected pieces.

CLASSROOM EXAMPLES

In addition to simply listening to stories, emerging readers can follow along in the text while they listen so they can better connect the spoken and printed word. Then, if necessary, they can read aloud what they have heard. Here the use of modeling methods such as shared reading, recorded reading, repeated reading, and choral reading are helpful (see Figure 5.2).

An effective strategy for helping students to fluently read challenging materials is the recorded book method, in which text is recorded at a slower pace than usual (about 85 words per minute), using natural-sounding phrasing and engaging expression. Usually, students listen to the recorded passage two to three times and then read it aloud. After discussing the selection with the teacher, students repeat this process with each two- to five- minute segment of text. Students can work with one or more segments at a sitting, depending on their interest and ability. (Carbo 1992)

In a study of thirty-three high school students with reading abilities ranging from the 2nd grade level to the 4th grade level, Queiruga (1992) reported a two-year gain in reading comprehension and improved speech patterns after four months of working with the recording method described above. Students were free to select any of 200 recorded stories, but they were encouraged to choose those that they could read back after two or three listenings. The recorded stories ranged in reading level from about 2nd through 10th grade (Carbo 1992).

REFERENCES

Adams 1990; Anderson, Heibert, Scott, and Wilkinson 1985; Carbo 1989, 1992; Chall, Jacobs, and Baldwin 1990; Chomsky 1976, 1978; Durkin 1966; Feitelson, Goldstein, Iroqui, and Shore 1993; Hoffman, Roser, and Battle 1993; Holdaway 1979, 1982; International Reading Association 1988; Kapinus, Gambrell, and Koskinen 1987; Manning 1990; Martinez and Teale 1988; McCauley and McCauley 1992; Morrow 1982, 1983, 1987, 1989; Samuels, Schermer, and Reinking 1992; Strickland and Morrow 1989; Teale and Sulzby 1986; Trelease 1982; Wasik and Slavin 1990.

● STRATEGY 5.2: CREATE A LITERACY-RICH ENVIRONMENT

Teachers provide students with motivating, high-quality reading materials that are developmentally appropriate, well-organized, varied in subject matter and level of difficulty, complementary to students' reading styles, and relevant to students' interests and abilities.

DISCUSSION

Students tend to become more motivated to read and will read for longer periods of time when they are given opportunities to choose reading materials that accommodate their interests, abilities, and reading styles. Emerging readers, particularly those from diverse linguistic, cultural, or socioeconomic backgrounds, often benefit from exposure to a wide variety of reading materials that promote and support literacy and print awareness and that honor different cultures. Challenging reading materials—neither too easy nor too hard—that are at or slightly above students' reading levels are usually most effective. Generally speaking, the common practice of keeping at-risk students at work on easy reading materials for long periods of time hinders reading achievement.

Figure 5.2
Continuum of Modeling Reading Methods

The goal of all the modeling strategies on this continuum is Sustained Silent Reading—reading alone with ease and enjoyment. Moving from bottom to top on the continuum, each strategy requires increasingly more reading independence of the student and less modeling of good oral reading from the teacher. The first three strategies provide the most modeling (Shared Reading, Recorded Books, and Repeated Reading), since the student hears the text read aloud by the teacher repeatedly before attempting to read some or all of it. The next two strategies (Neurological Impress and Choral Reading) require the student to read simultaneously with others. In the last strategy, Paired Reading, a passage is modeled, but usually by a peer, not the teacher, and the partner is expected to read the next portion of the story, not the part that was modeled. Teachers should select the strategy that is most appropriate for a student or a group. Generally, strategies that provide the most modeling should be used with beginning readers or those who cannot read a particular text fluently.

Sustained Silent Reading
Each person in the classroom, including the teacher, reads alone. The time period for a group can range from about ten to forty-five minutes per session, depending on the interests, ages, and abilities of the students. The emphasis is on self-selection of reading materials and reading for pleasure.

Paired Reading
Two students take turns reading a passage or story. Teachers may pair youngsters of similar or dissimilar reading abilities or interests, or children may select partners. The emphasis may be on reading for pleasure, or students may be given guidelines for assisting or evaluating their partner.

Choral Reading
Two or more students read a passage in unison. Less able readers try to follow the reading model provided by the more adept readers in the group. Group members may be teachers, parents or guardians, students, or others.

Neurological Impress
The teacher sits behind the youngster and reads into the child's ear. Both hold the book and read in unison. The child places his or her finger under the line of print being read by the teacher. The purpose is reading fluency; the teacher asks no comprehension questions (Heckelman 1969).

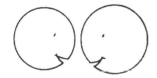

Repeated Reading
After discussing a passage, the teacher reads it aloud while the student (or group) follows along in the text. Then the teacher reads the first sentence aloud, and the student reads it back. This procedure continues until the passage is completed. In another version, Samuels (1979) recommended repeated, independent practice of easy passages until the student attains a reading rate of eighty-five words per minute.

Recorded Books
The youngster listens one or more times to a word-for-word recording while following along in the text, and then reads some or all of the book aloud (Chomsky 1976). Less able readers can listen one or more times to two- to five-minute segments of the text that have been recorded at a slower-than-usual pace (about eighty-five to ninety words per minute), and then read the passage aloud. Passages should be recorded with good expression, natural phrasing, and clear pronunciation (Carbo 1989).

Shared Reading
A high-interest book, often enlarged and containing many pictures and predictable language, is placed in front of students. The teacher reads the story while pointing to the words and pausing to ask questions. After a few readings, youngsters are encouraged to read along with the teacher.

Source: Carbo 1993. Copyright © 1994 Marie Carbo

Initially, teachers provide emerging readers with easy reading materials that allow them to experience success, such as dialogue journals, children's stories, books with repetitive phrases and predictable language, big books, recorded books, correspondence, picture books, and environmental print (words that youngsters encounter every day). Both the environmental print in classrooms and the books in class libraries should reflect students' first languages, as well as English.

The most effective teachers of reading expose students to a wide range of graded reading materials that become increasingly complex. They use well-organized textbooks that skillfully integrate relevant, subject-specific information. Articles from periodicals and newspapers help students connect reading to the topics and issues of the real world and introduce real-world materials into the classroom. Teachers must realize that basal readers, texts, and workbooks represent only a small sampling of the many available resources that encourage reading. Young people should be able to make extensive use of a variety of reading resources, especially high-quality children's and adolescent literature.

CLASSROOM EXAMPLES

Teachers can determine students' interests, abilities, and learning- or reading-style preferences through observations, interviews, checklists, and inventories. This information can guide the selection of materials and can also be shared with students.

In classrooms designed to encourage reading, teachers label many objects, post written charts and directions, and stock well-organized libraries with a variety of reading materials, including poetry, storybooks, newspapers, magazines, book recordings, reading games, and software. Physical features of libraries that increase children's voluntary use of books include a focal area, partitioned and private places to read, comfortable seating, a display of some attractive book covers, literature-oriented displays and props; and books organized into categories (Fractor, Woodruff, Martinez, and Teale 1993).

A large repertoire of written materials that reflect the students' interests and backgrounds should be available in classroom and school libraries. These materials should reflect the diverse cultures and experiences of the youngsters. Teachers can encourage students to write about their experiences, publish their writing in school, and share their writing with classmates. Youngsters may choose to write about topics such as their families, their interests, the country in which they were born, and holiday celebrations.

Teachers should provide time for students to browse through reading materials in the library and to choose, discuss, and share their reading interests and favorite reading materials with their peers. A student-devised card catalogue can list favorite books and why and for whom they are recommended. Teachers should help students keep records of what they read and the purposes for which they read in order to help youngsters become aware of the large role reading plays in their lives.

REFERENCES
Allington 1984; Anderson, Heibert, Scott, and Wilkinson 1985; Brophy and Evertson 1976; Carbo, Dunn, and Dunn 1986; Chall 1993; Durkin 1966; Fractor, Woodruff, Martinez, and Teale 1993; Freeman and Freeman 1993; Goodman, Goodman, and Hood 1989; Heald-Taylor 1987; Holdaway 1979, 1982; Huggins and Roos 1990; Salinger 1988; Strickland and Morrow 1989; Sulzby 1985; Teale 1984, 1987.

● STRATEGY 5.3: ENCOURAGE READING FOR PLEASURE

Teachers provide time and resources that enable students to read for pleasure and that increase reading motivation, fluency, and comprehension.

DISCUSSION

Not surprisingly, young people who enjoy reading and who spend a substantial amount of their free time reading tend to be better readers than those who do not invest themselves in reading. Many young people spend little time reading either in school or outside of school, and too few view reading as "fun." To stimulate interest in reading and to provide practice, teachers should design literacy-rich environments and provide time for students to read for pleasure.

Teachers need to find ways to build in uninterrupted periods of time (from ten to forty-five minutes, depending on the developmental ages, interests, and abilities of the students). During these periods, students are encouraged to become engaged with a variety of interesting, high-quality, developmentally appropriate reading materials; they can choose to read materials ranging from the readily understandable to the challenging. Teachers may permit students to freely choose any classroom materials or they may provide guidelines for students. For example, at times students may be required to select books from a list of biographies, books about history, or award-winning books.

Teachers may provide a variety of environments and activities to help students associate reading with pleasure. For example, students may interact with peers in discussion or reading groups, or they may form book clubs. The teacher can provide healthy snacks and comfortable seating areas, and emerging readers may work with tape recordings of challenging reading materials to help increase their confidence, comprehension, and fluency.

CLASSROOM EXAMPLES

After introducing students to a variety of reading materials, a teacher might help youngsters to identify various book clubs that they can form and join, based on their reading interests (for instance, the Mystery Club, the

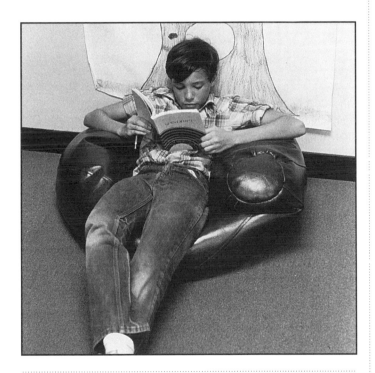

This middle-grade student is engrossed in a book of his choice. Sitting on a comfortable beanbag chair, under a tree created by his peers, makes for a relaxing and reassuring environment. Large amounts of reading done in and outside of school correlate positively with reading achievement. Experiences such as this one help students to associate reading with pleasure and increase the likelihood that they will voluntarily choose to read. Spending quality time reading, and doing this often, is a crucial step toward becoming a lifelong reader.

Adventure Club, or the History Club). The class can work together to design a poster for each book club, and students can sign their names on the poster if they are interested in reading a certain type of book with a group or after they have read a specific number of books of that type. Teachers can provide class time for students to meet and discuss their mutual interests and readings. Students can be encouraged to devise discussion questions for group meetings, and to lead discussion groups.

REFERENCES
Adams 1990; Anderson, Heibert, Scott, and Wilkinson 1985; Bloome 1985; Chall, Jacobs, and Baldwin 1990; Feitelson, Goldstein, Iroqui, and Shore 1993; Goodman 1984; Holdaway 1979; Karweit 1989; Knapp and Turnbull 1990; Morrow, Sharkey, and Firestone 1993; Passow 1990; Strickland and Morrow 1989; Sutfin 1990; Taylor, Frye, and Maruyama 1990; Teale and Sulzby 1986.

● STRATEGY 5.4: PROMOTE HOME/SCHOOL PARTNERSHIPS

Teachers enhance effective reading instruction through the use of home/school partnerships.

DISCUSSION

A great many young people of all ages in the United States today watch too much television and read too little. Voluntary reading and library use decline sharply throughout the grades, making it difficult for many youngsters, especially those at risk of academic failure, to learn to read well enough to function effectively in school.

Schools need to emphasize the importance of reading at home through a variety of activities with parents or guardians. Workshops can be offered at convenient times to:

• help parents understand the importance of reading at home;
• demonstrate techniques for reading with youngsters;
• provide hands-on practice with shared reading activities;
• show parents or guardians how to get a library card for their child;
• demonstrate how to use recordings of books in the home; and
• help parents or guardians understand their child's particular interests and style of learning.

Parents or guardians should be given specific activities that will enable them to play an active role in monitoring and assisting with assigned homework or school tasks. They need to be encouraged to read aloud to children regularly while limiting television viewing to less than ten hours weekly.

CLASSROOM EXAMPLES

To help parents or guardians provide books for their children at home, teachers might establish a classroom library of books that students can check out. During a workshop for parents or guardians, the procedures for securing and using a library card can be role played and discussed. Parents can learn how to create games that help children practice sight words and build their vocabulary. Parents usually enjoy learning how to read to their child and appreciate lists of possible books to borrow or purchase.

Teachers also might offer an intergenerational reading workshop in which parents and guardians are shown procedures for effectively reading a book to a child; for example, positioning the book during reading, involving the child in the story through questions and comments, and taking turns with the child to read the story using some of the modeling methods described in Figure 5.2 (on p.81).

To teach parents these modeling methods, teachers need to model the method first and then ask parents to practice the method. An effective procedure is to videotape a method being used correctly in the classroom, play the videotape for parents, model the method with a student, discuss the method and list the procedures with parents. Then parents can be asked to practice the method with their own child. At an intergenerational workshop, parents can practice a modeling method with their child.

REFERENCES
Anderson and Pearson 1984; Becher 1984, 1985; Binkley and others 1988, 1989; Chall 1993; France and Hager 1993; Freeman and Freeman 1993; Hansen 1987; Miller et al. 1986; Morrow 1982, 1983; Ollila and Mayfield 1992; Paschal, Weinstein, and Walberg 1984; Slade 1988; Strickland and Morrow 1989; Sulzby and Teale 1987; Taylor and Strickland 1986; Teale 1984, 1986, 1987; Tierney and Shanahan 1991; Trelease 1982; Walberg, Paschal, and Winstein 1985.

● STRATEGY 5.5: INTEGRATE LANGUAGE ACTIVITIES

Teachers who integrate reading, writing, listening, and speaking activities help students make natural connections among the disciplines and support their development as readers and communicators.

DISCUSSION

When students have the opportunity to engage in a range of language activities, they can observe and use the patterns of language in different ways. By listening to stories, for instance, they learn that stories have structure and similar components, such as characters and plot. This knowledge will guide their own reading. Story writing enables students to learn firsthand about the types of decisions that authors need to make. When writing a story, students can apply the knowledge of writing style, story structure, and language that they have gained from listening to, speaking about, and reading stories.

Talking with adults and peers about what they have read or written gives students insights into the meaning of texts and how that meaning is conveyed through language. Students develop these insights not only through listening to peers but also through the process of articulating their own perceptions and interpretations. When teachers are sensitive to and accepting of the differences in the expressive language abilities of diverse youngsters, they show that they value diversity and that they are ready to assist students in their language development.

Besides allowing students to make connections among the varied uses of language, integrated activities provide opportunities for students to perceive the differences in the uses of language for different purposes and in different contexts. For example, students learn that writing a story often requires language different from that used in retelling a story.

CLASSROOM EXAMPLES

To assist emerging readers and writers, teachers model and describe the purposes and writing styles of authors, and encourage students to draw parallels between these models and their own writings. They also encourage students to listen to the ideas and interpretations of their peers through student-directed discussions (possibly in small reading groups) of reading selections. As students develop their reading and writing abilities, teachers introduce them to more difficult and varied writing styles, which they may discuss, review, critique, and imitate.

Asking students to imitate the writing style of an author is an activity that helps students integrate reading, writing, listening, and speaking. It is appropriate for students who have listened to many stories by the same author. The teacher begins the activity by calling attention to the author's style, such as how the author usually begins a story, how she develops the plot, and how she describes the characters. Students then write stories in the same style. They might then send their stories to the author along with an invitation to visit their classroom to talk about writing.

REFERENCES

Anderson, Heibert, Scott, and Wilkinson 1985; Atwell 1987; Burnett and Berg 1987; Calkins 1983; Clay 1979, 1986; Goatley and Raphael 1992; Goodman, Goodman, and Hood 1989; Hansen 1987; Harste, Short, and Burke 1988; Heald-Taylor 1987; Holdaway 1979; Knapp and Turnbull 1990; Langer and Applebee 1983; Larrick 1987; Palincsar, Englert, Raphael, and Gavelek 1991; Strickland and Morrow 1989; Teale and Sulzby 1986; Tierney and Shanahan 1991; Tierney, Soter, O'Flahavan, and McGinley 1989.

On "Read-In Day" at Kempsville Meadows Elementary, Wendy Friedman, Chris Brown, Erin Mcdonald, and Zorran Watterson (left to right), are listening to Caps for Sale at the Listening Center. They're wearing their own caps, which adds to the enjoyment of the story and fosters a feeling of togetherness. Scheduled events like this can help to increase children's excitement about reading and improve their reading fluency.

● STRATEGY 5.6: ACCOMMODATE STUDENTS' INTERESTS, BACKGROUNDS, ABILITIES, AND READING STYLES

Teachers identify and accommodate their students' interests, backgrounds, abilities, and reading styles; they share this information with students and their parents to increase students' self-esteem, motivation, and learning ability.

DISCUSSION

According to William Glasser, students need to feel important in school; they need to be able to say, "Someone listens to me; someone thinks that what I have to say is important; someone is willing to do what I say." When their basic needs for recognition and power are ignored, many children "pay little attention to academic subjects" and, instead, engage "in a desperate search for . . . acceptance" that can lead to behavioral problems (Gough 1987, p. 657).

On the other hand, students whose teachers accommodate their interests, backgrounds, abilities, and styles tend to experience a sense of power, which can lead, in turn, to more effective learning and improved behavior. Instructional approaches that virtually force students to learn to read, ignoring what they have already learned and using materials that fail to engage them, tend to ensure failure and loss of self-esteem. Approaches that capitalize on students' strengths and interests tend to increase their self-confidence and their reading achievement.

At-risk students, in particular, need to learn how to capitalize on their learning strengths while compensating for their weaknesses. Teachers can identify young people's interests, backgrounds, abilities, and reading styles through observations, artwork, checklists, interviews, and inventories. They can then use this information to plan instruction; they can also share it with students and their parents, along with suggestions for work that be accomplished at home.

CLASSROOM EXAMPLES

Teachers can learn to observe students' reading styles and plan instruction based on their observations (see Figure 5.3). They might, for example, ask students to draw pictures related to reading. Students could draw pictures of where they like to read, such as a favorite reading chair

Figure 5.3
Reading Style Observation Guide (RSOG)

Observation: The student . . .	Reading Style Diagnosis: The student . . .	Suggested Teaching Strategies: The teacher might . . .
1 is distracted by noise, looks up from reading at the slightest sound, places hands over ears, tries to quiet others.	prefers to read in a quiet environment.	provide quiet reading areas (study carrels and magic carpet sections); use rugs, stuffed furniture, drapes; provide tape-recorded materials with headsets.
2 can read easily when other people are talking or music is playing.	prefers to read in an environment with talking and/or music.	permit student to listen to music through headsets while reading; establish small-group reading areas.
3 squirms, fidgets, squints when reading near a window on a sunny day.	prefers to read in soft or dim light.	use plants, curtains, hanging beads, dividers to block and diffuse light; add shaded lamps to reading sections; suggest student read in darker area of room.
4 seeks brightly lit areas for reading.	prefers to read in bright light.	allow student to read under bright lights and near windows.
5 wears many sweaters indoors.	prefers a warm environment.	encourage youngster to read in a warmer area and suggest sweaters.
6 perspires easily, wears light clothing.	prefers a cool environment.	encourage pupil to read in a cooler area and suggest light clothing.
7 is restless and moves in his seat when reading.	prefers an informal design.	allow the student to read while sitting on a pillow, carpeting, soft chair, or floor.
8 continually asks for teacher approval on reading work; enjoys sharing interests with teachers.	is teacher-motivated.	encourage child to discuss reading interests with you and to share work with you after doing it; praise him/her; try small, teacher-directed reading group.
9 enjoys reading with the teacher.	prefers reading with adults.	schedule youngster to read with you often; try older tutors and adult volunteers.
10 cannot complete lengthy assignments.	is neither persistent nor responsible.	give short reading assignments and check them frequently; try programmed reading materials or multisensory instructional packages.
11 becomes confused by many choices of reading materials.	requires structure.	limit choices; give clear, simple directions; try a structured reading approach such as a basal reader or programmed materials; provide a limited selection of reading resources based on child's interests.

Figure 5.3 (continued)
Reading Style Observation Guide (RSOG)

Observation: The student . . .	Reading Style Diagnosis: The student . . .	Suggested Teaching Strategies: The teacher might . . .
12 enjoys choices, demonstrates creativity when reading.	does not require structure.	provide many choices of reading materials; try an individualized reading program.
13 participates actively in group discussions; chooses to read with friends.	prefers to read with peers.	establish isolated small-group areas; provide reading games, activity cards; encourage writing and acting in plays or panels; try a language-experience approach.
14 shies away from others; reads best alone.	prefers to red alone.	provide programmed materials if structure is needed; tape-recorded books, computers, multisensory activities for tactile/kinesthetic or unmotivated child.
15 remembers details in pictures; is a good speller; does not confuse visually similar words or letters; has a good sight vocabulary.	is a visual learner.	try a whole-word reading approach; if the child also needs structure, try programmed learning sequences.
16 remembers directions and stories after hearing them; decodes words with ease; does not confuse similar-sounding words; enjoys listening activities.	is an auditory learner.	try a phonic or linguistic reading approach or structure; for variety, occasionally try a programmed learning sequence.
17 enjoys learning by touching; remembers words after tracing over and "feeling" them; likes to type, play reading games; is very active.	is a tactile/kinesthetic learner.	try a language-experience approach; use clay, sandpaper, and so on, to form words; try many reading games, model building, project work, and multisensory activities.
18 continually asks if it is lunch time or time for a snack when reading.	prefers intake while reading.	permit nutritious snacks during reading periods.
19 has difficulty reading in early morning; becomes more animated and attentive in the afternoon.	is better able to read in the late afternoon; may be even better at night!	schedule student to read in the late afternoon or send home "talking books" for evening work.
20 cannot sit still for long reading periods; becomes restless and sometimes misbehaves.	either requires mobility or different types of studies or methods.	allow snack breaks; provide manipulatives and reading games; have child read where movement is possible (floor, couch).

Source: Carbo 1994. Copyright © 1994 Marie Carbo.

or couch, and their preferred type of lighting. Or teachers might ask students to describe their favorite reading partner(s) and their favorite time of day for reading. Teachers could share their observations with other teachers, students, and students' parents or guardians. Inventories such as the *Reading Style Inventory* (Carbo 1988a) provide detailed, computerized profiles that describe students' reading styles and compatible reading strategies.

To identify students' reading interests, teachers can design a simple Reading Interests Inventory; youngsters could even help design this inventory as a class or school-wide project. The Reading Interest Inventory can be used as a guide for selecting and accumulating books for a class or school library. The inventory should, of course, include questions about students' interests, such as:

• their general interests (e.g., sports, food, software, baseball cars, chess, dancing, kites, music, machinery);
• the types of reading materials they enjoy (e.g., storybooks, books with facts, textbooks, readers, comic books, magazines, newspapers, plays, poems, picture books); and
• the types of books they enjoy (e.g., adventure, science fiction, humor, science, history, romance, mystery, mythology, fiction, nonfiction).

REFERENCES
Allington 1984; Anderson, Heibert, Scott, and Wilkinson 1985; Calfee and Drum 1986; Carbo 1987, 1988a, 1989; Carbo and Hodges 1988; Clay 1979; Dunn 1990; Garcia and Pearson 1990; Gough 1987; Grant 1985; Kapinus, Gambrell, and Koskinen 1987; Love 1988; Mohrmann 1990; Morrow, Sharkey, and Firestone 1993; Palincsar and Brown 1984; Paris, Cross, and Lipson 1984; Pearson, Roehler, Doler, and Duffy 1992.

● STRATEGY 5.7: USE SYSTEMATIC, VARIED STRATEGIES FOR RECOGNIZING WORDS

Teachers provide students with systematic instruction using a variety of strategies for recognizing words in meaningful contexts to promote fluency and to give students control over their reading.

DISCUSSION

Students need a repertoire of strategies for recognizing words, including the use of phonics, context, word family patterns, and structural analysis. Direct instruction and application in meaningful, authentic reading situations supports the development of reading fluency and independence, as students find that they can apply

strategies in an ever wider range of contexts. Inquiry is often useful for helping students discover for themselves patterns and relationships among words.

Instruction should be fun and thought-provoking; it should complement the interest and strengths of each student. Learning centers that contain interesting, challenging, "hands-on" materials enhance the learning of active learners—those who need to touch and experience what they are learning.

CLASSROOM EXAMPLES

When students cannot decode a word in context, the teacher might suggest a number of different strategies, such as reading ahead a bit and using context clues, sounding out the word, or thinking of words that resemble

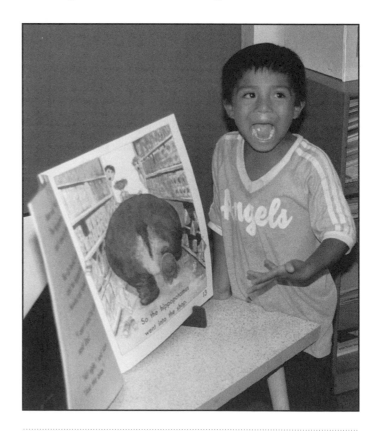

Absolute delight is expressed by Israel Felix, a young Mayan Indian child from Guatemala, at Hope Rural School in Indiantown, Florida. Hope Rural School was founded to meet the needs of a large migrant/immigrant population. To increase children's word recognition and comprehension the class can model a big-book story like the one shown here during shared reading. Students can discuss, reenact, and draw picture of the happenings in the story.

parts of the unknown word. Students who find inquiry methods frustrating may respond well to direct instruction; those who have difficulty with context clues may find phonics or structural analysis particularly helpful. Teachers should emphasize strategies that students find most beneficial rather than strategies that work well for teachers. For example, if students have difficulty sounding out words because they cannot hear or remember letter sounds, the teacher should emphasize context clues and other approaches that students find helpful. Ultimately, students should have a repertoire of strategies that they can apply flexibly in a variety of contexts.

REFERENCES

Adams 1990; Alverman and Swafford 1989; Anderson, Heibert, Scott, and Wilkinson 1985; Beck and Juel 1992; Brophy 1987; Brophy and Good 1986; Clay 1979; Dunn 1989, 1990; Garcia and Pearson 1990; Gough 1987; Grant 1985; Holdaway 1979; Juel 1991; Love 1988; Passow 1990; Samuels, Schermer, and Reinking 1992.

● STRATEGY 5.8: USE A VARIETY OF READING METHODS

To facilitate and accelerate the process of learning to read, teachers use a variety of reading methods that accommodate the interests, backgrounds, and reading strengths of students.

DISCUSSION

When students have the opportunity to use methods that make learning to read an interesting, enjoyable, and successful experience, they are likely to associate reading with pleasure and to perceive themselves as successful readers. This positive association increases the likelihood that students will choose to read on their own. On the other hand, reading methods that hamper learning can have a decidedly negative effect on reading ability, attitudes toward reading, and even self-esteem.

Teachers need to use methods that help students to master the complexity of reading rather than simply focus on isolated skills. Reading instruction should always support the notion of reading as a tool for building meaning and understanding. Young people who experience difficulty using one method should be given the opportunity to try an alternate approach that better accommodates their reading style.

CLASSROOM EXAMPLES

To accommodate students' reading strengths, teachers can adapt certain reading methods or substitute those that most benefit students. For example, they may allow students who don't enjoy the process of composing on paper to dictate stories to a teacher or to peers, or to use a word processor to facilitate the process. In a similar manner, teachers can encourage students who have difficulty distinguishing among, recalling, or blending sounds to illustrate letter sounds with drawings of words that begin with that sound. If the difficulty persists, then teachers can place less emphasis on phonics and more emphasis on alternative strategies and methods that do not require highly developed auditory abilities. For example, teachers can encourage students to write and read their own stories, listen to recordings of stories, and choral read stories (see Figure 5.2 on p. 81).

Students with visual reversals often benefit from touching and feeling letters, while students who have difficulty remembering may benefit from repeated reading methods and repeated listenings to recorded materials. For youngsters who are strongly tactile and kinesthetic, "hands-on" activities like board games and task cards can be helpful.

"Innovating on text" is a method that accommodates the interests, backgrounds, and reading strengths of many students. It involves making changes to a familiar word pattern or phrase. For instance students may substitute one word for another or two words for one word, or add words to the pattern, or delete words from the pattern. They may identify rhyming words and invent new rhymes by substituting words. Using the story "Five Little Monkeys," for instance, students may create a new story called "Five Little Bears":

> Five little bears jumping on stairs,
> One fell off and lost his hair.
> Mommy called the doctor,
> And the doctor declared,
> "No more bears jumping on stairs."

REFERENCES

Adams 1990; Anderson, Heibert, Scott, and Wilkinson 1985; Beck and Juel 1992; Bussis, Chittenden, Amarel, and Klausner 1985; Calfee and Drum 1986; Carbo, Dunn, and Dunn 1986; Carver and Hoffman 1981; Chall, Jacobs, and Baldwin 1990; Chomsky 1978; Dahl and Samuels 1979; Garcia and Pearson 1990; Harste, Short, and Burke 1988; Harste, Woodward, and Burke 1984; McCauley and McCauley 1992; Miller et al. 1986; Pearson, Roehler, Dole, and Duffy 1992; Samuels, Schermer, and Reinking 1992; Strickland and Morrow 1989.

● STRATEGY 5.9: ACTIVATE STUDENTS' PRIOR KNOWLEDGE

Teachers who activate students' prior knowledge and background experiences help students understand and respond to reading selections.

DISCUSSION

Students bring their own unique prior knowledge to the reading of any text. They often profit from guidance and support as they access their background experiences related to the information in a reading selection. To activate students' prior knowledge, teachers may ask students to draw on their personal experiences, perhaps by remembering a similar story, a place they visited, or something that happened to them. Teachers can assist this process by showing pictures, encouraging the sharing of anecdotes, and using graphic aids related to the story and vocabulary.

Teachers can help youngsters link their own language to unfamiliar language or to a "bookish" syntactical sequence. To do this, teachers might use language features contained in the story during the discussion of the story, carefully and deliberately enunciate unusual words, use particular sentence patterns two or three times, or ask the students to repeat several times difficult language or pronunciation after hearing the teacher's model. These techniques help ready the mind and ear of the students and enable them to process novel words, phrases, and concepts more easily (Clay 1991).

Teachers can ask questions to help students consider their relevant prior knowledge. Specific strategies—for example, KWL (what I know, what I want to learn, and what I learned)—help to structure the activation, application, and integration of students' prior knowledge. Reciprocal teaching allows students to consistently activate and apply prior knowledge as they make predictions about a reading selection.

CLASSROOM EXAMPLES

The teacher using KWL draws three columns on the board with the following headings: "Know," "Want to Learn," and "Learned." Students offer information that they already know about the topic to be written in the first column. Then, to guide their reading, students generate questions about what they want to find out from their reading. After completing the reading, students fill in the third column with descriptions of what they have learned.

In addition to the KWL strategy, previewing techniques such as probable passages and story frames, graphic organizers, and guided reading may be used in the classroom. To create a probable passage and story frame, the teacher chooses vocabulary words from a reading selection and helps students categorize the words according to the elements of a story frame (e.g., setting, characters, problem, solution, ending). The students use the story frame to predict a story line, writing the categorized terms into a "probable passage"—that is, the probably direction of the story. Students then read the selection. Finally, they modify the story frame and probable passage to reflect the actual reading selection.

To develop a graphic organizer, the teacher identifies and lists all of the vocabulary that students need to understand a story (or other type of text). The teacher chooses an appropriate diagram as a visual framework for the selection. This diagram, or graphic organizer, will help students grasp the text's organization and the relationships between the concepts. The teacher presents the graphic organizer by explaining the terms and their relationship to one another. Students may then elaborate on their experiences with the topic.

REFERENCES

Anderson and Pearson 1984; Anderson, Heibert, Scott, and Wilkinson 1985; Au 1980; Beck and McKeown 1981; Clay 1979, 1991; Kapinus, Gambrell, and Koskinen 1987; Ogle 1986; Paris 1986; Pearson, Roehler, Dole, and Duffy 1992; Pressley, Levin, and McDaniel 1987; Stahl and Vancil 1986; Strickland and Morrow 1989; Wang and Palincsar 1989.

● STRATEGY 5.10: PROVIDE AUTHENTIC PURPOSES, MATERIALS, AND AUDIENCES

Teachers increase students' motivation and engagement when they provide authentic purposes, materials, and audiences for reading, writing, listening, and speaking.

DISCUSSION

In the real world, people do things for real purposes. For example, adults write to entertain and inform peers, to persuade, to bring about action, to manage activities, to gain personal insights, or to keep records.

In school, students need audiences and purposes for reading, writing, and speaking that relate to the world outside the school. Teachers need to provide young people not only with well-written books and stories whose primary purpose is to entertain and inform, but also with materials related to the world outside the classroom, such as newspapers, maps, directions, brochures, advertisements, and directories.

CLASSROOM EXAMPLE

Students need to have authentic purposes, materials, and audiences for learning as they take part in activities in which they do some or all of the following activities: plan and implement a school fair, write and perform in a play, or raise money for a trip. During a project, youngsters might take notes, devise schedules, share work, make posters and costumes, discuss problems that arise, and report their findings.

Interdisciplinary teaching and learning occur quite naturally when youngsters work on large-scale projects. If, for example, students first identify a local environmental or community problem, they might then read newspaper items on the problem, science and social studies articles and texts, and relevant laws. After discussion, and possibly debates, they could write their own editorials, articles, and letters, and they might find it necessary to begin corresponding with people who are knowledgeable about the issue. Students might place key pieces of the information they accumulate in a large book or portfolio; they might also design bulletin boards to display their work. And they might share with other classes the knowledge they've gained. These are but a few of the multitude of activities and learning situations that could be classified as "authentic."

REFERENCES
Atwell 1987; Anderson, Heibert, Scott, and Wilkinson 1985; Beck and McKeown 1981; Brophy 1987; Bussis, Chittenden, Amarel, and Klausner 1985; Calfee and Drum 1986; Clay 1979; Garner 1992; Goodman, Goodman, and Hood 1989; Hansen 1987; Harste, Woodward, and Burke 1984; Jongsma 1989; Knapp and Turnbull 1990; Langer and Applebee 1983; Newman 1985; Pearson and Fielding 1991; Wolf 1989; Wixson, Peters, Weber, and Roeber 1987.

● STRATEGY 5.11: CONSTRUCT, EXAMINE, AND EXTEND MEANING

Teachers provide a variety of opportunities for students to construct meaning and respond to what they have read, thereby increasing students' comprehension of the text and helping them to make new and different connections to the real world.

Excitement over reading is evident in every classroom at Stemley Road Elementary, a model reading styles school in Talladega, Alabama. In this lesson, several strategies described in this chapter were used by Rita Pilkington, who was Teacher of the Year in 1993 for Stemley Road and received the Sanford Institute Teaching Excellence Award. Before reading a story to her students, Pilkington asked them questions to activate their prior knowledge (see strategy 5.9), then read the story aloud (see strategy 5.1), helped the children to reread the story (see strategies 5.1 and 5.7), and assisted the children as they composed a dramatized version of the story (see strategies 5.5, 5.10, 5.11, and 5.12). In this photograph, the youngsters (from left to right, Catrease Swain, Travis Fliker, Alphonso Truss, Latoya Pruett, Nicholas Watts, and Jason Jones) are role playing some of the characters in their story. Note the puppets on their hands (see strategies 5.5 and 5.10). Both federal funding and parent-teacher fund raisers (see strategy 5.4) provided each the resources, tape players, books, and the Reading Style Inventory *(see strategies 5.1, 5.2, 5.3, and 5.10).*

DISCUSSION

Readers' responses to a given text depend on their background knowledge and the information in the text. Interactions between the reader and the text should not be hierarchical; that is, less proficient readers need to be given opportunities to respond to texts on a variety of levels of thinking. All readers should be given opportunities to construct an initial understanding of the text, to interpret and examine the meaning of the text, and to respond "personally and critically" to the text (Carbo 1988a, p. 13).

CLASSROOM EXAMPLES

Students should be encouraged to interpret and respond to a reading selection in a variety of ways. For example, the retelling of stories, both oral and written, can provide students with broad understandings of what they have read. Artwork, role playing, and simulations in response to reading can provide literal and interpretive renderings of the ideas in the text. Interviews and questions can elicit a range of responses that may include personal and critical perceptions.

Student-led discussions allow for social interactions, and response logs provide a means of self-directed reflection on the meaning of the text. After students are exposed to a variety of ways of responding to text, they can be given more and more choices of how they will respond. The amount of choice provided depends on the learning styles of the youngsters.

Here is an example of how a teacher can provide a variety of opportunities for students to construct meaning and respond to what they have read: The teacher begins by asking students to read the book *Tikki Tikki Tembo* by Arlene Mosel (New York: Holt, 1968). After students have read the story, the teacher provides for the following activities:

• Read a nonfiction book about China from the library.
• Chant Tikki Tikki Tembo's full name with musical instruments.
• Discuss the illustrations in the book, and create Chinese kites using the colors of blue, green, yellow, and brown illustrated in the story.
• Reread the old man's description of his dream in the story; discuss dreams and share examples; and/or write about dreams and illustrate them.

REFERENCES
Anderson, Heibert, Scott, and Wilkinson 1985; Angeletti 1991; Atwell 1987; Beck and McKeown 1981; Burnett and Berg 1987; Carbo 1988a; Cazden 1983; Clay 1991; Harste, Short, and Burke 1988; Harste, Woodward, and Burke 1984; Hull and Shaw-Baker 1989; Morrow, Sharkey, and Firestone 1993; Ogle 1986; Paris 1986; Pearson and Fielding 1991; Simonsen and Singer 1992; Strickland and Morrow 1989.

● STRATEGY 5.12: USE MEANING-DRIVEN READING ACTIVITIES

Teachers help students understand that the goal of reading is the construction of meaning.

DISCUSSION

Too often, instruction in reading encourages youngsters to believe that the main goal of reading is to sound out words or to get the same answer that appears in the teacher's guide. Students need to understand that reading provides a means of building and extending an understanding of people, places, and things—and oneself. Teachers facilitate this meaning-making process by helping students make connections between their background experiences and knowledge and the new information they encounter in their reading.

Teachers can emphasize and focus on meaning by using inquiry strategies that promote divergent thinking, different levels of thinking, and personal responses. They can use meaningful materials for instructional and application activities. Engaging in substantive discussions with teachers and peers helps youngsters realize that meaning can be negotiated and revised.

CLASSROOM EXAMPLES

Even phonics generalizations or the development of insights about word patterns can be made meaningful for young people. To help students develop the skill of recognizing a certain pattern of letters in words, for instance, a teacher may ask students to locate examples of the pattern in a story. Students might then think of other words having the same pattern and use them in sentences related to the story.

To increase students' understanding of both the language and the concepts used in textbooks, teachers can employ various strategies that relate to the content and accommodate students' learning styles, including visuals (maps, pictures), imagery, reading aloud to students, retellings, questions, graphic overviews, study guides, summaries, outlines, and vocabulary previews.

Keeping a response log when studying literature or a learning log when doing content-area reading helps students focus on their own understanding of reading and the strategies they use to build those understandings. In teacher- or student-directed discussion groups, youngsters can share their responses to a range of questions posed by the teacher or by other students.

Semantic mapping is a strategy for teaching the meaning of words. It makes extensive use of classroom discussion in connection with a visual display (Johnson and Pearson 1984; Stahl and Vancil (1986) have described semantic mapping as follows: A teacher chooses a key word and other target words from material that the student will read. The key word is listed on the board and students are asked to suggest terms associated with the key word. The teacher writes the suggested words in a list on the board as the students suggest them. From this list, a map is constructed. The relationships between the key word and the target words are discussed thoroughly. Students are asked to try to categories each section of the map. A copy of an incomplete semantic map is handed out to the students. They are asked to fill in the words from the map on the board and any other additional categories or words they can add. The reading is assigned, with instructions for students to work on their maps during reading. After reading, the maps are discussed once more and new terms and categories are added.

REFERENCES
Adams 1990; Altwerger, Edelsky, and Flores 1987; Anderson, Heibert, Scott, and Wilkinson 1985; Chall, Conard, and Harris-Sharples 1983; Harste, Short, and Burke 1988; Johnson and Pearson 1984; Knapp and Turnbull 1990; Meyers 1992; Ogle 1986; Palincsar, Englert, Raphael, and Gavelek 1991; Paris 1986; Pearson, Roehler, Dole, and Duffy 1992; Pressley, Levin, and McDaniel 1987; Simonsen and Singer 1992; Stahl and Vancil 1986; Tierney and Pearson 1986.

● STRATEGY 5.13: PROVIDE EXPLICIT INSTRUCTION OF "WHAT," "WHEN," AND "WHY"

Teachers use modeling to provide explicit instruction in the "what,""when," and "why" of reading strategies; they offer students many opportunities to apply these strategies.

DISCUSSION

Students profit from explicit instruction in reading strategies. Modeling the use of strategies is an effective component of that instruction. Students need to know what a strategy is (declarative knowledge); how to use it (procedural knowledge); and when and why it should be used (contextual knowledge). For example, students need to know what a main idea is, how to figure out the main idea, and why it helps to think about the main idea.

Youngsters need opportunities to apply reading strategies in supportive contexts, so they can gradually assume responsibility for applying the strategies. Cues such as charts, posters, bookmarks, and logs help students make new strategies part of their repertoire.

CLASSROOM EXAMPLES

Reciprocal teaching is a structured approach that allows students to gradually and independently apply reading strategies within a meaningful context. First, the teacher reads a section of the text. Then she models a summary of what she read, asks a question about the text, clarifies potential areas of confusion, and predicts what will come next. After several instances of such modeling, the teacher turns over the leadership of the group to a student, and that student provides the modeling. This strategy can be varied to allow for the gradual introduction of strategies, one at a time, or the use of collaborative approaches, such as students working in pairs to develop their summaries, questions, clarifications, and predictions.

Another excellent approach is "Question-Answer-Relationships" or "QAR" (Raphael 1982), which involves teaching students how to analyze a question in order to find the correct answer or answers. Students try to place questions in one of three categories, according to the source of the information required for the answer: "Right There," "Think and Search," and "On My Own". The "Right There" category is for questions that have an answer explicit in the reading—that is, the words in the question and the words in the answer are "right there" in the same sentence. "Think and Search" also involves a question that has an answer in the reading, but this answer requires information from more than one sentence or paragraph. "On My Own" involves a question for which the answer must be found in the reader's own knowledge; in other words, the information is relevant to the story but doesn't appear in it. Students receive feedback concerning their ability to identify a QAR as "Right There," "Think and Search," or "On My Own," their ability to use the QAR to locate the answer, and their ability to provide an adequate answer.

REFERENCES
Adams 1990; Anderson, Heibert, Scott, and Wilkinson 1985; Calfee and Drum 1986; Cazden 1983; Hull, Shaw-Baker 1989; Jones 1986; Palincsar and Klenk 1991; Paris 1986; Pearson and Fielding 1991; Pearson, Roehler, Dole, and Duffy 1992; Raphael 1982; Strickland and Morrow 1989; Wang and Palincsar 1989.

● STRATEGY 5.14: ALLOW STUDENTS TO WORK IN A VARIETY OF GROUPINGS

Teachers provide opportunities for students to work in a variety of groupings or alone, acknowledge individual differences in background, interests, and styles, and foster the development of social language proficiencies, literary skills, and knowledge.

DISCUSSION

The meaning of reading selections can be clarified, extended, and revised through discussion. Groupings of all sizes allow for valuable learning to take place and develop students' abilities to use reading in a range of situations that reflect real-world contexts. Students need to be able to use reading as individuals and also to develop their understandings further through group activities.

For example, youngsters can modify or affirm their own perspectives by sharing ideas with their peers in discussion groups. Discussion groups can also help students learn many important social skills, such as taking turns, entering a discussion, and building on points made by others. Students also learn that listening is important for both understanding and contributing to a discussion.

Many youngsters have a strong learning-style preference for working in pairs or groups, rather than working alone. Some students have a strong preference for working with those perceived as authorities on a subject, such as older students, parents, or teachers. Students also need time to work alone, however, because solitary time can encourage reflection and is ideal for youngsters whose learning style requires them to process information quietly before sharing with others. When appropriate, students should also have the opportunity to tutor others as well as to be helped by students within and across their own grade level.

CLASSROOM EXAMPLES

A teacher asks students to write in a personal log their initial responses to a reading selection and then to share those responses in small-group discussions. This activity provides an opportunity for both individual and group learning. It is important to note, however, that students need models and guidance if they are to learn how to respond to and interpret reading and participate in and promote interesting, enlightening discussions. By presenting mini-lessons to the whole group, the teacher can support students' written responses, facilitate effective small-group discussions, and encourage students to function in large-group settings.

REFERENCES

Anderson et al. 1982; Bloome 1985; Carbo 1983; Carbo, Dunn, and Dunn 1986; Carbo and Hodges 1988; Dunn 1990; Hall, Nagy, and Linn 1984; Madden et al. 1986; Mooney 1986; Morrow 1989; Slavin 1980, 1986; Wasik and Slavin 1990.

BIBLIOGRAPHY

Adams, M.J. (1990). *Beginning to Read: Thinking and Learning About Print*. Cambridge, Mass.: Bradford Books/MIT Press.

Allington, R.L. (1984). "Policy Constraints and Effective Compensatory Reading Instruction: A Review." Paper presented at the annual meeting of the International Reading Association.

Altwerger, B., C. Edelsky, and B. Flores. (November 1987). "Whole Language: What's New?" *Reading Teacher* 41, 2: 144-154.

Alverman, D.E., and J. Swafford. (1989). "Do Content Area Strategies Have a Research Base?" *Journal of Reading* 32: 388-394.

Anderson, L.M., and others. (August 1982). "Principles of Small-Group Instruction in Elementary Reading." East Lansing: Michigan State University, Institute for Research on Teaching.

Anderson, R.C., E. H. Heibert, J.A. Scott, and I.A. Wilkinson. (1985). *Becoming a Nation of Readers: The Report of the Commission on Reading*. Urbana, Ill.: Illinois University, Center for the Study of Reading; Washington, D.C.: National Academy of Education.

Anderson, L.W., and L.O. Pellicer. (September 1990). "Synthesis of Research on Compensatory and Remedial Education." *Educational Leadership* 48, 1: 10-16.

Anderson, R.C., and P.D. Pearson. (1984). *A Schema-Theoretic View of Basic Processes in Reading Comprehension*. (Technical Report No. 306). Cambridge, Mass.: Bolt, Beranek and Newman; Urbana, Ill.: Illinois University, Center for the Study of Reading.

Angeletti, S.R. (December 1991). "Encouraging Students to Think About What They Read." *Reading Teacher* 45, 4: 288-296.

Atwell, N. (1987). *In the Middle: Writing, Reading, and Learning with Adolescents*. Upper Montclair, N.J.: Boynton/Cook.

Au, K.H. (Summer 1980). "Participation Structures in a Reading Lesson with Hawaiian Children: Analysis of a Culturally Appropriate Instructional Event." *Anthropology and Education Quarterly* 11, 2: 91-115.

Becher, R.M. (1984). *Parent Involvement: A Review of Research and Principles of Successful Practice*. Washington, D.C.: National Institute of Education.

Becher, R.M. (1985). "Parent Involvement and Reading Achievement: A Review of Research." *Childhood Education* 62, 1: 44-50.

Beck, I.L., and M.G. McKeown. (1981). "Developing Questions That Promote Comprehension: The Story Mao." *Language Arts* 58: 913.

Beck, I.L., and C. Juel. (1992). "The Role of Decoding in Learning to Read." In *What Research Has to Say About Reading Instruction*, edited by S.J. Samuels and A.E. Farstrup. Newark, Del. International Reading Association.

Binkley, M.R., and others. (March 1988). *Becoming a Nation of Readers: What Parents Can Do*. Lexington, Mass.: D.C. Heath; Washington, D.C.: Office of Educational Research and Improvement.

Binkley, M.R. (1989). *Becoming a Nation of Readers: What Principals*

Can Do. Boston, Mass.: Houghton Mifflin; Alexandria, Va.: National Association of Elementary School Principals; Washington, D.C.: U.S. Department of Education, Office of Educational Research and Improvement.

Bloome, D. (1985). "Reading as a Social Process." *Language Arts* 62: 134-142.

Brophy, J. (October 1987). "Synthesis of Research on Strategies for Motivating Students to Learn." *Educational Leadership* 45, 2: 40-48.

Brophy, J., and C.M. Evertson. (1976). *Learning from Teaching: A Developmental Perspective*. Boston: Allyn and Bacon.

Brophy, J., and T.L. Good. (1986). "Teacher Behavior and Student Achievement." In *Handbook of Research on Teaching*, 3rd ed., edited by M.C. Wittrock. New York: Macmillan; London: Collier Macmillan.

Burnett, E.H., and P.C. Berg. (January 1987). "Reading Instruction in the Schools: Improving Students' Critical Thinking Skills." *Clearing House* 61, 5: 208-210.

Bussis, A., E. Chittenden, M. Amarel, and E. Klausner. (1985). *Inquiry into Meaning: An Investigation of Learning to Read*. Hillsdale, N.J.: Lawrence Erlbaum.

Calfee, R., and P. Drum. (1986). "Research on Teaching Reading." In *Handbook of Research on Teaching*, 3rd ed., edited by M.C. Wittrock. New York: Macmillan; London: Collier Macmillan.

Calkins, L.M. (1983). *Lessons from a Child: On the Teaching and Learning of Writing*. Exeter, N.H.: Heinemann Educational Books.

Carbo, M. (February 1983). "Reading Styles Change Between Second and Eighth Grade." *Educational Leadership* 40, 5: 56-69.

Carbo, M. (1987). "Deprogramming Reading Failure: Giving Unequal Learners an Equal Chance." *Phi Delta Kappan* 69: 97-202.

Carbo, M. (1988a). *Reading Style Inventory*. Syosset, N.Y.: National Reading Styles Institute.

Carbo, M. (October 1988b). "What Reading Achievement Tests Should Measure to Increase Literacy in the U.S." *Research Bulletin* No. 7. (Available from *Phi Delta Kappa*, Center on Evaluation, Development, and Research, Bloomington, Ind.)

Carbo, M. (1989). *How to Record Books for Maximum Reading Gains*. Roslyn Heights, N.Y.: National Reading Styles Institute.

Carbo, M. (1992). "Eliminating the Need for Dumbed-Down Text Books." *Educational Horizons* 70: 189-193.

Carbo, M. (1993). "Release Your Students' Learning Power," p. 37. Syosset, N.Y.: National Readings Styles Institute.

Carbo, M. (1994). *Reading Styles Training Manual*. Level 2, 23a, b. Syosset, N.Y.: National Reading Styles Institute.

Carbo, M., R. Dunn, and K. Dunn. (1986). *Teaching Students to Read Through Their Individual Learning Styles*. Englewood Cliffs, N.J.: Prentice-Hall.

Carbo, M., and H. Hodges. (Summer 1988). "Learning Styles Strategies Can Help Students at Risk." *Teaching Exceptional Children* 20, 4: 55-58.

Carroll, J.B. (1987). "The National Assessments in Reading: Are We Misreading the Findings?" *Phi Delta Kappan* 68: 424-430.

Carver, R.P., and J.V. Hoffman. (1981). "The Effect of Practice Through Repeated Reading on Gain in Reading Ability Using a Computer-Based Instructional System." *Reading Research Quarterly* 16: 374-390.

Cazden, C.B. (1983). "Adult Assistance to Language Development Scaffolds, Models, and Direct Instruction." In *Developing Literacy: Young Children's Understanding of Language*, edited by R.P. Parker and F.A. Davis. Newark: Del.: International Reading Association.

Chall, J.S. (1983). *Stages of Reading Development*. New York: McGraw-Hill.

Chall, J.S. (1993). "Why Poor Children Fall Behind in Reading: What Schools Can Do About It." *Effective School Practices* 12, 2: 29-36.

Chall, J.S., S.S. Conard, and S. Harris-Sharples. (1983). "Textbooks and Challenge: An Inquiry into Textbook Difficulty, Reading, Achievement, and Knowledge Acquisition." A final report to the Spencer Foundation. Cambridge: Harvard University Graduate School of Education.

Chall, J.S., V.A. Jacobs, and L.E. Baldwin. (1990). *The Reading Crisis: Why Poor Children Fall Behind*. Cambridge: Harvard University Press.

Chomsky, C. (March 1976). "After Decoding: What?" *Language Arts* 53, 3: 288-296, 314.

Chomsky, C. (1978). "When You Still Can't Read in Third Grade: After Decoding, What?" In *What Research Has to Say About Reading Instruction*, edited by S.J. Samuels and A.E. Farstrup. Newark, Del.: International Reading Association.

Clay, M.M. (1979). *The Early Detection of Reading Difficulties*. Portsmouth, N.H.: Heinemann.

Clay, M.M. (1986). "Constructive Processes: Talking, Reading, Writing, Art and Craft." *The Reading Teacher* 39: 764-770

Clay, M.M. (1991). "Introducing a New Storybook to Young Readers." *The Reading Teacher* 45: 264-279.

Dahl, P.R., and S.J. Samuels. (1979). "An Experimental Program for Teaching High Speed Word Recognition and Comprehension Skills." In *Communications Research in Learning Disabilities and Mental Retardation*, edited by J.E. Button, T.C. Lovitt, and T.D. Rowland. Baltimore, Md.: University Park Press.

Dunn, R. (March 1989). "Survey of Research on Learning Styles." *Educational Leadership* 46, 6: 50-58.

Dunn, R. (October 1990). "Rita Dunn Answers Questions on Learning Styles." *Educational Leadership* 48, 2: 15-19.

Durkin, D. (1966). *Children Who Read Early: Two Longitudinal Studies*. New York: Teachers College Press.

Epstein, J.L. (1991). "Paths to Partnership: What We Can Learn from Federal, State, District, and School Initiatives." *Phi Delta Kappan* 72: 344-349.

Farr, R. (1993). "Putting It All Together. Solving the Reading Assessment Puzzle." *The Reading Teacher* 46: 26-37.

Farr, R., L. Fay, R. Myers, and M. Ginsberg. (1987). *Reading Achievement in the United States: 1944-45, 1976 and 1986*. Bloomington: Indiana University.

Feitelson, D., Z. Goldstein, J. Iroqui, and D. Shore. (1993). "Effects of Listening to Story Reading on Aspects of Literacy Acquisition in a Diglossia Situation." *Reading Research Quarterly* 28, 1: 71-79.

Foertsch, M.A. (1992). *Reading In and Out of School: Factors Influencing the Literacy Achievement of American Students in Grades 4, 8, and 12, in 1988 and 1990*. Washington, D.C.: Office of Educational Research and Improvement.

Fractor, G.S., M.C. Woodruff, M.G. Martinez, and W.H. Teale. (1993). "Let's Not Miss Opportunities to Promote Voluntary Reading: Classroom Libraries in the Elementary School." *The Reading Teacher* 46: 476-484.

France, M.G., and J.M. Hager. (1993). "Recruit, Respect, Respond: A Model for Working with Low-income Families and Their Preschoolers." *The Reading Teacher* 46: 568-572.

Freeman, D., and Y.S. Freeman. (1993). "Strategies for Promoting the Primary Language of All Students." *The Reading Teacher* 46: 552-559.

Garner, R. (1992). "Metacognition and Self-monitoring Strategies." In *What Research Has to Say About Reading Instruction*, edited by S.J. Samuels and A.E. Farstrup. Newark, Del. International Reading Association.

Garcia, G.E., and P.D. Pearson. (1990). *Modifying Reading Instruction to Maximize Its Effectiveness for All Students*. Cambridge, Mass.: Bolt, Beranek, and Newman Inc.

Goatley, V.J., and T.E. Raphael. (1992). "Non-traditional Learners' Written and Dialogic Response to Literature." In *Literacy Research, Theory, and Practice: Views From Many Perspectives*.

41st Yearbook of the National Reading Conference, edited by C.K. Kinzer, and D.K. Leu. Chicago: National Reading Conference.

Goodman, Y. (1984). "The Development of Initial Literacy." In *Awakening to Literacy*, edited by H. Goelman, A. Oberg, and F. Smith. Portsmouth, N.H.: Heinemann.

Goodman, H.S., Y.M. Goodman, and W.J. Hood. (1989). *The Whole Language Evaluation Book*. Portsmouth, N.H.: Heinemann.

Gough, P.B. (May 1987). "The Key to Improving Schools: An Interview with William Glasser," *Phi Delta Kappan* 68, 9: 656-662.

Grant, S.M. (October 1985). "The Kinesthetic Approach to Teaching: Building a Foundation for Learning." *Journal of Learning Disabilities* 18, 8: 455-462.

Griffin, J.L. (July 31, 1987). "Dropout Rate Tied to Early Failure," *Chicago Tribune*, p. 1.

Hall, W.S., W.E. Nagy, and R. Linn. (1984). *Spoken Words: Effects of Situation and Social Group on Oral Word Usage and Frequency*. Hillsdale, N.J.: Lawrence Erlbaum.

Hansen, J. (1987). *When Writers Read*. Portsmouth, N.H.: Heinemann.

Harste, J., K.G. Short, and C. Burke. (1988). *Creating Classrooms for Authors: The Reading-Writing Connection*. Portsmouth, N.H.: Heinemann.

Harste, J., V. Woodward, and C. Burke. (1984). *Language Stories and Literacy Lessons*. Portsmouth, N.H.:. Heinemann.

Heald-Taylor, G. (1987). "Predictable Literature Selections and Activities for Language Arts Instruction." *The Reading Teacher* 41: 6-12.

Hodges, H. (1989). "ASCD's 3-High Achievement Model." Unpublished manuscript for the ASCD Urban Middle Grades Network, Alexandria, Va.

Hodges, H. (1991). "Effective K-12 Reading Practices: A Research Synthesis". In *The Knowledge Base Reference Guide*.

Hoffman, J., N.L. Roser, and J. Battle. (1993). "Reading Aloud in Classrooms: From the Modal to a 'Model.'" *The Reading Teacher* 46: 496-503.

Holdaway, D. (1979). *The Foundations of Literacy*. Exeter, N.H.: Heinemann Educational Books.

Holdaway, D. (1982). "Shared Book Experience: Teaching Reading Using Favorite Books." *Theory into Practice* 21: 293-300.

Huggins, L.J., and M.C. Roos. (1990). *An Alternative to the Basal Reading Approach*.

Hull, S., and M. Shaw-Baker. (1989). "Questions Good Teachers of Reading Should Ask." Paper presented at the annual meeting of the International Reading Association.

International Reading Association. (May 1988). Statement adopted by the Delegates Assembly of the International Reading Association.

Johnson, D.D., and P.D. Pearson. (1984). *Teaching Reading Vocabulary*, 2nd ed. New York: Holt, Rinehart and Winston.

Jones, B.F. (April 1986). "Quality and Equality Through Cognitive Instruction." *Educational Leadership* 43, 7: 4-11.

Jongsma, K.S. (1989). "Portfolio Assessment." *The Reading Teacher* 43: 264-265.

Juel, C. (1991). "Beginning Reading." In *Handbook of Reading Research*, Vol. II, edited by R. Barr, M.L. Kamil, P. B. Mosenthal, and P.D. Pearson. New York: Longman.

Kameenui, E.J. (1993). "Diverse Learners and the Tyranny of Time: Don't Fix Blame, Fix the Leaky Roof." *The Reading Teacher* 46: 376-383.

Kapinus, B.A., L. B. Gambrell, and P.S. Koskinen. (1987). "Effects of Practice in Re-telling Upon the Reading Comprehension of Proficient and Less Proficient Readers." In *Research in Literacy: Merging Perspectives*, edited by J.E. Readence and R.S. Baldwin. 36th Yearbook of the National Reading Conference. Rochester, N.Y.: National Reading Conference.

Karweit, N. (1989). "Effective Kindergarten Programs and Practices for Students At Risk." In *Effective Programs for Students At Risk*, edited by R.E. Slavin, N.L. Karweit, and N.A. Madden. Boston: Allyn and Bacon.

Knapp, M.S., and B. Turnbull. (1990). *Better Schooling for the Children of Poverty: Alternatives to Conventional Wisdom. Volume 1: Summary*. Washington, D.C.: Prepared under contract by SRI International and Policy Studies Associates for the U.S. Department of Education, Office of Planning, Budget and Evaluation.

Langer, J.A., and A.N. Applebee. (1983). "Instructional Scaffolding: Reading and Writing as Natural Language Activities." *Language Arts* 60: 168-175.

Larrick, N. (1987). "Illiteracy Starts Too Soon." *Phi Delta Kappan* 69: 184-189.

LaShell, L. (1986). "An Analysis of the Effects of Reading Methods on Reading Achievement and Focus of Control When Individual Reading Style Is Matched for Learning Disabled Students." Doctoral diss., Fielding Institute, California.

Love, L. (May 1988). "The Effect of Reading Games on the Improvement of Fourth Grade Reading Skills Scores." Master's thesis, Kean College, New Jersey.

Madden, N.A., and others. (June 1986). "A Comprehensive Cooperative Learning Approach to Elementary Reading and Writing: Effects on Student Achievement." Baltimore, Md.: Center for Research on Elementary and Middle Schools.

Manning, M.L. (Winter 1989-1990). "Contemporary Studies of Teaching Behaviors and Their Implications for Middle Level Teacher Education." *Action in Teacher Education* 11, 4: 1-5.

Martinez, M.G., and W.H. Teale. (1988). "Reading in a Kindergarten Classroom Library." *The Reading Teacher* 41: 568-573.

Mason, J.M., and others. (July 1990). "Shared Book Reading in an Early Start Program for At-Risk Children." Urbana: Illinois University, Center for the Study of Reading.

McCauley, J.K., and D.S. McCauley. (1992). "Using Choral Reading to Promote Language Learning for ESL Students." *The Reading Teacher* 45: 526-533.

Miller, A., and others. (1986). "Parental Participation in Paired Reading: A Controlled Study." *Educational Psychology* 6, 3: 277-284.

Mohrmann, S.R. (1990). "Learning Styles of Poor Readers." Paper presented at the annual conference of the Southwest Educational Research Association, Austin, Texas.

Mooney, C. (May 1986). The Effects of Peer Tutoring on Student Achievement. M.A. thesis, Kean College, New Jersey.

Morrow, L.M. (1982). "Relationships Between Literature Programs, Library Corner Designs, and Children's Use of Literature." *Journal of Educational Research* 75: 339-344.

Morrow, L.M. (1983). "Home and School Correlates of Early Interest in Literature." *Journal of Educational Research* 76: 24-30.

Morrow, L.M. (1987). The Effect of One-to-one Story Readings on Children's Questions and Responses." In *Research in Literacy: Merging Perspectives*, edited by L.E. Readence and R.S. Baldwin. 36th Yearbook of the National Reading Conference, Rochester, N.Y.: National Reading Conference.

Morrow, L.M. (1989). "The Effect of Small-Group Story Reading on Students' Questions and Comments." In *Cognitive and Social Perspectives for Literacy Research and Instruction*, edited by S. McCormick and J. Zutell. 38th Yearbook of the National Reading Conference. Chicago, Ill.: National Reading Conference.

Morrow, L.M., E. Sharkey, and W.A. Firestone. (Spring 1993). "Promoting Independent Reading and Writing Through Self-directed Literary Activities in a Collaborative Setting." Reading Research Report No. 2. Athens, Ga.: National Reading Research Center.

Mullis, I.V.S., et al. (September 1990). *Accelerating Academic Achievement. America's Challenge. A Summary of Findings from*

20 Years of NAEP. Princeton, N.J.: Educational Testing Service; National Assessment of Educational Progress.

Mullis, I.V.S., et al. (1991). *Trends in Academic Progress: Achievement of U.S. Students in Science, 1959-70 to 1990, Mathematics, 1973 to 1990, Reading, 1971 to 1990, Writing, 1984 to 1990*. Prepared by Educational Testing Service under contract with the National Center for Education Statistics, Office of Educational Research and Improvement, U.S. Department of Education. Washington, D.C.: The Center. (For sale by U.S. G.P.O., ED 1.102:T 72/3)

National Assessment of Educational Progress. (1992). *Reading Framework for the 1992 National Assessment of Educational Progress*. NAEP Reading Consensus Project. (Report No. NAGB-92- 5002). Washington, D.C.: U.S. Government Printing Office.

Newman, J.M. (1985). "Insights from Recent Reading and Writing Research and Their Implications for Developing Whole Language Curriculum." In *Whole Language: Theory in Use*, edited by J.M. Newman. Portsmouth, N.H.: Heinemann.

Ogle, D. (1986). "K-W-L: A Teaching Model that Develops Active Comprehension of Expository Text." *The Reading Teacher* 39, 564- 570.

Ollila, L.O., and M.I. Mayfield. (1992). "Home and School Together: Helping Beginning Readers Succeed." In *What Research Has To Say About Reading Instruction*, edited by S.J. Samuels and A.E. Farstrup. Newark, Del.: International Reading Association.

Palincsar, A.S., and A.L. Brown. (1984). "Reciprocal Teaching of Comprehension-Fostering and Comprehension-Monitoring Activities." *Cognition and Instruction* 1, 12: 117-175.

Palincsar, A.S., C.S. Englert, T.E. Raphael, and J.R. Gavelek. (May-June 1991). "Examining the Context of Strategy Instruc-tion." *Remedial and Special Education* (RASE) 12, 3: 43-53.

Palincsar, A.S., and L.J. Klenk. (1991). "Learning Dialogues to Promote Text Comprehension." In *Teaching Advanced Skills to Educationally Disadvantaged Students*, edited by B. Means and M. Knapp. Washington, D.C.: Policy Studies Association.

Paris, S.G. (1986). "Teaching Children to Guide Their Reading and Learning." In *The Contexts of School-Based Literacy*, edited by T.E. Raphael. New York: Random House.

Paris, S.G., D.R. Cross, and M.Y. Lipson. (December 1984). "Informed Strategies for Learning: A Program to Improve Children's Reading Awareness and Comprehension." *Journal of Education Psychology* 76, 6: 1239-1252.

Paschal, R.A., T. Weinstein, and H.J. Walberg. (1984). "The Effects on Learning: A Quantitative Synthesis." *Journal of Educational Research* 78: 97-104.

Passow, A.H. (1990). *Enriching the Compensatory Education Curriculum for Disadvantaged Students*. New York: ERI Clearinghouse on Urban Education.

Pearson, P.D., and L. Fielding. (1991). "Comprehension Instruction." In *Handbook of Reading Research*, Vol II, edited by R. Barr, M.L. Kamil, P.B. Mosenthal, and P.D. Pearson. New York: Longman.

Pearson, P.D., L.R. Roehler, L.A. Dole, and G.G. Duffy. (1992). "Developing Expertise in Reading Comprehension. In *What Research Has to Say About Reading Instruction*, edited by S.J. Samuels and A.E. Farstrup. Newark, Del.: International Reading Association.

Pressley, M., J.R. Levin, and M.A. McDaniel. (1987). "Remembering Versus Inferring What a Word Means: Mnemonic and Contextual Approaches." In *The Nature of Vocabulary Acquisition*, edited by M. McGeown and M.E. Curtis, Hillsdale, N.J.: Lawrence Erlbaum.

Queiruga, L. (1992). "A Reading Styles Experiment with Learning Disabled, High School Students." Syosset, N.Y.: National Reading Styles Institute.

Raphael, T.E. (November 1982). "Question-Answering Strategies for Children." *Reading Teacher* 36, 2: 186-190.

Reading Styles Progress Report. (1990). Roslyn Heights, N.Y.: National Reading Styles Institute.

Salinger, T. (1988). *Language Arts and Literacy for Young Children*. Columbus, Ohio: Merrill.

Samuels, S.J., N. Schermer, and D. Reinking. (1992). "Reading Fluency Techniques for Making Decoding Automatic." In *What Research Has to Say About Reading Instruction*, 2nd ed., edited by S.J. Samuels and A.E. Farstrup. Newark, Del.: International Reading Association.

Simonsen, S., and H. Singer. (1992). "Improving Reading Instruction in the Content Areas." In *What Research Has to Say About Reading Instruction*, edited by S.J. Samuels and A.E. Farstrup. Newark, Del.: International Reading Association.

Slade, K. (August 1988). "Parents as Active Members in the School's Reading Program." Paper presented at the annual Rupertsland Regional Conference of the International Reading Association.

Slavin, R. (March 1980). "Cooperative Learning: Can Students Help Students Learn?" *Instructor* 96, 7:74-78.

Slavin, R. (1986). *Using Student Team Learning*, 3rd ed. Baltimore, Md.: Johns Hopkins University Press.

Stahl, S.A., and S.J.. Vancil. (October 1986). "Discussion Is What Makes Semantic Maps Work in Vocabulary Instruction." *Reading Teacher* 40, 1: 62-67.

Strickland, D.S., and L.M. Morrow. (1989). *Emerging Literacy: Young Children Learn to Read and Write*. Newark, Del.: International Reading Association.

Sudzina, M. (1987). "An Investigation of the Relationship Between the Reading Styles of Second Graders and Their Achievement in Different Basal Reader Programs." Doctoral diss., Temple University, Philadelphia.

Sulzby, E. (1985). "Children's Emergent Reading of Favorite Storybooks: A Developmental Study." *Reading Research Quarterly* 20: 458-481.

Sulzby, E., and W.H. Teale. (1987). "Young Children's Storybook Reading: Longitudinal Study of Parent-Child Interaction and Children's Independent Functioning." Final Report to the Spencer Foundation. Ann Arbor: University of Michigan.

Sutfin, H. (1990). "The Effects on Children's Behavior of a Change in Physical Design of a Kindergarten Classroom." Doctoral diss., Boston University.

Taylor, B.M., B.J. Frye, and G.M. Maruyama. (1990). "Time Spent Reading and Reading Growths." *American Education Research Journal* 27, 2: 351-362.

Taylor, D., and D.S. Strickland. (1986). *Family Storybook Reading*. Portsmouth, N.H.: Heinemann.

Teale, W.H. (1984). "Reading to Young Children: Its Significance for Literacy Development." In *Awakening to Literacy*, edited by H. Goelman, A. Oberg, and F. Smith. Portsmouth, N.H.: Heinemann.

Teale, W.H. (1986). "Home Background and Young Children's Literacy Development." In *Emergent Literacy: Writing and Reading*, edited by W.H. Teale and E. Sulzby. Norwood, N.J.: Ablex.

Teale, W.H. (1987). "Emergent Literacy: Reading and Writing Development in Early Childhood." In *Research in Literacy: Merging Perspectives*, edited by J.E. Readence and R.S. Baldwin. Needham Heights, Mass.: Allyn and Bacon.

Teale, W.H., and E. Sulzby, E. (1986). "Emergent Literacy as a Perspective for Examining How Young Children Become Writers and Readers." In *Emergent Literacy: Writing and Reading*, edited by W.H. Teale and E. Sulzby. Norwood, N.J.: Ablex.

Tierney, R.J., and P.D. Pearson. (June 1986). "Schema-Theory and Implications for Teaching Reading: A Conversation." *Reading Education Report No. 67*. Cambridge, Mass.: Bolt, Baranek and Newman.

Tierney, R.J., and T. Shanahan. (1991). "Research on the Reading-

Writing Relationship: Interactions, Transactions, and Outcome." In *Handbook of Reading Research*, Vol. II, edited by R. Barr, M.L. Komil, P.B. Mosenthal, P.D. Pearson, New York: Longman.

Tierney, R.J., A. Soter, J.F. O'Flahavan, and W. McGinley. (1989). "The Effects of Reading and Writing Upon Thinking Critically." *Reading Research Quarterly* 24: 134-173.

Trelease, J. (1982). *The Read-Aloud Handbook*. Middlesex, England: Penguin.

Walberg, H.J., R.A. Paschal, and T. Weinstein. (April 1985). "Homework's Powerful Effects on Learning." *Educational Leadership* 42, 7: 76-79.

Wang, M.C., and A.S. Palincsar. (1989). "Teaching Students to Assume an Active Role in Their Learning." In *Knowledge Base for the Beginning Teacher*, edited by M.C. Reynolds. New York: Pergamon.

Wasik, B.A., and R.E. Slavin. (1990). *Preventing Early Reading Failure with One-to-one Tutoring: A Best Evidence Synthesis*. Report No. 6. Baltimore Md.: The Johns Hopkins University Center for Research on Effective Schooling for Disadvantaged Students.

Wixson, K.K., C.W. Peters, E.M. Weber, and E.D. Roeber. (1987). "New Directions in Statewide Reading Assessment." *Reading Teacher* 40: 749-754.

Wolf, D.P. (April 1989). "Portfolio Assessment: Sampling Student Work." *Educational Leadership* 46, 7: 35-39.

Young, T.A., and S. Vardell. (1993). "Weaving Readers Theatre and Nonfiction into the Curriculum." *The Reading Teacher* 46: 396-406.

6

STRATEGIES FOR INCREASING ACHIEVEMENT IN WRITING

SALLY HAMPTON

Writing is a meaning-making process that is both complex and intellectually demanding. It requires thoughtfulness, precision, and time. It takes place on the blank page within the mind of the writer. As it creates meaning for the reader, it deepens understanding for the writer. It is a primary means of knowing.

— SALLY HAMPTON (1992)

In U.S. schools, students are afforded few opportunities to write. Two early studies document how little writing actually goes on in school. Applebee (1981) discovered that at the secondary level less than 3 percent of the time spent on classwork or homework required students to write a paragraph or more. At the elementary level, Graves (1978) likewise found that students spent little time actually writing. The National Assessment of Educational Progress (1986) pointed out that students at all levels were deficient in higher order thinking skills; the NAEP study recommended that students be afforded broad-based experiences that would integrate reading and writing into the entire curriculum. A further recommendation called for instruction in the writing process that would focus on teaching students how to think more effectively as they write.

Despite these recommendations, little of substance has changed in the schools' approach to writing. As revealed in Applebee's 1984 study, teachers today still give students little or no opportunity to revise their writing; those students most in need of help with their writing are no more likely to receive such help than are better writers; and teachers spend more time criticizing or correcting writing than they do actually teaching writing. Furthermore, these conditions persist despite the fact that student performance has shown no improvement after a decade of attention brought to bear by the so-called education reform movement, combined with the effects of attention to instruction in the writing process.

Enhancing Students' Writing Achievement

Curiously enough, many methods to improve student writing exist and are being used successfully, though on a limited basis. When teachers employ these methods, research shows that student writing improves. According to the NAEP (1990), such methods as having young people write frequently, using a workshop approach to instruction, encouraging multiple drafts of text, and fostering peer response groups all foster the development of student writing ability.

Data from the NAEP studies (1990) indicate that the most proficient writers:

- value writing and have positive attitudes toward it;
- use writing extensively for personal and social reasons;
- revise and edit their work;
- use a variety of strategies, including planning; and
- receive teacher feedback on their writing.

In addition, data from the California Assessment Program (1983) support the NAEP (1990) findings and indicate that students who have taken part in effective writing programs:

- believe that they have something important to say;
- are motivated to write and enjoy writing;
- are comfortable expressing their ideas in writing;
- write fluently, coherently, and correctly in various styles for a variety of purposes and audiences;
- employ a range of strategies for planning, revising, and editing texts; and
- recognize that writing is important in all content areas.

The State of the Art of Writing Instruction

The most recent data from the NAEP (1990) bring further reason to reevaluate the way in which writing is taught in U.S. schools. The NAEP tells us that:

- writing is valued by only half of the students in grades 4, 8, and 11;

- young people's attitudes about writing do not change dramatically as they progress through school;
- students in the upper grades are less likely to write on their own when they are not in school;
- the percent of students who give overt attention to planning has decreased over time; and
- the most frequently reported revision strategies involve the smaller units of text (spelling, punctuation, and grammar); the least frequently reported strategies are those that require the most extensive effort (moving sentences or paragraphs, starting over, and rewriting large chunks of text).

On the brighter side, the same NAEP report notes that teachers' feedback to young people about their writing increases as students progress to higher grade levels, and that there is some increase in the amount of writing done by students.

Assessing Students' Achievement in Writing

The evaluation of young people's writing abilities is a highly complex process. The ability to write in one genre or style does not necessarily correlate to the ability to write in various other genres. Any evaluation of writing abilities based on a single sample is open to question.

The use of student "portfolios"—that is, collections of student work generated over time—has gained prominence in recent years. When this collection also contains student-written rationales describing *why* each piece has been included in the portfolio, the writer must demonstrate a clear sense of what he or she values in text and what strategies have been consciously used to achieve what is valued. The best portfolios represent authentic learning, as opposed to the old-style, drill- and-practice type of activities.

Growth in students' writing ability should be measured against standards of adult proficiency, with students understanding that they are responsible for moving toward that standard. This view of writing development places less emphasis on the evaluation of any single piece of student work and more emphasis on the student's collection of work, which should show substantive growth over time or should contain evidence of having reached a certain level of proficiency.

FIGURE 6.1
A Summary of New Standards for Curriculum and Instruction in Writing

TRADITIONAL EMPHASIS ON	NEW EMPHASIS ON
teaching as a discrete subject area	integration of process and content
functional literacy	ability to construct meaning with and from written text
technical competence	wide variety of genre
mainstream culture and language	written language competency
passive learning experiences	students' home/community culture and experiences
	active learning experiences

TRADITIONAL EMPHASIS ON	NEW EMPHASIS ON
skills teaching: grammar, punctuation, spelling	strategy teaching: cognitive and metacognitive
writing exercises	real-life purposes
written feedback	oral dictation
independent seatwork	word processing
	discourse
	modeling of "thinking aloud" and guided practice
	scaffolding to guide students in completing complex tasks
	collaborative/team writing sessions
	peer tutoring

Source: Hodges 1989.

If a student is to be held accountable for his or her growth as a writer, then the student must be made aware of the rubrics that will be used to judge writing as successful; he or she must also be given regular feedback relative to these same criteria. Students should be afforded standards, models, and criteria that represent adult proficiency.

WRITING STRATEGIES THAT PROMOTE ACHIEVEMENT

The following strategies, which have been drawn from both research and experience in the field, are strongly recommended for accelerating writing ability and creating more good writers, particularly among the lower third of students in U.S. schools:

- providing students with opportunities to write routinely for a variety of purposes and audiences;
- encouraging writing as a meaning-making process and as a tool for learning;
- fostering student independence through self-selected topics and self-evaluations;
- emphasizing the quality of what is said, rather than simply attending to presentational features;
- modeling the writing process and emphasizing the need for thoughtful revision through conferencing;
- making the grading criteria accessible to students before they begin an assignment;
- teaching conventions in the context of students' own writing; and
- evaluating work over time through portfolios.

● STRATEGY 6.1: PROVIDE OPPORTUNITIES TO WRITE

Teachers provide young people with many and varied opportunities to write.

DISCUSSION

Students become more competent writers by writing and sharing their writing with others, not by practicing writing subskills (grammar, spelling, and so on) in isolation. Children must be free to experiment and grow up with written language, including invented spelling, scribbling, letter-like marks, and drawings.

When young children realize that writing is a powerful way of expressing their thoughts and needs, they will begin to write in ways appropriate to their age and development level. Although stages of emergent writing do exist, *not all children move through each stage sequentially.* Some children may skip certain stages completely, while others may "stall out" at one stage or another for an unusually long period of time. What is important is not that students progress through any set number of stages in a predictable way, but that children not be pressured and that the classroom be filled with printed materials and with many opportunities to write.

Teachers should model writing and encourage students to become writers. Teachers should also be less concerned than they have been traditionally about correct spelling. The use of inventive spelling is to be encouraged because it represents a developing understanding of sound/letter correlation. Furthermore, inventive spellings allow young writers to take risks with words in order to express themselves as naturally as possible, rather than be limited by the fear of correctness.

CLASSROOM EXAMPLES

Young children are invited to write every day for a number of different purposes that can include labels, letters, reminder notes, signs, stories, expository pieces, and books. All children must be encouraged to write in their own way, and they need to be reminded frequently that their writing does not have to look like "grown-up" writing. A variety of papers and writing utensils, made available in several centers, allow children to come to view writing as important and something that they are *able to do.*

Teachers support and advance children's ability to write when they read aloud to students every day. Regular reading allows students to learn story structure and to internalize the rhythms of language. Young writers often imitate familiar story structures and syntactic patterns to such an extent that it is possible to identify these elements in their writing.

REFERENCES
Adams 1990; Applebee 1981, 1984; Applebee and Langer 1983; Bereiter, Scardamalia, Anderson, and Smart 1980; Bissex 1980; Blount 1973; Bracewell, Frederiksen, and Frederiksen 1982; Britton, Burgess, Martin, McLeod, and Rosen 1975; Butler 1984; Calkins 1980; Cambourne and Turbill 1987; Chomsky 1971; Christensen 1967; Clarke 1988; Emig 1982; Farr and Daniels 1986; Falk 1979; Feitelson, Kita, and Goldstein 1986; Graves 1983, 1978; Henderson and Beers 1980; Heyes 1962; King and Rentel 1981; Lamme 1987; Read 1971; Sizer 1984; Strickland and Morrow 1989; Tway 1980.

● STRATEGY 6.2: USE WRITING IN ALL SUBJECT AREAS

Teachers use writing to promote learning in all subject areas, not just English.

DISCUSSION

Writing is a process of making meaning. A writer draws from a variety of sources—personal knowledge, observations, and primary-source data, among others—to construct text that allows never-before-made connections to emerge. This meaning making crosses disciplines and encourages students to explore relationships between the subjects they are studying and the real-world knowledge they bring to those subjects. What emerges from these connections represents new knowledge for the writer.

Teachers in all content areas should encourage *writing as a mode of learning.* In evaluating writing, teachers should emphasize the degree to which students are able to demonstrate content-specific understandings, make connections across disciplines, or apply their new understandings to real-world situations. (Less important is the student's ability to demonstrate knowledge of form or use of rhetorical strategies.) Once teachers focus on a student's ability to demonstrate an understanding of content or on the quality of thinking demonstrated in the writing, writ-

Teachers in all content areas should encourage writing as a mode of learning. Students with frequent opportunities to write are likely to improve as writers. Peer and teacher feedback encourage revision. Here, students are actively engaged in expressing their ideas in writing. They are also aware of their peers as an audience and as collaborators.

ing becomes less the province of the English teacher and more a means of examining what a student knows and how well a student thinks.

CLASSROOM EXAMPLES

Young science students, for instance, might construct observational diaries in which they record and reflect on temperature variations, weather patterns, animal habits, or other natural phenomena. Mathematics students might be encouraged to explain why a math answer is incorrect or tell at what point a student proposing the incorrect answer might have gone wrong. History students might be asked to write about the relationships they can identify among economic factors, unemployment, family relationships, and infant mortality.

Teachers who are working to help students develop various thinking strategies—regardless of the subject being considered— might use writing as a way of gauging improvement. Students might move through a series of assignments: for instance, moving from writing focused on developing the ability to see relationships in a very rudimentary context, to analyzing relationships within an increasingly complex situation, perhaps even to analyzing a whole series of complex relationships.

Specifically, a teacher might decide to construct a series of writing tasks that require students to examine the similarities between two things that are relatively alike— perhaps characters who are similarly motivated in a short story. The next assignment in the series might require students to consider how characters whose natures are similar may act differently. The following assignment might cause students to consider how, although a character fundamentally believes *X*, he or she does *Y* because of her interaction with another character. In all cases, however, the teacher's focus would be on whether students were improving their ability to define and analyze relationships. Students might well keep all these assignments and routinely review their work in order to assess their own progress.

REFERENCES

Applebee 1981, 1990; Barr, D'Arcy, and Healy 1982; Bereiter 1980; Britton, Burgess, Martin, McLeod, and Rosen 1975; Emig 1977, 1983; Farr and Daniels 1986; Fulwiler and Young 1982; Gere 1985; Glatthorn 1981; Lehr 1980; Langer 1986; Langer and Applebee 1987; Martin, D'Arcy, et al. 1976; National Assessment of Educational Progress June 1990; Scardamalia et al. 1984; Smithson and Sorrentino 1987; Yates 1987; Vygotsky 1962.

● STRATEGY 6.3: ENCOURAGE READING

Teachers encourage young people to read widely to help them become familiar with a wide variety of prose styles; reading is an integral part of instruction in writing.

DISCUSSION

The relationship between reading and writing is increasingly acknowledged to be an important one. Those who read widely internalize the patterns of organization of various types of writing and develop an understanding of and appreciation for the many structures of language. Moreover, attentive readers become more sensitive to writers' strategies and can make distinctions between strategies they find effective and those they do not.

Reading and writing are complementary cognitive processes; students should be encouraged to draw on their experience in one to solve problems in the other. Increasingly, reading and writing are being taught in integrated language arts blocks. At the very least, reading teachers should make specific references to features of writing when teaching students to read, and writing teachers should talk about accommodating the needs of readers when teaching students to draft text. As students read widely in particular genres, they begin to internalize the deep structures of those genres as well as the features distinctive to each genre. Students who read widely will also respond to various stylistic strategies employed by particular writers and will make connections between these strategies and their own strategies.

CLASSROOM EXAMPLES

To expand young students' repertoire of writing "voices," a teacher might read aloud various passages representing different voices and then ask students which voices invite them as readers. This technique fosters the idea that the choices students make as writers should be governed largely by the judgments about text they have made as readers.

Teachers can also encourage students to find examples of writing that they like. The idea here is for students to become aware of writing that they themselves judge to be effective and then to bring these pieces of effective writing before the class in order to analyze what makes the writing "work"—that is, the particular writing strategies used in the piece. Perhaps these strategies could be labeled and, with an example, placed into a class book of effective writing strategies that could serve as a resource for the whole class. This technique would make it possible for a student having problems with, say, getting started writing to refer to the strategy book and find a series of effective beginnings on which to model his or her own piece.

To the extent that we encourage young people to read as writers—looking for what works and what doesn't work—we will encourage discriminating writers, capable of accessing a range of options and strategies. To the extent that we require students to examine closely what makes writing effective, we will help them develop a repertoire of effective writing options.

REFERENCES
Atwell 1987; Blount 1973; Butler and Turbill 1984; Calkins 1983, 1986; Christensen 1965; Farr and Daniels 1986; Hansen 1986; Hidi and Hilgard 1983; Jensen 1984; Kucer 1985; Langer 1985; Strom 1960; Tierney et al. 1991.

● STRATEGY 6.4: USE AUTHENTIC WRITING TASKS

Teachers give students authentic writing tasks for specific audiences and purposes.

DISCUSSION

Writing is a highly recursive process that includes the steps of planning, drafting, revising, and editing text. Students learn to write by routinely engaging in this process to produce whole texts for specific purposes and audiences.

Students improve their writing when the writing task is "authentic"—that is, when the writing addresses a specific purpose and a real audience. Traditionally, students have worked from textbooks to practice discrete writing subskills, such as forming complete sentences, creating paragraphs, applying punctuation marks, and correcting usage errors within already constructed passages. The new emphasis on process encourages students to plan and generate their own text, continually rethinking and revising their writing by thinking about factors such as the purpose of the writing, the constraints of a particular audience, organizational strategies, considerations of rhetorical effectiveness, and—ultimately—correctness.

To the extent that students are given the opportunity to construct texts for a variety of purposes—from the highly personal, self-reflective writing that characterizes

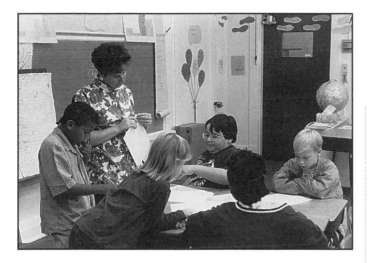

Photo courtesy of Helené Hodges, Alexandria, VA

By devoting time on a daily basis to writing, teachers can provide support to students on a full range of supportive skills: prewriting, planning, drafting, revising, and editing. When students become aware of what is valued in writing and are instructed in strategies for improving their writing, they will work to develop those strategies. In the top photo, elementary school students are engaged in a group task that involves reading and writing. Their teacher responds to a student query.

In the bottom photo, Key School students are seated comfortably on a couch as they work individually on a writing task. Elsewhere in the classroom, their teacher and another student are conferring one-to-one about the student's text.

journals to the public discourse that better serves the world of work—students will be able to value writing as a critical, lifelong skill. They will learn to use writing to serve their needs and to assess writing that affects their lives.

CLASSROOM EXAMPLES

A teacher who wants students to become good persuasive writers could ask them to write to the principal requesting permission for a perceived need—a field trip,

for example. Students will become fully engaged in this task when they realize that the responsibility to obtain permission rests with them. Because their writing has consequences more real than a grade, the writing task itself becomes real to them. Because they care about a favorable response to the proposal, they will take the task seriously and become quite conscious of both form and correctness.

Students could also study effective pieces of writing, including public health documents, political editorials, and contracts; their task would be to assess the writers' varying intents, their assumptions about audience, and the strategies they employed to make the writing effective. Students could revise these documents to make them more honest or effective.

Teachers might ask students to survey public data relevant to their own neighborhood; determine a problem relevant to their neighborhood and identify the public agency responsible for handling that problem; write a proposal for developing a possible solution to the problem; work in groups to bring about a product/service to solve the problem; produce a report on the project (and a manual to replicate the procedures); and create charts/graphs for an oral presentation to accompany the report. Various neighborhood problems might include teenage pregnancy, alcoholism, or the need for fire safety procedures (students raising funds for smoke detectors and producing brochures in Spanish and English on fire safety in the home).

REFERENCES
Applebee 1981; Atwell 1987; Booth 1963; Britton 1970; Calkins 1994; Falk 1979; Farr and Daniels 1986; Flower and Hayes 1981a; Graves 1976; Newkirk and Atwell 1988; Scardamalia, Bereiter, and Fillion 1981; Smith 1982; White and Karl 1980.

● STRATEGY 6.5: ADDRESS AUTHENTIC, MEANINGFUL TOPICS

Teachers use a variety of writing strategies to stimulate the quality and quantity of writing; they encourage students to select topics that are meaningful to them.

DISCUSSION

Students' ownership of their writing is of critical importance. For this reason, students should, whenever possible, initiate their own topics and be responsible for determining the pattern of organization that best serves the nature of the text they are developing. The teacher's goal is to help students become writers who are independent, resourceful, and capable of expressing themselves well in a variety of circumstances and for a variety of purposes and audiences.

Before being asked to address the matter of organizational structures for writing, students must write frequently on topics of genuine interest and for authentic purposes in order to develop fluency. The first requirement of a good writer is the ability to generate and develop ideas coherently.

When novice writers attempt to generate text to fit predetermined structures—a five-paragraph expository essay, for example—they are rarely able to become sufficiently engaged in the topic to enable them to coherently develop it. Instead of prescribing the format prior to the assignment—traditionally a fairly standard practice—teachers are now showing students various options for paragraph formation and essay organization at the revision stage.

CLASSROOM EXAMPLES

To help students develop strategies for organizing text, a teacher can encourage students to select and develop topics of interest to *themselves*. After students have completed their first draft, the teacher may introduce a mini-lesson on effective leads (or transition elements, or paragraphing strategies) and then encourage students to rethink and revise their text in light of the information presented in the mini-lesson.

Another teaching strategy is to distribute models of effective organization to the class as students begin a revision or editing session. The teacher asks students to discuss the models and determine which seem most effectively organized, pointing out the strengths or shortcomings of each model. Students then apply an effective organizational model to their own text or revise their text in terms of the discussion of organizational patterns, strengths, and shortcomings.

Still another way to address the joint issues of student ownership and effective development of topics is to ask students to choose something they would like to learn about as a major project—perhaps a particular culture or the life of a famous person. Such everyday topics as contemporary music, skateboards, fashion, or football will engage particular students. What is essential is that students have a serious interest in the subject. The teacher

should explain to students that they must become an expert on their topic and produce a piece of writing that demonstrates their expertise. Any genre or organizational style chosen by the writer is acceptable in this initial effort. Following the initial presentation, however, the student is expected to recast his writing in a second genre and then again in a third genre. So, for example, a student might first write a research report about the merits of high school football, then a short story whose theme is the merits of school football programs, and finally a persuasive essay on the importance of football programs. Upon completing these exercises, students are be expected to evaluate which form of presentation proved to be most effective.

REFERENCES
Anderson, Bereiter and Smart 1982; Atwell 1987; Bereiter and Scardamalia 1982; Burns and Culp 1980; Cooper 1975, 1977; Emig 1971; Farr and Daniels 1986; Graves 1975, 1983; Hillocks 1986; Odell 1974, 1980; Rohman and Wlecke 1964; Scardamalia et al. 1982; Stallard 1974; Woodruff, Bereiter, and Scardamalia 1981.

● STRATEGY 6.6: USE NUMEROUS EXAMPLES OF GOOD WRITING

Teachers expose students to numerous examples of good writing in a print-rich classroom environment that gives greater emphasis to encouraging students to express and refine their ideas and think more effectively as they write than to correcting their spelling and grammar.

DISCUSSION

The development of writing is shaped by the writer's interaction with a variety of symbolic media and with other people, including peers. The developing writer benefits particularly from writing that grows naturally from the writer's experiences in the classroom or elsewhere. The degree to which a writer can extend text or enrich it stylistically depends largely on the kinds of feedback available and on the creation of a risk-free environment that allows access to a variety of materials (such as "environmental print"—that is, words in a child's immediate environment: names of stores, streets, objects in display windows, magazines, books, etc.) and to other readers or writers.

Traditionally, instruction in writing has occurred largely at the secondary level. Research in composition, however, has demonstrated that even kindergarten children can construct text. The process of learning to write—like learning to speak—is an emergent skill. A child can, in fact, learn to write by using drawings and inventive spellings at the same time that he or she is learning to read. As mentioned earlier in this chapter, when students realize that writing is a powerful way to express their thoughts and needs, they will begin writing in ways that are developmentally appropriate for them. Teachers should surround students with print, should model writing, and should encourage children to write for many different purposes.

CLASSROOM EXAMPLES

Young children should be invited to write every day in a number of different styles: tables, letters, reminder notes, signs, stories, expository pieces, and books. Each child should be encouraged to write in his or her own way and should be reminded that student writing doesn't have to look like grown-up writing. A variety of paper and writing utensils should be available in several centers so that children come to view writing as something important that they can do. The emphasis should be on developing fluency among writers before emphasizing form and correctness. Similar methods apply to working with older students; the difference among writers of different ages resides mainly in the complexity of the writing.

Encouraging young people simply to tell one another what they will write about is an effective prewriting activity; it allows students to rehearse orally what they will write. Rehearsing a story orally allows the writer to become aware of a partner's degree of interest. In addition, hearing what a partner intends to write about may prompt ideas for the listener, and the sharing of ideas allows for dialogue among writers, which tends to reduce stress and also suggests interesting extensions or diversions in the intended writings.

Access to environmental print allows students to incorporate new words correctly spelled into their writing. Students often borrow language from published books to enrich their own writing when they are encouraged to use a variety of resources to expand or polish their own writing.

REFERENCES

Applebee 1981; Atwell 1987; Braddock, Lloyd-Jones, and Schoer 1963; Cambourne and Turbill 1987; Calkins 1979, 1980; Daniels and Zemelman 1985; Elley, Barham, Lamb, and Wylie 1975; Farr and Daniels 1986; Graves 1981; Hillocks 1986; National Council of Teachers of English 1989; Moffett 1968; Smith 1982; Strom 1960.

● STRATEGY 6.7: MODEL THE WRITING PROCESS

Teachers model the writing process; they also model how to read and write effectively in every area of the curriculum.

DISCUSSION

When students think the published writings they see flow effortlessly from the author's fingers, they are often overwhelmed by the idea of writing. Teachers of writing need to model their own writing processes, including rethinking, revising, and editing their text, to show students the reality of the writing process. By doing so, they will be encouraging students to take risks in their writing.

Traditionally, teachers taught writing; students wrote. Now most people concede that the best teachers of writing are teachers who themselves write and display to students both their writing and the process through which they created it. Especially effective, it seems, are those teachers who risk making their writing processes visible to their students. When teachers model their own planning strategies, talk through the constraints imposed by purpose and audience, and then attempt a first draft on an overhead transparency, they show students that even expert writers work tentatively, revise often, and still may need to start over—and over. When modeling is accompanied by thinking aloud, students can hear the teacher/writer sort through various options and questions and make choices appropriate for the intended purpose and audience.

CLASSROOM EXAMPLES

A teacher might first talk students through an assignment, explaining the purpose and audience for the writing and then detailing the scoring criteria to be used in evaluating the writing. This preamble to writing might be done on an overhead so that the students and teacher can negotiate a full understanding of what is expected. Since the only sure way to understand an assignment is to do it, the teacher might at this point—still at the front of the class and using an overhead—actually begin to do the assignment, going through some prewriting, drafting, and even revision. The most effective approach involves completing the assignment on transparencies, demonstrating to students the false starts, connections, and ongoing changes inherent in producing text.

A teacher might also model the writing process by bringing to class rough drafts of pieces he or she is working on outside of class (e.g., letters of recommendation, curriculum units, correspondence with parents) and soliciting feedback from students concerning clarity, focus, and so on. Or a teacher might routinely do assignments *with* students, joining in response groups and revising. The idea is to continuously reinforce the idea that the writing classroom is a workshop where teachers and students collaborate to become better writers.

REFERENCES
Atwell 1987; Calkins 1994; Calkins and Harwayne 1991; Cooper 1975; Farr and Daniels 1986; Graves 1983, 1990; Gunderson 1971; Macrorie 1970, 1984; Murray 1986.

● STRATEGY 6.8: USE CONFERENCING AND PEER REVIEW

Teachers give students many opportunities to engage in conferencing with each other and to participate in peer reviews.

DISCUSSION

Students' writing improves when they receive immediate feedback on their work. Immediate feedback helps students begin to ask relevant questions about the work, make decisions, and learn to evaluate the writing *while working on it* rather than after they have completed the writing and given it to the teacher for grading. While students are engaged in various stages of the writing process, teachers free themselves to conference individually with students and to work with small groups. And while the teacher is thus engaged, students must be able to help each other. Hence, each student must have an understanding of how to help peers develop and revise text.

The traditional classroom fosters learning in isolation: Teachers place students in straight rows, present a lesson using the lecture format, and then bombard students with independent seatwork that supposedly reinforces the concept just taught. In contrast to this traditional model of instruction, current research indicates that opportunities for student collaboration promote the development of writing skills. Teachers now cluster desks in small groups to allow for natural sharing and assistance with ideas, spelling, and mechanics. Children who are strong writers offer support to peers. Access to another

writer during the writing process creates a supportive atmosphere in the classroom, as well as making writing in the classroom more of a real-life task. Real writers get help on a text when they need help, and real writers usually get such help from trusted others who can offer useful insights. Working in a small-group setting, then, allows student writers the kind of access to critical feedback available in the real world and makes writing less stressful.

Shared writing is a powerful approach for promoting the development and enjoyment of writing. Learning the questions that writers ask to determine whether their text communicates effectively is a major learning task that is best accomplished through the teacher's modeling the use of such questions. This modeling takes place during student/teacher conferences when the teacher shows students how to be effective response partners, and during think-aloud revision activities.

CLASSROOM EXAMPLES

In a successful writing classroom, teachers can create a structure that permits peer conferences. At the beginning of the year, the teacher models appropriate responses to writing during individual conferences and class sharing time. By asking open-ended questions about the content of

Photo courtesy of Helené Hodges, Alexandria, VA

Students in a Key School classroom revise their work while others meet with the teacher. Frequent, brief teacher-student conferences are essential to the development of students' writing ability. Such conferences enable teachers to help students understand their individual writing process and its strengths and weaknesses. In this picture, the large poster behind the teacher makes clear his feelings about writing.

a piece of writing, teachers help student writers clarify their ideas. Young writers gradually internalize these predictable questions and start to apply them to their own writing.

When novice writers can get immediate feedback on their writing and apply the advice right away, their writing begins to improve. They begin to evaluate their own writing and will also be better able to evaluate the writing of their classmates (Calkins 1994). For example, if a teacher is helping students work on character development, one strategy might be to show writers how a single piece of telling dialogue can reveal more about a character than a lengthy narrative. The teacher could do a think-aloud—revising a piece of text and making sure the dialogue in question reflects the character's values. The teacher/writer might muse aloud, "Why am I having this character say these words?" . . . "What do these words reveal about this character's values or motivations?" . . . "Does this piece of dialogue help flesh out this character?" If the teacher uses these questions in teacher/student conferences every time characterization and dialogue are discussed, student writers will use the questions to construct dialogue that reveals character.

REFERENCES
Atwell 1987; Beaven 1977; Braddock, Lloyd-Jones, and Schoer 1963; Bruffee 1984; Calkins 1983, 1991, 1994; Clifford 1981; Cooper, Marquis, and Ayer-Lopez 1982; Diaute 1986; Diederich 1974; Dow 1973; Dyson 1985; Elbow 1973; Farr and Daniels 1986; Fine 1987; Freire 1968; Graves 1978, 1983; Hass, Childers, Babbit, and Dyalla 1972; Lagana 1972; Spear 1988.

● STRATEGY 6.9: USE WRITING CONFERENCES

Teachers schedule frequent one-to-one writing conferences with students to help them write better and think more critically about their writing.

DISCUSSION

Teacher/student writing conferences are essential to the development of students' writing ability. Such conferences can provide to-the-point instruction on particular problems that students are facing. Moreover, these conferences enable teachers to help students develop an awareness of their own writing processes, strengths, and weaknesses.

Traditionally, writing has been taught in a "first-draft-as-final-draft" manner: students wrote (*maybe* recopied the piece, usually for neatness), they handed in the text, and the teacher graded the text. Sometimes students were called on to revise the text after the papers had been graded and returned, but this practice was not widespread. Now we know that for writing to improve, students must rethink and revise text—often many times. This process, generally fostered through conferencing, takes place well before a student generates a final draft.

CLASSROOM EXAMPLES

During a teacher/student conference, the teacher may focus on a variety of subjects: features of writing the student finds troublesome, strategies used by the writer to develop a particular topic, the content of the writing, or the problems and strengths of the text. The teacher's role during the conference is to prompt student awareness by using a series of probing questions. Essentially, these questions cause the student to focus on a particular issue and to come to an understanding of the issue through the one-to-one dialogue with the teacher as mentor.

For example, if a student routinely opens with the phrase "One day" or "Once," the teacher may begin the conference by asking a question that would cause the student to become aware of this practice, to question its effectiveness, and then to consider alternatives. The goal of this particular conference would be to create an awareness in the student writer that writing leads or introductions are important and that good writers know a variety of means of inviting reader interest and acclimating the audience.

REFERENCES
Applebee 1984; Atwell 1987; Calkins 1983, 1994; Graves 1983; Farr and Daniels 1986; Freedman et al. 1987a; Murray 1968; Rief 1992; Parry and Hornsby 1985; Summers 1982; Sowers 1979.

● STRATEGY 6.10: TEACH STUDENTS "HOW TO WRITE"

Teachers devote explicit teaching time to the topic of "how to write."

DISCUSSION

Many children begin school without a well-developed set of literate behaviors that will allow them to succeed in school. These children have had limited exposure in their

In each of these elementary school classrooms, youngsters are engrossed in small-group discussions about writing. Their teachers have clustered desks to allow the sharing of ideas. Children who have received teacher guidance in understanding how to improve their writing can also learn to provide meaningful immediate feedback to their peers. In prewriting stages, sharing ideas in small groups can be among the varied strategies teachers use to assist children. Across all grade levels, the use of varied groups and peer feedback assist the writing process.

homes or communities to the kinds of labeling acts, listening behaviors, or question/answer patterns associated with schooling. Given exposure to modeling and the opportunity to interact with a wide range of texts through reading and writing, students will internalize much of what their background has failed to provide. In the interest of practicality, however, some explicit teaching of genre forms and language structure is appropriate.

In the past, teachers routinely "taught" for an entire class period and then expected students to do homework

that called for them to apply the content of the lesson; today, teachers routinely conduct "mini-lessons." These mini-lessons are the most appropriate form of instruction for writers because they take very little class time away from actual writing.

A mini-lesson is a form of explicit teaching: a whole-class, frontal teaching method that focuses on only one skill, subskill, strategy, or process at a time. A mini-lesson is short, rarely lasting more than seven minutes. Such lessons are not taught to mastery; the teacher will repeat the lesson at intervals during the year in order to introduce the material to students who were not developmentally ready to absorb it previously and to reinforce it for other students. After the mini-lesson, the teacher encourages students to think about the lesson as they create text or as they revise or edit text; the lesson may also serve as a focus for response-group discussion. As an alternative—in classes where students maintain writing folders—the teacher may direct students to use the information presented in the mini-lesson to revise several pieces from their folders.

CLASSROOM EXAMPLES

The teacher may prepare a mini-lesson focusing on how writers use quotation marks; the purpose of the mini-lesson would be to prompt a general understanding that the text within quotation marks is understood to be spoken by a character. The teacher may show the class examples of text that could be misread without quotation marks. She may also use examples from students' writing to give students some practice inserting the quotation marks. At the close of the lesson, the teacher encourages the student writers (where developmentally appropriate) to attend to quotation marks in their writing, or she asks them to review their writing folders, find a piece of text that calls for the use of quotation marks, and then insert them in the appropriate places.

A teacher who is working on improving student narratives might do a mini-lesson on the technique of foreshadowing or flashback, showing students examples of text that use this feature and then encouraging them to consider the strategy (if appropriate) when they revise their own narratives-in-progress.

A teacher might elect to work with a small group of students who share a similar problem. While other students in the room continue to work independently, in pairs, or in small groups, the teacher takes aside three or four students who are having problems with the same skill or concept (end punctuation, for example) and works with this group on proofing their papers for errors in end punctuation. The writing folder can always serve as a very personal sourcebook for writing exercises in need of revision or proofing and correction. In these folders, the writing is authentic and personal, and the idea of revisiting with an eye to improvement is ongoing.

REFERENCES
Anderson, Bereiter, and Smart 1980; Atwell 1987; Bloom 1985; Calkins 1983; Farr and Daniels 1986; Graves 1983; Scardamalia, Bereiter, and Goelman 1982; Tompkins 1990.

● STRATEGY 6.11: ALLOW TIME TO LEARN SUPPORTIVE SKILLS

Time is allocated daily for learning the supportive skills associated with excellence in writing: prewriting, planning, drafting, revising, and editing.

DISCUSSION

Student writers should be exposed to a variety of writing strategies—for example, invention strategies, revision strategies, and strategies of rhetorical effectiveness—so that they can recognize the range of strategies that writers have available to them. Student writers should also recognize that their own writing processes and strategies are both highly individual and quite dependent on context. In other words, what works for a writer under one set of circumstances will probably not be appropriate in every context. Furthermore, though all writers go through various stages when they are composing, they exhibit variety in the strategies that they use within these stages.

In the past, students were called on simply to generate text and an accompanying outline for most writing assignments. Research over the last fifteen years, however, has shown that writers naturally move *between* various stages when composing. Expert writers plan, draft, revise, and edit, through not necessarily in a linear sequence. As writers draft, they may also revise and edit. As they rethink their text, they may or may not seek responses to what they have written. They may—with or without response—refine and polish what they have produced, substantially change much of what they have written, or return to the planning stage and start over. Composing simply does not happen with rehearsal/planning on Monday, drafting on Tuesday, and revision/editing on Wednesday. Teachers now, therefore, encourage students to move among the various

stages of the composing process, often even requiring writers to turn in notes and early drafts with their final versions.

CLASSROOM EXAMPLES

Writers compose in their own way and at their own pace. Minute-by-minute shifts occur in the process of writing. Teachers need to provide students with daily blocks of time to compose at their own pace and to negotiate the various stages of the writing process. Furthermore, teachers should make students aware of effective strategies for generating, organizing, and refining their writing. A variety of strategies are available to help students generate text—from classical invention procedures to graphic organizers. Students learn the organizational structures of text and rhetorical techniques through a variety of means, including understanding genre distinctions, engaging in response groups, and discussing text during writing conferences.

REFERENCES
Bloom 1986, 1988; Calkins 1980b; Cooper 1977; Farr and Daniels 1986; Flower and Hayes 1981b; Graves 1982, 1983; Hansen 1978; Hayes and Flower 1986; Mohr 1984; Murray 1980; National Assessment of Educational Progress 1989; Perl 1980; Rohman and Wlecke 1964; Sommers 1982.

● STRATEGY 6.12: PROVIDE CRITERIA FOR EVALUATION

To help students revise their own work, teachers provide criteria by which various forms of writing are evaluated.

DISCUSSION

One goal of a writing teacher is to foster independence in student writers. Independence requires that students be able to evaluate what they write and to make appropriate revisions. One way to foster student independence in writing is to provide novice writers with rubrics (evaluation criteria) that are appropriate to the writing task *before* they begin to produce text. The criteria should be explained, discussed, and negotiated, and then students should be encouraged to use these criteria as one focus of their process of response and revision.

In the past, teachers simply assigned grades to papers, then returned the papers to students. The evaluation criteria were generally known only to the teacher. Research indicates, however, that when students are aware of the grading criteria before they submit their work, they use these criteria as tools in the process of revision, and their writing improves. Teachers can shift responsibility from the teacher to the learner by having writers assess and revise their own work using criteria that clearly define the features by which different types of writing are to be evaluated. Students now, therefore, are taught to evaluate their own work while internalizing these features for use in subsequent work.

CLASSROOM EXAMPLES

A rubric makes explicit the characteristics that distinguish one level of writing performance from another. When accompanied by exemplars, the rubric can serve as a fundamental instructional tool. For example, a teacher might show transparencies of student work on an overhead to illustrate how papers can be improved through the addition of various features or the refinement of these features. Suppose one feature of an A-level paper is coherent text, sometimes marked by the use of transitional elements. The teacher might use a paper that lacks coherence and add transitional elements to provide the coherence, structure, or organization. Once these elements have been added, the teacher point out that the paper could now receive a grade of A—all other factors being equal. The rubric thus serves as a guide to revision, allowing students to see how performance is measured and by what means performance might be improved.

As another example, a teacher might focus students on addressing more effectively the concept of audience awareness in their writing. After discussing why the notion of "audience" is a critical one for writers, the teacher then assigns a writing task in which audience is of primary importance—for example, asking students to devise an argument about an issue they find compelling. Next, the teacher distributes copies of the criteria to be used in evaluating the student papers (in this instance, audience awareness would be a prominent consideration). Students then begin to develop their texts. Upon completing their texts, students are directed to review their writing alone or with response groups and—using the assigned criteria—to edit for audience awareness. (When students have little experience with revision, the teacher might model the process of revising for audience following the discussion of the rubric.)

REFERENCES
Coleman 1982; Clifford 1978, 1981; Hillocks 1982, 1986; Odell and Hampton 1992; Sager 1973.

● STRATEGY 6.13: INCLUDE CONTEXTUAL INSTRUCTION IN GRAMMAR

Teachers include grammar instruction in the context of writing.

DISCUSSION

Research has shown that the study of grammar in isolation does not improve students' writing ability. Students should be taught strategies for learning such important skills *in context* rather than discretely and out of context, so that they can more readily apply their learnings to other contexts.

Traditionally, teachers have decided what young people need and have then taught the skill directly, often in a predetermined sequence; students then practiced the skill in isolation. Teachers emphasized practice and correct responses, controlling how much practice or how many exercises students required. Only rarely was the skill applied to new, meaningful contexts.

Now, however, with the use of strategy teaching, skills can be taught in a broader context because learners demonstrate a need for specific skills in the learning setting. The skill is taught because the learners *need* to use it, or because the teacher anticipates the learners' upcoming need to use the skill. The teacher guides students to determine for themselves the generalization and to think through possibilities in authentic contexts. Students are encouraged to make deductions and to consciously apply what they learn from one context to another. The major difference between skills teaching and strategy teaching is that the former is teacher-directed and the latter is student-directed.

Teachers routinely review student writing to determine the most common subskill errors. Teachers then plan mini-lessons that address these errors. During the mini-lesson, the teacher discusses the skill or concept and then uses the skill or concept in editing a piece of student writing (on a transparency). At the end of the mini-lesson, the teacher directs students to review the text on which they are working or a sample from their writing folders and to edit the work in terms of the skill featured in the mini-lesson.

CLASSROOM EXAMPLES

Let us assume that several students are having problems with end punctuation. The teacher might make transparencies of student papers that have numerous errors of this nature (obscuring the students' names, of course). The teacher could then edit these papers for end punctuation, referencing the appropriate rules and instructing students to edit their own work-in-progress for problems with end punctuation. The teacher's task becomes the identification of error patterns, rather than the correction of random errors.

If students maintain their writing in folders, teachers can use these caches of writing as rich resources for revision exercises. One way to use folders to focus on revision is to periodically review one piece of writing from a folder, affixing a Post-it note to the piece that details control of conventions, any features that distinguish the piece of writing, and any patterns of errors that mar it. The note will direct subsequent revision efforts, with students attending primarily to the pattern of errors noted to revise the selected piece and perhaps as many as two subsequent pieces. Students themselves may even choose to begin using this system of Post-it notes to document certain features of their own work.

REFERENCES
Bereiter, Scardamalia, Anderson, and Smart 1980; Braddock, Lloyd-Jones, and Schoer 1963; Calkins 1979, 1980; Elley et al. 1975; Farr and Daniels 1986; Graves 1982; Hailey 1978; Hillocks 1986; King and Rentel 1983; Loban 1976.

● STRATEGY 6.14: USE SENTENCE-COMBINING STRATEGIES

Teachers provide instruction in sentence-combining strategies.

DISCUSSION

Considerable research has highlighted the negative relationship between the teaching of formal grammar and the improvement of student writing abilities. Nonetheless, most teachers persist in conducting formal grammar lessons. Such lessons do provide students with a metalanguage with which to talk about sentences in written texts, but they consume tremendous amounts of classroom time, year after year. And though grammar lessons (at best) teach students about writing, they do *not* teach students to write. A better approach may be sentence combining, a strategy that gives students practice in combining short "kernel" sentences into longer, more complex sentences. Students learn to employ a variety of techniques to form various sentence patterns.

Teachers structure activities in which students combine short sentences to form longer sentences that correlate to a repertoire of sentence types. Students' knowledge of sentence patterns increases as they experiment with the formation of new sentence types and share the various possibilities of combinations.

CLASSROOM EXAMPLES

A teacher might put sets of kernel sentences on a chalkboard or transparency and then direct students to combine these sentences, either randomly or with the aim of producing specific sentence patterns—for example, compound sentences or sentences with final free modifiers. After students have worked independently on their combinations, they might form response groups to share their efforts, perhaps even determining the "most effective" sentences.

In this type of activity, students are not necessarily working to make all their sentences longer. Instead, the idea is to develop a sense of the best arrangement of clauses and modifiers to convey an idea. Suppose that students are working on making their writing more coherent.

One way for them to develop coherence is to examine each sentence to determine whether it provides new information or expands on another sentence. Those sentences that provide new information are left unchanged, but students try to combine the closely related sentences, usually by making the "expansion" sentence an independent clause that is the second part of the new sentence. After completing all the sentence combinations they think appropriate, students review the writing again and arrange both the new sentence combinations and the sentences left unchanged so that the text moves from old information to new information. Such a process helps students develop flow in the writing as well as coherence.

REFERENCES
Brant 1989; Cooper 1975; Evans et al. 1988, 1986; Faigley 1979; Freedman 1985; Farr and Daniels 1986; Hunt 1965; Hutson 1980; Lawlor 1983; Mellon 1969; O'Hare 1973; Morenberg, Daiker, and Kerel 1978; Strong 1986.

● STRATEGY 6.15: USE THE INQUIRY METHOD

Teachers use the inquiry method of instruction to improve the quality of students' writing.

DISCUSSION

For students to be proficient writers, they must be able to use a variety of strategies that address a range of purposes and audiences and often involve complex topics. The inquiry method calls on the teacher to structure specific tasks that require students to produce writing drawn from a variety of data. The assignments often involve teachers and students in determining the most effective strategies and the most appropriate mode of discourse. Such structured assignments allow students to develop the skills to work independently through comparable tasks. If students are not presented with such structured tasks, they may not explore a variety of writing types that require a range of strategies.

When students are allowed to work collaboratively on solving a writing problem—for example, how best to address a distant audience, or how best to organize text to persuade—the learning is less stressful than when students work independently. Teachers should structure writing problems that allow writers to collaborate and that develop specific writing strategies. Students should work through the problem collaboratively, exploring the data and determining effective strategies. Then students should work individually through a comparable assignment.

CLASSROOM EXAMPLES

As an introduction to this method of learning, the teacher presents students with a problem, such as writing a proposal to buy the class a computer. With the teacher's guidance, students conduct a needs assessment so they can write a convincing rationale for funding. They may interview businesses to glean concrete examples of the benefits of computers as a way of making their rationale more convincing. The teacher may suggest that students work in committees to develop different portions of the proposal, and then help students synthesize the various portions into a single proposal. At this point, the students are ready to apply this method of inquiry to a project that requires less teacher direction.

For example, high school students may be asked to revise the handbook of a community agency. Before the students can analyze the handbook, they need more information about the agency's purpose and function. Prior to the interviewing process, class members can analyze the current handbook and develop a series of questions. Students might interview staff members and volunteers at the agency to begin gathering data. Following the interview, students may plan visual or graphic methods to describe the agency's organization and services. After exploring the possibilities, student may determine that computer graphics should be used to generate a variety of visual displays for the handbook. They can analyze existing text in the handbook and revise it for clarity, adding missing information and deleting unimportant or outdated portions.

REFERENCES
Hillocks 1986; Knapp and Turnbull 1990; Farnham-Diggory 1990.

Calvin & Hobbes

I USED TO HATE WRITING ASSIGNMENTS, BUT NOW I ENJOY THEM.

I REALIZED THAT THE PURPOSE OF WRITING IS TO INFLATE WEAK IDEAS, OBSCURE POOR REASONING, AND INHIBIT CLARITY.

WITH A LITTLE PRACTICE, WRITING CAN BE AN INTIMIDATING AND IMPENETRABLE FOG! WANT TO SEE MY BOOK REPORT?

"THE DYNAMICS OF INTERBEING AND MONOLOGICAL IMPERATIVES IN *DICK AND JANE*: A STUDY IN PSYCHIC TRANSRELATIONAL GENDER MODES."

ACADEMIA, HERE I COME!

• STRATEGY 6.16: USE WRITING PORTFOLIOS

Teachers use writing portfolios to monitor students' growth in writing over a period of time.

DISCUSSION

The evaluation of students' writing abilities is a highly complex process. We know, for instance, that the ability to write in one genre does not necessarily correlate to the ability to write in various other genres. So, for example, students who construct well-developed narratives are not necessarily equally adept at writing reports or arguments. Therefore, any evaluation of students' writing abilities based on a single sample is open to question.

A more promising practice involves the review of student "portfolios," that is, collections of student work generated over time. A student portfolio has the potential to provide a complete picture of what a student is capable of doing. When this collection of student writing also contains student-written rationales describing *why* each piece has been included in the portfolio, the writer must demonstrate a clear sense of what he or she values in text and what strategies have been consciously used to achieve what is valued.

Portfolios should represent authentic learning, as opposed to the old-style, drill-and-practice type of activities. Students select portfolio pieces from their working folders. Whereas the working folder is a collection of *all* the work produced by a student, the portfolio is a representative sample of work deemed somehow significant or exemplary.

CLASSROOM EXAMPLES

Teachers should have students maintain all their writing in a working folder. Periodically, students should review these folders and select those pieces that they feel represent their best efforts, their most thoughtful work, their most extensively revised (and improved) work, or any other categories for portfolio inclusion that have been mutually agreed upon by teacher and students. Students should then write a rationale for including the pieces selected for their portfolios. The portfolio itself should continually grow and change; students can add, discard, or revise selections as they develop as writers.

Portfolios have tremendous power to change the dynamics of learning. When students have ownership of their portfolio—or at least are primarily responsible for determining its contents— a shift occurs in the relationship between teacher and student. By giving ownership of the portfolio to the student, a teacher says, in effect, "I will provide you with opportunity, expertise, and guidance; in return, you will demonstrate the degree to which you have learned." This shift in responsibility must occur before student self-assessment can take hold in a classroom. Once this transformation has occurred, the use of portfolios to demonstrate growth toward a performance standard can follow. When we speak of the use of portfolios as an instrument for school reform, it is this shift in responsibility from teacher to student, as much as the idea of the portfolio as an alternative to standardized assessments, that education reformers have in mind.

REFERENCES
Au, Scheu, Kawakami, and Herman 1990; Bloom and Bimes-Michalk 1991; Burham 1986; Howard 1991; Glazer and Brown 1993; Graves 1986; Graves and Sunstein 1992; Rief 1992; Tierney 1991.

• STRATEGY 6.17: INVOLVE STUDENTS IN THE EVALUATION PROCESS

Teachers involve students in several stages of the evaluation process and use multiple measures to assess students' literacy skills.

DISCUSSION

The development of students' writing abilities requires both a coherent writing program and continuing opportunities for students to engage in the writing process. Ideally, such growth in writing ability would be measured against standards of adult proficiency, with students understanding that they are responsible for moving toward these standards. This view of writing development places less emphasis on the evaluation of any single piece of student work and more emphasis on the student's collection (portfolio) of work, which should show substantive growth over time or should contain evidence of having reached a certain level of proficiency.

If students are to be held accountable for their growth as writers, then they must be made aware of the inventories, checklists, or scales used to judge writing as successful. And they must be given regular feedback relative to these same criteria. Just as students should be afforded evaluation criteria to work with in response groups, so should they be afforded standards, models, and criteria that represent adult proficiency.

When students become aware of what is valued in writing and are shown strategies for developing effective writing, *they will work to develop those strategies*. For example, once students who produce unelaborated text recognize that elaboration is a necessary component of effective writing, they can begin to judge the quality of their own work relative to the degree and kind of elaboration they provide. They may even decide to revisit earlier pieces in their portfolios and revise these pieces by successfully employing elaboration strategies. These same students may recognize that perhaps they do not elaborate as effectively as proficient adults, but they will also realize that they have the ability to elaborate more effectively than they once did. Teachers, too, see writing ability as evolving over time and recognize and celebrate the growth of student abilities.

CLASSROOM EXAMPLES

A teacher may encourage students to focus on developing proficiency in using a particular strategy or feature associated with various forms of discourse—the use of dialogue, for example. The teacher may conference with each student on effective ways to craft dialogue and how often or where to use a certain device. The teacher might ask students to bracket sections of text where they have used dialogue and to assess its effectiveness relative to earlier efforts or to a model piece of writing. This process allows students to appreciate their progress and encourages further effort and a willingness to revise.

Another effective strategy involves teachers asking students to review all work done prior to producing a final draft. After the review, students produce a reflective piece in which they describe the evolution of their writing, noting specifically what they did to make their work better and what might yet be done were they to consider a further revision. This reflective piece might actually be the primary basis for grade reporting and setting student goals.

Young writers can come to make judgments about the quality of their work by reviewing a collection of their past efforts and, perhaps, labeling the piece that was best received by their response group, the piece they worked hardest on, the piece they are proudest of, the piece they think needs most to be reworked, and so on. With novice writers, the notion of simply revisiting a collection of work in a judgmental way—rather than the discerning quality of

the judgment—is critical to the writing process. Nonetheless, a teacher/student conference following this kind of review can provide valuable insights into what young students value as writers. The conference also allows students to come to understand their own role in acting as responsible learners.

REFERENCES
British National Writing Project 1987; Clay 1975, 1977; Daniels and Zemelman 1985; Farr and Daniels 1986; Graves 1983; Hillcocks 1986; Jagger and Smith-Burke 1985; Newkirk and Atwell 1988; Sulzby 1985; Teale, Hiebert, and Chittenden 1987; Watson 1987.

BIBLIOGRAPHY

Adams, M.J. (1990). *Beginning to Read: Thinking and Learning About Print*. Cambridge, Mass.: Bradford Books/MIT Press.

Altwerger, B., C. Edelsky, and B.M. Flores. (November 1987). "Whole Language: What's New?" *Reading Teacher* 41, 2: 144-154.

Anderson, V., C. Bereiter, and D. Smart. (1982). "Activation of Semantic Networks in Writing: Teaching Students How to Do It Themselves." Paper presented at the annual meeting of the American Educational Research Association.

Applebee, A.N. (1981). *Writing in the Secondary School: English and the Content Areas*. Urbana, Ill.: National Council of Teachers of English.

Applebee, A.N. (1984). "Writing and Reasoning." *Review of Educational Research* 54. 4: 577-596.

Applebee, A.N., and J.A. Langer. (1983). "Instructional Scaffolding: Reading and Writing and Natural Language Activities." *Language Arts* 660: 168-175.

Applebee, A.N., et al. (November 1986). "The Writing Report Card: Writing Achievement in American Schools." Princeton, N.J.: National Assessment of Educational Progress.

Applebee, A.N., et al. (1990). *Learning to Write in Our Nation's Schools: Instruction and Achievement in 1988 at Grades 4, 8, and 12*. (Report No. 19-W-02). Princeton, N.J.: Educational Testing service and National Assessment of Educational Progress.

Atwell, N. (1987). *In the Middle: Writing, Reading, and Learning with Adolescents*. Upper Montclair, N.J. Boynton/Cook.

Au, K., J. Scheu, A. Kawakami, and P. Herman. (1990). "Assessment and Accountability in a Whole Literacy Curriculum." *The Reading Teacher* 43, 8: 574-578.

Barr, M., P. D'Arcy, and M. Healty, eds. (1982). *What's Going On? Language/Learning Episodes in British and American Classrooms, Grades 4-13*. Montclair, N.J.: Boynton/Cook.

Beaven, M. (1977). "Individual Goal Setting, Self-Evaluation, and Peer Evaluation." In *Evaluating Writing Describing, Measuring Judging*, edited by C. Cooper and L. O'Dell. Urbana, Ill.: National Council of Teachers of English.

Bereiter, C. (1980). "Development in Writing." In *Cognitive Processes in Writing*, edited by L.W. Gregg and E.R. Steinberg. Hillsdale, N.J.: Lawrence Erlbaum.

Bereiter, C., M. Scardamalia, V. Anderson, and D. Smart. (1980). "An Experiment in Teaching Abstract Planning in Writing." Paper presented at the annual meeting of the American Educational Research Association.

Bereiter, C., and M. Scardamalia. (1982). "From Conversation to Composition: The Role of Instruction in a Developmental

Process." In *Advances in Instructional Psychology*, Vol. 2, edited by R. Glaser. London: Longman.

Bissex, G.L. (1980). *Gnys at Work: A Child Learns to Write and Read*. Cambridge: Harvard University Press.

Bloom, D.S. (1985). "Understanding the Writing Process: Introducing Students to Composing." New Jersey State Dept. of Education, Trenton, New Jersey.

Bloom, D.S. (1986). "Assessing Higher-Order Thinking Skills Through Writing." A paper presented at the annual meeting of the American Educational Research Association, San Francisco.

Bloom, D.S. (1988). "The Graphic Pre-writing Representations of Selected Ninth-grade Writers During Formal Assessment of a Writing Sample." Doctoral diss., Rutgers—The State University.

Bloom, D.S., and B. Bimer-Michalak. (January 1991). "Making Sense of Writing in the Middle School." Paper presented at a meeting of ASCD's Urban Middle Grades Network.

Blount, N.S. (1973). "Research on Teaching Literature, Language and Composition." In *Second Handbook of Research on Teaching*, edited by R.M.W. Travers. Chicago: Rand McNally.

Booth, W. (October 1963). "The Rhetorical Stance." *College Composition and Communication* 14: 139-145. [Published by the National Council of Teachers of English, Urbana, Ill.]

Boyer, E.L. (1983). *High School: A Report on Secondary Education in America*. New York: Harper and Row.

Bracewell, R.J., C.H. Frederiksen, and J.F. Frederiksen. (1982). "Cognitive Processes in Composing and Comprehending Discourse." *Educational Psychologist* 17, 3: 146-164.

Braddock, R., R. Lloyd-Jones, and L. Schoer. (1963). *Research in Written Composition*. Champaign, Ill.: National Council of Teachers of English.

Brant, J.K. (May 2, 1989). "Sentence-Combining in the Secondary ESL Classroom—A Review of the Research Literature." (ERIC Document Reproduction Service No. ED 307-811)

British National Writing Project. (1987). *Ways of Looking at Children's Writing: The National Writing Project Response to the Task Group on Assessment and Testing*. (Occasional Paper No. 8). London: School Curriculum Development Committee Publications.

Britton, J. (1970) *Language and Learning*. Harmondsworth, Middlesex, England: Penguin.

Britton, J., T. Burgess, N. Martin, A. McLeod, and H. Rosen. (1975). *The Development of Writing Abilities (11-18)*. London: Schools Council Publications.

Bruffee, K.A. (1984). "Collaborative Learning and the `Conversation of Mankind.'" *College English* 46: 635-652

Burham, C. (1986). "Portfolio Evaluation: Room to Breathe and Grow." In *Training the Teacher of College Composition*, edited by C. Bridges. Urbana, Ill.: National Council of Teachers of English.

Burns Jr., H.L., and G.H. Culp. (August 1980). "Stimulating Rhetorical Invention in English Composition Through Computer-Assisted Instruction." *Educational Technology* 20: 5-10. (ERIC Document Reproduction Service No. ED 188-245).

Butler, A., and J. Turnbull. (1984). *Towards a Reading-Writing Classroom*. Rozelle, New South Wales, Australia: Primary English Teaching Association; Portsmouth, N.H.: Heinemann.

California State Department of Education. (1983). *Student Achievement in California Schools: 1982-83 Annual Report. California Assessment Program*. Sacramento: Calif. State Dept. of Educ., Planning, Evaluation, and Research Division. (ERIC Document Reproduction Service No. ED 250-376)

Calkins, L.M. (1979). "Andrea Learns to Make Writing Hard." *Language Arts* 56: 569-576.

Calkins, L.M. (1980). "When Children Want to Punctuate: Basic Skills Belong in Context." *Language Arts* 57: 567-573.

Calkins, L.M. (1983). *Lessons from a Child: On the Teaching and Learning of Writing*. Exeter, N.H.: Heinemann Educational Books.

Calkins, L.M. (1994). *The Art of Teaching Writing*. Portsmouth, N.H.: Heinemann.

Calkins, L.M., with S. Harwayne. (1991). *Living Between the Lines*. Portsmouth, N.H.: Heinemann.

Cambourne, B., and J. Turbill. (1987). *Coping with Chaos*. Rozelle, Australia: Primary English Teaching Association.

Chomsky, C. (1971). "Write Now, Read Later." *Childhood Education* 47: 296-299.

Christensen, M. (1965). "Tripling Writing and Omitting Readings in Freshmen English: An Experiment." *College Composition and Communication* 16: 123-124.

Christensen, F. (1967). *Notes Toward a New Rhetoric: Six Essays for Teachers*. New York: Harper and Row.

Clarke, L.K. (1988). "Invented Versus Traditional Spelling in First Grades Writings: Effects on Learning to Spell and Read." *Research in the Teaching of English* 22: 281-309.

Clay, M. (1975). *What Did I Write?* London: Heinemann.

Clay, M. (1977). "Exploring with a Pencil." *Theory into Practice*. 16: 334-341.

Clifford, J.P. (1978). "An Experimental Inquiry into the Effectiveness of Collaborative Learning as a Method for Improving the Experiential Writing Performance of College Freshmen in a Remedial Writing Class." *Dissertation Abstracts International* 38: 7289A.

Clifford, J.P. (1981). "Composing in Stages: The Effects of a Collaborative Pedagogy." *Research in the Teaching of English* 15: 37-52.

Coleman, D.R. (1982). "The Effects of Pupil Use of a Creative Writing Scale as an Evaluative and Instructional Tool by Primary Gifted Students." *Dissertation Abstracts International* 42: 3409-A.

Cooper, C.R. (1975). "Research Roundup: Measuring Growth in Writing." *English Journal* 64, 3: 111-120.

Cooper, C.R. (1977). "Holistic Evaluation of Writing." In *Evaluating Writing: Describing, Measuring, Judging*, edited by C.R. Cooper and L. Odell. Urbana, Ill.: National Council of Teachers of English.

Cooper, C.R, A. Marquis, and S. Ayer-Lopez. (1982). "Peer Learning in the Classroom: Tracing Developmental Patterns and Consequences of Children's Spontaneous Interactions." In *Communicating in the Classroom*, edited by L.C. Wilkinson. New York: Academic Press.

Daniels, H.A., and S. Zemelman. (1985). *A Writing Project: Training Teachers of Composition from Kindergarten to College*. Exeter, N.H.: Heinemann.

Diaute, C. (1986). "Do 1 and 1 Make 2? Patterns of Influence by Collaborative Authors." *Written Communication* 3: 382-408.

Diederich, P.B. (1974). *Measuring Growth in English*. Urbana, Ill.: National Council of Teachers of English.

Dow, R.H. (1973). "The Student-Writer's Laboratory: An Approach to Composition." *Dissertation Abstracts International* 34: 2435-A.

Dyson, A.H. (1985). "Second Graders Sharing Writing: The Multiple Social Realities of Literacy Event." *Written Communication* 2: 189-215.

Elbow, P. (1973). *Writing Without Teachers*. New York: Oxford University Press.

Elley, W.B., I.H. Barham, H. Lamb, and M. Wyllie. (1976). "The Role of Grammar in a Secondary School English Curriculum." *Research in the Teaching of English* 10: 5-21.

Emig, J. (1971). *The Composing Processes of Twelfth Graders*. (Research Report No. 13). Champaign, Ill.: National Council of Teachers of English.

Emig, J. (May 1977). "Writing as a Mode of Learning." *College Composition and Communication* 28: 122-128.

Emig, J. (February 1982). "Inquiry Paradigms and Writing." *College Composition and Communication* 33: 64-75.

Emig, J. (1983). *The Web of Meaning: Essays on Writing, Teaching, Learning and Thinking.* Upper Montclair, N.J.: Boynton/Cook.

Evans, R., et al. (April 1986). "The Effects of Sentence Combining Instructions on Controlled and Free Writing and on Scores for Standardized Tests of Sentence Structure and Reading Comprehension." Paper presented at the 70th annual meeting of the American Educational Research Association, San Francisco, Calif. (ERIC Document Reproduction Service No. ED 269-739)

Evans, R., et al. (September-October 1988). "The Effects of Sentence-Combining Instructions on Writing and on Standardized Test Scores." *Journal of Educational Research* 82, 1: 53-57.

Faigley, L.L. (1979). "The Influence of Generative Rhetoric on the Syntactic Maturity and Writing Effectiveness of College Freshmen." *Research in the Teaching of English* 13: 197-206.

Falk, J.S. (1979). "Language Acquisition and the Teaching and Learning of Writing." *College English* 41: 436-447.

Farnham-Diggory, S. (1990). *Schooling.* Cambridge: Harvard University Press.

Farr, M., and H. Daniels. (1986). "Language Diversity and Writing Instruction." New York: Columbia University, Institute for Urban and Minority Education; Urbana, Ill.: ERIC Clearinghouse on Reading and Communication Skills. (ERIC Document Reproduction Service No. ED 274-996)

Feitelson, D., B. Kita, and Z. Goldstein. (1986). "Effects of Listening to Stories on First Grader's Comprehension and Use of Language." *Research in the Teaching of English* 20: 339 356.

Fine, E.S. (1987). "Marbles Lost, Marbles Found: Collaborative Production of Text . . . " *Language Arts* 64: 474-487.

Flower, L.S., and J.R. Hayes. (1980). "The Dynamics of Composing: Making Plans and Juggling Constraints." In *Cognitive Processes in Writing,* edited by L.W. Gregg and E.R. Steinberg. Hillsdale, N.J.: Lawrence Erlbaum.

Flower, L.S., and J.R. Hayes. (1981a). "A Cognitive Process Theory of Writing." *College Composition and Communication* 32: 365-387

Flower, L.S., and J.R. Hayes. (1981b). "Plans That Guide the Composing Process." *In Writing: The Nature, Development and Teaching of Written Communication. Volume 2, Writing: Process, Development and Communication,* edited by C.H. Frederiksen and J.F. Dominic. Hillsdale, N.J.: Lawrence Erlbaum.

Freedman, A. (1985). "Sentence Combining: Some Questions." In *Carleton Papers in Applied Language Studies.* Volume II, edited by A. Freedman. Ottawa, Canada: Carleton University. (ERIC Document Reproduction Service No. ED 267 602)

Freedman, S., with C. Greenleaf and M. Sperling. (1987a). *Response to Student Writing.* (Research Report No. 23). Urbana, Ill.: National Council of Teachers of English.

Freire, P. (1986). *Pedagogy of the Oppressed.* New York: Seabury.

Fulwiler, T. (1979). "Journal-Writing Across the Curriculum." In *Classroom Practices in the Teaching of English, 1979-80: How to Handle the Paper Load,* edited by G. Stanford, chair, and the Committee on Classroom Practices. Urbana, Ill. National Council of Teachers of English.

Fulwiler, T., and A. Young. (1982). *Language Connections: Writing and Reading Across the Curriculum.* Urbana, Ill.: National Council of Teachers of English.

Gere, A.R., ed. (1985). *Roots in the Sawdust: Writing to Learn Across the Disciplines.* Urbana, Ill.: National Council of Teachers of English.

Glatthorn, A.A. (1981). *Writing in the Schools: Improvement Through Effective Leadership.* Reston, Va.: National Association of Secondary School Principals.

Glazer, S.M., and C.S. Brown. (1993). *Portfolios and Beyond: Collaborative Assessment in Reading and Writing.* Norwood, Mass.: Christopher Gordon Publishers, Inc.

Graves, D.H. (1975). "An Examination of the Writing Processes of Seven-Year-Old Children." *Research in the Teaching of English* 9: 227 241.

Graves, D.H. (1976). "Let's Get Rid of the Welfare Mess in the Teaching of Writing." *Language Arts* 53: 645-651.

Graves, D.H. (1978). *Balance the Basics: Let Them Write.* New York: Ford Foundation.

Graves, D.H. (1981). "Research Update: Writing Research for the Eighties: What Is Needed." *Language Arts* 58, 2: 197 206.

Graves, D.H. (1982). "Research Update: How Do Writers Develop?" *Language Arts* 59: 173-179.

Graves, D.H. (1983). *Writing: Teachers and Children at Work.* New Hampshire: Heinemann.

Graves, M.F. (1986). "Vocabulary Learning and Instruction." In *Review of Research in Education,* Vol. 13, edited by E.Z. Rothkopf. Washington, D.C.: American Educational Research Association.

Graves, D. (1990). *Lasting Impressions.* Portsmouth, N.H.: Heinemann.

Graves, D. (1990). *Discover Your Literacy.* Portsmouth, N.H.: Heinemann.

Graves, D., and B.S. Sunstein, eds. (1992). *Portfolio Portraits.* Portsmouth, N.H.: Heinemann.

Gunderson, D.V. (1971). "Research in the Teaching of English." *English Journal* 60: 792-796.

Hailey, J. (1978). *Teaching Writing, K 8.* Berkeley: School of Education, University of California.

Hansen, B. (1978). "Rewriting Is a Waste of Time." *College English* 39, 8: 956-960.

Hansen, J. (1987). *When Writers Read.* Portsmouth, N.H.: Heinemann.

Hass, V.P., R. Childers, E. Babbit, and S.N. Dyallay. (1972). "English Composition by Workshop." *Journal of Experimental Education* 40, 3: 33-37.

Hayes, J.R., and L.S. Flower. (1986). "Writing Research and the Writer." *American Psychologist* 41: 1106-1111.

Henderson, E.H., and J. Beers, J. (1980). *Developmental and Cognitive Aspects of Learning to Spell.* Newark, Del.: International Reading Association.

Heys Jr., F. (1962). "The Theme-a-Week Assumption: A Report of an Experiment," *English Journal* 51: 320-322.

Hidi, S., and A. Hildgard. (April-June 1983). "The Comparison of Oral and Written Production in Two Discourse Types." *Discourse Processes* 6, 2: 91-105.

Hillocks Jr., G. (1982). "The Interaction of Instruction, Teacher Comment, and Revision in Teaching the Composing Process." *RTE* 16: 261 78.

Hillocks Jr., G. (1986). *Research on Written Composition.* Urbana, Ill.: National Council of Teachers of English.

Hodges, H. (1989). "ASCD's 3-High Achievement Model." Unpublished manuscript for the ASCD Urban Middle Grades Network, Alexandria, Va.

Hodges, H. (1991). "Effective K-12 Writing Practices: A Research Synthesis." In *The Knowledge Base Reference Guide.*

Howard, E.F. (1989). *Aunt Flossie's Hats (and Crab Cakes Later).* Illustrated by J. Ransome. New York: Clarion.

Howard, K. (1990). "Making the Writing Portfolio Real." *The Quarterly* 12, 2: 4-7, 27

Hunt, K. (1965). *Grammatical Structures Written at Three Grade Levels.* Champaign, Ill.: National Council of Teachers of English.

Hutson, B.A. (1980). "Moving Language Around: Helping Students Become Aware of Language Structure." *Language Arts* 57: 614-620.

Jagger, A., and T. Smith-Burke, T. (1985). *Observing the Language Learner*. Urbana, Ill.: National Council of Teachers of English.

Jensen, J.M., ed. (1984). *Composing and Comprehending*. Urbana, Ill. National Conference on Research in English; Bloomington, Ind.: ERIC Clearinghouse on Reading and Communication Skills.

King, M.L., and V.M. Rentel. (1981). "Research Update: Conveying Meaning in Written Texts." *Language Arts* 59, 6: 721-728.

King, M.L., and V.M. Rental. (1983). *Transition to Writing*. Columbus: Ohio State University.

Knapp, M.S., and B. Turnbull, B. (1990). *Better Schooling for the Children of Poverty: Alternatives to Conventional Wisdom. Volume 1: Summary*. Washington, D.C.: Prepared under contract by SRI International and Policy Studies Associates for the U.S. Department of Education, Office of Planning, Budget and Evaluation.

Kucer, S.I. (1985). "The Making of Meaning: Reading and Writing as Parallel Processes." *Written Communication* 2: 317-336.

Lagana, J.R. (1972). "The Development, Implementation, and Evaluation of a Model for Teaching Composition Which Utilizes Individualized Learning and Peer Grouping." *Dissertation Abstracts International* 33: 4063-A. ED 079 726.

Lamme, L.L. (1987). *Growing Up Writing*. Washington, D.C.: Acropolis Books.

Langer, J.A. (1986). *Children Reading and Writing: Structures and Strategies*. Norwood, N.J.: Ablex.

Langer, J.A. (1987). "Children's Sense of Genre." *Written Communication* 2: 157-187.

Langer, J.A., and A.N. Applebee. (1987). *How Writing Shapes Thinking: A Study of Teaching and Learning*. (Research Report No. 22). Urbana Ill.: National Council of Teachers of English.

Lawlor, J. (1983). "Sentence Combining: A Sequence for Instruction." *The Elementary School Journal* 84, 1: 53-62.

Lehr, F. (1980). "ERIC/REC Report: Writing as Learning in the Content Areas." *English Journal* 69 8: 23-25.

Loban, W. (1976). *Language Development: Kindergarten Through Grade Twelve*. Urbana Ill.: National Council of Teachers of English.

Macrorie, K. (1970). *Uptaught*. New York: Hayden Book Company.

Macrorie, K. (1984). *Twenty Teachers*. New York: Oxford University Press.

Martin, N., P. D'Arcy, B. Newton, and R. Parker. (1976). *Writing and Learning Across the Curriculum, 11-16*. London: Ward Lock Educational.

Mellon, J.C. (1969). *Transformational Sentence-combining: A Method for Enhancing the Development of Syntactic Fluency in English Composition*. Champaign, Ill.: National Council of Teachers of English.

Moffett, J. (1968). *Teaching the Universe of Discourse*. Boston: Houghton Mifflin.

Mohr, M.M. (1984). *Revision: The Rhythm of Meaning*. Upper Montclair, N.J.: Boynton/Cook.

Morenberg, M., D. Daiker, and A. Kerek. (1978). "Sentence Combining at the College Level: An Experimental Study." *Research in the Teaching of English* 12: 245-256.

Murray, D.M. (1986). *A Writer Teaches Writing*. Boston: Houghton Mifflin.

Murray, D.M. (1984). *Write to Learn*. New York: Winston.

National Council of Teachers of English. (1989). *Motivating Reluctant Writers*. Urbana, Ill.: NCTE.

Newkirk, T., and N. Atwell. (1988). *Understanding Writing*. 2nd ed. Portsmouth, N.H.: Heinemann.

Odell, L. (1974). "Measuring the Effect of Instruction in Prewriting." *Research in the Teaching of English* 8: 228-240.

Odell, L. (1980). "Business Writing: Observations and Implications for Teaching Composition." *Theory into Practice* 19, 3: 225-232

Odell, L., and S. Hampton. (1992). "Writing Assessment, Writing Instruction, and Teacher Professionalism." In *A Rhetoric of Doing*, edited by S. Witte, N. Nokadale, and R. Cherry. Carbondale: Southern Illinois University Press.

O'Hare, F. (1973). *Sentence Combining: Improving Student Writing Without Formal Grammar Instruction*. Urbana, Ill.: National Council of Teachers of English.

Parry, J., and D. Hornsby. (1985). *Write-on: A Conference Approach to Writing*. Portsmouth, N.H.: Heinemann.

Perl, S. (1980). "Understanding Composition." *College Composition and Communication* 31: 363-369.

Read, C. (February 1971). "Preschool Children's Knowledge of English Phonology." *Harvard Educational Review* 41, : 1-34.

Rief, L. (1992). *Seeking Diversity*. Portsmouth, N.H.: Heinemann.

Rohman, D.G., and A. Wlecke. (1964). *Prewriting: The Construction and Application of Models to Concept Formation in Writing*. East Lansing: Michigan State University.

Sager, C. (1973). "Improving the Quality of Written Composition Through Pupil Use of Rating Scale." *Dissertation Abstracts International* 34: 1496-A.

Scardamalia, M., et al. (1982). "The Role of Production Factors in Writing Ability." In *What Writers Know: The Language, Process, and Structure of Written Discourse*, edited by M. Nystrand. New York: Academic Press.

Scardamalia, M., et al. (1984). "Teachability of Reflective Processes in Written Composition." *Cognitive Science* 8, 2: 173-190.

Scardamalia, M., C. Bereiter, and B. Fillion. (1981). *Writing for Results: A Sourcebook of Consequential Composing Activities*. Toronto: OISE Press; La Salle, Ill.: Open Court.

Sizer, T.R. (1984). *Horace's Compromise: The Dilemma of the American High School*. Boston: Houghton Mifflin.

Smith, F. (1982). *Writing and the Writer*. Portsmouth, N.H.: Heinemann.

Smith, F. (1983). "Reading Like a Writer." *Language Arts* 60: 558-567.

Smithson, I., and P. Sorrentino. (1987). "Writing Across the Curriculum: An Assessment." *Journal of Teaching Writing* 6, 2: 325-342.

Sommers, N. (1982). "Responding to Student Writing." *College Composition and Communication* 33: 148-156.

Spear, K. (1988). *Sharing Writing*. Portsmouth, N.H.: Boynton/Cook.

Sowers, S. (1979). "A Six-Year-Old's Writing Process: The First Half of First Grade." *Language Arts* 56: 829-835.

Stallard Jr., C.K. (1974). "An Analysis of the Writing Behavior of Good Student Writers." *Research in the Teaching of English* 8: 206-218.

Strom, I.M. (1960). "Research in Grammar and Usage and Its Implications for Teaching Writing." *Bulletin of the School of Education, Indiana University*, 36, 5: 13-14.

Strong, W. (1986). *Creative Approaches to Sentence Combining*. Urbana, Ill.: National Council of Teachers of English; Bloomington, Ind.: ERIC Clearinghouse on Reading and Communication Skills.

Strickland, D.S., and L.M. Morrow. (1989). *Emerging Literacy: Young Children Learn to Read and Write*. Newark, Del.: International Reading Association.

Sulzby, F. (1985). "Children's Emergent Reading of Favorite Storybooks: A Developmental Study." *Reading Research Quarterly* 20: 458-481.

Teale, W.H., E.H. Hiebert, and E.A. Chittenden. (1987). "Assessing Young Children's Literacy Development." *The Reading Teacher* 40: 772-777.

Tierney, R.J., M. Carter, and L. Desai. (1991). *Portfolio Assessment in the Reading and Writing Classroom*. Norwood, Mass.: Christopher Gordon.

Tompkins, G. (1990). *Teaching Writing: Balancing Process and Product*. Columbus, Ohio: Merrill.

Tway, E. (1980). "Teachers Responses to Children's Writing." *Language Arts* 57: 763-772.

Vygotsky, L.S. (1962). *Thought and Language,* edited and translated by E. Hanfmann and G. Vakar. Cambridge, Mass.: M.I.T Press.

Watson, D. (1987). *Ideas and Insights.* Urbana, Ill.: National Council of Teachers of English.

White, R.S., and H. Karl. (1980). "Reading, Writing, and Sentence Combining: The Track Record." *Reading Improvements* 17: 226-232.

Woodruff, E., C. Bereiter, and M. Scardamalia. (1981). "Computers and the Composing Process: An Examination of Computer-Writer Interaction." In *Computers in Composition Instruction,* edited by J. Lawlor. Los Alamitos, Calif.: SWRL Educational Research and Development.

Yates, J.M. (1987). *Research Implications for Writing in the Content Areas. What Research Says to the Teacher.* 2nd ed. Washington, D.C.: National Education Association.

Zinsser, W. (1985). *On Writing Well: An Informal Guide to Writing Non-Fiction.* New York: Harper and Row.

7

STRATEGIES FOR INCREASING ACHIEVEMENT IN MATHEMATICS

BEATRIZ D'AMBROSIO, HOWARD JOHNSON, AND LESLIE HOBBS

Photo courtesy of St. Elizabeth Seton School, Palo Alto, CA

Mathematics is important not just in the education of scientists, engineers, and economists but also in the education of every working citizen in the United States. It's hard to see how anybody can pull down anything better than a minimum wage job in the years ahead without quantitative skills.

— MSEB, *MAKING MATHEMATICS WORK FOR MINORITIES*, REPORT OF A CONVOCATION (1990), P. 2.

Results in mathematics from the 1990 National Assessment of Educational Progress (NAEP) indicate that a worrisome percentage of students score below the level of proficiency expected for their age and grade levels. More serious still is the evidence that some groups of students perform at lower levels than others of the same age and grade. These troubling differences in levels of achievement are related to race, ethnicity, gender, and socioeconomic background.

There *is* some evidence that scores have improved since 1982, but the improvement is limited to items focusing on basic computational skills. Items requiring problem solving, application of skills, or reasoning show achievement at very low levels.

Another indicator of young people's low level of achievement in mathematics is the high percentage of students who do not study math beyond the first year of high school. Only 6 percent and 8 percent of African American and Hispanic students, respectively, reported taking Algebra III, precalculus, or calculus at the high school level. The lower level of enrollment of some minorities in high school courses seriously limits their participation in college courses, as well as their career options.

Clearly the educational community must find ways to encourage young people to pursue mathematics at higher levels, and to provide instruction that will increase their mathematics abilities and, consequently, their mathematical achievement. In response to this need, the National Council of Teachers of Mathematics (NCTM 1989) has published a landmark document, *Curriculum and Evaluation Standards for School Mathematics*, which emphasizes the need for all students to develop mathematical literacy. The NCTM's five goals for all students are to:

- learn to value mathematics,
- become confident in their ability to do mathematics,
- become mathematical problem solvers,
- learn to communicate mathematically, and
- learn to reason mathematically.

ENHANCING STUDENTS' ACHIEVEMENT IN MATHEMATICS

Several conditions have been found to enhance students' mathematical ability and, consequently, their mathematical power. The following recommendations, which grew out of the 1990 NAEP report, suggest ways of increasing students' proficiency in mathematics:

- Provide instruction in pre-algebra and algebra.
- Link mathematics to everyday problems and situations.
- Develop students' reasoning and analytic abilities.
- Teach students how to communicate math ideas effectively.
- Test less, and involve students in small-group and individual projects more.
- Use calculators and computers.
- Assign homework every day.
- Monitor homework and school attendance.
- Emphasize less television and more reading.
- Encourage parents or care-givers to provide reading materials at home.
- Use flexible, heterogeneous grouping practices.

In addition, we must consider the relationship between success in school and young people's motivation and self- confidence. To promote increased mathematics achievement, educators must find strategies that increase students' self- esteem and self-confidence in their ability to do mathematics. We must also adopt strategies that motivate students to engage in mathematical activities and to pursue further study in mathematics.

THE STATE OF THE ART OF MATHEMATICS INSTRUCTION

Mathematics instruction in schools has changed little over the years: The teacher still tends to demonstrate a couple of problems for students; then the students work individually on examples similar to those demonstrated by the teacher and take a test to show that they have mastered the desired skill. The predominant materials used in mathematics instruction are textbooks and worksheets; more than half of the 4th graders surveyed by the NAEP reported solving problems from the textbook or worksheets on a daily basis. Even more reliance on individual, textbook-based work was reported at the 8th and 12th grade levels. And a considerable amount of testing was reported at all three grade levels.

Despite recent initiatives to encourage teachers to use both manipulative materials and small-group work to support students' mathematical learning, one-third of the students across the three grade levels reported *never* engaging in such activities. Moreover, the NAEP study revealed an alarming failure to use computers and calculators. More than half of the 4th graders reported never using calculators, and more than half of the 8th graders reported never using computers. In fact, as many as *two-thirds of the 12th graders never use computers at all.*

Teachers reported little attention to the development of students' thinking and reasoning abilities. In fact, many teachers seem to feel that higher order thinking skills can be emphasized only after students have mastered basic facts and procedures. Many more students from high-ability classes received instruction that emphasized higher order thinking skills than did their counterparts in lower-ability classes. Finally, little emphasis was placed on communication skills for most of the students studied.

Typically, mathematics instruction has been structured around the notion that students come to school with no mathematical knowledge and teachers will transmit all the knowledge they will need over the course of the years. This outdated view has contributed directly to the current state of achievement in mathematics. We can no longer think of mathematics instruction as a process in which the teacher transmits information and procedures to students. Instead, we must replace this instructional format with one in which the students construct their own understandings. This construction depends on the types of activities facilitated by the teacher as well as the previous knowledge brought to the learning situation by each individual.

THE CHARACTERISTICS OF GOOD MATHEMATICIANS

NCTM has proposed that the goal of mathematics instruction be to ensure that students gain mathematical power. "This term denotes an individual's abilities to explore, conjecture, and reason logically, as well as the ability to use a variety of mathematical methods effectively

FIGURE 7.1
A Summary of New Standards for Curriculum and Instruction in Mathematics

CURRICULUM

TRADITIONAL EMPHASIS ON	NEW EMPHASIS ON
spiral curriculum	core curriculum: topic integration, students' home/community, culture and experiences
teaching mathematics as a discrete subject area	integration of process and content
rigid sequencing of content	developmental
getting the "right answer"	broad range of topics: earlier exposure
	in-depth development of concepts
	application: novel problems, real-life problems

INSTRUCTION

TRADITIONAL EMPHASIS ON	NEW EMPHASIS ON
remediating weakness	building on students' knowledge base and experiences
textbook	challenging activities and opportunities
skills teaching: computation	wide variety of materials: calculators, computers, graphical representations, manipulatives
uniform instruction	strategy teaching: problem solving, focus on patterns
tracking	identifying individual student's learning style
independent seatwork	heterogeneous grouping
teacher delivering information	cooperative/team learning activities
students absorbing information	teacher as facilitator
	students constructing meaning and knowledge

Source: Hodges 1989.

to solve nonroutine problems" (NCTM 1989, p. 5). To attain this goal, NCTM has proposed more specific goals for all students. These include:

- that they learn to value mathematics;
- that they become confident in their abilities to do mathematics;
- that they learn to communicate mathematically;
- that they learn to reason mathematically (NCTM 1989, p. 5).

These goals can be attained, NCTM suggests, if each mathematics teacher shapes the classroom environment in ways that enhance students' involvement with mathematical problems and with each other as they engage in mathematical activity. The environment should enhance opportunities for students to communicate mathematically and to cooperate on problem-solving initiatives; it should also allow students to take risks as they explore mathematics. Changing the environment in the mathematics classroom is the first step toward reaching the goals proposed for all students.

ASSESSING ACHIEVEMENT IN MATHEMATICS

Knowledge of mathematics has traditionally been assessed by requiring students, using paper and pencil, to answer problems similar to those just taught. Grades on quizzes and tests are generally determined by the correctness of the final answers. Some teachers may give partial credit if the answer is incorrect but the process is correct. Scores are averaged and a report-card grade determined that can be defended as an accurate representation of student progress. This method of evaluation looks at the products of mathematics instruction, not the learning process.

Truly effective assessment, however, is an ongoing, integral part of instruction; it should be based on the overall goals of the curriculum. Assessment should be matched to instructional strategies. If being able to work cooperatively to solve problems is a desired outcome, and if instructional time is invested in achieving this outcome, then students should be assessed on this component of their program. Similarly, if students are taught to model concepts with manipulatives, then they should have manipulatives at hand when they are being evaluated.

If technology is used in instruction, then it should also be used during the assessment process. If the process of problem solving is being taught, students should be assessed on each component of the process: understanding the problem, planning strategies, finding a solution, and checking their answer.

Effective assessment incorporates a variety of approaches that recognize the strengths of students with different learning styles; it is a package containing various types of measures of progress. Although traditional multi-

FIGURE 7.2
Ten Keys to Mathematics Achievement

TO INCREASE STUDENTS' PROFICIENCY IN MATHEMATICS:

Provide instruction in pre-algebra and algebra.

Link math to everyday problems and situations.

Develop students' reasoning and analytic abilities.

Teach students how to effectively communicate math ideas.

Test less; involve students in small-group and individual projects more.

Use calculators and computers.

Assign homework everyday. Monitor homework and school attendance.

Emphasize less television and more reading.

Encourage parents to provide reading materials in the home.

Use flexible, heterogeneous grouping practices.

Source: Mullis et al. 1991.

ple-choice questions are easier for the teacher to grade, they usually do not require higher level reasoning or give students necessary opportunities to justify their reasoning and conclusions. In contrast to typical text-style word problems, authentic or performance-based assessments require the application of knowledge to the solution of real-life problems. If we are to have a complete picture of every student's progress, students need the opportunity to show both their ability to perform mathematics skills and their ability to apply them.

A mathematics portfolio provides an organized approach to ongoing assessment. It can contain final products of student work with a written explanation of the items included, and it can also contain materials such as journal pages, self-assessment checklists, observation and/or interview notes written by the teacher, a math autobiography, and other items to help portray the student as a learner of mathematics. It is appropriate to include examples of inadequate work and subsequent material illustrating progress, such as pretests and post-tests or skill inventories. Because it demonstrates the learning and understanding of ideas beyond mere facts and skills, the portfolio is valuable for student or parent conferences and at other times when an overall assessment is being made.

MATHEMATICS STRATEGIES THAT PROMOTE ACHIEVEMENT

The following strategies, intended to enhance students' learning of mathematics, are supported by research about how students learn most effectively. The strategies fall into three broad categories dealing with student learning, content applications and integration, and instructional approaches. Strategies most essential to increasing student achievement deal with:

- relating mathematics to the real-world experiences of young people;
- writing and talking about mathematics;
- working cooperatively to solve problems;
- exploring mathematics concepts with hands-on materials;
- using calculators and computers; and
- constructing one's own mathematical knowledge.

● STRATEGY 7.1: ENCOURAGE EXPLORATION AND INVESTIGATION

Teachers actively engage students in constructing mathematical knowledge through the use of activities that encourage them to explore and investigate mathematical ideas.

DISCUSSION

Students who engage in mathematical explorations and investigations reshape their understanding of mathematics as an area in which they can be creative. This type of activity develops flexibility in their reasoning skills and allows students to use their existing knowledge to explore new situations, hence extending their knowledge base.

As young people engage in mathematical activities, they raise questions that reflect their curiosity about mathematics. They ask "What if . . ." questions that explore the implications of those questions for the mathematical concept being explored. Students' success in mathematics is related to their ability to ask good questions and to raise interesting conjectures based on them.

CLASSROOM EXAMPLES

As students walk into the room, they see a problem on the board, which they are to work on in small groups. They immediately begin exploring the problem, which should be rich enough to allow many different strategies for its solution. Throughout the working session, the teacher circulates around to the different groups, observing the work and asking questions to help students verbalize the strategies they are using. After sufficient time for exploration, all groups share their solutions and compare the different approaches used to reach them.

Giving students an opportunity to explore concepts before being "taught the rules" is appropriate at all levels. At the high school level, students can use graphing calculators to explore the role of the coefficients in the graphical representation of linear functions. Measuring a table with paper clips, pencils, and notebooks helps younger children build number sense while coming to understand the need for standard units of measure.

REFERENCES
Blais 1988; Borasi 1992; Brown and Walter 1990; Campione, Brown, and Connell 1988; Davis, Maher, and Noddings 1990; Kroll 1989; Wearne and Hiebert 1989.

STRATEGY 7.2: USE STUDENTS' PRIOR KNOWLEDGE

Teachers build instruction on students' prior knowledge of mathematical ideas.

DISCUSSION

The knowledge that students bring to a new experience will greatly shape their understanding of new concepts. If we understand learning of mathematics as a constructive process, we can plan activities that will allow students to construct knowledge based on concepts they already understand. Given a problem-solving task, students must bring to that task what they already know in order to develop solutions that are personally meaningful to them. Their differing strategies and approaches to a problem will indicate the different mathematical constructions they rely on to solve a given problem.

To build instruction based on students' meanings and understandings, teachers must ask many questions throughout a teaching session. Students who reach the same answer for a problem may have solved it in very different ways. The process of sharing their solutions not only helps them see other possible solutions, but it also helps the teacher understand their thinking. Several successful programs of mathematics instruction use the instructional strategy of encouraging students to use what they know in order to invent procedures to solve problems whose answers they don't know.

CLASSROOM EXAMPLES

As 2nd graders think about subtraction problems, they are encouraged to use what they know to solve problems with new difficulties, such as 27 – 8. One child might think to himself that 28 – 8 = 20, so 27 – 8 must then be 19. Another child might think that 27 – 7 = 20, so one less would be 19. Yet another child might think of 27 – 8 as 10 – 8 = 2 + 17 = 19. Multiple strategies are possible for this problem, and children's understanding of subtraction *without* regrouping can lead to their successful solution of subtraction *with* regrouping, even if that algorithm has not yet been introduced.

Somewhat older students who can find the area of a rectangle can be challenged to discover a method for finding the area of a triangle or a parallelogram. Providing paper shapes and scissors or other tools and encouraging students to experiment will enable them to start with what

they already know and construct new knowledge that they will comprehend better and retain longer.

REFERENCES
Carpenter and Fennema 1992; Cocking and Mestre 1988; Garofalo 1989; Peterson, Fennema, and Carpenter 1991.

STRATEGY 7.3: USE MANIPULATVES

Teachers encourage students to use multiple representations to illustrate mathematical ideas.

DISCUSSION

Individuals who have made strong connections among different mathematical concepts demonstrate a greater conceptual understanding of those ideas. Teachers need to emphasize several different representations of mathematical ideas to help children make the many conceptual connections. These include concrete, oral, and graphic representations, as well as the traditional symbolic representations.

Students need to learn to "translate" from one of these "languages of mathematics" to another. For example, given an equation or number sentence, students should be able to draw a diagram or make a model with manipulatives and also write a problem that is represented by the equation. Similarly, given a verbal problem, students should be able to write an equation as well as represent it graphically or with manipulatives.

The use of manipulatives in classroom activities greatly enhances students' visualization of mathematical ideas. Manipulatives allow students to concretely explore and investigate mathematical relationships that will later be translated into symbolic form. They serve as an alternative representation of concepts and should be used whenever ideas are introduced. The key to the successful use of manipulatives lies in the bridge (which must be built by the teacher) between that artifact and the formalized statement of the underlying mathematical concepts. A weak link can defeat the purpose of the use of manipulatives.

The effective use of manipulatives requires three stages: (1) the use of the manipulatives alone, followed by (2) the use of the manipulatives side by side with symbolic paper-and-pencil representations, and then (3) the use of the symbolic representation alone. Not allowing sufficient time at the middle stage of this three-step process may leave students confused and unable to internalize the

Photo courtesy of Rebekah Neumann, Smithsburg Elementary School, Smithsburg, MD

Photo courtesy of Rebekah Neumann, Smithsburg Elementary School, Smithsburg, MD

Games are an excellent tool to reinforce learning and to help students share, explore, and extend their knowledge. In the process of sharing, students often negotiate meanings, verbalize and refine their knowledge, and point out inconsistencies. For tactile and kinesthetic learners, games improve time on task and retention of material.

concept being taught. When remediation is needed, these three stages should be reversed.

Contrary to popular belief, the use of manipulatives should not be restricted to younger students or to students having difficulties. At any grade level, manipulatives can facilitate students' exploration of new mathematical ideas at a concrete level, prior to the formalization of those ideas.

CLASSROOM EXAMPLES

Manipulatives range from commercial products (such as unifix cubes, base 10 blocks, or Cuisenaire rods) to everyday objects (bottle tops, dice, dominoes, or paper squares). They can also be teacher-made (game boards or geoboards) or student-made (pentominoes or three-dimensional shapes).

Chip-trading games in which students start in "three-for-one land," where they trade different-colored chips, give children an early introduction to place value, even before using base 10 blocks to understand basic arithmetic concepts. And geometric representations of tenths, hundredths, and thousandths make the understanding and ordering of decimals quite easy for most children. Algebra can be introduced using counters in two colors for positive and negative numbers and squares for variables.

The study of probability is enlivened by activities involving the collection of data from rolling dice, spinning spinners, grabbing objects from bags, or playing different games. Using such manipulatives spurs students' curiosity and motivates them to further explore simulations and other applications of actual and theoretical probability.

REFERENCES
Clements and Del Campo 1989; Gilfeather 1989; Hiebert and Lefevre 1986; Joyner 1990; Ross and Kurtz 1993; Skemp 1987.

● STRATEGY 7.4: USE REAL-WORLD PROBLEM-SOLVING ACTIVITIES

Teachers link mathematics and the real world through a wide range of problem-solving activities.

DISCUSSION

The use of real-world problems in the classroom helps students come to value mathematics as a useful tool that can be applied to out-of-school activities. Real-world

Story problems courtesy of elementary teachers, Washington County Public Schools, MD

In this activity, children created story problems and dictated them to their teacher. The children illustrated the story and wrote the appropriate number sentences. Through the use of real-world problems, students come to value mathematics as a useful tool that can be applied to out-of-school activities.

problems provide opportunities to relate mathematics to students' own interests and concerns; they draw on students' previous experiences; they link mathematics to other subjects; and they allow students to use their accumulated knowledge in mathematics as well as in other subjects. And applying mathematical knowledge to personally relevant situations is highly motivating for students.

CLASSROOM EXAMPLES

Real-world problem solving in mathematics takes many forms. Projects requiring the collection and analysis of data relevant to a genuine problem can lead to changes in the students' school or community. Younger children

can do surveys of food preferences and share them with the cafeteria manager; older students might analyze the results of community recycling efforts. Situations arising from student interest or community need are open-ended and encourage young people to generate their own creative directions for exploration and investigation. Students can visit appropriate sites and involve community members who have expertise in their area of inquiry.

Writing their own mathematics problems based on their personal experiences or those of family members is an important and effective way for students see the relevance of mathematics to their daily lives. The teacher can ask students to write problems involving their classmates or community members that are based on current topics of study such as multiplication, measurement, or square roots. These problems can then be used on a quiz, in a game of math Jeopardy, or in reviewing for a test. Students enjoy having their peers solve problems they have written.

REFERENCES
Austin 1991; Cobb, Yackel, Wood, Wheatley, and Merkel 1988; Kilpatrick 1987; Lesh, Landau, and Hamilton 1983; Lester 1989; Resnick 1991; Russell and Friel 1989; Swetz and Hartzler 1991.

● 7.5: INTEGRATE MATHEMATICS WITH OTHER CONTENT AREAS

Teachers integrate mathematics with other content areas in a meaningful way.

DISCUSSION

Students who have experiences that link mathematics to other subject areas are able to apply previously acquired knowledge to new situations. Teachers have many opportunities to integrate mathematics with other areas of the curriculum and enhance learning. Experiences of this type help students understand the power of mathematics to interpret problems in the social and physical sciences; such experiences also help them link the curricular subjects in ways that are real to them. Focusing on real-life, significant issues makes mathematics more relevant to students.

CLASSROOM EXAMPLES

Learning to communicate mathematical understandings is a critical element of instruction. As students keep journals, write math autobiographies, describe mathematical processes, make conjectures, and justify solutions to

128

problems, they enhance their oral and written language skills. Students discover that using what they learned in language arts strengthens their knowledge of mathematics.

Similarly, young people must come to use their mathematics skills as they study other subjects. Interdisciplinary activities organized around a common theme require students to connect mathematics to science, history, economics, art, physical education, and other subjects. Students may be asked to analyze measurements collected during a science experiment or to accumulate data on a presidential candidate's success in various regions of the country as indicated by the polls during an election campaign. Fractions are integral to reading music; geometry is an essential component of art; and measurement is vital in physical education. Challenging students to go through their school day *without* using mathematics (not just arithmetic) anywhere except in math class can open their eyes to the vital connections among mathematics and the learning of science, social studies, and other subjects.

The local newspaper is a wonderful tool for discovering the connections among math and other subjects. Every page uses numbers and shapes in news articles, advertisements, sports reports, and weather forecasts. Using the newspaper in mathematics is yet another vehicle for helping students see the importance of math for their future.

REFERENCES
Beyth-Maron and Dekel 1983; Jacobs 1993; Kurtzke 1990; Resnick 1991.

● STRATEGY 7.6: USE CULTURALLY RELEVANT MATERIALS

Teachers use culturally relevant materials as a springboard for mathematics instruction.

DISCUSSION

The process of legitimizing the mathematics practiced in different cultural settings is a way of increasing students' respect for their social and cultural heritage and, consequently, increasing their self-respect and self-confidence. Mathematics is practiced in different ways in different cultures. These practices can be valued and legitimized through their use in classroom instruction. Many of these mathematical activities are highly relevant to the students in a classroom, since they can be made to reflect students' own life experiences.

Integrating the history of mathematics with the study of new mathematical topics can show students how mathematics is linked to real-world problems and how mathematical knowledge evolved from the needs of different social or cultural groups. A study of the history of mathematics can also reveal, for example, how notions of rigor in mathematical proofs have evolved over time. What was considered a proof in the early history of mathematics would not meet today's standards of rigor. Students come to realize that these standards are socially agreed upon, and the classroom community can establish its own internal criteria for what will count as proof.

Culturally relevant materials can be used in multicultural experiences to motivate the development of mathematical topics, simultaneously stimulating young people's appreciation and understanding of other cultures and other realities. This type of experience reinforces the importance of valuing and respecting everyone's cultural heritage.

CLASSROOM EXAMPLES

Students can explore the differing evolution of the numeration system in varying cultural settings, such as in the Mayan, Chinese, Babylonian, or Arabic cultures. Comparison of these different systems of numeration and the needs from which they evolved can lead to a better understanding of the underlying structures of our own society's current numeration system.

Games from other cultures that use reasoning or other mathematics skills help students realize the importance of mathematics in every time and place: Senet and Wari originated in Africa; origami and the tangram puzzle came from Asia; Patolli and a walnut shell game are part of the Native American heritage. Having a collection of these activities in the classroom and using them for a change of pace is an effective way to apply this strategy.

Another way of using of culturally relevant materials is to teach concepts by relating them to students' current experiences. The local newspaper is a prime source of ideas for problem solving and applications of mathematics in the community. Teachers in Boston may relate instruction to the Boston subway system, while Florida teachers may create a unit on the tourism industry. Connecting mathematics to the local job market is culturally relevant and appropriate in any part of the United States.

REFERENCES
Arcavi 1991; D'Ambrosio 1985, 1990; Moses, Kamii, Swap, and Howard 1989; Secada 1991; Zaslavsky 1973, 1989.

● STRATEGY 7.7: USE TECHNOLOGY

Teachers provide students with opportunities to use technology.

DISCUSSION

Students benefit greatly from the use of technology as an alternative way of representing mathematical ideas. The ever- growing power of technology uses several dimensions to explore mathematics instruction.

First, technology can be used as a tool for problem solving. Calculators, spreadsheets, graphing utilities, and structured mathematical environments (such as Theorist and Mathematica) are used to engage students in solving problems that involve real data, problems that can be approached using many different strategies, and problems that would be cumbersome to solve without the use of such tools.

Second, technology can be used to generate exploratory mathematical environments called microworlds. Computer software such as Geometric Supposer, Geometer's Sketchpad, and Algebra Expresser, to name only a few,

create a mathematical environment in which students can explore mathematical ideas.

Finally, programming environments such as LOGO provide a means for students to construct mathematical ideas.

CLASSROOM EXAMPLES

Using geometry-based computer software to explore the effect of maximizing the area of a quadrilateral gives students insights that are difficult to acquire using only paper and pencil. The trial-and-error problem-solving strategy is easily applied when a student can quickly consider various options. Software programs exist that allow students to use such manipulatives as base 10 blocks to connect concrete materials with the appropriate picture representations and symbols. Computers can make the drill and practice of skills more interesting and can motivate students to continue practice—and eventually reach higher levels of achievement.

Scientific calculators facilitate solving statistics problems and relieve students of tedious calculations, so that they can spend their time on the more critical skills of data analysis. Simple four-function calculators could help elementary students explore patterns in multiplication, such as the results of multiplying numbers by 9, 99, or 999. After considering a few examples, students can analyze the pattern that emerges, predict other products, and verify their predictions by further exploring the products. The newer graphing calculators greatly expand the options for teaching algebra. Students can easily explore the effect on a curve of modifying its equation, or they can enter data and determine if it can be represented by an algebraic function. The graphing calculator can help students make important connections between algebra and geometry.

Teachers should spend time helping students understand appropriate uses of technology. Through experience, young people can determine what computations can be more efficiently done by mental math, by paper and pencil, or by calculator. High school students can see computer-generated fractals and realize that technology is opening the way to new discoveries and new frontiers of mathematics. Unless young people are taught mathematics with the use of technology, they are learning skills that may be obsolete by the time they finish high school.

Photo courtesy of Fran Burns, Nassau School, East Orange, NJ

This 1st grader is enjoying the cartoonlike graphics on this computer. The immediate, individualized feedback enables the student to progress at her own pace and to self-correct in privacy. The use of technology throughout the grades helps to prepare students for increasingly sophisticated learning tasks.

REFERENCES
Fey 1992; Kaput 1992; Olive 1991; Schwartz and Yerushalmy 1985; Thompson 1989.

● STRATEGY 7.8: ENCOURAGE ORAL AND WRITTEN EXPRESSION

Teachers facilitate mathematical communication through oral and written expression.

DISCUSSION

The sharing of mathematical thinking is an essential aspect of the classroom environment. Much of the current research on students' construction of knowledge points to social interaction as an important aspect of the construction process. Students should be encouraged to explain their thinking, to express their thinking to their colleagues, and to share their ideas. This process of sharing helps young people organize their thoughts and their solution strategies. It also helps them build a rationale for justifying the strategies they have chosen.

Mathematical communication is considered an essential part of the learning process, particularly in a classroom environment that encourages group work, student involvement, and student-generated solution strategies as well as student-generated problems. Communication provides a forum for students to negotiate meaning and to reflect on their solution strategies. Oral as well as written communication of mathematical thinking should be encouraged and sustained in classrooms.

CLASSROOM EXAMPLES

Students can be asked to keep journals in their mathematics classes. They write in their journals daily and report the results of their mathematics investigations and problem-solving episodes for the day. Journal entries can be on a topic of the student's choice or they can be prompted with open-ended statements such as these: "Division is called repeated subtraction because. . . . " "What would you most like more help with in math?" "Based on the graphs, I conclude...." The students' written work provides the teacher with evidence of each student's contributions to the group work, as well as each student's growth resulting from group activities.

Asking students to write a short paragraph summarizing new insights and areas of difficulty at the end of a homework assignment can help focus homework review sessions. Students can be given one minute at the beginning of class to write a summary of the previous day's lesson, instead of the teacher providing such a review, as is usually the case.

Writing courtesy of Cathy Scuffins, 4th grade teacher, Hickory Elementary School, Hagerstown, MD

Communicating mathematical understandings in written and oral form is an essential component of mathematics instruction today. This 4th grader describes the differences between area and perimeter and includes a drawing to illustrate the concept. Note the imaginative description likening area to the pie filling and perimeter to the surrounding crust.

REFERENCES

Borasi and Rose 1989; Collins, Hawkins, and Carver 1991; Countryman 1992; Johnson 1983; Keith 1988; Powell and Ramnauth 1992; Waywood 1992.

• STRATEGY 7.9: ENCOURAGE COLLABORATIVE PROBLEM SOLVING

Teachers provide students with the opportunity to engage regularly in collaborative problem-solving efforts.

DISCUSSION

Research indicates that student achievement rises in classroom environments in which students engage in collaborative problem-solving activities. Successful collaborative problem solving should be a crucial goal of mathematics instruction, because collaboration is the most prevalent problem-solving mode in the world of work for which students are preparing. Learners who are engaged cooperatively in problem-solving activities are all involved in sharing and negotiating meanings, in verbalizing their understandings, in trying to understand one another's strategies, in providing constructive criticism, and in being actively involved in learning. Cooperatively, students tackle challenging problems that are often beyond their individual abilities, and they are generally more highly motivated to persevere in finding solutions.

It is critical that the classroom environment be structured in a way that permits *all* students to make significant contributions to problem-solving experiences. Students must learn how to work in groups in order to get the most out of the collaborative experience. Elementary school teachers may need to organize the cooperative activity by assigning students specific roles or tasks. Generally, a group is given only one set of materials so that they must work together on the solution. There are a variety of collaborative problem-solving structures that ensure participation by each student in the group.

CLASSROOM EXAMPLES

Collaborative problem solving can take the form of long-term projects or shorter activities that can be completed in a single class period or less. Students enjoy puzzles in which each person in a group of four is given a different clue and the clues must be combined to reach the solution. Both number sense and mental math skills are developed when students are challenged to find a number which is even, is a multiple of three, has an integral square root, and has two digits.

Homework assignments can be efficiently reviewed in small groups. The teacher hopes, of course, that each problem will have been correctly solved by at least one person

Photo courtesy of Robert Kerly

These students are using geometry-based computer software. The possible insights generated by such computer graphics would be difficult to acquire with only paper and pencil. By pairing youngsters, teachers can use collaborative problem-solving approaches that encourage the exploration and investigation of mathematical concepts.

in each group. If not, by working together and sharing strategies, the group members can reach an answer that all understand. The teacher is called on only when everyone in the group is stumped. Students can also help one another prepare for tests by working collaboratively to determine what content will be covered and creating and reviewing sample questions together.

REFERENCES
Davidson 1985; Good, Reys, Grouws, and Mulryan 1990; Lindquist 1989; Noddings 1989; Slavin 1990; Yackel, Cobb, Wood, Wheatley, and Merkel 1990.

• STRATEGY 7.10: USE ERRORS TO ENHANCE LEARNING

Teachers value the individual's responses and ideas, and show respect for all thoughts shared throughout the course of instruction.

DISCUSSION

Many studies of student errors exist. Most significant, in terms of their implications for the classroom, are those that focus on using errors to enhance student learning. Borasi's work is particularly helpful in showing how errors can be a positive element in the learning process.

Children must realize that their way of thinking is important and will be heard and carefully reflected on by their peers. An environment that encourages the sharing of ideas will also encourage the development of students' self-confidence and willingness to contribute to group activities.

In a constructivist teaching environment, all students' ways of thinking are shared, explored, and extended. Instead of examining errors, teachers should question the processes used to obtain solutions. Often, in the process of sharing their thinking, young people refine their thoughts and point out inconsistencies in their previous expressions of ideas. The learning environment must encourage this level of reflection.

Too often in mathematics instruction, students' answers are simply assessed as correct or incorrect, and the discussion moves on to another problem. Simply telling a child that an answer is correct or incorrect discourages the reflection necessary to turn problem solving into a learning experience.

CLASSROOM EXAMPLES

Traditionally, classroom discussion has been a two-way dialogue between the teacher and one student at a time. Changing the teacher's role to that of a facilitator who expects students to respond to each other's questions

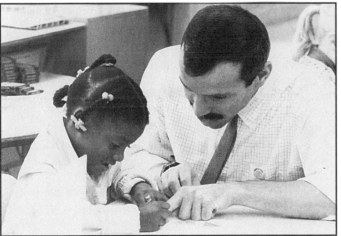

Photo courtesy of Enid Bloch, Bridgewater, NJ

By examining errors and noting their pattern, teachers help students understand the processes they use to obtain solutions. Here a teacher helps a young student think through a mathematical problem anew. Students who learn strategies in a supportive environment that demonstrates respect for their ideas are likely to learn from their mistakes.

communicates that the views of individual students are respected and that students are responsible for their own learning. Teachers and students must allow one another enough "think time," because not all students can respond immediately to questions.

Taking time regularly to talk with young people individually about their progress in mathematics communicates that the teacher values their ideas and cares whether they succeed. This kind of discussion can be a formal interview in which the teacher asks specific questions, or it can be less structured, focusing on journal entries or a review of student work. The suggestions dealing with communication and cooperative learning (see Strategies 7.8 and 7.9) are applicable here; the activities provide opportunities for students' ideas to be expressed and valued.

REFERENCES
Borasi 1987; Koehler 1990; Lappan and Schram 1989; Resnick 1987; Schoenfeld 1989; Sullivan and Clarke 1991; Wilson 1990.

● STRATEGY 7.11: OFFER AN ENRICHED CURRICULUM AND CHALLENGING ACTIVITIES

Teachers offer all students an enriched curriculum that goes beyond basic skills and incorporates a variety of challenging experiences.

DISCUSSION

Mathematics instruction—indeed, instruction in every subject—has been greatly hindered by the mistaken notion that mathematics should be "dumbed down" for underachieving students. This misconception is directly related to tracking and ability grouping, which increase both academic and social inequalities among children. This practice, in turn, increases students' feelings of inadequacy and helplessness regarding mathematics. Teachers' expectations of students' abilities to learn mathematics affect the type of instruction delivered to students in different ability groups.

All students should engage in challenging mathematical activities. They should experience mathematics as an inquiry-based discipline in which they ask many questions and allow their curiosity and creativity to guide their exploration and investigation of mathematical concepts. All students should investigate open-ended problem-solving experiences.

Photo courtesy of Mary Jo Kish, Weldon Elementary School, Clarke Community School District, Osceola, IA

Photo courtesy of Greg Eversole, E. Russell Hicks Middle School, Hagerstown, MD

Calculators provide immediate, accurate feedback. Besides helping younger students to check their own work, calculators enable students to approach problems using many different strategies. Students can also be freed from cumbersome, time-consuming calculations so that they can focus their efforts on solving problems that require higher order skills such as probability. A basic four-function calculator is appropriate for elementary school children. A secondary school student can use calculators with a greater variety of functions.

Unfortunately, underachieving students generally experience a much less interesting, less challenging, and, consequently, less motivating curriculum. To many such students, mathematics means merely rote memorization, and the work required of them is repetitive and mathematically trivial.

Mathematics instruction, if it is to be meaningful to all young people, must ensure that students will develop higher order thinking skills and engage in mathematical activity beyond the mere mastery of skills and procedures.

CLASSROOM EXAMPLES

Measurement, geometry, statistics, probability, and functions are a few of the topics identified by the NCTM as part of a complete mathematics curriculum. Unfortunately, these topics may be given little attention when the major portion of classroom time is devoted to computation skills. A richer curriculum attends to topics involving hands-on activities and demonstrating the applications of arithmetic. These activities are generally more motivating to students and require higher level thinking. In using calculators for computation, for instance, even students who have not mastered traditional algorithms can participate and benefit. Resource materials with enrichment activities, projects, and challenge problems must be readily available.

Interdisciplinary activities that connect mathematics with science and other subjects are also part of an enriched curriculum. Students enjoy opportunities to apply the math they are learning by undertaking projects that benefit the school and community. They may choose to delve deeper into a math topic such as the Fibonacci sequence, the golden rectangle, tesselations, or the history of mathematics or architecture.

Curriculum compacting is an effective way to generate time for activities that enrich the curriculum. Since the typical elementary and middle school text repeats topics each year, a chapter pretest will show what students have already mastered. Instead of repeating the concepts, more advanced students can work on other math activities of their choice and rejoin the class when it deals with a topic they have not yet mastered. Students who have "compacted out" of a unit may be asked to do a few problems from each assignment as a means of reinforcing the skill if the teacher feels it is necessary. Because some students may only rarely benefit from curriculum compacting, it is essential that enrichment activities be provided for the entire class on a regular basis.

REFERENCES
Carnegie Corporation of New York 1990; Haberman 1991; Knapp and Shields 1990; Levin and Hopfenberg 1991; Means, Chelemer, and Knapp 1991; Oakes 1986.

● STRATEGY 7.12: USE A VARIETY OF PROBLEM-SOLVING EXPERIENCES

Teachers challenge students with many types of problem-solving experiences, including solving nonroutine problems and open-ended problems.

DISCUSSION

Success in solving mathematical problems is related to students' experiences with problem solving. The lack of flexibility in students' thinking strategies reflects their lack of experience with nonroutine and open-ended problems. When confronting problem-solving situations, students often rely on such ineffective strategies as key words.

Many types of problems should be incorporated into the curriculum, including problems that can be solved in many different ways, problems that may have several correct answers, problems that may involve decision making and allow for various interpretations, and problems that may require students to determine what might be the interesting questions that merit exploration.

Experience with nonroutine problems and open-ended problems helps students shed the false perception that success in mathematics is linked to one's ability to recognize the correct procedure to use. When students recognize that they have many alternatives to use when they are faced with a problem, we see an increase in their level of perseverance and willingness to try new solutions.

CLASSROOM EXAMPLES

Textbooks illustrate a wide variety of problem-solving strategies, including drawing a diagram, making an organized list, working backwards, and solving a simpler problem. Students need many opportunities to learn and apply such strategies, which can be used to solve nonroutine problems. Too often, however, instructional time is devoted primarily to the most common strategy for solving an equation, while alternative strategies are given little attention.

Problems with multiple solutions can be presented as week- long challenges. Each Monday, the teacher can put one on a bulletin board:

- Find hexonimoes (grids of six adjacent squares) that can be folded into a cube.
- Find combinations of coins that total $1.00.
- Describe an illustration of the Fibonacci sequence.
- Write a rational number between 1/2 and 1.

During the week, students can post their solutions on the board for consideration on Friday.

Nonroutine problems are rich sources of collaborative work for small groups of students. Students find it exciting when several small groups reach a common solution by following different strategies. Such explorations prepare young people to apply mathematics in their out-of-school world and in their future jobs.

REFERENCES
Lester 1989; Peterson 1988; Schoenfeld 1989; Shavelson, Webb, Stasz, and McArthur 1989.

BIBLIOGRAPHY

Arcavi, A. (1991). "The Benefits of Using History." *For the Learning of Mathematics* 11, 2: 11.

Austin, J. D., ed. (1991). *Applications of Secondary School Mathematics*. Reston, Va.: National Council of Teachers of Mathematics.

Beyth-Maron, R., and S. Dekel. (1983). "A Curriculum to Improve Thinking Under Uncertainty." *Instructional Science* 12, 1: 67-82.

Blais, D.M. (1988). "Constructivism—A Theoretical Revolution for Algebra." *Mathematics Teacher* 81, 8: 624-631.

Borasi, R. (1992). *Learning Mathematics Through Inquiry*. Portsmouth, N.H.: Heinemann.

Borasi, R. (November 1987). "Exploring Mathematics Through the Analysis of Errors." *For the Learning of Mathematics—An International Journal of Mathematics Education* 7, 3: 2-8.

Borasi, R., and B. Rose. (1989). "Journal Writing and Mathematics Instruction." *Educational Studies in Mathematics* 20, 4: 347-365.

Brown, S.I., and M.I. Walter. (1990). *The Art of Problem Posing*. 2nd ed. Hillsdale, N.J.: Lawrence Erlbaum.

Campione, J.C., A.L. Brown, and M.L. Connell. (1988). "Metacognition: On the Importance of Understanding What You Are Doing." In *The Teaching and Assessing of Mathematical Problem Solving*, edited by R.I. Charles and E.A. Silver. Reston, Va.: National Council of Teachers of Mathematics.

Carnegie Corporation of New York. (Summer/Fall 1990). "Ensuring Minorities' Success in Mathematics, Engineering, and Science: The MESA Program." *Carnegie* 35, 3-4: 7.

Clements, M.A., and G. Del Campo. (1989). "Linking Verbal Knowledge, Visual Images, and Episodes for Mathematical Learning." *Focus on Learning Problems in Mathematics* 11, 1-2: 25-33.

Cobb, P., E. Yackel, T. Wood, G. Wheatley, and G. Merkel. (September 1988). "Creating a Problem-Solving Atmosphere." *Arithmetic Teacher* 36, 1: 46-47.

Cocking, R.R., and J. Mestre, eds. (1988). *Linguistic and Cultural Influences on Learning Mathematics*. Hillsdale, N.J.: Lawrence Erlbaum.

Collins, A., J. Hawkins, and S.M. Carver. (1991). "A Cognitive Apprenticeship for Disadvantaged Students." In *Teaching Advanced Skills to At-Risk Students: Views from Theory and*

Practice, edited by B. Means, C. Chelemer, and M.S. Knapp. San Francisco: Jossey-Bass.

Countryman, J. (1992). *Writing to Learn Mathematics: Strategies That Work, K-12.* Portsmouth, N.H.: Heinemann.

D'Ambrosio, U. (1985). "Ethnomathematics and Its Place in the History and Pedagogy of Mathematics." *For the Learning of Mathematics* 5, 1: 44-48.

D'Ambrosio, U. (1990). "The Role of Mathematics in Building Up a Democratic Society and the Civilizatory Mission of the European Powers Since the Discoveries." In *First International Conference on the Political Dimensions of Mathematics Education,* edited by R. Noss. London: Institute of Education, University of London.

Davidson, N. (1985). "Small-Group Learning and Teaching in Mathematics: A Selective Review of the Literature." In *Learning to Cooperate, Cooperating to Learn,* edited by R. Slavin, S. Sharan, S. Kagan, R. Lazarowitz, C. Webb, and R. Schmuck. New York: Plenum.

Davis, R.B., C.A. Maher, and N. Noddings. (1990). "Constructivist Views on the Teaching and Learning of Mathematics." *Journal of Research in Mathematics Education* Monograph No. 4. Reston, Va.: National Council of Teachers of Mathematics.

Fey, J. T., ed. (1992). *Calculators in Mathematics Education.* Reston, Va.: National Council of Teachers of Mathematics.

Garofalo, J. (1989). "Beliefs, Responses, and Mathematics Education: Observations From the Back of the Classroom." *School Science and Mathematics* 89: 451-455.

Gilfeather, M. (1989). "Conceptually Based Mathematics Instruction: An Investigation with a Classroom of Fourth and Fifth Grade Students." Doctoral diss., Indiana University.

Good, T., B. Reys, D. Grouws, and C. Mulryan. (December/January 1990). "Using Work Groups in Mathematics Instruction." *Educational Leadership* 47, 4: 56-62.

Haberman, M. (December 1991). "The Pedagogy of Poverty Versus Good Teaching." *Phi Delta Kappan* 73, 4: 290-294.

Hiebert, J., and P. Lefevre, eds. (1986). *Conceptual and Procedural Knowledge: The Case of Mathematics.* Hillsdale, N.J.: Lawrence Erlbaum.

Hodges, H. (1989). "ASCD's 3-High Achievement Model." Unpublished manuscript for the ASCD Urban Middle Grades Network, Alexandria, Va.

Jacobs, H.H. (February 1993). "Mathematics Integration: A Common-Sense Approach to Curriculum Development." *Arithmetic Teacher* 40, 6: 301-302.

Johnson, M.L. (1983). "Writing in Mathematics Classes: A Valuable Tool for Learning." *Mathematics Teacher* 76, 2: 117 119.

Joyner, J.M. (1990). "Using Manipulatives Successfully." *Arithmetic Teacher* 38, 2: 6-7.

Kaput, J. (1992). "Technology and Mathematics Education. In *Handbook of Research on Mathematics Teaching and Learning,* edited by D.A. Grouws. New York: Macmillan.

Keith, S.Z. (December 1988). "Explorative Writing and Learning Mathematics." *Mathematics Teacher* 81, 9: 714-719.

Kilpatrick, J. (1987). "Problem Formulating: Where Do Good Problems Come From: In *Cognitive Science and Mathematics Education,* edited by A.H. Schoenfeld. Hillsdale, N.J.: Lawrence Erlbaum.

Knapp, M., and P. M. Shields. (June 1990). "Reconceiving Academic Instruction for the Children of Poverty." *Phi Delta Kappan* 71, 10: 753-758.

Koehler, M.S. (1990). "Classrooms, Teachers, and Gender Differences in Mathematics." In *Mathematics and Gender,* edited by E. Fennema and G.C. Leder. New York: Teachers College Press.

Kroll, D.L. (1989). "Connections Between Psychological Learning Theories and the Elementary Mathematics Curriculum. In *New Directions for Elementary School* (1989 Yearbook), edited by P.R. Trafton. Reston, Va.: National Council of Teachers of

Mathematics.

Kurtzke, J.F. (1990). "The Baseball Schedule: A Modest Proposal." *Mathematics* 83, 5: 346-350.

Lappan, G., and P. Schram. (1989). "Communication and Reasoning: Critical Dimensions of Sense Making in Mathematics." In *New Directions for Elementary School of Mathematics,* edited by P. Trafton. Reston, Va.: National Council of Teachers of Mathematics.

Lesh, R., M. Landau, and E. Hamilton. (1983). "Conceptual Models in Applied Mathematical Problem Solving." In *Acquisitions of Mathematics Concepts and Processes,* edited by R. Lesh and M. Landau. New York: Academic Press.

Lester, F.K. (November 1989). "Mathematical Problem Solving In and Out of School." *Arithmetic Teacher* 37, 3: 33-35.

Levin, H., and W. Hopfenberg. (January 1991). "Don't Remediate: Accelerate!" *Principal* 70, 3: 11-13.

Lindquist, M. (1989). "Mathematics Content and Small-Group Instruction in Grades 4-6." *Elementary School Journal* 89, 5: 625-632.

Means, B., C. Chelemer, and M. Knapp, eds. (1991). *Teaching Advanced Skills to At-Risk Students: Views from Theory and Practice.* San Francisco: Jossey-Bass.

Moses, R.P., M. Kamii, S.M. Swap, and J. Howard. (1989). "The Algebra Project: Organizing in the Spirit of Ella." *Harvard Educational Review* 59, 4: 423-443.

Mullis, I.V.S., J.A. Dossey, E.H. Owen, and G.W. Phillips. (June 1991). *The State of Mathematics Achievement: NAEP's 1990 Assessment of the Nation and the Trial Assessment of the States.* Princeton, N.J.: Educational Testing Service and National Assessment of Education Progress.

NCTM. (1989). *Curriculum and Evaluation Standards for School Mathematics.* Reston, Va.: National Council of Teachers of Mathematics.

Noddings, N. (1989). "Theoretical and Practical Concerns About Small Groups in Mathematics." *Elementary School Journal* 89, 5: 607-623.

Oakes, J. (1986). "Tracking, Inequality, and the Rhetoric of School Reform: Why Schools Don't Change." *Journal of Education* 168, 1: 61-80.

Olive, J. (1991). "Logo Programming and Geometric Understanding: An In-Depth Study." *Journal for Research in Mathematics Education* 22, 2: 90-111.

Peterson, P.L. (1988). "Teaching for Higher-Order Thinking in Mathematics: The Challenge for the Next Decade." In *Perspectives on Research for Effective Mathematics Teaching,* edited by D.A. Grouws and T.J. Cooney. Hillsdale, N.J.: Lawrence Erlbaum; Reston, Va.: National Council of Teachers of Mathematics.

Peterson, P., E. Fennema, and T. Carpenter. (1991). "Using Children's Mathematical Knowledge." In *Teaching Advanced Skills to At-Risk Students: Views from Theory and Practice* edited by B. Means, C. Chelemer, and M. Knapp. San Francisco: Jossey-Bass.

Powell, A. B., and M. Ramnauth. (June 1992). "Beyond Questions and Answers: Prompting Reflections and Deepening Understandings of Mathematics Using Multiple-Entry Logs." *For the Learning of Mathematics* 12, 2: 12-18.

Resnick, L. (1987). "Constructing Knowledge in School." In *Development and Learning: Conflict or Congruence?,* edited by L.S. Liben. Hillsdale, N.J.: Lawrence Erlbaum.

Resnick, L. (1991). "Thinking in Arithmetic Class." In *Teaching Advanced Skills to At-Risk Students: Views from Theory and Practice,* edited by B. Means, C. Chelemer, and M. Knapp. San Francisco: Jossey-Bass.

Ross, R., and R. Kurtz. (1993). "Making Manipulatives Work: A Strategy for Success." *Arithmetic Teacher* 40, 5: 254-257.

Russell, S.J., and S.N. Friel. (1989). "Collecting and Analyzing Real

Data in the Elementary School Classroom." In *New Directions for Elementary School Mathematics*, edited by P. Trafton. Reston, Va.: National Council of Teachers of Mathematics.

Schoenfeld, A. (1989). "Problem Solving in Context(s)." In *The Teaching and Assessing of Mathematical Problem Solving*, edited by R.I. Charles and E.A. Silver. Reston, Va.: National Council of Teachers of Mathematics.

Schwartz, J., and M. Yerushalmy. (1985). *The Geometric Supposer*. Pleasantville, N.Y.: Sunburst Communications.

Secada, W.G. (1991). "Selected Conceptual and Methodological Issues for Studying the Mathematics Education of the Disadvantaged." *Better Schooling for the Children of Poverty: Alternatives to Conventional Wisdom*, edited by M.S. Knapp and P.M. Shields, Berkeley, Calif.: McCutchan.

Shavelson, R.J., N.M. Webb, C. Stasz, and D. McArthur. (1989). "Teaching Mathematical Problem-Solving: Insights from Teachers and Tutors." In *The Teaching and Assessing of Mathematical Problem Solving*, edited by R.I. Charles and E.A. Silver. Reston, Va.: National Council of Teachers of Mathematics.

Skemp, R.R. (1987). *The Psychology of Learning Mathematics*. Hillsdale, N.J.: Lawrence Erlbaum.

Slavin, R. (December/January 1990). "Research on Cooperative Learning: Consensus and Controversy." *Educational Leadership* 47, 4: 52-54.

Sullivan, P., and D. Clarke. (1991). "Catering to All Abilities Through Good Questions." *Arithmetic Teacher* 39, 2: 14-18.

Swetz, F., and J. S. Hartzler, eds. (1991). *Mathematical Modeling in the Secondary School Curriculum*. Reston, Va.: National Council of Teachers of Mathematics.

Thompson, P. (1989). "Artificial Intelligence, Advanced Technology, and Learning and Teaching Algebra." In *Research Issues in the Learning and Teaching of Algebra*, edited by S. Wagner and C. Kieren. Reston, Va.: National Council of Teachers of Mathematics.

Waywood, A. (1992). "Journal Writing and Learning Mathematics." *For the Learning of Mathematics* 12, 2: 34-43.

Wearne, D., and J. Hiebert. (1989). "Constructing and Using Meaning for Mathematical Symbols: The Case of Decimal Fractions." In *Number Concepts and Operations in the Middle Grades*, edited by J. Hiebert and M. Behr. Hillsdale, N.J.: Lawrence Erlbaum; Reston, Va.: National Council of Teachers of Mathematics.

Wilson, P.S. (Summer Fall 1990). "Inconsistent Ideas Related to Definitions and Examples." *Focus on Learning Problems in Mathematics* 12, 3 4: 111-129.

Yackel, E., P. Cobb, T. Wood, G. Wheatley, and G. Merkel. (1990). "The Importance of Social Interaction in Children's Construction of Mathematical Knowledge." In *Teaching and Learning Mathematics in the 1990s*, edited by T.J. Cooney. Reston, Va.: National Council of Teachers of Mathematics.

Zaslavsky, C. (November 1973). "Mathematics in the Study of African Culture." *Arithmetic Teacher* 20: 532-535.

Zaslavsky, C. (September 1989). "People Who Live in Round Houses." *Arithmetic Teacher* 37, 1: 18-21.

137

8

STRATEGIES FOR INCREASING ACHIEVEMENT IN ORAL COMMUNICATION

JIM CHESEBRO, ROY BERKO, CAROL HOPSON, PAMELA COOPER, AND HELENÉ HODGES

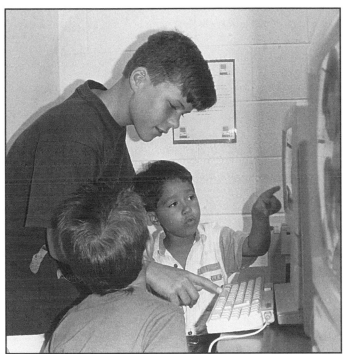

Photo courtesy of Barbara Skorija, Orlando, FL

Communication competence requires not only the ability to perform adequately certain communication behaviors, [but] also . . . an understanding of those behaviors and the cognitive ability to make choices among those behaviors.

— MCCROSKEY (1984, P. 264)

Authors' note: The authors thank Anne Curran for her contributions to this chapter.

Research suggests that students graduate from U.S. schools unable to function as effective oral communicators. Vangelisti and Daly (1989) concluded that 25.6 percent of the nation's young people cannot adequately communicate orally. Their study focused on conveying basic information, not on the more complex issues involved in communicative interactions. Thus, for example, they observed that 62.9 percent of young people cannot explain how to get to a local grocery store so that another person can understand the directions.

Among disadvantaged students, performance in oral communication constitutes an even more serious problem. In a survey of 2,793 academically at-risk middle-grade students that compared their performance to national norms, Chesebro and his colleagues (1992) found that disadvantaged students were significantly more apprehensive of communicating orally and also had a significantly lower perception of their ability to function as competent oral communicators.

At the elementary and secondary levels, a more intensified national interest in competence in oral communication can be traced to 1978, when Congress revised Title II of the Elementary and Secondary Education Act, emphasizing the need for instructional improvement so that "all children are able to master the basic skills of reading, mathematics, and effective communication, both written and oral." In 1990, in association with President Bush's education initiative, the National Governors' Association adopted national education goals that included a commitment to having students "demonstrate an advanced ability" to "communicate effectively" (see National Governor's Association 1990). The Association also specified that "achievement tests must not simply measure minimum competencies,

139

but also higher levels of reading, writing, speaking, reasoning, and problem-solving skills."

Even more recently, in its blueprint for high performance, the Secretary of Labor's Commission on Achieving Necessary Skills identified speaking and listening skills among its list of necessary foundation skills for U.S. workers (see U.S. Department of Labor 1992). The list of speaking skills included:

• organizes ideas and sends oral messages appropriate to listeners and situations;

• participates in conversation, discussion, and group presentations;

• selects an appropriate medium for conveying a message;

• uses verbal language and other cues such as body language in a way appropriate in style, tone, and level of complexity to the audience and the occasion;

• speaks clearly and communicates a message;

• understands and responds to listener feedback; and

• asks questions when needed.

Despite all the evidence indicating the need for improved oral communication, K-12 teachers are generally provided with only a very limited education in oral communication. Indeed, in many school districts, school speech therapists are the only trained providers of instruction in oral communication—and their services are targeted primarily to meet the needs of students who have been deemed "language deficient." We must place greater emphasis on preparing future teachers to provide instruction in oral communication to young people, especially in light of the increasingly multicultural environment of today's elementary and secondary schools.

ENHANCING STUDENTS' ACHIEVEMENT IN ORAL COMMUNICATION

Significant improvement in oral communication might well be difficult to achieve, however, given the lack of curricular emphasis and instructional attention to this crucial topic in U.S. schools. Reading and writing occupy far greater prominence on our instructional and assessment agendas, though research increasingly points to the value of an integrated, holistic approach to the development of competence in communication.

When we provide students with opportunities to understand the process of oral communication, and when we complement such efforts with instructional strategies designed to improve students' oral communication skills, we can realize significant gains in related student achievements. A sizable body of research (for example, McCroskey 1970, Newmark and Asante 1976, Trank and Steele 1983) has established a correlation between competence in oral communication and such related student achievements as:

• the ability to articulate one's own desires, assumptions, and beliefs;

• the mastery of a broad range of language codes acquired by face-to-face oral interactions;

• the production of clearer and more persuasive messages, both oral and written;

• greater flexibility in adjusting to different environments without losing one's own basic values;

• the development of a self-concept that fosters trust, open-mindedness, ego strength, and the ability to accept ambiguity and diversity among people; and

• increased confidence in social interactions, for competence in oral communication reduces social apprehension, increases the number of positive responses directed toward a speaker, and increases young people's belief in themselves as competent social agents.

THE STATE OF THE ART OF ORAL COMMUNICATION

In sharp contrast to the positive outcomes that can be achieved through effective instruction in oral communication, the actual state of education in oral communication is characterized by a less desirable set of circumstances, including the following aspects:

• Instruction in oral communication is seldom a discrete component of a language arts curriculum, in part because of the misconception that oral communication is a natural ability that all students possess before entering a classroom.

• Education in oral communication is seldom supervised by teachers from the earliest stages to the completion of an individual's formal education, as are such other communication skills as reading and writing.

FIGURE 8.1
A Summary of New Standards for Curriculum and Instruction in Oral Communication

CURRICULUM

TRADITIONAL EMPHASIS ON	NEW EMPHASIS ON
teaching as a discrete subject area	integration of talking and listening activities across all content areas
classical public speaking	ability to use and understand spoken language in a variety of educational and social settings
general audience analysis	knowledge and analysis of topic, audience, task. and messages
mainstream culture and language (standard American dialect)	use of appropriate language and dialect for the situation
	knowledge of varied cultural influences

INSTRUCTION

TRADITIONAL EMPHASIS ON	NEW EMPHASIS ON
uniform instruction	identifying diverse language needs of individual students
remediating weakness	building on students' existing language competencies
lecture and workbooks	dialogue and discussion ("student talk," "thinking aloud")
rote, drill, practice	wide variety of media and telecommunications
skills teaching: voice, diction, pitch	modeling and interactive guided practice (verbal and nonverbal)
ability grouping	integrated whole-language techniques
	strategy teaching: cognitive (audience analysis); feedback, listening, and speaking skills; metacognitive (problem solving, critical thinking, etc.)
	heterogenous grouping: flexible (native and non-native language speakers), cooperative/team learning activities, peer tutoring

Source: Hodges 1989.

Tom Toles—The Buffalo News Universal Press Syndicate. Reprinted with permission.

The Characteristics of Effective Oral Communicators

Oral communication is a complex process that should be approached from different perspectives at each age level. Competence in communication is reached when the person communicating can be understood and can understand the intended message. This competence and understanding can be developed through skills training, modeling, and the reinforcement of positive behaviors.

Any instruction in oral communication must begin with a definition of oral communication and what it means to be an effective oral communicator in a specific setting. To be effective, this process must include strategies for understanding and dealing with communication anxiety, as well as activities in active listening, vocabulary, pronunciation, diction, and fluency. Also included must be attention to critical thinking, speaking, and listening; vocal delivery; and the means of appropriate nonverbal communication (body language and gestures, for example). Effective oral communicators must also understand how to give directions, describe and make requests, summarize, ask questions, respond to questions, develop ideas, organize information, deliver messages, and give feedback.

Naturally, competence in oral communication of many kinds is required to become an effective speaker. Before a teacher begins to impart skills in oral communication, however, he or she must consider three important variables that affect oral communication in the classroom. These variables include:

- the teacher's own oral competence, including the ability to listen to the child's message;
- the student's fears about oral communication; and
- the multiculturalism that now defines the American experience.

As the quotation from James McCroskey at the beginning of this chapter suggests, to become competent in oral communication, a student must be exposed to two kinds of instruction. First, in classroom environments, teachers must provide specific prescriptions for improving actual speaking techniques. The teacher essentially functions as a change agent and suggests how alternative speaking techniques can enhance a student's clarity and persuasiveness

- When instruction *is* provided, oral communication is generally treated solely as a skill requiring performance drills and repetitions (i.e., the behavioral domain) rather than as a complex social process that students must come to understand (i.e., the cognitive domain).

- In other curricular areas, oral teacher/student interactions are seldom viewed as the most immediate and direct method for determining student understanding.

- Most teachers are not adequately trained to provide students with an understanding of the variables affecting the process of oral communication, nor are most teachers adequately trained to provide students with performance activities and critiques that systematically increase their ability to function as clear and persuasive speakers.

- Unfortunately, the integrated language arts curriculum remains only an ideal. While language arts textbooks advocate integration, they contain separate chapters on reading, writing, speaking, and listening. In most schools, the integration of the language arts peaks in kindergarten and declines throughout the grades; by the time a child reaches secondary school, instruction in language arts is neatly fragmented into separate courses.

Oral communication is not perceived as essential to the curriculum, even though research indicates that instruction in this area can dramatically enhance significant dimensions of a student's academic life. Oral communication remains the neglected component of the comprehensive language arts program.

as a speaker. But improving speaking techniques in the classroom alone is not enough. The classroom is an extremely specialized communication environment. Students must also receive a second kind of instruction that allows them to generalize beyond the classroom and to adapt classroom speaking techniques to a variety of other situations.

If students are to be able to apply their skills appropriately to other speaking environments, teachers must provide students with a second kind of instruction: namely, an understanding of the nature and functions of oral communication as a social and interactive human process. Teachers thus need to provide both behavioral and cognitive instruction in oral communication. When both behavioral and cognitive instruction are provided, a competent oral communicator should:

• understand the unique functions and appropriate uses of the oral medium of communication;

• possess methods and techniques for understanding audience motivations and needs, as well as use analysis to achieve his or her objectives;

• understand the potential functions and limitations of language and identify when language is either overcoming barriers or creating barriers;

• possess methods and techniques for identifying different types of nonverbal communication, as well as techniques that allow the coordination of verbal and nonverbal modes of communication;

• be able to identify the role, functions, and limitations of the vocal process, as well as use articulation techniques to enhance an oral performance;

• identify the range of different speaking styles available (for instance, conversational, formal, confrontational, consensus, etc.), as well as use the most appropriate speaking style in a given situation;

• understand an audience's expectation for systematic and patterned information, as well as employ organizational patterns that enhance an oral performance;

• be able to identify the range of factors that affects an audience's impression of a speaker's credibility and be able to employ techniques that allow the speaker to adjust his or her image to a specific audience;

• identify the range of logical and emotional appeals that can be used by a speaker, specifying logical and emotional appeals available to a speaker on a given topic in front of a specific audience;

• identify differing kinds of speaking occasions and determine which situations exist in terms of a specific audience;

• identify the unique features of oral communication and use these features as resources in constructing an oral message; and

• specify the function of feedback and use feedback to change an oral message during a presentation.

ORAL COMMUNICATION AND DIVERSE STUDENT LEARNERS

The diversity of our nation's school population underscores the importance and the challenge of improving young people's skills in oral communication. In some school systems, the diversity of languages spoken within the system—and even within a single school—can be mind-boggling. In Dade County, Florida, for example, children attending school represent more than one hundred nationalities (National Governors' Association 1989)! Students who speak a nonstandard dialect or who speak English as their second language have steadily increased in number. According to data released by the U.S. Census Bureau in April 1993, one in seven U.S. residents speaks a language other than English at home. The use of Spanish, the most commonly spoken language after English, has increased by 50 percent since 1980.

Improving the competence in oral communication of students whose primary language is English in itself represents a formidable challenge to the education community. Widespread (and growing) diversity in languages compounds that challenge manyfold. Dialogue, debate, and discussion—both within every neighborhood and community and at the state and national levels—are essential to the survival of democracy.

Multiculturalism can certainly enrich the communication process, but teachers must be prepared for the kinds of *mis*communications that can occur in a culturally diverse environment. Multiculturalism requires teachers to understand the systems of knowledge, societal norms and preferences, and verbal and nonverbal patterns of alternative cultures. It may be helpful for teachers to view themselves as public speakers who must analyze their "audiences" before speaking, seeking to understand and anticipate the cultural backgrounds that their listeners will use to assess their ideas and strategies. These understandings can only benefit the quality of instruction they provide. Even in schools not characterized by cultural variation, it is important to prepare students for life in a pluralistic America and a global society.

ASSESSING ACHIEVEMENT IN ORAL COMMUNICATION

The assessment of competence in oral communication is an ever-changing (and rapidly developing) area of concern, which is being shaped by both practitioners and researchers. As with any emerging area, some difficulties exist. In some cases, recognition is a problem. For example, the National Assessment of Educational Progress (NAEP) does not assess oral communication. In other cases, the tools available for assessment can be complicated or involved. Since 1982, for instance, the Speech Communication Association[1] has distributed the CCAI or Communication Competency Assessment Instrument (Rubin 1982), an assessment tool used by trained observers to rate a speaker's listening and speaking behaviors according to standards specified for one or more of nineteen competencies. The CCAI must be administered individually and requires approximately a half hour to complete. Cost, time, and a shortage of trained personnel are among the factors that hinder its usage. Many teachers have found that the CCAI provides operational definitions of key concepts in oral communication, is extremely comprehensive, and, with experience, is increasingly easy to use.

A useful body of materials exists that can direct the teacher who wishes to undertake the assessment of competence in oral communication. Information and documents related to assessing oral communication are available on a limited basis, with additional sources being developed constantly. For example, guidelines for what should be included in a program of oral communication have been developed and are distributed by the Speech Communication Association (SCA) in two publications, "Essential Speaking and Listening Skills for Elementary School Students" (SCA 1980) and "Speaking and Listening Competencies for High School Graduates" (SCA 1987). Several standardized evaluation systems, which are based on these guidelines, can provide assessments of listening,[2] oral language,[3] speaking,[4] nonverbal communication,[5] and communication apprehension.[6]

In November 1991, the SCA identified criteria relevant to any assessment of oral communication competencies[7] that included a set of general criteria, criteria for the content of assessment, criteria for assessment instruments, criteria for assessment procedures and administration, criteria for assessment frequency, and criteria for the use of assessment results. Among the several criteria recommended, the SCA specifically noted that the assessment of oral communication must go beyond the ability to generate acceptable oral speech; it must include an understanding of the oral communication process itself and the desire and willingness to communicate orally:

> Assessment of oral communication should view competence in oral communication as a gestalt of several interacting dimensions. At a minimum, all assessments of oral communication should include an assessment of knowledge (understanding communication process, comprehension of the elements, rules, and dynamics of a communication event, awareness of what is appropriate in a communication situation), an assessment of skills (the possession of a repertoire of skills and actual performance of skills), and an evaluation of the individual's attitude toward communication (e.g., value placed on oral communication, apprehension, reticence, willingness to communicate, readiness to communicate) (SCA 1990, p. 3).

An ongoing revision of an older work (Rubin and Mead 1984), when completed, will also assist teachers in assessing the performance of student communicators.

Beyond these considerations, SCA has recommended that the assessment of oral communication "should include assessment of both verbal and nonverbal aspects of communication and should consider competence in more than one communication setting. At a minimum, assessment should occur in the one-to-many setting (e.g., public speaking, practical small-group discussion) and in the one-to-one setting (e.g., interviews, interpersonal relations) (SCA 1990, p. 3). In this context, SCA particularly emphasized the importance of employing assessment instruments that "meet acceptable standards for freedom from cultural, sexual, ethical, racial, age, and developmental bias" (SCA 1990, p. 3).

Assessment of competence in oral communication can be performed using both holistic and atomistic[8] methods; that is, oral communication performance can be judged by looking at oral performance either as a whole or by assessing its component parts, such as what is said and how it is said. The holistic approach gives the teacher an

FRANK & ERNEST BOB THAVES

opportunity to include all elements of an assignment in the evaluation and therefore provides for assessment that attends to every aspect of the activity. The atomistic approach allows both teacher and student to concentrate on specific, identified skills and to assess the student's progress toward achieving them.

Both holistic and atomistic approaches are necessary in the assessment of oral communication competence, just as a forest ranger must assess the health of the entire forest as well as determine the well-being and value of individual trees. Consider this example: A student is asked to direct the class to the cafeteria. Holistic assessment allows the teacher to give a relatively positive evaluation of the activity, while an atomistic assessment of individual components of the presentation reveals that the student used many distracting vocalized pauses.

COMMUNICATION STRATEGIES THAT PROMOTE ACHIEVEMENT

Understanding and mastering oral communication is not just a classroom task; it is a lifelong process. As young people grow and develop, new motivations and different circumstances require that old skills be replaced by newer, more appropriate, and sophisticated systems of oral communication. For teachers as well as their students, this lifelong process is necessary. Yet, for a number of teachers, training in and knowledge of oral communication have not been a significant part of their professional preparation. We have this group of teachers specifically in mind as we discuss the following teaching strategies for developing the oral communication competence of young people.

Let us note first that it is possible to develop oral communication skills in students and to develop students' understanding of the process through skills training, modeling, active guided practice, and reinforcement of positive behaviors. While oral communication can be taught in a variety of ways, opportunities for participating in oral activities—with chances for improvement and mastery through practice, repetition, and reinforcement—must also be provided. Students should be given more than just the chance to speak; they should be encouraged to learn what makes oral presentations effective in face-to-face, classroom, and group settings as well as when speaking to a larger audience.

The strategies that occupy the remainder of this chapter provide a preliminary but immediately useful guide for teachers who seek to develop the oral communication skills of their students. The summary below provides a foundation for examining the recommended teaching strategies for developing students' competence in oral communication. The strategies to be described in this chapter include the following:

• Provide ample time for student-generated dialogue and discussion.
• Use interdisciplinary, holistic experiences.
• Focus on understanding as a universal goal of communication.
• Reduce students' speaking anxiety.
• Encourage both native and standard systems of dialect and language.
• Promote intercultural understanding and communication.
• Build on students' home, community, and cultural experiences.
• Foster the analysis of topic, audience, message, and purpose.

145

• Encourage the use of coordinated verbal and non-verbal systems of communication.

• Emphasize higher order thinking.

• Use real-world experiences.

• Develop awareness of appropriate articulation and pronunciation.

• Use a wide variety of methods, materials, and technologies.

• Use both self-assessment and peer evaluation.

• Encourage accurate reporting.

• Introduce logical and emotional strategies as conflict-resolution techniques.

This summary provides a foundation for examining the first recommended teaching strategy for developing students' oral communication competency.

● STRATEGY 8.1: PROVIDE AMPLE TIME FOR STUDENT-GENERATED DIALOGUE AND DISCUSSION

Teachers encourage a quantity and variety of student-generated talk in classrooms at all grade levels and in all content areas.

DISCUSSION

Effective instruction in oral communication includes increasing the percentage and variety of total student "talk time" in the classroom. Young people need to be engaged in speaking activities through a wide variety of literacy experiences throughout their schooling; these experiences should be integrated across all content areas.

In some cases, especially when the typical instructional technique is the lecture, teachers discourage student talk. When student-generated talk increases, students articulate how they are internalizing what they have learned. Thus, teachers receive feedback in terms of what students do and do not know and are better able to modify their instruction to meet individual and group needs. In addition, students begin to feel responsible for what they learn, and student empowerment increases. In a highly interactive environment that includes both student-to-student and teacher-to-student exchanges, students become more proficient communicators. Cross-cultural understandings are also promoted.

Teachers cultivate a classroom climate that supports oral communication when they invite "student talk" on many varied topics of mutual interest to both teacher and students. Student-generated talk should increasingly reflect what students know, the information they have acquired within their own culture, and how they understand themselves, others, and their environments. In this sense, student-generated talk should become increasingly interpersonal, reflecting what students understand. Accordingly, student-generated talk should enable students to believe in themselves, to trust their own judgment, and to appreciate the cultural experiences they have gained outside the classroom.

CLASSROOM EXAMPLES

In the early grades (kindergarten through 3rd grade), teachers should provide structured and unstructured as well as evaluated and unevaluated oral experiences. For example, in the oft-used "show-and-tell" activity, instead of simply saying, "Bring in something to talk about," teachers can provide an assignment that teaches children to structure and develop by saying, "Bring in one of your favorite storybooks and give us two reasons why you like it." Or children could be asked to draw an illustration of their favorite holiday and then provide two reasons why they enjoy that holiday. This activity allows the child to develop the structure needed to orally communicate a message that can be easily understood by others. After each child's presentation, the teacher can assess the activity by asking other students to identify the speaker's favorite toy or game and the two reasons given for its selection. If the class did not receive the information, the teacher should communicate specifically what needs to be done to transmit the intended message. The teacher should repeat the show-and-tell assignment with an alternative task, so that the students have the opportunity to take the corrective action prescribed.

A second assignment, which has the objective of allowing a child to express an idea or view without fear of rejection, is to have the child say what he or she liked best about the noon meal or about a game that has been played on the playground. There is no right or wrong answer, and the child's views are not challenged. This activity allows the child to realize that his or her views have value; it also encourages the child to think creatively.

At higher grade levels, after completing a science experiment, for instance, students may discuss their conclusions with a partner and then record them on a joint lab report. Opportunities for working with a partner or a small group on an interdisciplinary task or project extend the possibilities for students to share ideas, questions, learnings, and talents. In the 4th through 8th grades, "news" assignments can be given that require students to interview one another about different cultural values and then share their findings with the class.

References
Adams 1990; Basic Skills Proficiency Act 1978; Berko 1993; Chesebro, McCroskey, Atwater, Bahrenfuss, Cawelti, Gaudino, and Hodges 1992; Cooper 1990; Daniel 1992; Ecroyd 1973; Gorham 1988; McCroskey 1970, 1984; Naremore and Hopper 1990; Rubin 1982; Rubin and Mead 1984; Slavin 1986; SCA 1991; Trank and Steele 1983; U.S. Department of Labor 1992; Vangelisti and Daly 1989; Wood 1976.

A language-rich, supportive environment is essential to the development of willing, competent communicators. Teachers who are successful in nurturing children's oral communication skills recognize the value of talking and reading in a variety of modes, including small groups. Aides and volunteers are helpful in providing appropriate models for pupils. Youngsters can hear and imitate the words pronounced by appropriate adult models. They also have more occasion to respond to the probing questions of adults. Also important, the youngsters learn that effective communication skills are valued and that their ideas are considered important.

● STRATEGY 8.2: USE INTERDISCIPLINARY, HOLISTIC EXPERIENCES

Teachers integrate reading, writing, listening, and speaking activities in a stimulating, literacy-rich environment to help students focus and make connections among different subject areas.

DISCUSSION

While oral communication can be (and most often is, unfortunately) taught as a discrete subject area, it is important to integrate the teaching of effective speaking and listening activities across *all* content areas. Traditionally, the emphasis has been on teaching only public speaking (oratory), but the new emphasis is on the ability to communicate both orally (by speaking and listening) and nonverbally (by using space, behavior, kinesics,[9] paralanguage,[10] and other nonspoken messages) in a variety of settings. This new emphasis centers on understanding the relationship between sender and receiver, including the participants, the setting, and the purpose in both one-to-one and one-to-many situations. This emphasis also recognizes the crucial need for a knowledge of varied cultural influences.

CLASSROOM EXAMPLES

Despite the existence of a body of unique skills and strengths that must be taught independently of other disciplines, oral communication can be integrated—and should be integrated— into all academic content areas. For example, the teacher may have students first read a story, then write their opinions of the story, and finally tell the story orally. The objective here is to allow students to develop their skills of critical thinking, writing, structuring, and oral presentation. Beginning this technique with any discipline may be helpful; however, teachers must take care to provide a structure for the oral communication component that assures the student has all the information needed to present the material in a way that allows for relieving anxiety that may be created by the oral mode of presentation. Thus, the teacher must be certain of the expectations and the evaluation methods to be used.

The following exercise is an effective one for middle school children: Ask the students to form groups of six to eight participants and sit facing one another. As one student reads a short paragraph, the others write down exactly what they hear. Each child then reads aloud what he or she wrote.

• For grades 3 to 5, play Treasure Chest. The teacher writes several clues (directions) related to a story the class has been reading and hides them around the room. The class forms small groups and searches for the clues. One person in each group is designated as the reader. When each clue is located, this person reads the clue, and the group follows the directions contained in the clue. The last clue leads the group to a "treasure."

• For math, in grades 5 to 9, the teacher can instruct the class to take a simple math problem and turn it into a word problem. Then each child gives his or her problem to another student to solve. Finally, the writer shares his or her problem orally with the entire class and sees if the second student solved it correctly. Here's an example of a math problem turned into a word problem: $2 \times (3 + 1 + 2) = 12$ becomes "Mrs. Jones has three pairs of tennis shoes, one pair of black flats, and two pairs of heels. How many shoes does she have?"

REFERENCES
Cronin and Grice 1991; DeVito 1991; Holdaway 1979; Knapp and Turnbull 1990; Martinello and Cook 1992; Strickland and Morrow 1989; Teale 1987.

● STRATEGY 8.3: FOCUS ON UNDERSTANDING AS A UNIVERSAL GOAL OF COMMUNICATION

Teachers emphasize that the purpose of effective communication is to understand and to be understood.

DISCUSSION

Oral communication is a two-way interactive process—one-to- one as well as one-to-many—that always includes speaking and listening. Students will not become effective communicators unless they are motivated by the understanding that competence in oral communication is a lifetime skill that will enhance their personal relationships, their ability to obtain and progress in employment, and their effectiveness in changing the ideas, beliefs, or actions of others.

To ensure that each student speaker develops the ability to be understood, the teacher must help young people realize the importance of establishing a common ground on which to build. This need for common ground becomes especially important in a multicultural classroom. Words and phrases that originate in one culture are often adopted by other cultures, and this language acceptance can be used to help enrich a multicultural class; in a homogeneous class, it can be used to help students focus on other cultures.

CLASSROOM EXAMPLES

Teaching strategies in this area will differ depending on the grade level of the students and their prior learning activities. One particularly effective activity is to ask students to bring a current newspaper to class and to read aloud several articles; the class then divides into small groups to review the articles and identify and discuss the origins of as many of the words as possible. This activity encourages the interaction of reading, writing, listening, and speaking; it also provides an opportunity for multicultural activities.

Students might point out words in the text such as "patio homes" or "wok" that relate to specific cultures yet are understood and appreciated by people of many cultures. Teachers can find examples of miscommunicated words or phrases; for example, an ad that reads "Chester Drawers on Sale." After asking students to correct the ad, the teacher shows a picture of a chest of drawers, and the students make the correct association. Another example might be hearing or reading the phrase "first come, first served," which is often heard or seen as "first come, first serve." Students can discover for themselves the difference in meaning by being asked to perform the action called for in each phrase. If students do not respond to this stimulus, the teacher may have to rephrase the statements as "first to come, first to be served" and "first to come, first to do the serving." The teacher must then reiterate that the purpose of effective communication is to understand and to be understood.

One final example of the types of activities that can be used to establish the need for oral and written language skills is to have students listen to paired phrases that sound identical but that have vastly different meanings, which become immediately apparent when the words are seen in written form—for instance: "Gladly, the cross I'd bear" and "Gladly, the cross-eyed bear."

REFERENCES
Albert 1986; Argyle 1985; Bassett and Boone 1983; Beatty 1988; Berko 1993; Broome 1991; Heath 1983; Reardon 1971; Ting-Toomey 1986; Wood 1976.

"They caught me passing notes in my communication class."

● STRATEGY 8.4: REDUCE STUDENTS' SPEAKING ANXIETY

Teachers work to reduce students' anxiety regarding oral communication and to promote students' confidence in the use of language.

DISCUSSION

About 20 percent of the children in any given classroom exhibit high levels of apprehension in most speaking situations. They feel unsure about when to talk, how much to talk, and how to talk. The percentage who fear speaking in public climbs to between 50 percent and 70 percent.

Children develop speaking anxiety for a variety of reasons, including heredity, childhood reinforcement, communication or language deficiency, and cultural patterns (McCroskey and Richmond 1991). Being reared in environments in which standard English is not spoken or is a second language may also limit a child's opportunity to learn the standard form of language and can affect classroom performance as well as later job-seeking and job-performance situations (McCroskey and Richmond 1991). Children who are, for whatever reason, deficient in the mainstream language often find themselves uncomfortable when speaking English; consequently, they may avoid

presenting their ideas. Moreover, some cultures prize shyness and discourage assertive communicative behavior. Children from such cultures tend to withdraw from the types of communicative situations that those from more assertive cultures have been taught to face.

In any case, students need to become skillful and comfortable in their use of oral communication, regardless of the language they use. Teachers must take responsibility for assisting children who are communication-deficient to gain facility in mainstream language and attitudes while respecting individual cultural customs. Oral communication experts suggest using a combination of these interventions:

• Create a friendly, nonthreatening, noncritical classroom environment.
• Assign structured tasks that clearly outline what is expected.
• Encourage students to work in small groups with peers.
• Allow students to present short speeches.
• Always provide holistic evaluation that contains more positive than negative feedback.
• Provide ample opportunities for students to share ideas orally without fear of being evaluated.

Communication apprehension in a public speaking situation is often referred to as "stage fright." The basic cause of stage fright is the fear of negative evaluation. Stage fright is normal; most people experience it at some point in their development. The degree of stage fright depends on the person or situation (Daly et al. 1989; Ayres 1986; McCroskey, Fayer, and Richmond 1985; McCroskey, Ralph, and Barrack 1970). In his book *Understanding Social Anxiety*, Leary (1983, p. 18) observes that two main factors determine the degree of stage fright: (1) the speaker's prediction of the success of the performance, and (2) the speaker's evaluation of the importance of the performance.

The teacher exerts a significant influence on how students predict (anticipate) and evaluate (define) their own communication performances. In this sense, the teacher is a significant model of effective oral communication for students. It is generally the teacher who establishes the rules regulating oral communication, the norms for language reinforcement and feedback, and the range and kinds of oral communication roles permitted in the classroom (see, for example, Ecroyd 1973). Therefore, the teacher must be aware of student apprehensions about oral communication, especially among students for whom English is a second language (see, for example, McCroskey, Fayer, and Richmond 1985). Another instructional must is that all descriptions, interpretations, and assessments of competence in oral communication recognize the multicultural nature of U.S. society.

Students must be helped to recognize that not every effort to communicate orally in class is going to be subject to formal instructional evaluation. The teacher should encourage the free flow of ideas so that students become comfortable with the use of oral language as a medium for sending messages, without apprehension concerning the way their speech will be judged by others, even though the teacher may be using any given speaking opportunity as an occasion for developmental evaluation (that is, comparing the child's language development with the norm).

CLASSROOM EXAMPLES

In the lower elementary grades, the teacher might arrange an after-lunch discussion in which children talk about what they ate and what they liked or disliked about the meal. Each child's opinion is valued; there are no right or wrong answers. No effort should be made to correct either the child's speech or the choices of likes and dislikes; however, the teacher could follow this discussion with his or her own views and perhaps even a discussion of good nutrition.

In the middle or upper elementary grades, students can expand on these discussion sessions by discussing in small groups their views of recent events they may be studying, or they might visit lower grades to discuss current events with younger students or to explain the rules of a game the children are learning. By incorporating cooperative or collaborative learning activities across grade levels and across all content areas, teachers can further provide students with opportunities to speak in smaller group settings that many will find less intimidating than speaking to the entire class.

One activity is to have students, working in groups, list situations in which the members of the group experienced apprehension and those in which they did not. Relaxation exercises can be important means of reducing anxiety in many situations, especially in reducing stage fright in speaking situations. Teachers in the lower grades might have their students sit quietly on the floor with eyes closed and tell the children a story designed to promote the dispelling of fear- provoking thoughts.

In the middle and upper grades, teachers may identify several models of relaxation and ask the students to try them and decide which they prefer. One group might concentrate on breathing exercises; another might try the four components developed by Benson and Klipper (1976) in *The Relaxation Response*. The authors suggest that to relax one must have a quiet environment, a mental device to crowd out fear-provoking thoughts, a passive attitude, and a comfortable position (p. 17).

REFERENCES
Ayres 1986; Ayres and Hopf 1990; Beatty 1988; Benson and Klipper 1976; Booth-Butterfield 1989; Cooper 1991; Cooper and Galvin 1982; Daly et al. 1989; Ellis 1963; Ecroyd 1973; Fremouw and Scott 1979; Leary 1983; McCroskey 1972, 1977; McCroskey and Richmond 1991; McCroskey, Fayer, and Richmond 1985; McCroskey, Ralph, and Barrack 1970; Phillips and Metzger 1973; Slavin 1987; Wolpe 1958.

● STRATEGY 8.5: ENCOURAGE THE USE OF BOTH NATIVE AND STANDARD DIALECT AND LANGUAGE SYSTEMS

Students are taught the differences between their native dialect and the standard elements of conversational and formal speech and helped to identify the contexts in which each style is appropriate.

DISCUSSION

A person's language does much to reflect who the person is, for one's language is necessarily a reflection of one's culture. Thus, each student should be encouraged to develop language skills that will best serve him or her with the people with whom he or she must communicate daily; those language skills must serve the student in a wide variety of social settings. When teaching oral communication, it is therefore essential to deal with the *appropriateness* of language in a given situation.

At the same time, the importance of effective communication and a common language cannot be underestimated. The desire to inculcate standard English proficiency among students is generally well-intentioned, for both speaker and listener must understand the message if it is to have its desired effect. Nonetheless, even the standard English dialect is ultimately only one of several language choices; each choice needs to be assessed in terms of its appropriateness in a given situation.

For communication to be successful, the listener must be able to *understand*, not just hear, the message.

Without a proper framework, however, this goal can do more harm than good, especially for those young people who are not adept in standard English. The communication environment is further complicated when there are multiple first languages in one class. Students' self-concept and the attitude of the teacher toward students who are not fluent in standard American English are critical to students' academic success. A broad understanding of oral communication, both speaking and listening, and a sensitivity to cultural differences are both needed before any decision can be made to influence a student's language choices or dialect. The diversity in the classroom itself must be considered.

CLASSROOM EXAMPLES

The teacher can ask students to identify and research their spoken cultural dialects and/or accents; this research can be shared with fellow students. The teacher can then explain that no single dialect or accent is used by a majority of people in the United States. Students' speech patterns can be traced to particular geographic regions. The importance of speaking a standard dialect when necessary should be noted, particularly as standard speech allows a listener to comprehend a message more easily.

The teacher can generate a series of interpersonal scenarios, each with a different cultural orientation. These should include scenarios in which the use of standard dialect is most appropriate as well as scenarios in which the use of a different dialect might also be appropriate. Students can role play their opinions of the most appropriate oral communication behaviors in each scenario, and then discuss the importance of recognizing and appropriately modifying one's speech in different contexts.

The entire class can discuss the differences between standard English and regional dialects in an informative, neutral manner. Teachers should impart the differences between students' native dialects and the standard elements of conversational and formal speech and help students to identify the contexts in which each style is appropriate. Teachers should take care not to criticize or ridicule a student for using his or her dialect in the classroom. Dialects are not "inferior" to standard English; they simply differ from it in a variety of predictable, rule-governed ways.

Teachers should explain—through modeling and guided, interactive student activities—that certain speech styles are more appropriate for some speaking situations than others. They may point out that it is perfectly accept-

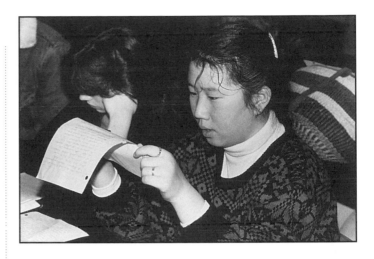

Students gain confidence in their use of language in school settings that respect their cultural heritage and offer a variety of communication opportunities. This young girl is revising a piece of writing about holiday customs in her family. She will later share it with her classmates in a small-group setting. Following peer feedback and writing revisions, class members will compile a class holiday resource file and calendar. On a weekly or monthly basis, students will share appropriate holiday information and display holiday-related objects.

able (and in fact advisable) to use one's dialect among family and friends, but that in school (and later in college and in one's career) it may be preferable and even necessary to use standard English. Indeed, individuals who can make informed judgments about which speech style to use in a given situation, and who can effectively "code-switch" from dialect to standard English and back again depending on the situation, are often some of the most effective communicators.

Teachers can incorporate discussion about dialect and standard English into language arts and reading activities in a variety of ways. Most important, teachers should strive to convey an acceptance of young people's attempts to communicate, regardless of the style of communication used. For example:

Teacher: Marcus, would you like to tell us what you did this weekend?
Marcus: My sister bike got stole.
Teacher: Oh no! Your sister's bike was stolen? Then what happened?

In this instance, the teacher did not correct Marcus, but instead rephrased his statement using standard English. She also affirmed the communicative context of his statement by asking him to continue his story. Correcting Marcus's grammar during this conversation would have distracted listeners from the content of his message—and, most important, might have made him reluctant to talk or to share information in the future. Later, the teacher may present a language arts/grammar activity in which the grammatical differences between standard English and the dialectical variation Marcus used can be examined in a neutral manner, as part of the lesson.

REFERENCES

Albert 1986; Delpit 1988; Heath 1982; Hecht, Collier, and Ribean 1993; Nelson-Barber 1982; Ting-Toomey 1986; Tzeng, Duvall, Ware, and Fortier 1986.

● STRATEGY 8.6: PROMOTE INTERCULTURAL UNDERSTANDING AND COMMUNICATION

Teachers develop students' understanding of the process of intercultural communication, including the factors that lead to misunderstanding between and among people from different cultures.

DISCUSSION

Each culture has its own unwritten rules for communication. When two people from different cultures try to communicate, even though they may have a common language, there can be a mismatch of expectations about how the conversation should proceed that may cause misunderstandings. Teachers need to guide students in developing sensitivity to the existence of such differences.

Young people grow up with different ways of talking that emulate the speech patterns of their home and community. Teachers must cultivate students' awareness of these differences. Teachers can ask students to discuss the ways in which others talk that surprise them, or ask them how they talk with different people in their homes, such as their brothers and sisters, their parents or care-givers, and their grandparents. Different social rules of communication apply with different speech partners, depending on their age and role. Young people have probably picked up some awareness of these rules by observing what is allowed with their friends but is considered inappropriate with their grandparents. Teachers can extend this knowledge to show students that unwritten rules of communication are different in different cultures.

A multicultural perspective requires that every speaker anticipate how alternative cultural experiences could change the meanings a speaker is trying to convey. For example an Anglo teacher who offers students suggestions to improve their performance should be aware that Hispanic students are more likely than other students feel an element of shame that the teacher did not intend them to feel. Likewise, a white teacher should be aware that African-American students may react far more strongly than the teacher anticipates to implications of social alienation, within-group favoritism, and between-group hostility.

CLASSROOM EXAMPLES

It is not uncommon for the children in any given classroom to come from three or more cultural backgrounds. In general, for a teacher to enhance the oral communication skills of dissimilar groups of students, there must be a high level of "talk" between the teacher and students so that each recognizes appropriate speaking and listening skills for that particular class. For example, a Hispanic girl may expect everyone to look at her while she is speaking, but a young man from Ghana would regard such behavior as inappropriate. Teachers should acknowledge and discuss these cultural communication differences with their students.

Teachers may show videos of two people from different cultures interacting and attempting to communicate, then ask students to analyze and identify the factors that cause misunderstandings. These factors may include such differences as the amount of time each person wants to talk about the task, acceptable amounts of eye contact, body language, expectations of the sequence of turn taking, and honorific forms of address.

Students may also be shown a segment of videotape and then asked to write a report of what they have seen using their base dialect. These reports are then shared with the class to allow students to see how the same situation may be perceived and reported from different cultural aspects. Younger students may be asked to create a puppet representing any culture in the world and then act out the part of that puppet. This activity allows students to investigate and learn about other cultures, thus increasing their own awareness of different styles of oral communication.

REFERENCES

Albert 1986; Delpit 1988; Gudykunst, Ting-Toomey, and Wiseman 1991; Hecht, Collier, and Ribean 1993; McCroskey and Richmond 1990; Nelson-Barber 1982; Osgood 1974a, 1974b; Ting-Toomey 1986; Tzeng, Duvall, Ware, and Fortier 1986.

● STRATEGY 8.7: BUILD ON STUDENTS' HOME, COMMUNITY, AND CULTURAL EXPERIENCES

Teachers construct classroom lessons in ways consistent with students' home-community culture and language to take advantage of students' cognitive experiences and to allow students opportunities to engage in achievement-related behaviors.

DISCUSSION

Learning is more likely to occur when there is a match between young people's expectations about how to interact with adults and other children and the expectations of the teacher and school administration. Teachers must express their empathy for, and willingness to learn about, different ethnic and cultural groups and show a desire to experience the world from their students' perspectives through their use of oral communication. In doing so, they show that they value and appreciate each child's culture and language. Whenever possible, teachers should infuse the curriculum with lessons on diverse topics that are meaningful to their students. Teachers should also allow students to practice oral language, thinking, reading, and writing skills in real, meaningful, interactive situations that give students opportunities to speak and listen.

The valuing of students' culture and language differences need not compromise standards and expectations for student learning. Instead, by recognizing and using differences in constructive ways, teachers can heighten student awareness of the importance of human communication and guide students in cultivating skills that will serve them well in varied roles and situations. Au and Jordan (1981) have shown that when teachers incorporate the home culture's expected patterns of interaction and discourse, students feel more comfortable about being in school and about participating in learning situations. In the truly diverse classroom, however, the teacher cannot adapt to all diverse cultures simultaneously. Therefore, the teacher and the class should agree on the common ground on which to approach each other.

CLASSROOM EXAMPLES

Results of the Kamehameha Early Education Project (KEEP) provide one example of increased student participation and learning that is tied to understanding, respect-

ing, and incorporating students' culture into the school context. When participatory patterns in reading discussions permitted the use of "talk story" (a Hawaiian-Polynesian conversational style that involves collaboration), students' reading skills improved. In a different study, Heath's work with teachers in the Piedmont Carolinas focused on the use of talk, especially questions, in children's out-of-school and in-school experiences. Differences between teacher and student dialects became a source of school investigation for increasing student learning rather than an insurmountable barrier between teachers and the school community.

In the middle to high school grades, the teacher can assign a process (how-to-do-it) speech in which each student's presentation must follow a prescribed format:

1. Introduce the subject.
2. List or name the materials needed.
3. Tell or show how to do the process.
4. Summarize or review.

The students must choose as a topic something that reflects their primary culture. Some examples: A student

Reading, writing, listening, and speaking activities are integrated in this classroom. Most important, connections are made among different content areas and with real-world contexts. The class bulletin board titled "Writing for the Community" includes student writing based on a range of community-related issues. Student voices, both oral and written, are empowered in this class setting; the teacher is a facilitator of learning. At the same time, students are instructed in options regarding language usage and the need to match audience, message, and style so as to communicate successfully.

from South Louisiana might demonstrate Cajun dancing, a Hawaiian girl might teach the Hula, or an African-American student might show how to make calas (fried cakes made mainly of rice).

Similarly, when implementing cooperative or collaborative learning approaches, teachers need to be aware of students' backgrounds and attitudes. Cambodian students, for example, may perform better with cooperative rewards rather than competitive rewards. Students from Vietnam and China, who are likely to come from backgrounds influenced by Confucian ideas, may be more resistant to cooperative learning.

REFERENCES

Au 1980; Au and Mason 1981; Broome 1991; Calfee, Cazden, Duran, Griffin, Martus, and Willis 1981; Heath 1983, 1986; Au and Jordan 1981; Phillips 1983.

● STRATEGY 8.8: FOSTER THE ANALYSIS OF TOPIC, AUDIENCE, MESSAGE, AND PURPOSE

Teachers provide students with direct instruction and practice in analysis of audience, choice of topic, development of ideas, and purpose of message.

DISCUSSION

Unless a speaker understands the need for analysis of a specific audience and development of appropriate communication strategies to address that audience, there is a strong likelihood of misunderstanding and unsuccessful communication. The receiving audience affects the topic selected, the language and examples used, and the purpose of the message. In order to become a more effective oral communicator, both as speaker and listener, a student must recognize and practice the major process components.

Class instruction and practice in oral communication can include instruction in one-to-many communication, practice in large-group games, "show-and-tell" activities, and cooperative learning activities. Teachers should include a variety of interpersonal communication and public speaking situations.

Teachers should instruct students in the primary principles associated with speaking to an audience of one, to a small group, or to many listeners. Activities should be carefully planned to include both the development of

content and the delivery of the material. If this is to be an effective strategy, students must have more than one opportunity to give a speech. Once the teacher critiques a student's first speech, that student must have an opportunity to make the needed corrections and then to present the speech again. The basic speaking principles learned in this activity can then be applied to speaking opportunities in classes such as history, civics, English, or mathematics.

CLASSROOM EXAMPLES

Students in the middle grades can be asked to role play selected situations, paying particular attention to the language choices made. Here's an example of a role-playing task: "Your major project is late, and you receive a low grade. Explain this to your parents, your teacher, and your best friend."

Students can be given a list of topics, a list of different audiences, and a list of different places. For example:

Topic: school
Audience: other students, parents
Places: at school, at home

Students are then asked to identify what they might say about school to other students at school, then what they might say about school to their parents or care-givers at home.

High school students can learn to analyze the audience and to prepare information by engaging in exercises such as these:

• Give students a current-events topic and ask them to develop a one-minute speech on it. After they develop their ideas on the topic, ask them to adapt the topic so they can present it to:

1. the class,
2. the faculty,
3. a group of young people who have never heard of the topic, or
4. a group of politicians or businesspersons who are very familiar with the topic.

• Ask each student to complete a short evaluation form on several topics chosen by the teacher or by a group of students. For each topic, ask the students to use a Likert scale to show response to the following statements:

1. I believe I know about this topic.
2. I am interested in this topic.
3. I have strong feelings about this topic.

The class then joins in an analysis of the audience (themselves) to see graphically that each listener must be treated differently.

• Teach students that there are four major purposes for giving speeches: to entertain, to inform, to inspire, and to persuade. Play parts of several speeches and ask students to discuss the purpose of each. For example, the opening monologue of the "Tonight" show is meant to entertain; Martin Luther King's well-known "I Have a Dream" speech had dual purposes: to inspire and to persuade.

• Even in the lower elementary grades, teachers can help young students learn the importance of audience by encouraging the children to share an experience, such as visiting the neighborhood firehouse. The children can tell what they saw to another class and to their parents. The teacher might suggest ways of sharing this information with the two different audiences.

REFERENCES

Berko, Wolvin, and Wolvin 1992; Berko, Bostwick, and Miller 1989; Cooper 1990; Galvin, Cooper, and Gordon 1988; Hopson, Rouzan, DeKemel, and Hopson 1992; Wolvin, Berko, and Wolvin 1993.

Teaching strategies addressing the use of nonverbal and verbal communication are necessary for effective instruction in oral communication. One of the students pictured here is using hand gestures to reinforce the point he is making verbally. In addition to emphasizing the appropriate uses of nonverbal communication, teachers should discuss with students the different norms for nonverbal communication that exist in different cultures. By providing students with many opportunities to observe and practice a range of speaking styles, teachers help students become more comfortable and proficient communicators.

● STRATEGY 8.9: ENCOURAGE THE USE OF COORDINATED VERBAL AND NONVERBAL COMMUNICATION SYSTEMS

Among a repertoire of approaches, teachers include modeling, oral and written instructions, quizzes, discussions, and rehearsal to improve students' use of their nonverbal communication skills as well as their understanding of the nonverbal language of others.

DISCUSSION

Students become more effective oral communicators when they can select nonverbal behaviors that support the verbal messages they wish to communicate. Students need opportunities to observe and discuss the roles, functions, and limitations of nonverbal communication in face-to-face oral interactions. Illustrations of specific methods and techniques that students can use to communicate more effectively are also helpful.

Student-generated talk should increasingly be coordinated with nonverbal communication. Verbal and nonverbal communication should reinforce each other and ultimately clarify the message conveyed to audience members. Some class assignments, such as reading oral reports, will necessarily work against this objective because oral reports detract from direct eye contact, restrict the use of hand gestures (because students generally hold the written report), and prevent students from moving. Teachers should make a point of including assignments that coordinate verbal and nonverbal communication.

In addition, teachers must assist students in recognizing that differing norms for appropriate nonverbal communication (i.e., eye contact, physical distance, gestures, touch, etc.) exist in different cultures. Student should discuss different cultures' use of nonverbal cues and then act out the ways in which different groups might use certain gestures. The verbal message and the nonverbal message must be congruent and prepared for the intended audience.

CLASSROOM EXAMPLES

Ask students to explore the difference in audience feedback between the use of verbal instructions only and the use of coordinated verbal and nonverbal behaviors. Ask each student, for example, to describe without using any

In this class, students are exploring the culture and customs of West Africa. Such class projects involve students in developing topics, research questions, and study groups focused on individual interests. Students also can engage in decision making and program planning that may lead to assembly or class programs for other students or evening programs open to parents and other community residents. The variety of communication opportunities in such student-motivated endeavors allow teachers to integrate instruction with practice in audience analysis and with the development and presentation of high-interest material.

nonverbal communication a simple process such as making a peanut-butter-and-jelly sandwich, tying a shoe or necktie, or jumping rope. Students should raise their hands whenever the directions are unclear. Following this portion of the activity, each student should be asked to demonstrate the process using only *nonverbal* means, with feedback from the audience whenever the "directions" are unclear. The class should discuss the results of the activity.

In regard to cultural differences in nonverbal communication, teachers can ask students to prepare a list of words that are frequently expressed nonverbally (e.g., yes, no, maybe, go, stop, etc.) and then ask students to indicate how the meanings are conveyed in their cultures. Students can identify those nonverbal behaviors that seem to be common among cultures and those that are more likely to be unique to a particular culture.

Following a discussion about facial expressions, students can be asked to select pictures and paste them on posterboard. Students can be asked to indicate what emotions are conveyed by the various expressions. A discussion about emotional expressions and how we develop our ability to "see" the expressions should then take place.

REFERENCES

Anderson and Withrow 1981; Argyle 1985; Bassett and Boone 1983; Berko, Bostwick, and Miller 1989; Ekman 1976; Galvin, Cooper, and Gordon 1988; Hegstrom 1979; Henley 1977; Leathers 1975; McCroskey 1976; Weimann and Weimann 1975.

● STRATEGY 8.10: EMPHASIZE HIGHER ORDER THINKING

Teachers encourage students to respond to many questions at different cognitive levels and ask probing questions to help students further explain or elaborate on their responses.

DISCUSSION

Analytical and critical thinking are vital parts of competence in oral communication. Critical thinkers are aware of their own biases; they are objective and logical. The effective communicator can identify, select, and anticipate the information needed by audience members in order to analyze the material and to accept the arguments as logical. It is imperative for young people to learn that problem solving is a complex process, that a variety of means may be used to reason critically to reach a solution, and that strategies exist that may be used to evaluate conclusions critically. In the teaching of listening skills, it is imperative for students to learn to critically evaluate the arguments of others.

CLASSROOM EXAMPLES

Teachers promote young people's cognitive growth when they engage them in higher order tasks that involve problem solving. Providing many opportunities for students to learn and apply new information, concepts, and skills in meaningful and diverse oral contexts also aids the learning process.

Teachers should ask questions of varying levels of difficulty, taking care to include higher level questions for all students at all grade levels. Questions involving factual recall should not be allowed to dominate the instructional process. For example, before reading the conclusion of a story, students might be asked to predict its outcome or to offer solutions to a problem faced by one of the characters. In all content areas, students can be given opportunities to solve problems aloud and to describe how they arrived at their conclusions.

Classroom experiences and exercises designed to foster higher order thinking should depend on the developmental level of the students involved, particularly when students are asked to develop higher order thinking about their own oral communication behavior. Indeed, classroom teachers can view the development of higher order thinking as a series of developmental activities, phases, or stages. Students will first need to develop the ability to describe their own activities as oral communicators. When they have mastered description, students should begin the process of understanding how to interpret their oral communication behaviors. Once they have mastered interpretation, students should learn how to evaluate their own communication behaviors.

REFERENCES
Cooper 1990; Covert and Thomas 1978; Dunkins and Biddle 1974; Gall and Rhody 1987; Wilder 1971.

● STRATEGY 8.11: USE REAL-WORLD EXPERIENCES

Teachers provide students with many opportunities to observe, compare, and contrast a wide range of speaking styles in a variety of real-world contexts.

DISCUSSION

Traditionally, instructional strategies in oral communication emphasized the ideal speaking style as one in which a speaker addressed a large audience; the speaker spoke, and the audience listened. The speaker functioned as an expert; employed a formal, if not impersonal, style in language choices and references; and spoke as if his or her address were designed for the multitudes. Today's instructional emphasis recognizes that a wide range of speaking styles is available to speakers and that the most appropriate style must fit the immediate audience, topic, occasion, and speaker. To be effective, oral communicators must be familiar with a range of different speaking styles (e.g., conversational and formal) and the various reactions that may result from their use. Different circumstances and social settings necessarily influence the selection of speaking style.

Students become more effective oral communicators if teachers identify and illustrate specific methods and techniques, which students can then practice. This approach lessens student anxiety and increases student confidence. As the student learns to concentrate on what needs to be said, anxiety will be reduced.

CLASSROOM EXAMPLES

Teachers can ask young people to observe, compare, and contrast a wide variety of speaking situations and speakers. For example, students might observe a sermon, a Presidential address, a student council meeting, a group of friends at a party—or even analyze their own delivery and style in a variety of speaking situations. Students can then discuss in small groups or write in journals their ideas about how appropriate style and delivery differ with different audiences, topics, occasions, and speakers.

High school students might work in pairs; for a week, each student might keep a journal reflecting on the speaking style of the other. When did the student appear most comfortable speaking? Least comfortable? Did the partner use different tones or speaking patterns with different people? (Proper cautions should be given to team members to avoid unnecessarily negative reporting.)

REFERENCES
Addington 1965; Berko, Wolvin, and Wolvin 1992; Delpit 1988; Faries 1963; Dedmon and Kowalzik 1964; Heath 1982; Lass and Puffenberger 1971; Mohrmann 1966; Pearce and Brommel 1972; Reardon 1971; Wolvin, Berko, and Wolvin 1993.

● STRATEGY 8.12: DEVELOP AWARENESS OF APPROPRIATE ARTICULATION AND PRONUNCIATION

Teachers develop students' awareness of vocal characteristics and the need for appropriate articulation and pronunciation and include relevant practice in supportive settings.

DISCUSSION

As individuals find themselves in varying environments, they encounter situations that require the use of appropriate language. Speaking at home and speaking at a club meeting or at a job site require the use of appropriate articulation and pronunciation. Effective communicators learn to fit their language and language usage to the setting.

Teachers should provide students with opportunities to learn pronunciation patterns that allow them to be understood in various settings. For individuals who speak languages other than English as their primary language or who speak dialects, opportunities should be provided to hear and learn alternative pronunciations.

CLASSROOM EXAMPLES

Teachers can provide young people with a list of words and a review of standard pronunciation. The word list should be developed by the teacher in response to areas of common need identified by the students themselves. (Students can also develop their own unique lists.)

The teacher should provide students with opportunities to record their own voices in a variety of activities so that they can assess how they respond and sound to others. Students can videotape one another in class activities. The teacher can review the tape either with the entire group or individually to help identify pronunciation and inflection patterns that may not be appropriate for some situations important to the student. Non- native English speakers can be required to listen to certain television shows, particularly news shows, and to record words or phrases they do not understand. These words or phrases can become the basis for group discussions.

Teachers can ask students in 9th through 12th grades to identify actors, politicians, and religious leaders for whom English is a second language. This activity can serve to hone the students' listening ability, increase their confidence in using English, and build their self-esteem. Ask

students to identify what the speaker does differently and how it is that people understand the speaker despite the fact that English is not his or her native tongue. Together, teacher and students should identify well-known individuals and discuss with the entire class their effectiveness as speakers and the ability of audiences (listeners) to receive and understand their messages. The list of speakers might include Pope John Paul II, Arnold Schwarzenegger, and Gloria Estefan.

REFERENCES
Addington 1965; Berko, Bostwick, and Miller 1989; Daniel 1992; Naremore and Hopper 1990; Nelson-Barber 1982; Reardon 1971; Thomas 1969.

● STRATEGY 8.13: USE A WIDE VARIETY OF METHODS, MATERIALS, AND TECHNOLOGIES

Teachers incorporate a wide variety of methods, materials, and technologies into activities to help students improve their communication skills.

DISCUSSION

Because oral communication includes a combination of speaking, listening, and nonverbal messages, learning experiences should also include the use of many types of resources. Research suggests that students should be exposed to a wide variety of methods and materials that address their individual instructional styles and needs as they learn to improve their speaking and listening skills. Speeches, debates, one-to-one and small-group discussions, private conferences, oral reports, and storytelling may be used in all content areas to provide students with opportunities to use and practice language in meaningful ways.

Teachers of ethnically diverse students should bridge cross- cultural communication gaps by exposing their students to instructional resources that address concerns common to all cultures. Students must be helped to understand and use words and concepts that are understood by most cultures and ethnic groups. In addition, instructional materials that recognize, incorporate, and accurately reflect the contributions of the groups represented among students in the classroom, as well as other cultural groups, are essential.

Photo courtesy of Nancy Curran, District Learning Resource Center, Decatur, IL

Exposing students to a wide variety of methods and materials helps them improve their speaking and listening skills. This young boy is motivated to tell a story about his hand puppet's adventures. Across all grade levels, the use of props, including puppets, musical instruments, articles of clothing, and other objects, stimulates storytelling and engages the eyes and ears of the audience. Visual, tactile, and auditory methods appeal to divergent learning styles and interests.

Under the teacher's guidance, students can work in whole group situations, in pairs, in cooperative learning groups, and individually. Groupings may be based on students' instructional levels, rates of progress, interests, or various strategies for effective instruction. These groupings provide students with structured situations in which they can share ideas about their learning and develop greater skill and confidence as communicators. Heterogeneous groupings can make use of the diversity among students and provide opportunities for discussion. Members of homogeneous groups need opportunities for exchanges with groups of differing composition.

The use of computers, audiotapes, videotapes, and other technologies can stimulate student interest and help in assessing strengths and needs in communication competence.

CLASSROOM EXAMPLES

The teacher may ask class members to audiotape their individual oral presentations, conduct small-group discussions, or simply read materials aloud. Interactive videos, in which a student uses computer-assisted instruction to learn listening skills, is yet another technique. The practice of videotaping oral presentations allows students to see and hear their presentations as an outsider might. This helps each student to perform an objective self-critique.

Whenever possible, students should be videotaped while performing class activities. The teacher can review the tape either with the whole group or with individual students. Videotaping can be used to help a student identify both positive and negative nonverbal behavior patterns, pronunciation and inflection patterns, and choice of words.

Teachers can involve students in projects that include interviewing members of the community and seeking information to develop their own print and nonprint resources.

REFERENCES
Berko 1993; Dunn 1990; Gage 1984; Osgood 1974a, 1974b; Palincsar and Klenk 1991; Valverde, Feinberg, and Marquez 1980; Wong-Fillmore and Valadez 1986.

● STRATEGY 8.14: USE BOTH SELF-ASSESSMENT AND PEER EVALUATIONS

Teachers incorporate various types of feedback on oral communication competence, including self-assessment and peer evaluation, in order to respond to individual students' needs.

DISCUSSION

Relying solely on the teacher as audience does not provide students with sufficient feedback to assess their effectiveness in oral communication. Students improve their speaking skill more thoroughly when a variety of audiences, including teachers, peers, and many others, give them feedback about their performance. Feedback may be written, oral, videotaped, or audiotaped.[11]

Through the use of written and oral feedback from different audiences, students can identify their strengths and their needs as oral communicators. The use of self-assessment before a performance or speaking task is also beneficial because it helps students assess the validity of their self-analysis. With this feedback, students can plan for improvement.

Research has not identified a differential effect of feedback types on speaker performance (Book 1985). Although there is much more to learn about the influence of various types of feedback, experts in the field generally agree that the following strategies demonstrate the greatest instructional value in improving students' speech performance. Strategies are listed in descending order from the most to the least influential:

1. Viewing one's own performance on videotape, accompanied by peer or teacher commentary.

2. Positive oral feedback by the teacher that is specific and personal and that delivers criticism in a supportive manner.

3. Positive or negative written feedback by teacher or peers that is specific and impersonal and that offers suggestions about needed areas of improvement in content and delivery.

4. Listening to one's own performance on audiotape, accompanied by teacher or peer commentary.

CLASSROOM EXAMPLES

Teachers and students collaborate in developing a checklist prior to the delivery of a brief oral report on an inventor or some other topic. This checklist helps students to structure and present the report; students also use it to assess their peers' presentations.

Oral presentations may be videotaped and later reviewed by individual students in concert with the feedback data. Students may then choose to redo a presentation, making use of suggested improvements. The teacher may use one of many available evaluation instruments or create one to fit specific needs. For example, one student in a group can be charged with charting the "talk" of others so that the group can see who leads, who talks most and least, who listens, and who asks questions.

REFERENCES
Book 1985; Book and Simmons 1980; Bostrom 1963; Diehl, Breen, and Larsen 1970; Fuller, Veldman, and Richek 1966; Porter and King 1972; Potter and Emanuel 1990; Richmond 1990; Vogel 1973.

● STRATEGY 8.15: ENCOURAGE ACCURATE REPORTING

Teachers encourage students to be accurate in reporting what they hear, read, or see.

DISCUSSION

The words of a persuasive speaker can often change what is happening. If a person learns to persuade others through speaking, that person has acquired a truly powerful ability. President Ronald Reagan was referred to as the "Great Communicator" because of his persuasive speaking skills. All speakers must realize that the ability to speak can be used for good or ill, depending on the speaker's motives; therefore, it is important for teachers to include in any program of oral communication the importance of ethical behavior on the part of the speaker. This crucial component of oral communication can be taught even to young children by showing them the difference between speakers who are credible and those who are not.

Accurate reporting is an exceedingly complex issue, however. On one level, the issue is whether a speaker seeks to describe what really exists. Certainly, the failure to knowingly provide accurate descriptions generates ethical concerns. At the same time, more is involved than the speaker's effort to report accurately. Regardless of the speaker's truthfulness, an audience will make judgments about his or her integrity. Indeed, a speaker needs to be aware that an audience's judgment of his or her credibility may have little or nothing to do with the accurate reporting of facts. When we consider an audience's assessment of a speaker's image as an accurate reporter, we are dealing with questions of credibility or ethos.

Students become more effective oral communicators if instructional strategies: (1) include discussions of the range of factors affecting the impression a speaker makes on an audience; and (2) identify and illustrate specific methods and techniques that students can employ to select and use the most effective linguistic choices and nonverbal behaviors that enhance a speaker's credibility with an audience.

Thus a speaker needs to be aware of two different dimensions that affect accurate reporting. One dimension deals with the speaker's intention and effort to report accurately. The second dimension deals with the audience's perception of the speaker's honesty. Both dimensions affect the outcomes of speaker/audience interactions.

CLASSROOM EXAMPLES

In the lower grades, teachers can talk with children about why they don't go off with strangers or take candy from people they don't know. (While caution is certainly required, the teacher does not want to foster a fear of all strangers in young children.) This exercise should be designed to highlight those factors that determine whether someone can be trusted.

In the upper grades, the teacher might find numerous examples of speakers in the local newspapers. Pictures of the speakers, together with the text of their speeches, can stimulate a discussion of whether the students believe the speaker is telling the truth. This discussion should focus on two levels: (1) the speaker's probable intention and his or her speaking behaviors, and (2) the audience's perceptions and beliefs.

REFERENCES

Berko, Wolvin, and Wolvin 1992; Cooper 1990; Daniel 1992; Galvin and Book 1990; Galvin, Cooper and Gordon 1988; McCroskey and Richmond 1991; Phillips and Metzger 1973; Wilbrand and Rieke 1983; Wilder 1971.

These students are clarifying a point with their teacher. By structuring cooperative learning activities, the teacher has included numerous opportunities for pupils to articulate their ideas, respond to questions from each other, and reconsider a point of view upon gaining new information. When stymied and in need of additional guidance, however, students are quick to get needed support from the teacher. Through a carefully guided instructional process, the teacher is able to incorporate multicultural groups that function effectively and use conflict resolution skills.

● STRATEGY 8.16: INTRODUCE LOGICAL AND EMOTIONAL STRATEGIES AS CONFLICT-RESOLUTION TECHNIQUES

Teachers incorporate the use of logical and emotional arguments in oral communication activities and assist students in using these strategies to resolve conflicts.

DISCUSSION

People are influenced by ideas associated with both logical and emotional appeals. A logical appeal casts an idea as consistent with established tests of validity and reasoning. Using statistics to support a claim is one example of how a logical argument might be constructed. An emotional appeal, on the other hand, links an idea with certain subjective psychic and physical reactions. In some television commercials, for example, sociability (the emotion of wanting to be liked by others) may be associated with the use of certain products.

Both logic and emotion are part of the fabric of our existence. Some maintain that all human discourse should adhere to standard tests of logic, while others maintain equally strongly that human discourse should reflect a commitment to the emotional profile that defines humanity and links all people into one human race. Naturally, it is difficult to imagine a world governed only by scientific and technological logic, but it is just as difficult to imagine a world governed solely by personal desires and needs. Both logical and emotional systems operate within the human domain, and they are equally powerful forces in the decision-making process.

Students become more effective oral communicators if instructional strategies: (1) include discussions of the types and functions of logic and emotions as appeals that can be used by speakers to influence audiences, and (2) identify and illustrate specific methods and techniques that students can employ to identify, select, and anticipate audience reactions to specific logical and emotional appeals.

CLASSROOM EXAMPLES

Classroom debates constitute some of the most useful exercises for revealing the use of both logical and emotional appeals in the process of human communication. Besides the fact that the mode of communication in a debate is oral, debates are composed of a series of logical and emotional appeals designed to influence the judge and the larger audience. Moreover, debate involves both team-work (i.e., the cooperative effort required by the partners on each side of a question) as well as competition (i.e., the "win"/"lose" structure of debates). Debate functions as an excellent classroom device for instruction in oral communication, for, as other researchers have noted, parents want their children to learn to function as part of a team that also teaches them to compete.

Even for younger children, debate functions as a potentially instructive activity for introducing students to the nature of logical and emotional appeals. Lybbert (1985) has maintained that the discipline of debate has three goals: (1) the enhancement of critical thinking and reasoning abilities, (2) academic advancement and development, and (3) the promotion of communication skills. For young children, Lybbert concluded, the focus can be on the development of oral communication skills.

Kathy Littlefield and Robert Littlefield (1988) have developed an innovative after-school program for grades 3 through 6 that was specifically designed to teach oral communication skills to young children. The program, called KIDSPEAK, was initiated in 1987. The debate units contained in the program are oral reading, listening, creative expression, storytelling, and communication etiquette. Interested teachers were given a training session and access to additional help if they felt they needed it.

The Florida Department of Education has recommended that debate be introduced into the school curriculum as early as middle or junior high school. The Florida program outlines its major concepts/content as follows: oral communication, techniques of group discussion, fundamentals of parliamentary procedure, elements of debate and debate activities, basic techniques of public speaking, and techniques of evaluation (see Aiex 1990).

REFERENCES

Aiex 1990; Berko, Wolvin, and Wolvin 1992; Carre 1986; Littlefield and Littlefield 1989; Lybbert 1985; Wolvin, Berko, and Wolvin 1993.

NOTES

[1] The Speech Communication Association or SCA is a professional education association whose purpose is "to promote the study, criticism, research, teaching, and application of the artistic, humanistic, and scientific principles of communication." In June of 1992, some 6,500 individuals were members of SCA. SCA is the largest organization in the world devoted to the study of oral communication.

[2] For example, see: Brown-Carlson Listening Test (for high school students); CIRCUS Listening Test (for K-3 students); Cloze Listening Test (for secondary students); Durell Listening Series: Primary, Intermediate, and Advanced; Massachusetts Assessment of Basic Skills Listening Test (for grades 7-12); Metropolitan Achievement Test: Listening Comprehension (for K-4 students); Stanford Achievement Tests: Listening Comprehension (for grades 1-6); and the Test for Listening Accuracy in Children (for grades K-6).

[3] For example, see: CIRCUS Say and Tell (Pre-K through 3rd grade); the Communicative Evaluation Chart from Infancy to Five Years.

[4] For example, see: Dyadic Task-Oriented Communication Test (for elementary grades); the Language Facility Test (for ages 3 through 15); the Massachusetts Assessment of Basic Skills Speaking Test (for grades 7-12); the Utah Test of Language Development (ages 2-14); and Speech in the Classroom: Assessment Instruments of Speaking Skills (grades 1-12).

[5] For example, see: Profile of Nonverbal Sensitivity (grades 3 through 6, and high school); PRI Oral Language Skill Clusters (for grades K-3); and the Test of Listening Accuracy in Children (for grades K-6).

[6] For example, see: McCroskey's two different measures— the Willingness to Communication Test (WCT), and the Personal Report on Communication Apprehension (PACA).

[7] These criteria were developed within the context of the standards recommended by the National Commission on Testing and Public Policy (1990).

[8] Atomic assessment is the isolation of one specific aspect of the communications transaction for assessment.

[9] Kinesics is the study of the communicative dimension of movements (DeVito 1991, p. 68).

[10] Paralanguage is the vocal, but nonverbal, aspect of speech that includes vocal' quality, vocal characteristics, vocal qualifiers, and vocal strategies (DeVito 1991, p. 9).

[11] These generalizations may not apply to a first speaking situation. Following a first speaking situation, a teacher may wish to exercise direct control over feedback in order to ensure that the feedback students receive will be encouraging and will motivate students to want to speak again. Indeed, the teacher may wish to avoid any negative feedback following a first speech, focusing instead upon activities that can be taken by all speakers in the class to improve their speeches on a subsequent speaking assignment.

BIBLIOGRAPHY

Adams, M.J. (1990). *Beginning to Read: Thinking and Learning About Print*. Cambridge, Mass.: Bradford Books/MIT Press.

Addington, D.W. (1965). "The Effect of Mispronunciations on General Speaking Effectiveness." *Communication Monographs* 32: 159-163.

Aiex, N.K. (September 1990). "Debate and Communication Skills." *ERIC Digest*. Bloomington, Ind.: ERIC Clearinghouse on Reading and Communication Skills.

Albert, R.D. (1986). "Communication and Attributional Differences Between Hispanics and Anglo-Americans" In *International and Intercultural Communication Annual*. Vol. 10, edited by Y.Y. Kim. Newbury Park, Calif.: Sage.

Anderson, J.F., and J.G. Withrow. (October 1981). "The Impact of Lecturer Nonverbal Expressiveness on Improving Mediated Instruction." *Communication Education* 30: 342-353.

Argyle, M. (1985). *The Psychology of Interpersonal Behavior*. Baltimore: Penguin.

Au, K.H. (Summer 1980). "Participation Structures in a Reading Lesson With Hawaiian Children: Analysis of a Culturally Appropriate Instructional Event." *Anthropology and Education Quarterly* 11, 2: 91-115.

Au, K., and C. Jordan. (1981) "Teaching Reading to Hawaiian Children: A Culturally Appropriate Solution." In *Culture and the Bilingual Classroom: Studies in Classroom Ethnography*, edited by H. Trueba, G. Guthrie, and K. Au. Rowley, Mass.: Newbury House.

Au, K.H., and J.M. Mason. (1981). "Social Organizational Factors in Learning to Read: The Balance of Rights Hypothesis." *Reading Research Quarterly* 17: 115-152.

Ayres, J. (July 1986). "Perceptions of Speaking Ability: An Explanation for Stage Fright." *Communication Education* 35, 3: 275-287.

Ayres, J., and T.S. Hopf. (1990). "The Long-Term Effect of Visualization in the Classroom: A Brief Research Report." *Communication Education* 39, 1: 75-78.

Bassett, R.E., and M.E. Boone. (1983). "Improving Speech Communication Skills: An Overview of the Literature." In *Improving Speaking and Listening Skills*, edited by R.B. Rubin. San Francisco: Jossey-Bass.

Beatty, M.J. (April 1988). "Increasing Students' Choice-Making Consistency: The Effect of Decision Rule-Use Training," *Communication Education* 37, 2: 95-105.

Beebe, S.A. (January 1974). "Eye Contact: A Nonverbal Determinant of Speaker Credibility." *Speech Teacher* 23, 1: 21-25.

Benson, H., and H.Z. Klipper. (1976). *The Relaxation Response*, New York: Avon.

Berko, R. (1993). *Effective Instructional Strategies: Increasing Speaking/Listening Achievement in K-12*. Annandale, Va.: Speech Communication Association.

Berko, R., A.D. Wolvin, and D.R. Wolvin. (1992). *Communicating*. Boston: Houghton-Mifflin.

Berko, R., R. Bostwick, and M. Miller. (1989). *Basic-ly Communicating: An Activity Approach*. Dubuque, Iowa: William C. Brown.

Birdwhistell, R.L. (1970). *Kinesics and Context: Essays in Body Motion Communication*. Philadelphia: University of Philadelphia Press.

Book, C.L. (Spring/Summer 1985). "Providing Feedback: The Research on Effective Oral and Written Feedback Strategies." *Central States Speech Journal* 36, 1-2: 14-23.

Book, C.L., and K.W. Simmons. (May 1980). "Dimensions and Perceived Helpfulness of Student Speech Criticism." *Communication Education* 29, 23: 135-145.

Booth-Butterfield, M. (April 1989). "The Interpretation of Classroom Performance Feedback: An Attributional Approach." *Communication Education* 38, 2: 119-131

Bostrom, R.N. (1963). "Classroom Criticism and Speech Attitudes," *Central States Speech Journal* 14, 1: 32.

Broome, B.J. (1991). "Building Shared Meaning: Implication of a Relational Approach to Empathy for Teaching Intercultural Communication." *Communication Education* 40: 235-250.

Calfee, R.C., C.B. Cazden, R.P. Duran, M.P. Griffin, M. Martus, and H.D. Willis. (1981). *Designing Reading Instruction for Cultural Minorities: The Case of Kamehameha Early Education Program*. Cambridge, Mass.: Harvard University, Graduate School of Education. (ERIC Document Reproduction Service No. ED 215 039).

Carre, C. (1986). *Curriculum Frameworks Grades 6-8, 1986-1987*. Tallahassee: Florida State Department of Education.

Chesebro, J.W., J.C. McCroskey, D.F. Atwater, R.M. Bahrenfuss, G. Cawelti, J.L. Gaudino, and H. Hodges. (October 1992). "Communication Apprehension and Self-Perceived Communication Competence of At-Risk Students." *Communication Education* 41: 345-360.

Cooper, P.J. (1990). *Activities for Teaching Speaking and Listening: Grades 7-12*. Annandale, Va.: Speech Communication Association.

Cooper, P.J. (1991). *Speech Communication for the Classroom Teacher*. 4th ed. Scottsdale, Ariz.: Gorsuch Scarisbrick.

Cooper, P.J., and K. Galvin. (1982). *Improving Classroom Communication*. Washington, D.C.: Dingle Association.

Covert, A., and G.L. Thomas. (1978). *Communication Games and Simulations*. Theory & Research into Practice series. Urbana, Ill.: ERIC Clearinghouse on Reading and Communication Skills; Annandale, Va.: Speech Communication Association.

Cronin, M.W., and G.L. Grice. (1991). "Implementing Oral Communication Across the Curriculum." Unpublished paper. (Available from the Speech Communication Association, Annandale, Va.)

Daly, J.A., et al. (Winter 1989). "Pre-performance Concerns Associated with Public Speaking Anxiety." *Communication Quarterly* 37, 1: 39-53.

Daniel, A.V. (1992). *Activities for Integrating Oral Communication Skills for Students Grades K-8*. Annandale, Va.: Speech Communication Association.

Dedmon, D.N., and J.F. Kowalzik. (May 1964). "The 'Elocution' Specter and the Teaching and Researching of Speech Delivery." *Central States Speech Journal* 15, 2: 100-106.

Delpit, L.D. (1988). "The Silenced Dialogue: Power and Pedagogy in Educating Other People's Children." *Harvard Educational Review* 58: 280-298.

DeVito J. (1991). *The Communication Handbook: A Dictionary*. New York: Harper Collins.

Diehl, E.R., M.P. Breen, and C.U. Larsen. (1970). "The Effects of Teacher Comment and Television Video Tape Playback on the Frequency of Non-fluency in Beginning Speech Students." *Communication Education* 19: 185-189.

Dunkins, M.J., and B.J. Biddle. (1974). *The Study of Teaching*. New York: Holt, Rinehart and Winston.

Dunn, R. (October 1990). "Rita Dunn Answers Questions on Learning Styles." *Educational Leadership* 48, 2: 15-19.

Ecroyd, D.H. (1973). "The Relevance of Oral Language Development to Classroom Teaching." *Communication Quarterly* 21, 1: 11-17.

Elementary and Secondary Education Act (ESEA). (1978). H.R. 15-PL 95-561, signed into law November 1, 1978. Title II—Basic Skills.

National Governors' Association. (1990). *Educating America: State Strategies for Achieving the National Education Goals*. Washington, D.C.: NGA.

Ekman, P. (1976). "Movements with Precise Meanings." *Journal of Communication* 26, 1: 14-26.

Ellis, A. (1963). *Reason and Emotion in Psychotherapy*. New York: Stuart.

Faries, E. (1963). "A Defense of Elocution." *Southern Speech Communication Journal* 29, 2: 133-140.

Florida State Department of Education. (1986). "Oral Communication Guidelines," Tallahassee, Fla.: FSDE.

Fremouw, W.J., and M.D. Scott. (May 1979). "Cognitive Restructuring: An Alternative Method for the Treatment of Communication Apprehension." *Communication Education* 28: 129-133.

Fuller, F.F., D.J. Veldman, and H.G. Richek. (1966). "Tape Recordings, Feedback and Prospective Teachers' Self-Evaluation." *Alberta Journal of Educational Research* 12: 301-307, cited by R.F. Peck and J.A. Tucker, "Research on Teacher Education," *Second Handbook of Research on Teaching*, edited by R.M. Travers. Chicago: Rand McNally.

Gage, N.L. (1984). "What Do We Know about Teaching Effectiveness?" *Phi Delta Kappan* 66, 2: 87-93.

Gall, M., and T. Rhody. (1987). "Review of Research on Questioning Techniques." In *Questions, Questioning Techniques and Effective Teaching*, edited by W. Wilen. Washington, D.C.: National Education Association.

Galvin, K.M., and C.L. Book. (1990). *Person to Person*. Lincolnwood, Ill.: National Textbook Company.

Galvin, K.M., P.J. Cooper, and J.M. Gordon. (1988). *The Basics of Speech: Learning to Be a Competent Communicator*. Lincolnwood, Ill.: National Textbook Company.

Gorham, J. (1988). "The Relationship Between Verbal Teacher Immediacy Behaviors and Student Learning." *Communication Education* 37: 40-53.

Gudykunst, W., S. Ting-Toomey, and R.L. Wiseman. (1991). "Taming the Beast: Designing a Course in Intercultural Communication." *Communication Education* 40: 272-285.

Heath, S.B. (1982). *Ways with Words*. New York: Cambridge University Press.

Heath, S.B. (1983). *Ways with Words: Language, Life, and Work in Communities and Classrooms*. New York: Cambridge University Press.

Heath, S.B. (1986). "Sociocultural Contexts of Language Development." In *Beyond Language: Social and Cultural Factors in Schooling Language Minority Students*, developed by the Bilingual Education Office, California State Department of Education. Los Angeles: National Evaluation, Dissemination and Assessment Center, California State University.

Hecht, M.L., M.J. Collier, and S.A. Ribean. (1993). *African American Communication*. Newbury Park, Calif.: Sage.

Hegstrom, T.G. (Spring 1979). "Message Impact: What Percentage Is Nonverbal?" *Western Journal of Speech Communication* 43, 2: 134-142.

Henley, N. (1977). *Body Politics: Power, Sex, and Nonverbal Communication*. Englewood Cliffs, N.J.: Prentice-Hall.

Hodges, H. (1989). "ASCD's 3-High Achievement Model." Unpublished manuscript for the ASCD Urban Middle Grades Network, Alexandria, Va.

Hodges, H. (1991). "Effective K-12 Oral Communication Practices: A Research Synthesis." In *The Knowledge Base Reference Guide*.

Holdaway, D. (1979). *The Foundations of Literacy*. Exeter, N.H.: Heinemann Educational Books.

Hopson, C.S., L. Rouzan, K. DeKemel, and C.M. Hopson. (1992). "The Live Oak Project: Strengthening the Oral Communication Skills of Urban Middle School Students". Unpublished report.

Hunsaker, R. (1993). *Classroom Practices in the Teaching of Listening*. Annandale, Va.: Speech Communication Association.

Knapp, M.S., and B.J. Turnbull. (1990). *Better Schooling for the Children of Poverty: Alternatives to Conventional Wisdom. Volume 1: Summary*. Washington, D.C.: Prepared under contract by SRI International and Policy Studies Associates for the U.S. Department of Education, Office of Planning, Budget and Evaluation.

Lass, N.J., and M.D. Puffenberger. (February 1971). "A Comparative Study of Rate Evaluations of Experienced and Inexperienced Listeners." *Quarterly Journal of Speech* 57: 89-93.

Leary, M. (1983). *Understanding Social Anxiety*. Troy, N.Y.: Sage.

Leathers, D.G. (1975). *Nonverbal Communication Systems*. Boston: Allyn and Bacon.

Littlefield, K.M., and R.S. Littlefield. (September 29, 1988). "KID-SPEAK: An Innovative Activity Program for Children." Paper presented at the 11th annual meeting of the Plains Regional Council of the International Reading Association, Fargo, N.D. (ERIC Document Reproduction Service No. ED 298-586)

Lybbert, B. (August 8 11, 1985). "What Should Be the Goals of High School Debate?" Paper presented at the National Forensic League Conference on the State of Debate, Kansas City.

Martinello, M.L., and G.E. Cook. (1992). "Interweaving the Threads of Learning: Interdisciplinary Curriculum and Teaching." *Curriculum Report* 21, 3: 1 6. (Available from the National Association of Secondary School Principals, Reston, Va.)

McCroskey, J.C. (1970). "Measures of Communication-Bound Anxiety." *Speech Monographs* 37: 269-277.

McCroskey, J.C. (1972). The Implementation of a Large-scale Program of Systematic Desensitization for Communication Apprehension. *Speech Teacher* 21: 255-264.

McCroskey, J.C. (1977). *Quiet Children and the Classroom Teacher*. Annandale, Va.: Speech Communication Association.

McCroskey, J.C. (1976). "The Effects of Communication Apprehension on Nonverbal Behavior." *Communication Quarterly* 24: 39-44.

McCroskey, J.C. (1984). "The Communication Apprehensive Perspective." In *Avoiding Communication: Shyness, Reticence and Communication Apprehension*, edited by J.A. Daly and J.C. McCroskey. Beverly Hills, Calif.: Sage.

McCroskey, J.C., D.C. Ralph, and J.E. Barrack. (1970). "The Effect of Systematic Desensitization on Speech Anxiety." *Speech Teacher* 19: 32-36.

McCroskey, J.C., J. Fayer, and V.P. Richmond. (1985). "Don't Speak to Me in English." *Communication Quarterly* 33: 185-192.

McCroskey, J.C., and V.P. Richmond. (Fall 1990). "Willingness to Communicate: Differing Cultural Perspectives." *The Southern Communication Journal* 56, 1.

McCroskey, J.C., and V.P. Richmond. (1991). *Quiet Children and the Classroom Teacher*. 2nd ed. Annandale, Va.: Speech Communication Association.

Mohrmann, G.P. (1966). "The Language of Nature and Elocutionary Theory." *Quarterly Journal of Speech* 52: 116-124.

Naremore, R.C., and R. Hopper. (1990). *Children Learning Language*. New York: Harper and Row.

National Commission on Testing and Public Policy. (1990). *From Gatekeeper to Gateway: Transforming Testing in America. Report of the National Commission on Testing and Public Policy*. Chestnut Hill, Mass.: Boston College.

Nelson-Barber, S. (1982). "Phonologic Variations of Pima English." In *Language Renewal Among American Indian Tribes: Issues, Problems, and Prospects*, edited by R. St. Clair and W. Leap. Rosslyn, Va.: National Clearinghouse for Bilingual Education.

Newmark, E., and M.K. Asante. (1976). *Cultural Communication*. Urbana, Ill.: ERIC Clearinghouse on Reading and Communication Skills; Annandale, Va.: Speech Communication Association.

Osgood, C.E. (1974a). "Probing Subjective Culture, Part 1: Cross-Linguistic Tool-Making." *Journal of Communication* 24, 1: 21-35.

Osgood, C.E. (1974b). "Probing Subjective Culture, Part 2: Cross-Cultural Tool-Using." *Journal of Communication* 24, 2: 82-99.

Palincsar, A.S., and L.J. Klenk. (1991). *Learning Dialogues to Promote Text Comprehension*. Research report. Ann Arbor: University of Michigan.

Pearce, W.B., and B.J. Brommel. (1972). "Vocal Communication in Persuasion." *Quarterly Journal of Speech* 58: 298-306.

Phillips, J.R. (1983). *The Invisible Culture: Communication in Classroom and Community on the Warm Springs Indian Reservation.* New York: Longman.

Phillips, J.R., and N.J. Metzger. (1973). "The Reticent Syndrome: Some Theoretical Considerations about Etiology and Management." *Speech Monographs* 40: 220-230.

Porter, D.T., and G.W. King. (1972). "The Use of Videotape Equipment in Improving Oral Interpretation Performance." *The Speech Teacher* 21: 105.

Potter, W.J., and R. Emanuel. (1990). "Students' Preferences for Communication Styles and Their Relationship to Achievement." *Communication Education* 39: 234-249.

Reardon, R.C. (1971). "Individual Differences and the Meaning of Vocal Emotional Expressions." *Journal of Communication* 21: 72-82.

Richmond, V.P. (1990). "Communication in the Classroom: Power and Motivation." *Communication Education* 39: 181-195.

Rubin, D.L. (1982). *Communication Competency Assessment Instrument (CCAI).* Annandale, Va.: Speech Communication Association.

Rubin, D.L., and N.A. Mead. (1984). *Large-Scale Assessment of Oral Communication Skills: Kindergarten Through Grade 12.* Urbana, Ill.: ERIC Clearinghouse on Reading and Communication Skills; Annandale, Va.: Speech Communication Association.

Slavin, R. (1986). *Using Student Team Learning.* 3rd ed. Baltimore, Md.: Johns Hopkins University Press.

Slavin, R. (1987). "Cooperative Learning: Can Students Help Students Learn?" *Instructor* 96, 7: 74-78.

SCA. (1980). *Speech Communication Guidelines: Essential Speaking and Listening Skills for Elementary School Students.* Annandale, Va.: Speech Communication Association (SCA).

SCA. (1987). *Speech Communication Association Guidelines: Speaking and listening Competencies for High School Graduates.* Annandale, Va.: Speech Communication Association (SCA).

SCA. (1990). *The Speech Communication Association's Criteria for the Assessment of Oral Communication.* Annandale, Va.: Speech Communication Association (SCA).SCA. (1991). *Guidelines for Developing Oral Communication Curricula in Kindergarten Through Twelfth Grade.* Annandale, Va.: Speech Communication Association (SCA).

Strickland, D.S., and L.M. Morrow. (1989). *Emerging Literacy: Young Children Learn to Read and Write.* Newark, Del.: International Reading Association.

Teale, W.H. (1987). "Emergent Literacy: Reading and Writing Development in Early Childhood." In *Research in Literacy: Merging Perspectives,* edited by J. Readence and R.S. Baldwin. Rochester, N.Y.: National Reading Conference.

Thomas, S.H. (June 1969). "Effects of Monotonous Delivery on Intelligibility." *Speech Monographs* 36: 110-113.

Ting-Toomey, S. (1986). "Conflict Communication Styles in Black and White Subjective Cultures." In *Inter-ethnic Communication: Current Research,* edited by Y.Y. Kim. Newbury Park, Calif.: Sage.

Trank, D.M., and J.M. Steele. (April 1983). "Measurable Effects of a Communication Skills Course: An Initial Study." *Communication Education* 32: 227-236.

Tzeng, O.C.S., C.J. Duvall, R. Ware, and R. Fortier. (1986). "Subjective Intergroup Distances of Blacks and Whites." In *International and Intercultural Communication Annual.* Vol. 10, edited by Y.Y. Kim. Newbury Park, Calif.: Sage.

U.S. Census Bureau. (April 28, 1993). Commerce Department Press Release CB 93-78, Report CPH-L-133: "Language Spoken at Home and Ability to Speak English for U.S. Regions and States: 1990."

U.S. Department of Labor. (1992). *Learning a Living: A Blueprint for High Performance. A SCANS Report for America 2000.* Washington, D.C.: Secretary's Commission on Achieving Necessary Skills, U.S. Department of Labor. (For sale by U.S. G.P.O.)

Valverde, L., R.C. Feinberg, and E.M. Marquez. (1980). *Educating English-Speaking Hispanics.* Alexandria, Va: ASCD.

Vangelisti, A.L., and J.A. Daly. (1989). "Correlates of Speaking Skills in the United States: A National Assessment." *Communication Education* 38: 132-143.

Vogel, R.A. (1973). "An Analysis of the Relationship Between Teacher and Written Criticism and Improvement in Student Speech Performance," Doctoral diss., Purdue University.

Weimann, M.O., and J.M. Weimann. (1975). *Nonverbal Community in the Elementary Classroom.* Theory & Research into Practice series. Urbana, Ill.: ERIC Clearinghouse on Reading and Communication Skills; Annandale, Va.: Speech Communication Association.

Wilbrand, M.L., and E. Rieke. (1983). *Oral Communication in Elementary Schools.* Belmont, Calif.: Wadsworth.

Wilder, L. (June 1971). "Spoken Rehearsal and Verbal Discrimination Learning." *Communication Monographs* 38, 2: 113-120.

Wolpe, J. (1958). *Psychotherapy by Reciprocal Inhibition.* Stanford: Stanford University Press.

Wolvin, A.D., R. Berko, and D.R. Wolvin. (1993). *The Public Speaker. The Public Listener.* Boston: Houghton-Mifflin.

Wong-Fillmore, L., and C. Valadez. (1986). "Teaching Bilingual Learners." In *Handbook of Research on Teaching,* edited by M.C. Wittrock. New York: Macmillan.

Wood, B. (1976). *Children and Communication: Verbal and Nonverbal Language Development.* Englewood Cliffs, N.J.: Prentice-Hall.

9

ASCD Talks Back

INTRODUCTION

In this final chapter of *Educating Everybody's Children*, we have provided an opportunity for a number of forward-looking educators who are closely involved with ASCD affiliates worldwide to respond to the ideas in this book. We selected a wide variety of respondents who work in many different kinds of educational settings, from classroom teachers to university professors. Each respondent was asked two questions:

1. Where do we start instructionally tomorrow with the recommendations of this publication?

2. What are the barriers to effective instruction that prevent practitioners from implementing these recommendations? How can we best eliminate the barriers to effective instruction?

We believe that the responses in this chapter add a new and extremely useful dimension—straight from the real world of the ASCD member—to the findings and recommendations in this publication.

JUDY WILSON STEVENS
Executive Director of Elementary Instruction
Spring Branch Independent School District
Houston, Texas

Where do we start?

The teachers of America should understand and use the strategies in this book to facilitate instruction for all students. Once the recommendations are internalized, teachers should honestly reflect on their current practices to determine the degree to which the recommendations are used consistently. Only through personal reflection and analysis will the information provided in this book benefit the students for whom it is intended. Successful implementation depends on the degree to which we educators admit that we are not now using these methods with all of our students.

It has often been said that, as educators, "we know more than we do." If teachers scan the suggestions in this book and quickly decide, "I'm already doing this," then these recommendations will meet the fate of the many proposals that have preceded them. Everyone concerned with the future of America's children, and anyone who is interested in making decisions that affect education, should discuss these recommendations, include them in a heightened set of expectations for quality educational practice, and continually strive to ensure that every single student receives exemplary instruction. These measures provide a platform for analyzing—and, consequently, beginning to use—diverse teaching strategies to significantly improve the quality of instruction.

What are the barriers?

One of the most significant barriers to effective instruction is the ability of our all-too-human brain to allow us to espouse a set of beliefs, act in ways that are diametrically opposed to these beliefs, and still remain unconscious of the gap between what we say and what we do. Practitioners who believe that they are already using the kinds of recommendations in this book are frequently unaware of the poor quality of implementation or the small amount of time actually spent using such techniques. These educators sincerely believe that they are teaching diverse learners in an exemplary manner. As a result, they perceive no cognitive dissonance between their current reality and any vision of a desired state of affairs—and thus they are unable to seek improvement.

To eliminate this barrier, teachers and administrators must engage in honest reflection and feedback so that they will be able to discern existing gaps between such practices as espousing a "real-world application of mathematics" and spending the majority of instructional time on drill and practice of math facts or on textbook problems. Only by confronting this incongruence can the teacher *choose* to select more appropriate instructional strategies.

Another barrier to effective instruction is the lack of adequate training for many educators in how to use these recommendations to teach diverse learners. The statement "teachers can't teach what they don't know—even when they're mandated to do so" is an accurate assessment of the current state of many educators who fail to implement recommended strategies. To overcome this barrier, it is imperative that time for staff development be allocated or created. Elaborate staff development designs are not necessary. Organizing book studies or minicourses using the contents of this book can be a very effective method for overcoming the lack of adequate training that bars the path to successful implementation.

CHERYL COX
Assistant Superintendent for Instruction
San Felipe Del Rio, Consolidated Independent
  School District
Del Rio, Texas

Where do we start?

First, we must start with an instructional leader who has a clear vision and high expectations for all students. The leader should know three things: (1) where he is going, (2) why he is going there, and (3) how he is going to

get there. Only committed top-level management can make lasting changes. Second, we must develop a long-range plan that can serve as a road map for change. This plan should identify expected outcomes for all students. Third, we must develop a comprehensive staff development program. Fourth, we must develop a multidisciplinary or interdisciplinary curriculum aligned with the expected outcomes for all students. Finally, we must identify high-yield strategies for improving the learning of all students—especially the low achievers—and then correlate these strategies with the objectives of the curriculum.

The staff development program needs to focus on providing training to teachers on how to deliver the curriculum through the high-yield strategies mentioned above. These strategies should include an emphasis on learning styles. Styles research indicates that most students, particularly those most at risk, tend to be "hands-on" learners. When they can touch and feel objects, they learn faster and with better retention; furthermore, they become actively involved in their own learning. Another high-yield strategy that I recommend be used to deliver the curriculum is cooperative learning. Also, there should be an emphasis on higher-order thinking skills for lower achievers. For too long, these students have been required only to memorize facts and details.

What are the barriers?

The main barrier that prevents practitioners from implementing the recommendations in this book is a lack of adequate funding. Funding is needed to develop and maintain strong instructional leaders. A comprehensive staff development program is also very costly. For instance, the cost of substitute teachers is expensive; in addition, teachers' absence from the classroom occasions criticism, even when the cause of the absence is staff development. Furthermore, the top-quality consultants that provide necessary training often carry a high price tag.

The cost of developing the curriculum and purchasing the resources needed to deliver the curriculum can be prohibitive for many districts, especially smaller, property-poor districts with very limited financial resources. Most low achievers profit from using hands-on materials, but these materials are relatively expensive. Although powerful strategies exist for maximizing the learning of low achievers, implementation of these strategies is extremely difficult without adequate funding.

BARBARA TALBERT JACKSON
Executive Director, Grants Administration
District of Columbia Public Schools
Washington, D.C.
ASCD President 1993-94

Where do we start?

Starting right away, every educator should enter the classroom with a positive attitude and newly acquired skills to carry out the recommendations in this publication. Student grouping for instruction should change from whole-group instruction to a combination of approaches that includes collaborative and cooperative activities. Emphasis needs to be placed on individualizing the instructional program to meet the needs of remedial, average, and accelerated students.

We need to revise the curriculum to incorporate an interdisciplinary approach. Instruction and assignments for students could be made according to their documented learning and reading styles. All students would have an opportunity to be actively involved in instructional activities. Instructional approaches would encompass cultural experiences and the language of the various ethnic groups in the classroom.

Student assessment should be changed from the traditional paper-and-pencil, fill-in-the-blank, multiple-choice, true/false, or yes/no answers. Alternative assessment activities could include demonstrated performances, construction of projects, and audiovisual presentations, as well as essay-type responses. Students could participate in a continuous learning process that would allow them to achieve academically at their own pace.

Learning activities for these children would not be limited to classroom or textbook-based experiences. Students could be assigned challenging, reality-based instructional activities. The instructional program would not be limited to the confines of the classroom; the greater community and the business district would be an integral part of the learning environment. Parents would be invited and trained to be active partners in the education of their children.

What are the barriers?

The many barriers to effective instruction discussed in this book are indeed daunting. Practitioners can begin the process of eliminating these barriers by adopting an attitude toward teaching and learning that promotes positive thinking and high expectations for student achievement. Many existing institutional practices and policies must be revised or eliminated. Education must become a top priority for those citizens in governing positions and in the business community. Parents will have to become active partners in the education of their children. A large part of parents' involvement is ensuring that their children are ready to learn when they enter school. Practitioners will have to participate in training and retraining programs to keep abreast of rapidly changing, state-of-the-art instructional strategies.

BRUCE McDONNELL DAVIS
Principal, Ralph W. Emerson Elementary School
Garvey School District
Rosemead, California

Where do we start?

At each school, educators should make it crystal clear that they place a high value on education. Students and their parents should be required to sign a letter of agreement signaling their commitment to academic excellence, exemplary behavior, and regular attendance. When that agreement is not honored, the school principal must seek a recommitment from the home.

Using the "bully pulpit" of the principalship, the principal must preach the gospel of learning via daily presentations, either orally or in print, using the services of translators if needed.

Teachers, the foot soldiers of the struggle for a more enlightened populace, groan under the weight of their responsibilities. This book correctly reports that many educators lack the necessary training to be as effective as possible in teaching diverse learners. In these situations, school administrators need to provide leadership and demonstrate sensitivity by providing and participating in staff-generated inservice training designed to alleviate weaknesses.

It would be a serious mistake to forget the important role played by instructional aides. Aides and teachers must establish a partnership that facilitates student learning. The Developing a Partnership Program, created by the Los Angeles County Office of Education, serves as an excellent model in such efforts.

169

What are the barriers?

Educators simply do not have time to do all that is demanded of them. Even worse, long-ignored societal problems, left on the back burner by myriad government agencies, exert a horrendous impact on our schools. Furthermore, school districts must break the habit of embracing every new panacea that comes along.

We are severely hampered by archaic education codes, a deterioration in the quality of school board candidates, and educators who have lost the confidence of the public by using a shotgun expenditure approach that has often missed the target. A plethora of union rhetoric, which hamstrings more than it helps, ambushes those educators who are attempting to limp along the pathway to progress. We must streamline the laws under which we operate. School board candidates need to have at least minimal academic qualifications.

We need to support educators who have the courage to speak out and stand up against unreasonable union demands. We need to replace contrariness with courage. When we provide educators with time for reflection and with the proper degree of assistance, we will be walking, not hobbling, along the path to success.

BEVERLY E. CROSS
Assistant Professor, University of Wisconsin at Milwaukee

Where do we start?

ASCD can assume a leadership role in providing support to school districts in implementing the recommendations in this book. Knowledgeable teams who are fluent in these ideas could assist school districts in assessing current practices, planning for curricular and instructional innovations, and moving ahead into implementation. Top-level district support is crucial.

It seems imperative that school districts build a holistic instructional framework within which these recommendations can be included. ASCD can provide critical external support in this effort. If the recommendations quickly become fragmented elements of instruction, they will have little impact. The ideas as they appear here represent a rather exhaustive compilation of research and practices; their relevance to instruction, while strong, needs to be conceived as part of a larger framework. If this is done, the results could prove powerful for practitioners and for children.

The instructional ideas herein are not prescriptive, but they do require thinking, sorting out of ideas and dilemmas, and integrating into practice. Practitioners need time to connect the book's ideas with their own context; they need time to confront their own beliefs about curriculum, diverse learners, and instructional practices.

Along with rethinking instructional practices, practitioners need to embrace the powerful notion of engaging in inquiry about ideas. ASCD could be instrumental in shifting views of implementation from a mechanistic process performed by teachers to a thinking, inquiring, collaborative, planning process. This way of thinking requires that teachers have the time and support necessary to build a framework for integrating these ideas into their practice in a systematic, personal way.

What are the barriers?

Building a support base for the implementation of the practices outlined in this book is a crucial step. This support base must be built within a political context that expects *immediate results* from educational change. It must be built within a societal climate in which, unfortunately, children appear to be of little value and in which we eschew responsibility for poor children and children of color. Within both the political and educational arenas, ASCD could be a major force in shaping the implementation of the kinds of systemic, research-based practices included in this book. This intervention could be achieved through an extensive public information campaign and through distinct commitment to the education of poor and minority children.

Practitioners need the time for thoughtful and reflective examination, analysis, inquiry, and discourse about this book. Practitioners must feel free to take informed risks within their particular political, social, and education contexts. Practitioners need to be able to articulate their ideas about these instructional innovations. This will mean more than simply glancing through the contents of the book.

Financial support must be provided for curricular and instructional innovations—support not only for materials, but also to enable practitioners to study, plan, and design instructional practices that fit within their own context. Careful understanding and implementation strategies are equally important to ensure the success of the instructional strategies discussed herein.

Practitioners need systematic professional development, coaching, feedback, and practice to implement these innovations. Once the instructional plan is designed, implementation can occur in each classroom. Support for individual implementation is necessary to effect improvement in practice.

Practitioners need to become students of their students. The aims of the instructional practices are not likely to be achieved without practitioners' first developing an active curiosity about those they teach. This interest needs to be supported with resources and the time to learn about students.

LISA MOWEN
Assistant Principal, West Jefferson High School
Harvey, Louisiana
President, Louisiana ASCD, 1993-1994

Where do we start?

I congratulate the authors and editor of *Educating Everybody's Children: Diverse Teaching Strategies for Diverse Learners* for producing a very readable work filled with specific ideas and activities for schools and classrooms. Some of my recommendations for prompt implementation would include the following:

• The school-based educational leaders who read this book should promptly synthesize its recommendations and disseminate this information. Many educators and parents will be gratified to know that their philosophies and practices for working with children from diverse backgrounds are supported by research and expert thinking; others may learn new ways of responding to diverse young people.

• Professional organizations, including ASCD and its affiliates, should ensure access to speakers familiar with the content of the work (and even to the authors and editor themselves when appropriate) in planning upcoming conference programs.

• Higher education administrators and faculty should begin to develop coursework for preservice teachers and administrators based on the book's content, if they have not already done so.

What are the barriers?

Many school systems have no time available to provide inservice training for their employees on important new educational developments. Administrative and teacher groups must work collaboratively to keep abreast of constantly shifting concepts of good instructional practice.

Another barrier to the implementation of the book's recommendations is the mindset of many educators that having to work with culturally diverse students represents a career setback. Educators of this ilk need to be encouraged and inspired as to the importance of education's great mission: to teach and reach *every* child.

BETTY SUE SPARKS
Elementary Supervisor, Knox County Schools
Knoxville, Tennessee
President, Tennessee ASCD, 1992-1993

Where do we start?

We must begin with the belief that each day in the classroom is a *new* day, full of promise and expectation. Each child deserves the benefit of an educator who is dedicated to making school the most inviting, exciting place imaginable! We need to allow our students to understand that while we do not have all the answers, we have the dedication and caring commitment to *find* what works for them. I am convinced that we have the skill and leadership to develop approaches to reading, writing, oral communication, and mathematics that will enable each child to experience success.

My responsibility as an instructional leader is to ensure that the teachers I work with have access to the strategies and techniques outlined in *Educating Everybody's Children*. I must also facilitate the use of resources by ensuring the time to plan and reflect on those strategies that are best suited to the individual needs of youngsters. I must see that teachers receive the support and encouragement they need in order to meet the challenges of today's classroom. Finally, I must model the enthusiasm and commitment that will enable these methods to work.

What are the barriers?

Barriers to effective instruction come in many forms, yet it seems that there are always those dedicated individuals who have a special talent for breaking down barriers and building bridges. ASCD and its membership are in the business of building bridges, as evidenced by the following goal statement: "By the year 2001, ASCD will mobilize resources to ensure that schools serving children of the poor have access and appropriate opportunity to widely use and effectively implement our programs, products, and services."

The information and strategies outlined in this publication represent a synthesis of best practices and research-based strategies. We can demonstrate authentic commitment by providing copies of *Educating Everybody's Children* to media centers and teacher resource centers in schools that serve poor children. In addition, training opportunities and support must be provided in ways that facilitate the implementation of this wealth of ideas.

EDWARD PAJAK

Professor, Department of Educational Leadership
University of Georgia, Athens
President, Georgia ASCD, 1994-1995

Where do we start?

A number of ideas come to mind, including:

• Policymakers, administrators, and supervisors should permit and encourage teachers to take risks, think creatively, and diversify instructional practice. Educational leaders should themselves become facilitators of teachers' work, if their expectation is for teachers to be facilitators of student learning.

• Teachers must become more aware of the rich diversity of our nation and the world to help students avoid withdrawal into a narrowly defined sense of self that is focused solely on their own cultural orientation.

• Schools must provide students with an anchor by fostering a sense of safety and stability, since young people's family and community environments may be troubled and chaotic. Interagency, communitywide collaboration may help in this effort.

• Time and resources should be allocated for staff development and peer coaching to develop teachers' repertoires in diagnosis, instruction, and assessment.

• Teachers must be convinced with concrete evidence that tracking is *not* an effective way to address the needs of students of varying abilities. They then need specific practical methods, such as those presented in this book, to serve as alternatives to tracking.

• Teachers should be helped to recognize that a multitude of methods can provide the variety needed to keep *all* students interested and involved, not only those with unique learning styles and diverse cultural roots.

• Financial resources are needed to bring *all* schools up to minimum standards in terms of materials and facilities before the possibilities of computer and information technologies can be exploited.

What are the barriers?

• During the 1980s, many districts and states adopted teacher evaluation procedures and criteria that presume direct instruction based on a teacher-centered model of (so-called) effective teaching. The evaluation models and the outmoded perspectives of evaluators must be changed.

• Most teachers lack a detailed understanding of other cultures. Success with children of other cultures demands more than superficial impressions or romantic stereotypes. Advanced coursework and even travel may prove to be necessary.

• Many schools that serve students who are poor or members of minorities lack such fundamentals as adequate facilities and the most basic instructional materials (see, for instance, the many horrifying examples in Jonathan Kozol's book *Savage Inequalities* [New York: Crown, 1991]). These necessities must be provided before the wonders of modern technology can begin to make a difference for children. All schools require equitable funding to be able to successfully educate all children.

• Teachers need time, resources, and incentives to redefine their roles and to acquire skills in diagnosis, instruction, and assessment of student performance. A substantial investment in training and coaching is necessary.

• Television and other forms of passive entertainment often emphasize (in both the medium and the message) immediate sensation over applied effort toward long-term goals and personal gratification over respect for others. Educators should band together—and ally themselves with other concerned groups—to pressure corporate leaders in the electronic media industry into presenting responsible messages to young people.

• Some cultures, other than mainstream American cultures, are themselves sexist, racist, and xenophobic. Members of such cultures, bound by age-old prejudices and animosities, are likely to resist efforts toward multicultural appreciation and tolerance. The road to achieving full multicultural appreciation is certain to be a rocky one.

ETTA RUTH HOLLINS
Professor, California State University, Hayward

Where do we start?

Implementing the recommendations in this book will require changing preservice and inservice teacher education programs to emphasize the importance of teachers' responsiveness to students' attributes and experiences. These programs need to help teachers: (1) become more aware of how their own cultural heritage, early socialization, experiential background, perceptions, and values influence classroom practices and expectations for their students; (2) get to know their students well enough to determine how they are similar to and different from themselves and to identify ways of accommodating the differences that influence learning; (3) identify ways of creating a social context for school learning that is physically and psychologically comfortable and supportive for all students; and (4) enhance instruction.

For example, many low-income "latchkey" children spend considerable amounts of time watching television. These students can be asked to read or write reviews of their favorite television programs or to compare program ratings. Such activities can improve children's literacy and mathematics skills.

What are the barriers?

In my opinion, the most significant barriers to effective instruction are teachers' beliefs about and responses to ethnic minority and low-income students. (This phenomenon is well documented in research studies.) Teachers' beliefs about the students they teach influence the nature and quality of instruction provided, the effort put into planning and instruction, the framing of curricular content, the nature of the social context of learning, and the attribution of blame for academic failure.

When teachers examine the impact of their personal beliefs and responses on student learning and the quality of the social context in their classrooms, they may be better prepared to assume responsibility for planning productive, meaningful classroom instruction.

JOHN M. SCHROEDER
Principal, Welborn Middle School
High Point, North Carolina
President, North Carolina ASCD, 1993-1994

Where do we start?

As a principal, I believe that the place to begin is to have the staff read various sections of this book and to then conduct seminars on it. The discussion should lead to a plan to make these concepts come alive for students. The principal must passionately paint the vision of all students learning, vividly enough to infect the staff with the desire to own the vision and to work toward its accomplishment.

The principal must then serve in a dual role. With pom-poms in one hand, he or she must serve as chief cheerleader of the faculty, encouraging their growth. In the other hand, the principal wields the staff of Moses, shielding the faculty from a narrow view of education reform that would measure quality solely through test scores.

What are the barriers?

The barriers to change are numerous and seem almost insurmountable. They include such seemingly inflexible practices as the test-driven curriculum, as well as the following:

• Schools are told to focus, but also to address a lengthy laundry list of "valued outcomes."

• Short-sighted goals crowd out attention to long-term improvement.

• A host of external pressures discourage innovation.

• The normal response to discipline problems is to tighten up, not to try more open models of instruction.

• Site-based management (positive in the long run) demands planning time that conflicts with the time required for additional team and individual class planning, as well as for inservice training.

• Some principals don't see the big picture or are buried by paperwork and the demands of the central administration; they have little time or energy left to develop a vision and to lead.

• Too many teachers have low expectations of students.

• For a variety of reasons, parents are uninvolved in their children's education.

• Money for materials, manipulatives, and technology is often scarce and seldom equitably distributed.

• "One-size-fits-all" inservice training is inadequate, as is the notion that a one-shot inservice effort should last forever.

• The media focus on self-gratification and violence. Need we wonder that so many children subscribe to this kind of thinking, rather than learning and service to humanity?

Each school must overcome these barriers. Each principal must stand up for his or her faculty. The principal must have vision and must infect the staff with the desire to plan and accomplish the vision. The site-based leadership team can then move the school toward accomplishing the vision of all children learning. The principal must give the credit and take any blame; only then is the staff free to experiment.

HAYDEÉ PIRIS-MALDONADO
Professor, Pontifical Catholic University of Puerto Rico, Ponce
President, Puerto Rico ASCD, 1993-1994

Where do we start?

In no other period of history have families turned to school (especially preschool and kindergarten) for help with their children. And never before has so much pressure has been put on the government in the form of demands for more and better schools. Based on these new and sometimes uncomfortable realities, we should start by considering the earliest level of education development.

The importance of an adequate setting is determined during the earliest years. We should be very concerned about the quality of our day-care centers and kindergartens. Education for children in these primary school settings should be very active, emphasizing cognitive learning. The learning climate should be conducive to creativity, the building of self-confidence, and social adjustment.

In the area of language arts—especially reading and writing—we should offer a material-rich environment. For example, make use of a wide variety of books, both commercially produced and written and illustrated by the children themselves. Every experience in the classroom should be an opportunity to read and write.

In the area of mathematics and science (and in other subjects, too), youngsters can measure objects, paint murals, draw maps, and use magnifying glasses to observe animals or plants and to draw conclusions from their observations. They can read and write about their activities. They won't be bored at school if they are taught though their own interests, curiosity, and experiences.

All of the recommendations in this book are quite possible. What we need is *commitment* to making these changes—and then we need just to *start*. When? Today. Tomorrow will be too late.

What are the barriers?

We have come a long way in the past twenty years, but we approach the new millennium faced with many barriers that prevent teachers from implementing the recommendations made in this book. Based on my experience working with bilingual education, I see the following major barriers:

Communication. Our society is a multicultural one, so language and culture affect education directly. Minority students usually score low academically; many of them are forced to drop out of school. When they seek employment, they generally obtain only the lowest-level jobs. Bilingual and multicultural education will help to overcome this barrier.

Curriculum. Content often represents a barrier to effective education. Pertinent and significant curricular materials can help to remove this barrier by taking into account the capabilities, potentialities, and interests of young people, as well as the needs of the work force. The U.S. Departments of Labor and Education need to work cooperatively to develop educational programs that address the goals and needs of the labor market, thus providing one avenue to help lower unemployment and ease poverty.

High-quality teaching. High-quality professional development for practitioners is a vitally important means of helping to counteract and anticipate the effects of change in schools. If quality education is our goal, we need to update and train teachers both in content and methods. A vigorous, continuous, and well-planned inservice training program is a "must" in every school.

Assessment. New ways of assessing students' mastery of the processes of analytical reasoning, problem solving, and critical thinking are being developed. True/false or multiple-choice tests do not have the analytical power we need today.

Cooperation and commitment. Gaining the ready assistance of school, family, and government agencies should be our focus if we wish to overcome the barriers to the full and rapid implementation of the recommendations in this book.

GERRY SCHIELE
Teaching Principal, Buechel Elementary School
Germany
President, Germany ASCD, 1993-1994

Where do we start?

To get started tomorrow, every teacher in my school needs to learn, in the most personal way possible, that I want the recommendations implemented and that our superintendent wants the same thing.

Moreover, the following groups clamor for the recommendations: the School Advisory Committee (the school board in the United States), the PTA, and every family associated with the school. In addition, each teacher needs to have a checklist of the recommendations so that he or she can see quickly what is already being done and what still needs to be accomplished.

What are the barriers?

The biggest barrier to implementing something new is the awkward feeling experienced by the teacher when he or she first experiments with the new behavior. At first it feels phony, then it feels mechanical, and eventually it becomes natural. Teachers need to understand that they will be supported when they have problems implementing change—and when they hear complaints from parents or community members about the change. Teachers need to be reassured as they pass through the stages of change.

We can best eliminate the barriers to effective instruction through a comprehensive staff development program that is long-term and collegial, and that celebrates experimentation and risk taking.

JOYCE R. TAYLOR
Teacher, Reading Even Start Program
Reading, Pennsylvania

Where do we start?

Our true master teachers (as shown by student results, not just popularity contests) should be encouraged to give workshops, allow their classes to be videotaped, and be monitored by students and other teachers. We need to create ways of allowing the teaching practices of the best to influence the rest.

Teacher training classes at the university level *must* include practice in using proven cross-cultural instruction in the classroom. Prospective teachers require preparation in recognizing cultural differences that may cause problems for new teachers (for example, refusing to make eye contact or being overly demonstrative).

The curriculum should stop being clock-driven and become *needs-driven*. A cross-cultural class may need four hours a day of reading-related activities in order to incorporate vocabulary building, comprehension, oral work, and reading for pleasure. This kind of intensive work cannot be accomplished in classrooms where children move to a different room every hour.

We need to discard all tests geared to true/false and one-word answers of any kind. Even at the 1st grade level, students should learn to answer questions in complete sentences with the question in the answer. This technique helps the student think clearly, and it enables the teacher to follow the student's thought processes.

Encourage Even Start programs. Although Head Start is a commendable program that encourages parent participation, Even Start parents are active participants at every step of the way. (Even Start programs vary considerably throughout the country; I speak from experience only with the sites in Reading, Pennsylvania.) Parents become excited about their own education while their children enjoy low-stress developmental and readiness activities. Parents spend a half hour daily learning good parenting practices and another half hour daily practicing parenting activities with their own children. As a result, Even Start children will have been in cross-cultural classes for as long as four years before they enter formal schooling. They speak English, they are school-ready, and their parents are able and eager to be active partners in their children's education.

What are the barriers?

• Lack of teacher preparation in cultural differences is a huge barrier to progress. We may be encouraging more good black and Hispanic teachers to enter teaching, but how have we prepared them to deal with Vietnamese and Afghani students?

• Despite all that has been said and written, we still see the teacher as a source of information. In a cross-cultural classroom, the student's *perception* of what is being taught is far more important, especially in a non-native, English-speaking situation.

• Bilingual education in most school systems simply does not work. Even students who begin in kindergarten are soon hopelessly behind and can never rejoin their age peers.

• Perhaps kindergarten and 1st grade classes could become more success oriented than they are now.

• Concentrate on the three Rs plus oral expression. Show-and-tell is an important part of learning in the early grades and should be planned to include every child.

• Hands-on activities and care with vocabulary will usually result in children's not only speaking English within six months in the early grades, but also in their assimilating necessary basic information.

• Let's eliminate our education ghettoes!

CELIA STEWART
St. Peters Hillside School
St. Maarten, Netherlands Antilles
President, St. Maarten ASCD, 1993-1994

Where do we start?

Re-education is the key factor in spreading the word about this publication. This book needs to be distributed to all the key players in education in the countries served by ASCD. Through ASCD affiliates, the strategies advocated in this book could be made the central focus of workshops, seminars, and other staff development programs. ASCD can influence practitioners via its technological and human resources by pulling out all stops to make these strategies known worldwide. The inclusion of classroom examples will encourage teachers to use the suggested strategies.

In small, developing nations outside the United States, where the problems facing educators are somewhat different than those in the United States, educators will need to discuss which of the book's recommended strategies are most suitable before implementing staff development programs. (It will be important to keep in mind that not all developing nations have funds to use technology in individual classrooms.) I believe that programs of teacher education should include these recommendations in their courses so that new teachers can implement the strategies suggested. Administrators and supervisors will need to discover which strategies are already in use in their schools and then find ways of implementing those deemed necessary.

The reeducation of the teaching force will be a necessary first step toward using these powerful teaching strategies to improve student achievement in the key areas of reading, mathematics, writing, and oral communication in diverse classrooms.

What are the barriers?

Unfortunately, teachers themselves tend to be the biggest barrier to effective instruction. Many teachers are not aware of current research and what it says about teaching strategies that improve achievement. Others are aware but do not want to change because change is uncomfortable. Still others would like to use new strategies, but are not given support by colleagues and therefore do not implement changes.

Classroom teachers first need to examine themselves carefully and assess their attitudes toward change; then, with their administrators, they need to take a long, hard look at themselves and decide how they are going to influence the performance of those students who do not fit the "norms."

In small, developing nations—where funds for education are sorely lacking—legislators need to assess their priorities in terms of effective instruction. There would need to be a nationwide staff development program in which strategies for effective instruction are made known, especially to teachers who received their training over five years ago; much of the more recent research will be unknown to them. Unless teachers, parents, and administrators are made aware of diverse teaching strategies, there will always be barriers to effective instruction.

JAMES E. TAYLER
Teacher, H.D. Cartwright Junior High School
Calgary, Alberta
President, Alberta ASCD, 1993-1994

Where do we start?

Many of the instructional strategies in this book are already very much a part of our best teachers' repertoires. Unfortunately, our best teachers are not always the ones who are teaching the children who need them the most. Those who are working in situations of great cultural and ethnic diversity must believe that their choice of instructional strategies makes a powerful difference in their students' lives.

In the "new" normal classroom that many of us face each Monday morning, our choice of instructional practices may need to be as diverse as the backgrounds, experiences, and understandings of the world that the students bring with them every day. In addition, empathetic teachers who understand the real needs of their students will provide much of what is required for these children to achieve success; obviously these young people need the support of colleagues, administrators, school districts, and the community if their schooling experience is to make a positive and lasting difference in their lives. To provide less than this is both a disservice to the children and a mistake that society seems to insist on making over and over again, even when it is glaringly clear what needs to be done and how to do it.

What are the barriers?

One critical barrier to be overcome is the staffing procedures for "high needs" schools. Rarely is staffing done with the real needs of the school in mind. Staff members who are "selected" or transferred to such schools are often (though not always) mediocre practitioners who are placed there against their wishes. A teacher's academic qualifications or subject specialty are usually considered first, before attention is given to that teacher's beliefs and attitudes about teaching and learning in a school with a diverse population. Unfortunately, many teachers who are working with some of our neediest children are unprepared, unwilling, limited in their own personal experiences—and are simply marking time until retirement.

Too few teachers in high-needs schools see the world with the broad, open-minded view that is essential to succeed with diverse students. We need more teachers who passionately wish to work with our neediest children—and to be a part of their world. We need more teachers who are willing to experience profound professional and personal growth as a result of the multitude of challenges in schools where stagnation and mediocrity are too common. Other barriers outside the classroom can be overcome if we have dedicated, highly motivated teachers who enjoy providing all children with the best possible instruction every day.

BRUCE JOHNSON
Superintendent, Kodiak Island Borough
  School District
Kodiak, Alaska
President, Alaska ASCD, 1993-1994

Where do we start?

As this book suggests, we know how to teach students successfully; therefore, there can no longer be any excuses for continued failure to do so. Translating what we know into the reality of reaching all students in every classroom demands that we break down the artificial divisions that chop up the curriculum and create instead a rich, integrated curriculum and collaborative teamwork involving students, parents, teachers, and administrators. This transformation must begin with education for understanding, with pilot projects that provide demonstrations of success, and with negotiations to break down the myriad barriers that confront students on a daily basis.

On a practical level, policymakers must encourage change while simultaneously supporting parents and educators with dynamic, relevant training opportunities aimed at developing and implementing instructional strategies designed to assure success for all students. Obviously, I am assuming that this publication provides a "tool chest" of effective instructional strategies that can be shared tomorrow with educators worldwide to assist with this effort. In doing so, classroom instruction and teacher behaviors will be affected positively, creating success-oriented classrooms.

What are the barriers?

The greatest existing barriers to success include lack of time and the dominance of traditional teaching practices. Educators are frequently faced with demanding teaching loads; they have little opportunity to stop and consider precisely what they might do differently to create a better lesson. Team collaboration (in the form of common planning periods, for instance) is still foreign to many schools, thereby forcing most teachers to rely on their own best judgment, which too often allows them to revert to instructional techniques that have always worked reasonably well for a certain percentage of students. I believe that educators truly desire to reach all students; given the constraints of time, however, they can only achieve so much.

Another barrier focuses on traditional practices that have evolved over decades. Frontal teaching and multiple-choice exams, for example, are comfortable approaches that have worked for many students. Therefore, many teachers continue to cling to them as their primary teaching tools, even though the nature of the student population has changed dramatically in recent years.

The barrier of time can be eliminated if policymakers recognize that educators need time for collaborative planning and for staff development. Many school districts have secured the time necessary for planning and training by first accepting the need for staff development and planning as an integral component of improving education. They have created such time by, for example, establishing a shortened school day once a week for staff collaboration, devising child-care opportunities on those days when students are out of school, and so forth. With training opportunities and available time, traditional practices that have adversely affected some students can be eliminated from classrooms. If school systems supply the opportunities for acquiring improved instructional strategies, we can hope to extinguish ineffective practices.

APPENDIX
CRITERIA FOR SELECTING RESEARCH

The following criteria were used in selecting the research included in this publication:

CRITERION 1

The study addresses a significant issue related to students' academic achievement.

Studies included had to deal with an important aspect of students' learning. The results also had to be meaningful in school settings. Researchers who conduct experiments speak of the trade–off between internal and external validity. Internal validity refers to how well the rules for experimentation are followed. External validity concerns the relevance of the study to settings in the real world—in this case, the schools. Studies included have high external validity and represent strategies that teachers will recognize as having practical value in the classroom. Some of the research included represents new ideas and approaches that appear to offer the promise of substantially improving students' academic achievement.

CRITERION 2

The study was conducted with a coherent theoretical framework.

Studies had to be based on a theory well established in some area of the sciences or social sciences. The researchers had to make the theoretical orientation of their work clear and show how their findings related to other major studies in the area. This criterion does not exclude any particular theories and allowed the inclusion of research from a number of different orientations—for example, whole language and schema theory.

CRITERION 3

The study observed conventions of design and method associated with its particular type of research.

Studies had to be designed and executed in a manner consistent with the technical requirements for research of its type. Each kind of research (for example, ethnographic or experimental) follows its own rules for design and methodology. This criterion does not exclude any particular type of research and allowed the inclusion of research conducted with a range of methods.

CRITERION 4

The study reported results for students, so benefits to students of diverse backgrounds were known.

Studies had to present systematic information about what students had gained. Students' learning can be assessed in many ways, through writing samples, statements made during classroom discussion, hypotheses generated during science experiments, and so on. Students' attitudes can be assessed through interviews and classroom observations. Studies were not limited to those reporting results from standardized tests. Standardized tests have the advantage of being economical and convenient, but they are not good measures of many forms of complex thinking. Because all measures are limited in some way, the best means of demonstrating benefits to students are monitored over a period of years and shown to be long lasting.

CRITERION 5

The study showed sensitivity to the issues involved in the learning of students of diverse backgrounds.

Studies had to show a respect for the learning abilities of students of diverse backgrounds. Studies could not be conducted from a deficit perspective, which assumes that students of diverse backgrounds are deficient in language or mental ability. Studies could not stereotype, penalize, or denigrate students because of their cultural or linguistic background. Special significance was attached to research that dispelled myths about the learning of students of diverse backgrounds.

OTHER FACTORS

Beyond the usual descriptive terms of types of research—i.e., empirical, quantitative, literature, teaching/best practice, and so on—the criteria included these broad definitions:

• Application of research findings in a variety of settings.

• Longitudinal monitoring (standing the test of time).

• New research that has promise—the group's consensus that the body of research has the potential to bring about real outcome differences.

• Research that dispels myths and stereotypes about how diverse children learn.

• Research offering strategies that teachers will accept as capable of being implemented in the classroom setting.

Any programs mentioned have not only strong research and evaluation components but also the strong endorsement of the schools and school districts involved. They also demonstrate student outcomes on a variety of measures.

ACKNOWLEDGMENTS

The work of the ASCD Urban Middle Grades Network (UMGN), the ASCD Advisory Panel on Improving Student Achievement, and the ASCD Improving Student Achievement Research Panel contributed to the development of this book. The authors appreciate the knowledge and insights provided by the individuals and school districts participating in these groups. Kendel Taylor provided administrative support to the project and helped to compile the extensive bibliographic information included in the book. Special thanks to Robert W. Cole for reviewing the manuscript with a keen and critical editorial eye.

ASCD URBAN MIDDLE GRADES NETWORK 1989-1991

Atlanta Public Schools
Crawford Long Middle School
Alger S. Coleman, Jr.
Principal
Atlanta, GA

Birmingham City School System
Lincoln Middle School
Ruth Strong
Assistant Superintendent
Birmingham, AL

Cleveland City Schools
Harry E. Davis Middle School
James Coleman
Area Superintendent
Cleveland, OH

Dade County Public Schools
Mays Middle School
Robert Stinson
Principal
Miami, FL

Denver Public Schools
Morey Middle School
Rhoda Imhoff
Principal
Denver, CO

Denver Public Schools
Rishel Middle School
Irene Jordan
Principal
Denver, CO

Detroit Public Schools
Winterhalter Middle School
Herman Carroll
Principal
Detroit, MI

Long Beach Unified Schools
Benjamin Franklin Middle School
Linda Moore
Principal
Long Beach, CA

New Orleans Public Schools
Live Oaks Middle School
Armand Devezin
Principal
New Orleans, LA

Norfolk Public Schools
Lake Taylor Middle School
Margaret Saunders
Assistant Superintendent, Middle Schools
Norfolk, VA

Richland Co. School District One
Crayton Middle School
Mary Beach
Associate Superintendent of
    Curriculum/Instruction
Columbia, SC

San Antonio Independent School District
Mark Twain Middle School
David Splitek
Associate Superintendent of Instruction
    Services
San Antonio, TX

Seattle Public Schools
Washington Middle School
Bruce Hunter
Principal
Seattle, WA

Tucson Unified School District
Mansfeld Middle School
Arnie Adler
Principal
Tucson, AZ

Wichita Public Schools
Jardine Middle School
Cynthia Rutherford
Area II Secondary Director
Wichita, KS

Helené Hodges, UMGN Project Director
Director, Research and Information
ASCD
Alexandria, VA

ASCD Advisory Panel on Improving Student Achievement 1991

Sheryl Denbo
President
Mid-Atlantic Equity Consortium, Inc.
Washington, DC

Alan Ginsburg
Director, Planning and Evaluation Service
U.S. Department of Education
Washington, DC
Lois Hirst
Associate Professor
Northern Michigan University
Marquette, MI

Shirley Jackson
Director of Comprehensive School Health
Education Program
U.S. Department of Education
Washington, DC

J. Michael O'Malley
Supervisor of Assessment and Evaluation
Prince William County Public Schools
Manassas, VA

Lorraine Valdez Pierce
Associate Professor
George Mason University
Fairfax, VA

Stuart Rankin
Visiting Professor
University of Michigan
Ann Arbor, MI

Harriet Doss Willis
Director
Southwest Regional Laboratory for
Educational and Regional Development
Los Alamitos, CA

Helené Hodges, Advisory Panel Project
Director
Director, Research and Information
ASCD
Alexandria, VA

ASCD Improving Student Achievement Research Panel 1992-1994

Carol Ascher
Senior Research Associate
ERIC Clearinghouse on Urban Education
Institute for Urban and Minority
Education
Teachers College, Columbia University
New York, NY

Kathryn Hu-pei Au
Educational Psychologist
Kamehameha Schools
Honolulu, HA

Roy Berko
Director of Education Services
Speech Communication Association
Annandale, VA

Denise Borders
Chief of Accountability
Student Assessment Planning and
Program Audit
Baltimore Public Schools
Baltimore, MD

Marie Carbo
Executive Director
Research and Staff Development
National Reading Styles Institute
Roslyn Heights, NY

Jim Chesebro
Professor
Department of Communication
Indiana State University
Terre Haute, IN

Pam Cooper
Visiting Scholar
English Language Teaching Unit
The Chinese University of Hong Kong
Shatin, New Territories, Hong Kong

Beatriz D'Ambrosio
Assistant Professor of Mathematics
Education
University of Georgia
Athens, GA

Rita Dunn
Professor and Director
Center for the Study of Learning and
Teaching Style and Chairperson, Division
of Administrative and Instructional
Leadership
St. John's University

Jamaica, NY
Eugene Garcia
Director
Office of Bilingual Education and
Minority Language Affairs (OBEMLA)
U.S. Department of Education
Washington, DC

Sally Hampton
Director of Writing and Reasoning Skills
Forth Worth School District
Fort Worth, TX

Carol Hopson
Vice President
Academic Affairs
Nuñez Community College
Chalmette, LA

Kenji Ima
Professor of Sociology
Department of Sociology
San Diego State University
San Diego, CA

Howard Johnson
Associate Vice-Chancellor for Academic
Affairs
Syracuse University
Syracuse, NY

Barbara Kapinus
Senior Program Officer
Council of Chief of State School Officers
Washington, DC

Marietta Saravia-Shore
Director
Cross-Cultural Literacy Center
Associate Director
Institute of Urban and Minority
Education
Teachers College, Columbia University
New York, NY

Warren Simmons
Senior Associate
The Annie E. Casey Foundation
Baltimore, MD

Floraline Stevens
Science Education Evaluation Analyst
National Science Foundation
Washington, DC

Helené Hodges, Research Panel Project
Director
Director, Collaborative Ventures
ASCD
Alexandria, VA

The Authors

Carol Ascher is a senior research associate with the ERIC Clearinghouse on Urban Education, and the Institute on Education and the Economy at Teachers College, Columbia University, where she specializes in research and policy on equity issues concerning urban students. Ascher is also a widely published fiction writer.

Kathryn Au is an educational psychologist at Kamehameha Schools, an institution dedicated to the education of students of Native Hawaiian ancestry. She has published on the school literacy learning of students with diverse cultural and linguistic backgrounds.

Roy Berko is Associate Director of the Speech Communication Association. Author of numerous books on speech communication and education, Berko has received six national teaching recognition awards.

Denise Borders serves as Chief of Educational Accountability with the Baltimore City Public Schools. With experience in school leadership at every level, Borders is interested in linguistics, has several publications, and has recently co-authored *Language Diversity in Classroom Discourse*.

Marie Carbo is Executive Director of the National Reading Styles Institute and an international reading consultant. Author of the *Reading Style Inventory* and originator of the Carbo Recorded Book Method, Carbo has published more than 100 articles and books for children, parents, and teachers.

Jim Chesebro is Chair and Professor in the Department of Communication at Indiana State University. He has served in numerous leadership positions in communication and was Director of Education Services at the National Office of the Speech Communication Association from 1989 through 1992. Frequently published in leading communication journals, Chesebro has received many honors, including the SCA's "Golden Anniversary Award" for outstanding monograph of the year.

Robert W. Cole is vice president and chief operating officer of the Center for Leadership in School Reform. Chairperson of the Urban Education Advisory Board of ASCD, Cole is a past president of the Education Press Association of America and former editor of *Phi Delta Kappan* magazine. His research investigations

have focused on the effects of education reform and on changes in rural America.

Pamela Cooper is professor of Communication Studies at Northwestern University. A past chair of SCA's Educational Policies Board, Cooper is currently vice-chair of the Instructional Development Division of SCA and editor of SCA's Education and Instructional Development Publication Series. Author of several texts on speech communication, she taught middle and high school students prior to teaching at the university level.

Anne Curran is an assistant principal at South Hagerstown High School in Hagerstown, Maryland. Before completing her doctoral program and research in high school restructuring, Curran taught and supervised K-12 language arts programs in Maryland and Connecticut. Her publications include the final report of the ASCD Restructuring Consortium, *Visions That Guide Change*.

Beatriz D'Ambrosio is an Assistant Professor of Mathematics Education at the University of Georgia. Her research interests lie in bridging the gap between research and practice in mathematics education. With the intent of empowering teachers, she has focused on building preservice and inservice experiences that develop the teacher-researcher.

Harriet Doss Willis is the director of the Southwest Regional Laboratory's Center for Educational Equity, a desegregation assistance facility serving the school districts of Arizona, California, and Nevada. She has previously worked on urban education initiatives for the New Jersey Department of Education and both the North Central and Central Midwestern Regional Educational Laboratories.

Rita Dunn is professor in the Division of Administrative and Instructional Leadership and Teaching Styles, St. John's University, New York. Widely recognized for her work on learning styles, Dunn was recently honored with the Mensa Education and Research Foundation Award for Excellence in Research. In 1988, she was honored with the National Association of Elementary School Principals' "Educator of the Year" award.

Eugene Garcia, Director, Office of Bilingual Education and Minority Affairs, U.S. Department of Education, is the former Dean of the Division of Social Sciences, and Professor of

Education and Psychology at the University of California, Santa Cruz. Having published extensively in the areas of language teaching and bilingual development, Garcia also served as Co-Director of the National Center for Research on Cultural Diversity and Second Language Learning.

Sally Hampton directs the writing and reasoning skills program in the Fort Worth, Texas, schools. Her work connects in-class learning with out-of-school problems and tasks. She is currently involved in an assessment project examining the contrasts between work-world writing, and the writing taught in schools.

Leslie Hobbs is supervisor of mathematics for the Washington County, Maryland, school system. With teaching experience in middle and high schools, she also serves on the Mathematics Coordinating Committee for the Maryland State Department of Education, and the Mid-Atlantic Eisenhower Consortium for Mathematics and Science.

Helené Hodges is Director of Collaborative Ventures at ASCD. Responsible for coordinating the two-year collaborative writing project resulting in the publication of *Educating Everybody's Children*, Hodges researched, developed, and wrote the strategies that authors ultimately describe throughout this publication. She is widely recognized for her work in improving the performance outcomes of diverse learners and has worked in this area for more than twenty years.

Carol Hopson is acting president of Nuñez Community College in Chalmette, Louisiana. She has worked with groups of at-risk students for nearly thirty years, and has a background in planning and development.

Kenji Ima is Professor of Sociology at San Diego State University. Author of numerous publications on Asian Americans and Asian refugees, Ima has held teaching positions at the Illinois Institute of Technology and the California School for Professional Psychology.

Howard C. Johnson is associate Vice Chancellor for Academic Affairs at Syracuse University, where he is also Chair of Mathematics Education. He has authored and co-authored many publications, among them a recently published mathematics textbook series for grades K-8, *MATHEMATICS PLUS* (Harcourt Brace Jovanovich).

Barbara A. Kapinus is Senior Program Coordinator for the Council of Chief State School Officers, working on curriculum and assessment projects. With teaching experience at every level of education, Kapinus has also worked with the National Assessment Governing Board and is active in the International Reading Association, serving on the editorial board of *The Reading Teacher*.

Lloyd Kline works independently as a commissioned writer, editor, and education consultant, and has been active in teaching and writing throughout his career.

Marietta Saravia-Shore is Associate Director of the Institute for Urban and Minority Education (IUME) for Professional Development and Educational Programs at Teachers College, Columbia University. Founder and Director of the IUME Cross-Cultural Literacy Center, she also co-directs the Cross-Cultural, Interdisciplinary, Cooperative Learning Project with Community District Five in New York City.

Warren Simmons is Senior Associate, The Annie E. Casey Foundation, and former Director of Equity Initiatives for the New Standards Project, a partnership of 17 states and 6 school districts developing a performance-based examination system that embodies world-class standards. With interests in multicultural education and black male achievement, Simmons is also Acting Co-Director of the National Alliance for Restructuring Education.

Floraline I. Stevens is Program Director in the Evaluation Unit for the Division of Research, Evaluation, and Dissemination of the National Science Foundation. She was the American Educational Research Association's second Senior Research Fellow at the National Center for Education Statistics, and served as a vice president of Division H of AERA.